Converting Britannia

Studies in the Eighteenth Century
ISSN: 2398–9904

This major series from Boydell & Brewer, published in association with the British Society for Eighteenth-Century Studies, aims to bring into fruitful dialogue the different disciplines involved in all aspects of the study of the long eighteenth century (c.1660–1820). It publishes innovative volumes, singly or co-authored, on any topic in history, science, music, literature and the visual arts in any area of the world in the long eighteenth century and particularly encourages proposals that explore links among the disciplines, and which aim to develop new cross-disciplinary fields of enquiry.

Series editors: Ros Ballaster, University of Oxford, UK; Matthew Grenby, Newcastle University, UK; Robert D. Hume, Penn State University, USA; Mark Knights, University of Warwick, UK; Renaud Morieux, University of Cambridge, UK

Previously published

Material Enlightenment: Women Writers and the Science of Mind, 1770–1830, Joanna Wharton, 2018

Celebrity Culture and the Myth of Oceania in Britain, 1770–1823, Ruth Scobie, 2019

British Sociability in the Long Eighteenth Century: Challenging the Anglo-French Connection, edited by Valérie Capdeville and Alain Kerhervé, 2019

Things that Didn't Happen: Writing, Politics and the Counterhistorical, 1678–1743, John McTague, 2019

British Catholic Merchants in the Commercial Age: 1670–1714, Giada Pizzoni, 2020

Lessons of Travel in Eighteenth-Century France: From Grand Tour to School Trips, Gábor Gelléri, 2020

Political Journalism in London, 1695–1720: Defoe, Swift, Steele and their Contemporaries, Ashley Marshall, 2020

Fictions of Presence: Theatre and Novel in Eighteenth-Century Britain, Ros Ballaster, 2020

Ephemeral Print Culture in Early Modern England: Sociability, Politics and Collecting, Tim Somers, 2021

The Geographies of Enlightenment Edinburgh, Phil Dodds, 2022

Changing Pedagogies for Children in Eighteenth-Century England, Michèle Cohen, 2023

Converting Britannia

Evangelicals and British Public Life, 1770–1840

Gareth Atkins

THE BOYDELL PRESS

Published in association with

BSECS
British Society for
Eighteenth-Century Studies

First published 2019
The Boydell Press, Woodbridge
Paperback edition 2024

ISBN 978 1 78327 439 0 (Hardback)
ISBN 978 1 83765 126 9 (Paperback)

The Boydell Press is an imprint of Boydell & Brewer Ltd
PO Box 9, Woodbridge, Suffolk IP12 3DF, UK
and of Boydell & Brewer Inc.
668 Mt Hope Avenue, Rochester, NY 14620–2731, USA
website: www.boydellandbrewer.com

A CIP catalogue record for this book is available
from the British Library

The publisher has no responsibility for the continued existence or accuracy of URLs for
external or third-party internet websites referred to in this book, and does not guarantee that any content on such websites is, or will remain, accurate or appropriate

To my parents

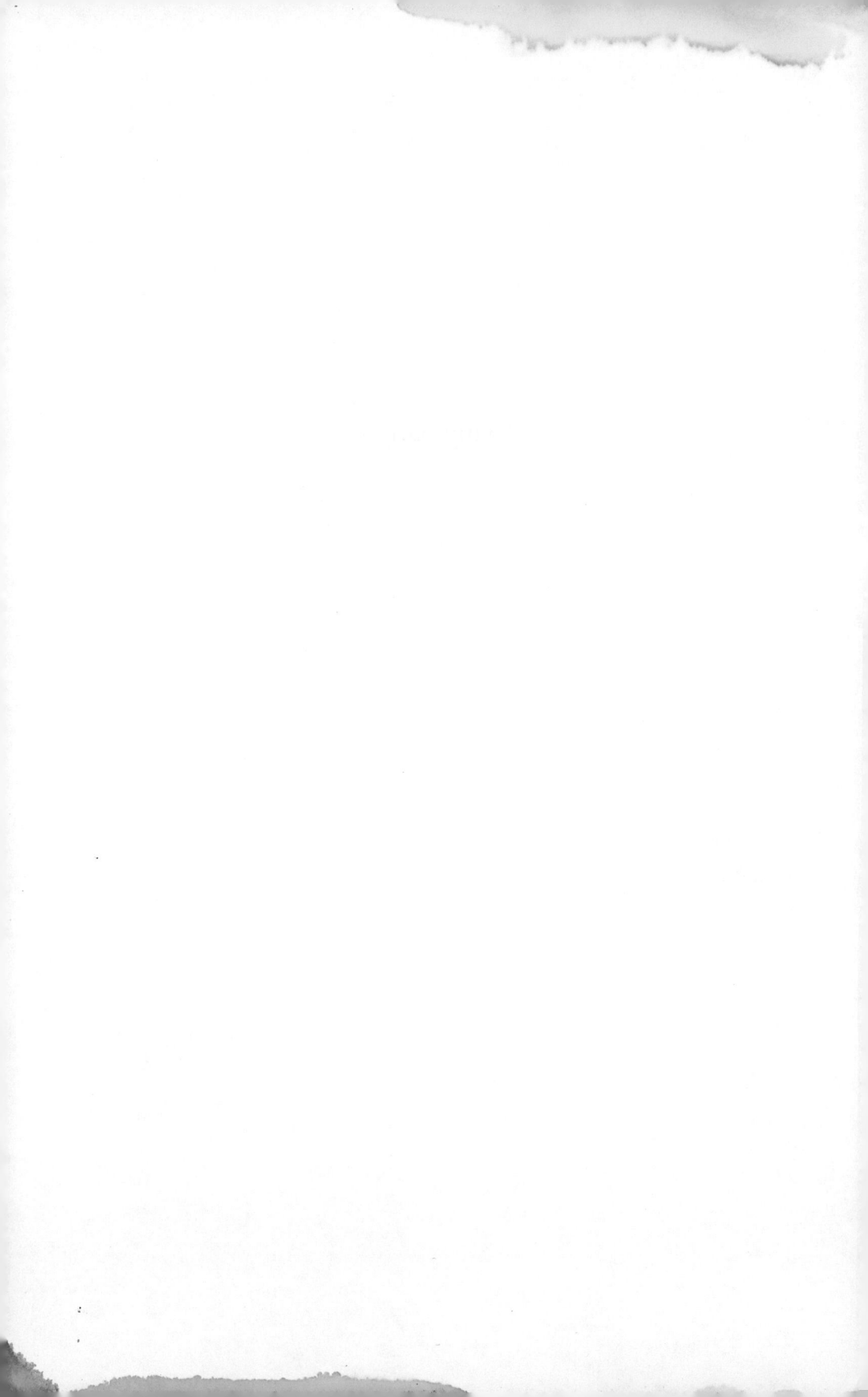

Contents

Illustrations

Plates

Figures

Tables

Map

The author and publishers are grateful to all the institutions and individuals listed for permission to reproduce the materials in which they hold copyright. Every effort has been made to trace the copyright holders; apologies are offered for any omission, and the publishers will be pleased to add any necessary acknowledgement in subsequent editions.

Abbreviations

Alum. Cantab.	J. and J.A. Venn, *Alumni Cantabrigienses: a Biographical List of all Known Students, Graduates and Holders of Office at the University of Cambridge, from the Earliest Times to 1900. Part 1. From the Earliest Time to 1751*, 4 vols (Cambridge, 1922–7); *Part 2. From 1752 to 1900*, 6 vols (Cambridge, 1940–54)
Alum. Oxon.	J. Foster, *Alumni Oxonienses: the Members of the University of Oxford, 1715–1886*, 4 vols (Oxford, 1887–8)
BDEB	Donald M. Lewis (ed.), *The Blackwell Dictionary of Evangelical Biography, 1730–1860*, 2 vols (Oxford, 1995)
BFBS	British and Foreign Bible Society
BL Add. MS	British Library Additional Manuscript
BMS	Baptist Missionary Society
Bodl.	Bodleian Library, Oxford
CBF	Colonial Bishoprics' Fund
CCS	Colonial Church Society
CMS	Church Missionary Society (originally Society for Missions to Africa and the East)
CPAS	Church Pastoral Aid Society
CRL	Cadbury Research Library, University of Birmingham
CUL	Cambridge University Library
EIC	East India Company
Fisher, *HoP*	D.R. Fisher (ed.), *The History of Parliament: the House of Commons, 1820–32*, 7 vols (London, 2009)

LMS	London Missionary Society (originally the Missionary Society)
LPL	Lambeth Palace Library
LSPCJ	London Society for Promoting Christianity Among the Jews
Namier and Brooke, *HoP*	L.B. Namier and John Brooke (eds), *The History of Parliament: the House of Commons, 1754–90* (London, 1964)
NMBS	Naval and Military Bible Society
ODNB	*Oxford Dictionary of National Biography* online
PBHS	Prayer Book and Homily Society
RTS	Religious Tract Society
SBCP	Society for Bettering the Condition of the Poor
SLC	Sierra Leone Company
SPCK	Society for Promoting Christian Knowledge
SPG	Incorporated Society for the Propagation of the Gospel in Foreign Parts
Thorne, *HoP*	R.G. Thorne (ed.), *The History of Parliament: the House of Commons, 1790–1820*, 5 vols (London, 1986)
Wilberforce, *Life*	Robert Isaac Wilberforce and Samuel Wilberforce, *The Life of William Wilberforce*, 5 vols (London, 1838)

Notes on the Text

1. Most of the protagonists of this book are referred to as 'Evangelicals' (with an upper-case 'E'). This is not intended to denote an organized ecclesiastical party. This was a movement whose edges were blurred, often to the point of their being unrecognizable. Nevertheless, 'Evangelical' does usefully set apart churchpeople and their fellow travellers, for despite the commonalities of belief between all those who held vital beliefs ('evangelicals') the social and doctrinal divisions that distinguished its establishment proponents from their dissenting counterparts could be considerable, and were in some respects becoming wider.
2. In quotations and references, capitalization and punctuation have sometimes been altered and abbreviations expanded in order to clarify the meaning.
3. Unless otherwise specified, biographical details are drawn from standard reference works: *Alum. Cantab.*, *Alum. Oxon.*, *BDEB*, *ODNB*, History of Parliament volumes and the Clergy of the Church of England Database. In order to avoid unwieldy footnotes, these are not generally referenced separately.
4. Wherever possible, individuals' date ranges have been given the first time they appear.
5. The spellings of place-names usually follow contemporary rather than modern conventions (e.g. Calcutta for Kolkata; Serampore for Srirampur).

Acknowledgements

Any book that takes this long to research and write is likely to incur a mountain of debts. Precious few of them can be satisfactorily acknowledged. Some of mine are material. I could not have undertaken postgraduate study without the safety net of Arts and Humanities Research Board/ Council funding. I could not have concluded my Ph.D. without generous support from Cambridge University's Lightfoot Fund and a Scouloudi Fellowship from the Institute of Historical Research. A British Academy Postdoctoral Fellowship and a Research Associateship at the Centre for Research in Arts, Social Sciences and Humanities (CRASSH) diverted me into new areas, but they also gave space for me and my ideas to mature.

Other debts are practical. Unpublished papers held in many libraries and archives have allowed glimpses of what lay behind the selective omissions of Victorian hagiographers. I am especially grateful for the assistance of the staff at the Bodleian Library, the British Library, the Cadbury Research Library at the University of Birmingham, the Hampshire Record Office and the Leicestershire, Leicester and Rutland Record Office. I should also like to thank the Earl of Harrowby for permission to consult manuscripts held at Sandon Hall, and the National Maritime Museum at Greenwich, which generously awarded me a Caird Visiting Fellowship. With so much printed primary material now available online, it is easy to forget the hours I have spent in the Rare Books Room at Cambridge University Library, and hours of work put in by the staff there, whose unfailing kindness, patience and efficiency is remarkable given the demands placed on them.

I have benefited hugely over the years from the generosity, support and insight of academic friends and colleagues. It is not possible to name all of them here, but I owe particular thanks to David Bebbington, Arthur Burns, David Craig, Simon Ditchfield, Eamon Duffy, Michael Gladwin, Michael Hetherington, Philip Hobday, Bill Jacob, Matt Jenkinson, Tim Larsen, Tom Licence, Mary Newbould, Peter Nockles, Jon Parry, Rob Priest, Nicholas Rodger, Nigel Scotland, Simon Skinner, Mark Smith, Clare Stancliffe, Anne Stott, John Walsh, Alex Walsham and Carl Watkins. I am grateful for chances to air work in progress at seminars in Cambridge, Edinburgh, Oxford and Winchester, at the Institute of Historical Research, and at the Armed Forces Chaplaincy Centre, Amport House. Between 2012 and 2017 I was privileged to be part of the ERC-funded Bible and Antiquity in Nineteenth-Century Culture Project at CRASSH. During many hours spent discussing forgotten Victorian worthies over piles of Limoncello sandwiches some significant friendships were made. All the 'Biblants' are dear to me, but Simon Goldhill's energy, Scott Mandelbrote's rigour, Brian Murray's capacity for late-night conversation and Kate Nichols's varied and infectious enthusiasms stand out.

It is time to acknowledge two major intellectual debts. The first is to my Ph.D. supervisor, Boyd Hilton, whose humanity, humour, forensic attention to detail and above all interest in what I was doing both encouraged and prodded me to think for myself. This was necessary: to his credit, Boyd was not fazed – at least, not perceptibly so – by the arrival of a gauche new-comer with only the vaguest inkling of a subject and no idea where to start. His generosity allowed me to flourish. The second debt is to Michael Ledger-Lomas, another Biblant, a friend and a fellow collector of long-deceased religious eccentrics, but one whose seemingly inexhaustible appetite for chewing through drafts, and incisive, insightful advice has lent my work a breadth of perspective it did not really deserve. Thank you.

I should like to thank my Ph.D. examiners, John Wolffe and David Thompson, whose painstaking attention I appreciated and whose advice shaped this project for the better over many years. Thanks, too, to everyone at Boydell and Brewer, especially Mari Shullaw, and to the two anonymous readers whose comments and corrections provided helpful food for thought. The substance of Chapter 5 was first published as 'Religion, Politics and Patronage in the Late-Hanoverian Navy, c. 1780–c. 1820', in *Historical Research*, 88 (2015), 272–90. I am grateful to John Wiley and Sons for permission to reproduce it here.

Friends and family raise the thought that for better, and, just occasionally, for worse, academic work does not take place in a vacuum. Various of them kindly accommodated me during research trips, most notably Vicki Tibbits (née McGregor) and her family in Turnham Green, back in early 2006. Others did not really contribute to this project at all, but they tolerated it and sometimes showed an interest. More importantly, they were and are friends: you know who you are! Magdalene College Chapel Choir provided singing, sanity, lifelong friends and much else besides during my early years in Cambridge. I will always be grateful to the fellows of Magdalene and, latterly, Queens' College, for electing me to their number: those richly varied and humane communities have helped make me who I am. My family have, I hope, kept me rooted. Sarah has graciously and lovingly borne with me, and somehow still does, while Anna and Adam provide frequent and occasionally forcible reminders that there is more to life than work. Last of all, my parents. They have supported and encouraged me (and us) unstintingly every single step of the way, as only parents can. This book is dedicated to them.

22 February 2019

The publication of this book has been made possible by a grant from
The Scouloudi Foundation in association with the Institute of Historical Research

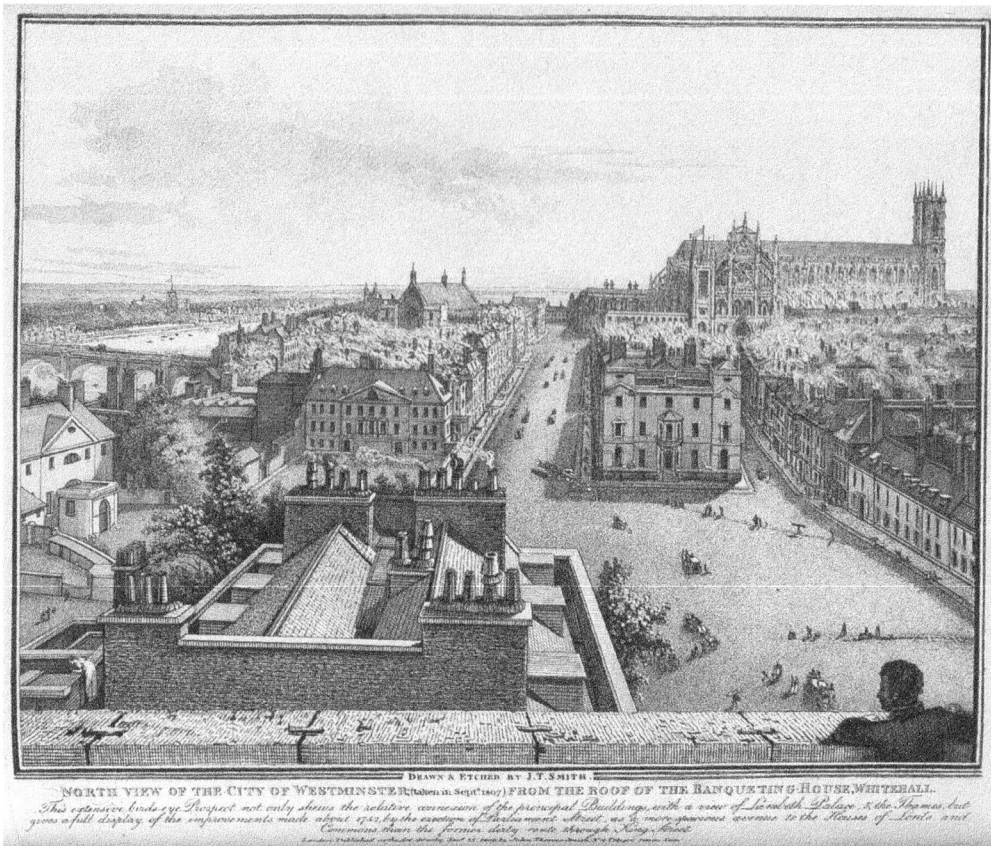

Plate 1: J.T. Smith, *North View of the City of Westminster, taken in September 1807, from the Roof of the Banqueting House, Whitehall*. Etching, 1809.

Introduction:
Redefining 'the Age of Wilberforce'

The roof of Banqueting House in Whitehall offers a bird's-eye view of Westminster in late 1807. Through the smoke of countless chimneys juts Westminster Hall and the jumble of parliamentary buildings around it. Down Parliament Street in the centre it is just possible to see Old Palace Yard, half hidden by the bulk of Westminster Abbey. Crane your neck and you might be able to glimpse William Wilberforce's house, the epicentre of the parliamentary campaign for the abolition of the British slave trade, which concluded only a few months before the engraving was done. A well-informed celebrity spotter might also look towards the higher ground beyond the River Thames, knowing that somewhere along the horizon lay the village of Clapham, home of the pious coterie known to contemporaries as the 'Saints' and to posterity as the Clapham Sect. The notion that this small group and its spheres of activity formed the main point of contact between Evangelicals and British public life was once a historiographical staple. Such ideas drew on decades of hagiographical commentary, and in particular on the affectionate 1844 retrospective in which Sir James Stephen (1789–1859) coined the term 'Clapham Sect'.[1] Stephen himself was brought up at the centre of that milieu, and his essay was deeply personal, as well as being avowedly 'whimsical', not least since those he eulogized did not all live there at the same time.[2] It was also selective, excluding figures who were impeccably pious but whose faces did not fit.[3] Nevertheless, the idea that this 'faithful band' changed the complexion of British politics and culture proved attractive to academic and popular commentators alike

---

[1] [Sir James Stephen], 'The Clapham Sect', *Edinburgh Review*, 80, 161 (1844), 251–307.

[2] Sir James Stephen to Joseph Sturge, 4 Oct. 1844, Sturge Papers, BL Add. MS 43845, fo. 25.

[3] J. R. Oldfield, 'Literary Memorials: Clarkson's *History* and *The Life of William Wilberforce*', in Oldfield, *'Chords of Freedom': Commemoration, Ritual and British Transatlantic Slavery* (Manchester, 2007), 33–55.

well into the twentieth century, and for obvious reasons.[4] Around William Wilberforce (1759–1833) and his friends they wove a grand tale of national sin and humanitarian redemption: a narrative that allowed the British to see theirs as an empire of godliness as well as guineas and gunboats.[5] The publication of Eric Williams's *Capitalism and Slavery* in 1944 punctured this self-satisfied story. Since then the scholarly pendulum has swung markedly away from heroic narratives, even if popular biographers, confessional writers and film-makers remain fascinated by them. Academic accounts of anti-slavery now tend to eschew eminent personalities, focusing instead on grassroots abolitionism[6] and the agency of enslaved people.[7]

The shift was a necessary one. Yet it has not been without its drawbacks. Although scholars now pay far more attention to 'small-e' evangelicalism than they once did, we know surprisingly little about how it operated at the political and cultural 'centre'. It is often portrayed as a species of grassroots piety whose exponents forced moral reform on their contemporaries through pressure-group campaigning, a view that underestimates the hard-edged power wielded by its spokespeople, and the institutional structures that gave them access to it. A re-examination is necessary. It is also timely: the best surveys of the so-called 'Age of Wilberforce' are now a generation or more old,[8] while the most nuanced account of Evangelical politics – albeit one that confines itself to Westminster – remains unpublished.[9]

This book aims to map the world of establishment Evangelicalism from c. 1770–1840, and in so doing to show how it became so influential. It ranges far beyond the predictable lines of Clapham and the House of Commons, tracing networks that spanned the Church, universities, armed forces and imperial officialdom, and which connected London and the regions with Europe and the world. Wilberforce and those he knew and corresponded with were certainly important, but not always, as we shall see, in the sense

---

4   For an excellent summary of this vast literature and its eclipse, see Christopher Leslie Brown, *Moral Capital: Foundations of British Abolitionism* (Chapel Hill, NC, 2006), 1–30.

5   Roshan Allpress, 'William Wilberforce and "the Saints"', in Gareth Atkins (ed.), *Making and Remaking Saints in Nineteenth-Century Britain* (Manchester, 2016), 209–25.

6   Again, the scholarship is extensive: see Seymour Drescher, 'Whose Abolition? Popular Pressure and the Ending of the British Slave Trade', *Past and Present*, 143 (1994), 136–66, for a summary.

7   See Brown, *Moral Capital*, esp. 21–2.

8   Ford K. Brown, *Fathers of the Victorians: the Age of Wilberforce* (Cambridge, 1961); Roger Anstey, *The Atlantic Slave Trade and British Abolition, 1760–1810* (London, 1975).

9   Ian Bradley, 'The Politics of Godliness: Evangelicals in Parliament, 1784–1832' (unpublished D.Phil. thesis, University of Oxford, 1974).

that Victorian and Edwardian commentators assumed. This was a ramifying web of pious individuals, tied together by shared beliefs, to be sure, but cemented by social contact and intermarriage and lubricated – or perhaps driven – by patronage and ambition. Put another way, *Converting Britannia* seeks to make the self-evident but often forgotten point that the Fathers of the Victorians were Hanoverians: that while they were fleet-footed in their willingness to adopt the pressure-group techniques and mass-subscription voluntarism that would later become the standard model for philanthropic organization, they also had a shrewd appreciation of existing levers of power and how one might gain access to them. It seeks to anatomize a particular period with its own logic and *modus operandi*: one that arguably stands between early modern confessionalism and religious 'modernity'.

This has important implications for how we read what Arthur Burns and Joanna Innes have called the 'Age of Reform', the years between roughly 1780 and 1850 in which conservative change, more often piloted from within government and institutions than forced on them from without, averted revolution, largely exonerated the establishment from accusations of 'Old Corruption' and produced the variegated patchwork of public, private, old and new that comprised mid-Victorian Britain.[10] Evangelicals, I suggest, were some of the best exponents of the languages and methods of that 'Age'. Being concerned with building a Christian nation, they sought new 'pulpits' in public life from which they hoped to reshape discourses of national character, professionalism and individual behaviour. This perspective opens up new angles on what happened to Protestantism and 'national identity' in the first half of the nineteenth century. For if scholars have rightly been sceptical of the notion that Protestantism and xenophobic anti-Catholicism unproblematically united the diverse sects and fissiparous tendencies of eighteenth-century Britain, they have tended to accept the more limited proposition that the political establishment united, broadly speaking, around Anglican Protestantism.[11] What that meant, however, was always open to debate, and such discussions became more heated in our period, as empire, social and demographic developments, campaigns for constitutional change, 'popular opinion' and changing conceptions of religious liberty placed unprecedented strain on inherited structures and ideas. Evangelicals were clearly not the only purveyors of the language of

---

[10] Arthur Burns and Joanna Innes (eds), *Rethinking the Age of Reform: Britain, 1780–1850* (Oxford, 2003).

[11] For an excellent summary of this scholarship, see Tony Claydon and Ian McBride (eds), *Protestantism and National Identity: Britain and Ireland, c. 1650–c. 1850* (Cambridge, 1998), 3–29.

religious nationhood. But the powerful part they played in shaping it has seldom received the attention it deserves.

What follows also seeks to explain how evangelicalism and evangelical-style language acted as a catalyst for probably the dominant political debate between the 1820s and the 1870s: that of how to define the sacred and the secular and where to draw the line between them. To understand why this was the case we need to be aware that debates about secularization were in many ways an amplification of older discourses. Ambitious movements to stiffen the religious and moral backbone of the body politic were, after all, nothing new. At the turn of the eighteenth century and again in its middle decades, pulpits, politics and the print sphere resounded with calls to revival and denunciations of luxury, effeminacy and corruption. Societies were formed to proselytize at home and abroad, while the degradation and illiteracy of the poor, the grubby commercialism of the moneyed orders and the flamboyant immorality of the rich all generated heated commentary.[12] If Evangelicals inherited the same urgency, they also inherited many of the same concerns. Central among them, as Brent Sirota has recently argued for the period between 1680 and 1730, was the conflict between 'general benevolence' and doctrinal specificity, between moral and confessional prescriptions for behaviour, between associational and parochial models of charity. In an age that prized religious tolerance, Sirota suggests, breadth won out, despite the jeremiads of late-Stuart and early Hanoverian highchurchmen.[13] Christian life now took place *within* civil society, and through free association and commercial enterprise rather than providing the defining framework for them.

The 'Age of Wilberforce', as we shall see, saw another swing of the same pendulum. For in projecting their own brand of Christian establishment into new spheres, and in harnessing new tools to spread it, Evangelicals unsettled the broad consensus that had solidified around such questions. What follows therefore suggests that we should see conflict between them and a range of opponents as ecclesiological as much as theological: it concerned definitions of what the role of the established Church was, what it ought to be for and where the limits of its writ ran. Most obviously their embrace of voluntarism and fuller lay leadership sat uneasily with a parochial system and the ecclesiastical hierarchy. Equally, though, their propensity for working from within the establishment often riled dissenters

---

[12]   Brent Sirota, *The Christian Monitors: the Church of England and the Age of Benevolence, 1680–1730* (New Haven, CT, 2014); Bob Harris, *Politics and the Nation: Britain in the Mid-Eighteenth Century* (Oxford, 2002), 278–323.

[13]   Sirota, *Christian Monitors*, 252–60.

and other champions of freedom from state interference. Most interesting, perhaps, is how their attempts to re-sacralize commerce, the professions and the public sphere were variously interpreted. The movement's spokesmen came to define success in terms of money raised, Bibles distributed, friends in high places and rhetorical commitment to moral values, seeing all these as evidence of a truly Christian nation. For many of their Anglican opponents, as well as for dissident voices within the Evangelical movement later on, such developments represented secularization by the back-door: a reduction of the demands and particularities of Christianity to pounds, shillings and pence on a balance-sheet and – perhaps surprisingly – a denial of the importance of individual commitment. In some senses these reactions bespeak the difficulties inherent in holding together a broad movement. But I am also making a bigger claim: that in seeking to reshape civil society and to define its values Evangelicals also helped to decentre and fragment religious authority in ways that would also prove damaging to their universal vision. It is no coincidence that the relative eclipse of the movement in the 1840s and 50s was marked by a tighter drawing of the lines between the private sphere of belief and a more plural and in some ways more secular political sphere.

Returning to our vantage point atop Banqueting House, we can begin to sketch some of the main lineaments of the Evangelical world. Immediately surrounding us, in and around Whitehall, lies a warren of buildings containing government offices. Turn, for instance, to the right, to look across the street to the majestic Admiralty Building, the headquarters of the Royal Navy, vacated only the previous year by an Evangelical First Lord. Turn further right to gaze north around the curve of the river to neoclassical Somerset House on the Strand, home of several major government offices, including the Navy Board and Transport Board, both hotbeds of Evangelical influence. Also on and around the Strand lie the inns of court, the centre of the English legal profession: they too contain pious connections. Perhaps a mile beyond is the City of London, whose banking and mercantile aristocracy provide the Evangelical movement with much of its financial clout and some of its most eminent supporters. Their votes ensure the repeated re-election of Evangelical directors at the great institutions of the City: the Bank of England and the East India Company. Through the latter and later also through favourable personnel in the War and Colonial Office, the Evangelical movement also reaches out into Britain's expanding overseas possessions. City church towers serve as a reminder that in the Church of England lay sponsorship ensures openings across the country and further afield for 'gospel clergymen', many of them products of Evangelical-dominated colleges at Oxford and Cambridge. This is the world that *Converting Britannia* will lay bare.

Networks, Patronage, Power

Although the chronology of this book is intentionally drawn more broadly than the conventional 'Age of Wilberforce', which usually runs from his conversion in the mid 1780s until his death in 1833, the choice of its periodization is relatively uncontroversial. It has long been known that evangelicalism in various guises was part of a broader reshaping of British society and culture in the decades either side of 1800.[14] In the last thirty years the influence of the new piety on this period has loomed increasingly large in the historiography. Leonore Davidoff and Catherine Hall's seminal *Family Fortunes* (1987) influentially placed it at the centre of their account of pre-Victorian class and gender formation. Boyd Hilton's *Age of Atonement* (1988) showed how evangelical metaphors of sin, debt and redemption pervaded 'the mentality of the *haute bourgeoisie* that dominated British politics from 1784 to the 1840s'.[15] David Bebbington's *Evangelicalism in Modern Britain* (1989) further underlined the importance of evangelicalism as an engine of intellectual change and religious 'modernity'. Yet although we know a great deal more about evangelical thought and action than we once did, the networks through which vital religion spread remain hazy. This matters because, as recent historians of early nineteenth-century empire have been quick to point out, the British imperial state was a fluid and relatively open world whose webs and circuits enabled a variety of competing groups and interests to advance sectional agendas.[16] The establishment Evangelicalism with which this book is chiefly concerned thought of itself not just as a form of piety but as a movement: a takeover bid that sought to capture the commanding heights of late-Hanoverian Britain and to transform it from the top down.

Apposite parallels for what this book seeks to do are to be found in the ongoing Legacies of British Slave Ownership Project, led by Catherine

---

[14]   See e.g. Maurice J. Quinlan, *Victorian Prelude: a History of English Manners, 1700–1830* (repr. London, 1965); Muriel Jaeger, *Before Victoria: Changing Standards and Behaviour, 1787–1837* (2nd edn: London, 1967).

[15]   Boyd Hilton, *The Age of Atonement: the Influence of Evangelicalism on Social and Economic Thought, 1785–1865* (Oxford, 1988), 7.

[16]   See e.g. Alan Lester, *Imperial Networks: Creating Identities in Nineteenth-Century South Africa and Britain* (London, 2001); Zoe Laidlaw, *Colonial Connections, 1815–45: Patronage, the Information Revolution and Colonial Government* (Manchester, 2005).

Hall, Nicholas Draper and Keith McClelland.[17] Working outwards from the compensation payments made to absentee slave owners when slavery was abolished in the British Empire in 1833, that project demonstrates the rich potential of detailed prosopographical study to give insights into the interlocking networks, personal relationships and business connections that tied together the British elite and professional classes.[18] There are significant differences: whereas they are concerned with revealing how far slave ownership or involvement in aspects of that economic system had quietly penetrated that world, the networks examined here were more public, to the delight of their supporters and the consternation of their opponents. Indeed, the longevity of the heroic narrative that Hall and her collaborators are bent on undermining testifies to the success of the Evangelical endeavour. Nevertheless, like the 'Legacies' project, *Converting Britannia* aims to uncover the material realities that underlay contemporary rhetoric and later mythology: material realities, indeed, that have often been downplayed. My book also mirrors theirs in using connections to throw new light on how institutional Britain operated. Thus, as well as re-examining well-trodden ground, it also touches on spheres that have seldom, if ever, been closely examined by historians of religion.

This approach, however, raises methodological questions. Among the chief challenges in drawing any network is how to capture the varying intensity of the relationships that comprise it. Another is how to demonstrate change over time. While the Legacies project works outwards from one high-resolution image – the compensation awarded when slavery ended – this book necessarily explores the growth and development of Evangelical milieu across a much longer period. It draws on an extensive database detailing family relationships, education, society membership and patron-and-client connections, information which it also cross-references with other prosopographical works: the *ODNB*, the *Blackwell Dictionary of Evangelical Biography*, the History of Parliament. If the resulting book employs different analytical tools at different points, it should be emphasized that this is a deliberate decision. Evangelicalism was a protean phenomenon: it touched people in a variety of ways and varied considerably according to its context. It was a grassroots movement that could also boast privileged access to the corridors of power; it campaigned alongside reforming and radical tendencies while also drawing strength from the

---

[17] See 'Legacies of British Slave Ownership', https://www.ucl.ac.uk/lbs/, last accessed 16 August 2018.

[18] Catherine Hall, Nicholas Draper, Keith McClelland, Katie Donington and Rachel Lang, *Legacies of British Slave-Ownership: Colonial Slavery and the Formation of Victorian Britain* (Cambridge, 2014).

moral-minded upper middle classes; it was at once an innovative social movement and an establishment coup. The challenge, then, has been to develop an account that is sufficiently multi-layered to do justice to a movement while retaining a coherent sense of what it meant to be part of it. Hence some sections focus on particular events, while others explore in detail how networks developed in specific environments; elsewhere I map the physical geography of church attendance and sociability, while in other places I analyse the membership of philanthropic societies and involvement in them. In many ways this approach reflects the insights of Actor-Network Theory, a tool developed by sociological scholars such as Bruno Latour and John Law, which proposes that everything in the social world exists in constantly shifting networks of relationship. Instead of seeking to 'explain' why social activity takes place, they argue, we should simply seek to describe it, seeing analyses that go beyond the empirical as conjuring up abstract theoretical concepts that do not genuinely exist. In other words, I have resisted imposing a false coherence on the world I have been studying: I am not concerned with the spread of a single, easily identifiable idea or the propagation of one organization, but with how a set of not-always-coherent beliefs and connections functioned as they reproduced and metamorphosed over time.[19]

The idea that evangelicalism in the long eighteenth century was inherently a connection-making creed emerges clearly from a number of recent studies.[20] Mark Noll in particular has urged scholars to see networks as written into a piety that defined itself in opposition to its contemporaries socially as much as theologically.[21] This idea is also reflected in older literature on the 'Age of Wilberforce', notably in Ford K. Brown's widely read but now dated *Fathers of the Victorians* (1961). Like E.P. Thompson in *The Making of the English Working Class* (1963), Brown argued forcefully that the adoption of vital religion by the ruling orders cloaked a cynical attempt to justify social inequalities through the invocation of Providence and the threat of eternal punishment.[22] Critics have not always accepted this thesis, and have also pointed to practical flaws in Brown's analysis, the main

---

[19]   See Bruno Latour, *Reassembling the Social: an Introduction to Actor-Network Theory* (Oxford, 2005).

[20]   D. Bruce Hindmarsh, *John Newton and the English Evangelical Tradition: Between the Conversions of Wesley and Wilberforce* (Oxford, 1996); Grayson Carter, *Anglican Evangelicals: Protestant Secessions from the Via Media, c. 1800–1850* (Oxford, 2001).

[21]   Mark Noll, *The Rise of Evangelicalism: The Age of Edwards, Whitefield, and the Wesleys* (Leicester, 2004).

[22]   Brown, *Fathers of the Victorians*, 4–6, 123–55; E. P. Thompson, *The Making of the English Working Class* (rev. edn: London, 1980), esp. 385–440.

problem being his cavalier use of the label 'Evangelical', which he applied indiscriminately to almost every moral, benevolent or religious society active between 1787 and 1844.[23] Changes in the historiographical landscape since 1961 have, moreover, rendered other aspects of Brown's work problematic. Since the publication of J.C.D. Clark's *English Society, 1688–1832* (1985) the idea that evangelicalism was a reaction against a secular-minded age has looked less convincing. The revisionist turn in Hanoverian religious history has emphasized the institutional robustness, flexibility and socio-cultural centrality of the established churches.[24] Naturally, Evangelical controversialists frequently decried their clerical contemporaries as lazy squarsons or 'idol shepherds'. But to see such rhetoric as reflecting reality, as both High and Low Church Victorians liked to do, is to ignore the piety and energy of many of those supposedly somnolent clergy, as well as causes in which Evangelicals and the 'Orthodox' (i.e. mainstream) clergy were practically indistinguishable. Nevertheless, although ecclesiastical specialists will readily see the problems with Brown's picture, there are important truths in it. The rakish, rumbustious, sexual licentious world of late eighteenth-century London so brilliantly evoked by Vic Gatrell undoubtedly gave way to a more decorous, more buttoned-up, more overtly pious culture in the second quarter of the nineteenth century, and Evangelicals had much to do with that.[25] They punched above their numerical weight, not least because they were quick to innovate organizationally, founding Bible and missionary societies whose deliberately pragmatic goals were designed to appeal to as broad a spectrum of opinion as possible. These endeavours were well-publicized and astutely presented, employing discourses of patriotism and civic philanthropy to further enhance their appeal to the moral-minded (and upwardly mobile) urban middle classes, and to confer cultural authority on those who used such language.

Most importantly, as Brown was well aware, they combined all of this with an intimate knowledge of the levers of power. 'We see the marshalling and deployment of influence, "interest" and social power', he explained, 'the intense zeal and passionate fervour of moral suasion, the subtlety of

[23] See especially David Newsome, 'Father and Sons', *Historical Journal*, 6 (1963), 295–310; see also reviews by John Clive, *Journal of Modern History*, 34 (1962), 337–8, and J. M. Prest, in *Economic History Review*, n.s., 15 (1963), 555–6.

[24] See e.g. John Walsh, Colin Haydon and Stephen Taylor (eds), *The Church of England, c. 1689–c. 1833: from Toleration to Tractarianism* (Cambridge, 1993). For an assessment of this scholarship, and of its limitations, see Mark Goldie, 'Voluntary Anglicans', *Historical Journal*, 46 (2003), 977–90.

[25] Vic Gatrell, *City of Laughter: Sex and Satire in Eighteenth-Century London* (London, 2006), 417–82.

ecclesiastical intrigue.'[26] This would certainly have come as no surprise to contemporary critics, who damned the new piety as a neo-puritan conspiracy. Among the fiercest proponents of this notion was the Whig churchman Sydney Smith (1771–1845), who wrote frequently and vehemently against the new piety in the *Edinburgh Review*:

> The party which [they have] formed in the Legislature, and the artful neutrality with which they give respectability to their small numbers, – the talents of some of this party, and the unimpeached excellence of their characters, all make it probable that fanaticism will increase, rather than diminish. [They] have made an alarming inroad into the Church, and they are attacking the Army and Navy. The principality of Wales, and the East India Company, they have already acquired. All mines and subterraneous places belong to them; they creep into hospitals and small schools, and so work their way upwards. They beg all the little livings, particularly in the north of England, from the ministers for the time being; and from these fixed points they make incursions upon the happiness and common sense of the vicinage.[27]

Others were just as scathing. 'The mongrel SAINTS of our days are as keen for places, pensions, contracts and jobs as the inhabitants of any perjured borough in the kingdom,' jeered the Tory radical William Cobbett (1763–1835), who reckoned them to be 'the main prop of the PITT system'. 'Indeed if I were to be put to it to find out the most consummate knaves in all England, I should most assuredly set to work amongst those who are ironically denominated SAINTS.'[28]

One of the advantages of studying Evangelicalism in terms of networks is that it enables us to cut decisively through the 'artful neutrality' that Smith and Cobbett found so objectionable: to reinject politicking into accounts of the Evangelical movement, and to show where Evangelicalism fitted into contemporary politics. Historians have long been sceptical about the Saints' self-proclaimed independence. The ethical overlap between Evangelical rectitude and Pittite reformism has attracted plenty of scholarly attention; so too has the confluence of pious anti-slavery with Whig humanitarianism.[29]

---

[26] Brown, *Fathers of the Victorians*, 7.

[27] [Sydney Smith], 'Ingram on Methodism', *Edinburgh Review*, 11, 22 (Jan. 1808), 361.

[28] William Cobbett, 'Dissenters' [1811], in John M. Cobbett and James Paul Cobbett (eds), *Selections from Cobbett's Political Works*, 6 vols (London, 1835), IV: 53, 59.

[29] Anstey, *Atlantic Slave Trade*; Boyd Hilton, *A Mad, Bad, and Dangerous People: England, 1783–1846* (Oxford, 2006), 174–94; Simon Devereaux, 'Inexperienced

Yet this book shows that there were also concrete reasons to see the Saints as political players. Thriving connections in officialdom and the City of London drew them into the orbit of government, especially during the Pitt ministries of 1784–1801 and 1804–6. If such connections remained relatively strong during the administrations of Spencer Perceval (1762–1812) and Lord Liverpool (1770–1828) between 1809 and 1827, the Saints also aligned themselves with the Whigs on humanitarian questions, such as during the slave trade abolition campaign of 1806–7, and in the 1830s when the Liberal Evangelical Lord Glenelg (1778–1866) was President of the Indian Board of Control from 1830–4 and then Secretary of State for the Colonies from 1835–9. Nevertheless, the Saints seldom seem to have felt beholden to ministers for long. 'Mr Wilberforce', complained George Canning (1770–1827) in 1820, '[is] as regular a suitor at the Treasury for the disposal of offices in the revenue in favour of his friends, as any other ministerial member.' 'On that account ... the Ministers [should have] an equal right to his vote and support.'[30] To some extent Canning's frustration can be ascribed to parliamentary arithmetic, for although the Saints were of little significance numerically in the House of Commons, there were times when their votes held the balance. Also significant was the growth of a formidable 'religious public' that made the pronouncements of Evangelical parliamentarians harder to ignore. Evangelicals were not, then, independent in the way we might understand it, but they did not need to follow anyone else's agenda slavishly.

Central to the argument of this book is the fact that this would have been cheerfully acknowledged by Evangelicals themselves. Their unpublished correspondence, diaries and personal papers are littered with references to place-finding and clientage. Such references are, however, striking by their absence from published accounts. By the time the sons and daughters of the Wilberforce generation came to write up their illustrious forebears, the world had changed.[31] Patronage still existed, of course. But by the late 1830s and certainly by the 1840s the naked exercise of it ('Old Corruption')

Humanitarians? William Wilberforce, William Pitt, and the Execution Crisis of the 1780s', *Law and History Review*, 33 (2015), 839–85; A. D. Kriegel, 'A Convergence of Ethics: Saints and Whigs in British Antislavery', *Journal of British Studies*, 26 (1987), 423–50.

30 Cited in [Thomas Creevey], *A Guide to the Electors of Great Britain upon the Accession of a New King* (London, 1820), 5.

31 Christopher Tolley, *Domestic Biography: the Legacy of Evangelicalism in Four Nineteenth-Century Families* (Oxford, 1997).

was becoming a dirty word.[32] Biographers referred to it obliquely or not at all. Other developments exacerbated this wilful amnesia, not least the changing relationship between politics and religion. Late-Hanoverian Evangelicals thrived in a world in which the state offered powerful support to one version of Christianity. They adapted readily to – and in some cases cheered on – campaigns for religious toleration, but the Whig reforms of the 1830s, militant nonconformity and intense partisanship within the Church of England meant that by the middle of the century politicians and public figures were coming to regard the state as impartial in religious matters.[33] Although the sphere occupied by religion remained far larger than it does today, faith was increasingly thought of as a private matter. Hence the uncontroversial emphasis of Victorian memoirists on moral statesmanship and charisma: the great campaigns for the abolition of the slave trade and the reform of the nation's morals. Hence, too, the selective editing that downplayed what had once been seen as the legitimate manipulation of patronage, and the impression, implicit in the silence of many modern accounts, and explicit in others, that such activity was somehow illicit. And hence, therefore, the importance of excavating this world in order to examine how it really worked. Wilberforce's biographer John Pollock, for example, mistakes his subject's renunciation of the use of interest on behalf of friends and family for a complete disavowal of patronage: in reality this marked his determination to deploy it in the interests of religion.[34] The *ODNB* article on Thomas Babington Macaulay (1800–1859) suggests that he shared the 'otherworldly' attitude of his parents' generation, the 'Saints': 'political influence', it declares in a statement that they would probably have found puzzling, 'was less important than doing God's work'.[35] I have therefore been at pains to show that the subjects of this book were men and women of their time. It is anachronistic to pigeonhole them as 'reformers' or 'reactionaries', both of which labels are still frequently ascribed to them. They pursued their own priorities, often measuring their success in terms of appointments and influence, and talking openly about this in terms that later generations would have found deeply cynical.

This book, therefore, is concerned chiefly with the pursuit of power. If that sounds strange it is because recent historiography has tended to look

[32]   Philip Harling, *The Waning of 'Old Corruption': Economical Reform, 1779–1846* (Oxford, 1996), 208–16, 229–40.

[33]   Stewart J. Brown, *The National Churches of England, Ireland and Scotland, 1801–46* (Oxford, 2001), 324–410.

[34]   John Pollock, *Wilberforce: God's Statesman* (Eastbourne, 2001), 130.

[35]   William Thomas, 'Macaulay, Thomas Babington, Baron Macaulay (1800–1859)', *ODNB*.

elsewhere, rightly emphasizing how evangelicalism shaped gender, class, racial and familial identities.[36] This has, however, sometimes obscured the breadth of Evangelical ambitions. Against the suggestion that even their adoption of the slavery issue cloaked a narrowly moralistic agenda – 'a chance to win over those otherwise suspicious of campaigns against vice', as one historian puts it – what follows insists that Evangelicals pursued a universal vision of a Christian nation that was about far more simply encouraging individuals to embrace their own conversion.[37] It follows from this that accounts focusing on grassroots activism tell only a partial story. For although Evangelicals certainly found ways to remould the public sphere around their priorities,[38] they were also obsessed with securing a grip on institutions. This combination of campaigning and the cultivation of influence helps to explain not just the nature of Evangelical strength but its timing, too. It could be argued that late-Hanoverian Britain lay on the cusp of political and religious modernity. At a time of unsettling techno-logical innovation, social change, political reform, religious pluralism and imperial expansion, Evangelicals were prepared to embrace new forms of organization and activity while at the same time taking full advantage of older structures.

It may therefore come as no surprise to learn that this book deals mainly with male-dominated milieux. Recent scholarship on evangelicals and gender has naturally and rightly led to an emphasis on women. It has revealed how ideas about pious femininity ('separate spheres') limited middle-class women, but also paradoxically empowered them to become arbiters of domestic piety and moral causes.[39] It has also demonstrated the importance of families and kinship ties, a finding which will be amply con-firmed in what follows. And it has also contributed to a widening in our notion of what constitutes politics.[40] This book contains many women who

---

[36]　From a vast scholarship, see Leonore Davidoff and Catherine Hall, *Family Fortunes: Men and Women of the English Middle Class, 1780–1850* (London, 1987); John Tosh, *A Man's Place: Masculinity and the Middle-Class Home in Victorian England* (New Haven, CT, 1999); Catherine Hall, *Civilising Subjects: Metropole and Colony in the English Imagination, 1830–1867* (Chicago, IL, 2002); Alison Twells, *The Civilising Mis-sion and the English Middle Class, 1792–1850: the 'Heathen' at Home and Overseas* (Basingstoke, 2009); Anne Stott, *Wilberforce: Family and Friends* (Oxford, 2012).

[37]　Brown, *Moral Capital*, 387–9.

[38]　Hall, *Civilising Subjects*; Richard Huzzey, *Freedom Burning: Anti-Slavery and Em-pire in Victorian Britain* (Ithaca, NY, 2012).

[39]　Clare Midgley, *Women Against Slavery: the British Campaigns, 1780–1870* (London, 1992).

[40]　Kathryn Gleadle, *Borderline Citizens: Women, Gender and Political Culture in Brit-ain, 1815–1867* (Oxford, 2009); Elizabeth J. Clapp and Julie Roy Jeffrey (eds), *Women,*

were active as ecclesiastical patrons, authors and activists, and recognizes that they found ways to participate in both formal and informal politics. But in what follows, these insights lead us full circle to consider afresh the powerful men: to how they defined power, why they sought it and what they wanted to do with it once they had it. For as William Van Reyk has suggested in an important article, the influential assumption of John Tosh and others that public masculinity was an essentially secular construct, being performed by irreligious males to an irreligious audience, flies in the face of considerable evidence to the contrary. Davidoff and Hall's equation of the masculine 'public sphere' with the middle-class world of work, meanwhile, excludes a range of contexts where Christian manliness was, and had always been, articulated.[41] The sustained attention given to the relationship between femininity, religiosity and ideas about Britishness has been largely asymmetrical.[42] This book will argue that Evangelical attempts to take control of British public life were also attempts to market their own ideas about what manliness ought to look like. Converting Britain was for them about far more than bringing the individuals that comprised it to faith, imperative though that was. Appropriating and reshaping discourses of national character and individual behaviour was no less important. Institutional takeover, then, was about finding vantage points from which to proclaim their message and to implement change.

Evangelicals in Public Life

Having set out the broad lines of argument, it is worth asking why Evangelicals became so heavily involved in public affairs when they did. To anyone who had lived through the 1740s, 50s and 60s it might have seemed surprising that Evangelicals were interested in politics at all, for then they occupied a place on the social and political fringes. Their marginalization was partly self-imposed, since the corrupting effect of 'worldliness' was seldom far from the serious mind. 'Politics', wrote one eighteenth-century cleric, 'are Satan's most tempting and alluring baits… A Christian observes what God is doing on the Earth but he studies politics more as a divine providence

---

Dissent, and Anti-Slavery in Britain and America, 1790–1865 (Oxford, 2011); Sarah Richardson, *The Political Worlds of Women: Gender and Politics in Nineteenth-Century Britain* (Abingdon, 2012).

[41] William Van Reyk, 'Christian Ideals of Manliness in the Eighteenth and Early Nineteenth Centuries', *Historical Journal*, 52 (2009), 1053–73.

[42] Judith S. Lewis, *Sacred to Female Patriotism: Gender, Class, and Politics in Late Georgian Britain* (London, 2003), 159–90; Emma Major, *Madam Britannia: Women, Church, and Nation, 1712–1812* (Oxford, 2012).

than a worldly system.'[43] 'If you will believe the children of Satan,' the MP Sir Richard Hill (1732–1808) warned a relative in 1763, 'they will tell you that you may be conformed to the world and love God too.'[44] By the time Hill's biography was published in 1839, however, the cultural goalposts had shifted. Respectability was taming the vices of the poor and had even taken the edge off aristocratic immorality.[45] Hill's eccentric 'opposition from the world', his biographer conceded, was difficult now to comprehend, but 'we who live under very different circumstances can scarcely appreciate what a man of his station in society had to sacrifice to his zeal and opinions'.[46] Simultaneously, though, Evangelicalism had also undergone a shift in its priorities.[47] Crucial to this was its spread within the bounds of the social and ecclesiastical establishment. From as early as the 1760s there existed a small group of clergymen, distinct from Methodism, who identified themselves as 'gospel ministers'. They were joined in the 1780s and 90s by a new generation of lay activists drawn from among the professional and commercial classes, many of them Anglicans, who brought with them tactical awareness and a fuller appreciation of the advantages of influence. Whereas the boast of John Wesley (1703–1791) that he 'designed plain truth for plain people' had epitomized the temper of the early revival, innovators now sought 'to do within the Church, and nearer the throne what Wesley has accomplished in the meeting and amongst the multitude'.[48] This went hand in hand with a move towards political activism, for if the urgent public moralism of the years after the loss of America was not peculiar to Evangelicals, it was undoubtedly conducive to the spread of 'seriousness' in public life.[49]

These developments were underpinned by and in turn reinforced a broad shift in soteriology among evangelicals. The vicious Calvinistic controversies of earlier decades, which pitted Wesley against George Whitefield (1714–1770), and Augustus Montague Toplady (1740–1778) against

[43]   John Owen, *Memoir of the Rev. Thomas Jones* (London, 1851), 161–2.

[44]   Edwin Sidney, *The Life of Sir Richard Hill* (London, 1839), 45.

[45]   M.J.D. Roberts, *Making English Morals: Voluntary Association and Moral Reform in England, 1787–1886* (Cambridge, 2004), 96–142; Gatrell, *City of Laughter*, 417–573; David Spring, 'Aristocracy, Social Structure, and Religion in the Early Victorian Period', *Victorian Studies*, 6 (1962–3), 263–80.

[46]   Sidney, *Richard Hill*, 249.

[47]   John Wolffe, *The Expansion of Evangelicalism: the Age of Wilberforce, More, Chalmers and Finney* (Nottingham, 2006), 151–215.

[48]   Wilberforce, *Life*, I: 130.

[49]   Hilton, *Age of Atonement*, 3–26; 203–11; Harling, *Waning of 'Old Corruption'*, 31–55; Roberts, *Making English Morals*, 17–58; Joanna Innes, *Inferior Politics: Social Problems and Social Policies in Eighteenth-Century Britain* (Oxford, 2009), 109–226.

John Fletcher (1729–1785), had for the most part waned, giving way to a profound distaste for wrangling about how salvation took place. The new mood, broadly shared across the denominational spectrum, was resolutely anti-systematic. 'Nothing seems important to me but so far as it is concerned with *morals*,' declared the prominent London cleric, Richard Cecil (1748–1810). 'The end – the *cui bono?* – enters into my view of every thing [*sic*].'[50] 'I do not know any opinions separate from their practical uses that are worth contending for,' sniffed the Hull clergyman Joseph Milner (1744–1797).[51] In some ways this reflected a generational shift, as younger figures such as Charles Simeon of Cambridge (1759–1836), Thomas Robinson of Leicester (1749–1813) and John Venn of Clapham (1759–1813) rose to prominence, but it was also evident in the changing thinking of older men such as John Newton (1725–1807), whose Calvinism softened considerably during the 1770s and 80s.[52] Either way, a deliberately unsystematic 'Moderate Calvinism' – or 'Bible Christianity', as it was sometimes pointedly called by its advocates – was rapidly becoming the norm among the gospel clergy.[53] Only a few die-hard High Calvinists continued to revel in the details of 'fixed fate, free will and knowledge absolute': justification by faith alone, not predestined election, was becoming for most the touchstone of Evangelical orthodoxy.[54] Grace was to be offered to all because Christ had died for all. Reacting against accusations that predestinarianism left men 'saved, do what they will ... [or] damned, do what they can', as Wesley scorchingly put it, preachers scrutinized their congregations less for correct beliefs than for the works that were evidence of genuine faith.[55] 'Be ye doers of the word and not hearers only' was the watchword of Thomas Scott (1747–1821) during his influential chaplaincy of London's Lock Hospital between 1785 and 1803, where he struggled to convince cultured Calvinists that without evidential works their 'faith' was delusory.[56] While collections of systematic

[50]   Josiah Pratt, *The Works of the Rev. Richard Cecil*, 3 vols (2nd edn: London, 1816), III: 532.

[51]   Isaac Milner (ed.), *The Works of the Late Rev. Joseph Milner*, 8 vols (London, 1810), VI: 174.

[52]   Hindmarsh, *John Newton*, 166–8.

[53]   John D. Walsh, 'The Yorkshire Evangelicals in the Eighteenth Century, with Especial Reference to Methodism' (unpublished Ph.D. thesis, University of Cambridge, 1956), 27–36; Bebbington, *Evangelicalism*, 63–5. I am also deeply indebted to Dr John Walsh for the loan of his superb unpublished paper, 'Evangelicals and Predestination, 1730–1830.'

[54]   John Milton, *Paradise Lost*, II: 560.

[55]   John Wesley, *The Consequence Proved* (London, 1771), 4–7.

[56]   John Scott, *The Life of the Rev. Thomas Scott* (4th edn: London, 1822), 224–59.

theology gathered dust, volumes of *Practical Sermons* poured from the presses, packed with moral guidance.

If undiluted Calvinism was falling out of vogue among churchmen, many up-and-coming laymen viewed it with positive distaste. Wilberforce, for one, avowed himself to be 'no predestinarian' in 1797, later admitting to his son Samuel that 'every year that I live I become more impressed with the unscriptural character of the Calvinistic system'.[57] Whenever the High Calvinist Robert Hawker of Plymouth (1753–1827) was invited to preach at the Lock, the Wilberforces instead decamped to Bentinck Chapel to hear Basil Woodd (1760–1831), who was less apt to spout 'poison'.[58] For Wilberforce, as for many others, Calvinism was pernicious because it bred a dangerous antinomianism which undermined the importance of moral vigilance. 'Very doctrinal and unprofitable', noted Wilberforce of one unnamed sermonizer. 'Alas how much easier to make a profession of religion than to govern the temper!'[59] Such comments also underline a pronounced mistrust among laymen for doctrinal abstractions of any sort. The Leeds surgeon William Hey (1736–1819) saw the Bible as a '*practical* book' which was not to be imprisoned in 'the fetters of any received system'.[60] 'I value all speculative opinions little, except as they influence practice and are connected with it', Wilberforce told the agriculturalist Arthur Young (1741–1820). Christ's message, he added, had been entrusted to unlettered men, and was to be interpreted with common sense, 'not with logical precision'.[61] 'I see more and more that religion is far from the doctrinal thing which some make it', confessed the banker Henry Thornton (1760–1815) in his diary, suggesting that he would go so far as to avoid both the word 'Trinity' and the 'higher Calvinistic points' for the sake of ecclesiastical unity.[62] Theology was not abandoned, but the frameworks which earnest laymen used to interpret their experience were pared down to functional essentials. 'By their fruits ye shall know them' (Matt. 7: 20) could have been their motto, for although Evangelicals held that salvation was by faith alone, they also knew that faith

---

[57] Wilberforce, *Life*, V: 162.

[58] *Ibid.*, IV: 473. He also avoided the evening preacher, C. E. de Coetlogon, for similar reasons. 'I told you what to expect if you went to the Lock in an Ev[enin]g', he chided a friend, sending him a volume of Hooker as an antidote. Cited in *Ibid.*, I: 286; Wilberforce to Arthur Young, n.d., 1797, Arthur Young Letters, BL Add. MS 35127, fo. 453.

[59] Wilberforce, *Life*, III: 473.

[60] John Pearson, *The Life of William Hey*, 2 vols (London, 1822), II: 210, 215.

[61] Wilberforce to Arthur Young, 20 Jul. 1799, Arthur Young Letters, BL Add. MS 35128, fo. 122.

[62] Henry Thornton Diary, CUL, Thornton Family Letters and Papers, MS Add.7674/1/R, fos 163, 166.

without works was dead. It was actions rather than beliefs that showed whether an individual was on the way to heaven: an idea that stoked an anxious sense that this world was a probation for the next, but which also justified active involvement in public affairs. The bestselling behaviour manuals of Wilberforce, Hannah More (1745–1833) and Thomas Gisborne (1758–1846) found a receptive audience among busy laypeople for whom arguments based on social interests, professional ambitions, reason and practicality carried more weight than systematic intellectual abstractions.[63]

The swing away from Calvinism also reflected a growing canniness among Evangelicals about how they presented themselves. When Scott read Wilberforce's *Practical View* he was struck by the fact that his friend 'seem[ed] afraid of Calvinism, and is not very systematical'. 'Perhaps it is so much the better', Scott reflected, realizing that – given its associations with extravagance and puritan fanaticism – 'Calvinism' was a difficult pill for polite hearers to swallow.[64] The same could be said of other eccentricities. 'It is really a thing greatly to be regretted', complained Wilberforce to John Venn in 1797, 'that some persons of solid piety should not feel it their duty to divest themselves of any peculiarities of manner, and to acquire some powers of conciliation in an age like this, when there is a prejudice against the evangelical doctrines themselves.'[65] Concerns over respectability assumed greater importance in the 1790s, as the *Anti-Jacobin Review* lumped together 'Methodists' of all varieties and damned them as enthusiasts, levellers and would-be revolutionaries.[66] Many Evangelicals blamed the prevalence of unhelpful caricatures on the naïve failure of their predecessors to cultivate ecclesiastical and political influence. Henry Thornton, for instance, was deeply critical of his father's patronage of openly Calvinistic divines, reckoning that 'he therefore rendered the Bishops his enemies'. 'While he was doing much good to thousands and perhaps tens of thousands of the common people to whom he both sent preachers and distributed books innumerable', he added, 'he made little progress with the

---

[63]   See Anne Stott, *Hannah More: the First Victorian* (Oxford, 2003), 97–8; John Wolffe, 'William Wilberforce's *Practical View* (1797) and its Reception', *Studies in Church History*, 44 (2008), 175–84.

[64]   Scott, *Thomas Scott*, 347.

[65]   Wilberforce to Venn, 18 Jan. 1797, cited in Wilberforce, *Life*, I: 153.

[66]   Stott, *Hannah More*, 232–57; Peter B. Nockles, 'The Waning of Protestant Unity and Waxing of Anti-Catholicism? Archdeacon Daubeny and the Reconstruction of "Anglican" Identity in the Later Georgian Church, c. 1780–c. 1830', in William Gibson and Robert G. Ingram (eds), *Religious Identities in Britain, 1660–1832* (Aldershot, 2005), 179–230.

rich.'[67] Thornton junior, in contrast, was only too aware that appearances mattered, justifying the expenditure of £300 on a new coach by pointing out to his wife-to-be that 'we must do good both to the bodies and the souls of men, and that to gain an influence over the minds of our equals is perhaps most necessary which cannot be done if we are not equally free from austerity and ostentation'.[68] 'By becoming a little more respectable,' he later put it more pithily, 'we become much more dangerous'.[69] Image-savvy Evangelicals, in short, were painfully conscious of the need to woo the rich and influential, and battled hard to do so.

This mattered all the more because the spread of the new piety among the well-to-do was opening up prospects for far-reaching change. Moral reform became an urgent imperative in the 1780s, but it was invested with fresh urgency in the 1790s, when the triumphs of atheistic republicanism in France, the execution of Louis XVI (1754–1793), military reverses on the continent and Napoleon's invasion of Egypt pushed a wide range of religious commentators to search the prophetic portions of the scriptures for evidence of Britain's likely fate.[70] While extremists such as the naval-officer-turned-prophet Richard Brothers (1757–1824) predicted imminent apocalypse, establishment Evangelicals saw such events as a call to action. Armageddon might be averted, they argued, if the nation repented of its sins.[71] Campaigns against vice, sabbath-breaking and the slave trade could thus be presented as part of the war effort, with successes and failures of British arms being read as a barometer of divine favour.[72] From around the turn of the century new national societies capitalized on this temper. Endeavours such as the British and Foreign Bible Society, founded in 1804, were marketed as endeavours that sought not just to save souls but also to rejuvenate Britain as a Christian nation: a project that all true patriots ought to invest in. It was a seductive formula, and the burgeoning receipts of Bible, tract and missionary societies in the early 1810s speak volumes for its appeal beyond narrowly evangelical constituencies. Integral to the growth of the new societies was their wholehearted embrace of this-worldly

---

[67] Henry Thornton, 'Recollections', CUL, MS Add.7674/1/N, fo. 4.

[68] Marianne Sykes (later Mrs Henry Thornton) to Mrs Sykes, Feb. 1796, CUL, 'Family Letterbook and Recollections', MS Add.7674/1/N, fos 57–8.

[69] Henry Thornton to Hannah More, 26 Jan. 1811, 'Family Letterbook and Recollections', CUL, MS Add.7674/1/N, fo. 286.

[70] Stuart Semmel, *Napoleon and the British* (New Haven, CT, 2004), 72–106.

[71] John Coffey, '"Tremble, Britannia!": Fear, Providence and the Abolition of the Slave Trade, 1758–1807', *English Historical Review*, 127 (2012), 844–81.

[72] Gareth Atkins, 'Christian Heroes, Providence and Patriotism in Wartime Britain, 1793–1815', *Historical Journal*, 58 (2015), 393–414.

tools – print technology, publicity, business know-how – which were now re-interpreted not as 'worldly' crutches but as divinely appointed 'means' to salvation.[73] By 1815, the eschatological gloom of earlier years was evaporating in the face of a sunny postmillennialism that emphasized the role of human agency in paving the way for Christ's second coming. For many it was a vision in which British global dominion, maritime trade and civilization would play a central part.[74] Behind the grandiloquent sloganizing lay a flinty determination to employ all means necessary to ensure that it came to pass.

Redefining Evangelicalism in the 'Age of Wilberforce'

Little has been said so far about the boundaries of the movement, or about what precisely is meant here by 'Evangelical'. It will be clear already that the ambitious expansiveness of our period meant that doctrinal niceties were often subsumed in broad-based coalitions.[75] Yet such ecumenism was selective. It birthed temporary alliances on particular issues, but this seldom progressed far towards pan-evangelical union, on the one hand, or assimilation into the ecclesiastical mainstream, on the other. Among the main reasons for that was the evaporation of the promiscuous cross-denominationalism of the earlier revival in the face of a heightened awareness of the importance of social respectability and ecclesiastical regularity – i.e. adherence to the disciplines of the Church of England.[76] The gap between churchmen and dissenters was widening, especially among the clergy, who were generally more squeamish about crossing denominational boundaries than laymen. Although they co-operated with dissenters on particular projects, they were generally careful to stress that these were practical rather than religious endeavours. This raises a further point that is not original but needs to be re-emphasized: Evangelicalism was neither monolithic nor unchanging. While their Victorian friends and enemies conspired to give the impression that Evangelicals had always comprised a distinct party whose members were easily identifiable by peculiarities of doctrine

---

[73] Joseph Stubenrauch, *The Evangelical Age of Ingenuity in Industrial Britain* (Oxford, 2016).

[74] Gareth Atkins, '"Isaiah's Call to England": Doubts about Prophecy in Nineteenth-Century Britain', *Studies in Church History*, 52 (2016), 381–97.

[75] Roger H. Martin, *Evangelicals United: Ecumenical Stirrings in Pre-Victorian Britain, 1795–1830* (Metuchen, NJ, and London, 1983).

[76] Charles Smyth, *Simeon and Church Order: a Study of the Origins of the Evangelical Revival in Cambridge in the Eighteenth Century* (Cambridge, 1940).

or speech, they occupied a range of positions on most issues. Their place within the Church of England was, as Grayson Carter has suggested, a case in point, for if the vast majority of the gospel clergy were loyal Anglicans, their reasons for this ranged from a pragmatic desire to inhabit prominent pulpits to a sacramentally and historically rooted churchmanship that later generations would have thought distinctly high-flown.[77] Anglican Evangelicalism proved durable, but it was never a stable amalgam. To all of this can be added the truism that real life does not map consistently onto party lines. Indeed, the closer we examine those lines, the more blurred they often appear.

It should be stressed at this point that I do not want to dispute what has become the accepted set of criteria for what constitutes evangelicalism: David Bebbington's famous 'quadrilateral' of conversionism, activism, biblicism and crucicentrism.[78] Yet while Bebbington purposely sought to avoid becoming ensnared in the perspective of a particular period by advancing a general account, this book insists on the value and indeed the necessity of examining the 'Age of Wilberforce' on its own terms. It makes sense, to be sure, to think of it as a generational phase within the longer story of evangelicalism. Equally, though, it is possible to frame it as a late reflex of 'heart religion', a Europe-wide phenomenon of the long eighteenth century affecting both Protestants and Catholics that, as David Hempton has suggested, represents the intersection of intensely personal forms of inherited spirituality with optimistic eschatology, 'enlightened' rationalism and an expansive missionary urge generated by imperial expansion and encounter.[79] For the 'Age of Wilberforce' was a period in which 'seriousness', 'vital religion', 'true Christianity', or any of the numerous other contemporary labels for it referred more to a temper or frame of mind than a rigid creed. It involved conversion, to be sure, fervent Bible reading and acceptance of the sacrifice of a crucified saviour. But it was expressed publicly chiefly through activism and forms of association that facilitated it: clerical meetings, philanthropic societies, professional acquaintanceship, business connections. Its appeal lay in a reformist outlook that eschewed separatism, reaching out to potential allies and like-minded people and engaging wholeheartedly with society and politics in order to bring about

---

[77] Carter, *Anglican Evangelicals*, 7–30; Christopher J. Cocksworth, *Evangelical Eucharistic Thought in the Church of England* (Cambridge, 1993), 72–100.

[78] D.W. Bebbington, *Evangelicalism in Modern Britain: a History from the 1730s to the 1980s* (London, 1989), 1–17.

[79] David Hempton, *The Church in the Long Eighteenth Century* (London, 2011), 35–55; see also John Coffey (ed.), *Heart Religion: Evangelical Piety in England and Ireland, 1690–1850* (Oxford, 2016).

universal change. 'Action is the life of virtue,' Hannah More told her fashionable readers, 'and the world is the theatre of action.'[80] The networks thus produced were porous, being comprised of fluid and often ambiguous relationships in which piety is impossible to disentangle from patronage, personal connections, family and friendship. Where relevant I have tried to explain what individuals believed, and how closely they fitted into broader networks. Being aware, however, that this can turn into a circular exercise ('people were Evangelical because they belonged to Evangelical networks'), I have often simply indicated familial linkages or acquaintanceship, seeing such connections as significant whether or not those who comprised them were 'truly' Evangelical – which is, in any case, often impossible to discern.

This approach has the advantage of reflecting how Evangelicals themselves operated. They cultivated close social connections across denominational divides. Notwithstanding his horror of 'Socinianism,' Wilberforce was, for instance, intimate with the Unitarian MP William Smith (1756–1835), a longstanding resident of Clapham who, in Ian Bradley's words, was 'rightly regarded by contemporaries to have been one of the Saints,' and was numbered by Stephen in his 'Clapham Sect.'[81] Evangelicals exulted in the ecumenism of the Bible Society, whose deliberately undogmatic aim of distributing the scriptures 'without note or comment' was calculated to attract as wide a constituency as possible. Anglicans, Roman Catholics, Quakers and Methodists jostled alongside Baptists, Congregationalists, Presbyterians and Unitarians on its subscription lists. 'For my own part,' averred the flamboyant clergyman Rowland Hill (1744–1833), 'I should be glad to get a Mahometan to receive and disperse our bibles; he might get good and would do good.'[82] Such ecumenism was, however, calculated. The Bible Society commanded broad support because it presented itself not as a religious organization but as a hard-headed business concern: one that simply printed and circulated the scriptures as cheaply as possible.[83] Although the interlocking directorates of the London-based missionary, Bible and tract societies provided a measure of political co-ordination, denominational identities proved persistent. This, too, made pragmatic sense. Proximity to power mattered, and only by being close to but in some respects distinct

---

[80]   Hannah More, *An Estimate of the Religion of the Fashionable World* (London, 1808), 146.

[81]   Bradley, 'Politics of Godliness,' 278; [Stephen], 'Clapham Sect,' 268–9. See also R. W. Davis, *Dissent in Politics, 1780–1830: the Political Life of William Smith, MP* (London, 1971), 105–19.

[82]   Edwin Sidney, *The Life of the Rev. Rowland Hill* (London, 1834), 372.

[83]   Martin, *Evangelicals United*, 80–98; Leslie Howsam, *Cheap Bibles: Nineteenth-Century Publishing and the British and Foreign Bible Society* (Cambridge, 1991), 1–34.

from dissenters could Anglicans lobby effectively on their behalf. 'The Quakers ... and other well-meaning persons ... might have spoken or written as much as they pleased, it would have been merely a vain outcry had means not been found to bring [slave trade abolition] before Parliament, and make it the cause of the nation,' observed one contemporary.[84]

Similar points may be made about how Evangelicals related to their contemporaries within the Church of England. Although there was considerable suspicion of 'enthusiasm', there was also much overlap between Evangelicals and the Orthodox majority regarding moral causes and the crucial importance of the Church of England. Bishops Shute Barrington (1734–1826) of Salisbury and Durham and Beilby Porteus (1731–1809) of London would not have described themselves as Evangelicals, but from the 1780s onwards they were intimate with the circle around Wilberforce, More and the 'Saints', collaborating with them on efforts to reform public behaviour and to abolish the slave trade, and advancing cultured Evangelical moderates such as Thomas Gisborne, who became a prebendary of Durham in 1823.[85] In the new century Barrington's onetime chaplain Thomas Burgess (1756–1837), Bishop first of St David's and then of Salisbury, was an ardent defender of the Bible Society,[86] while Reginald Heber (1783–1826), second Bishop of Calcutta, supported the CMS and BFBS in addition to the older, Orthodox-dominated SPG.[87] Samuel Horsley (1733–1806) of Rochester was among several High Church figures who were deeply critical of 'disorderly zeal' but admired the spiritual intensity of Methodist and Evangelical devotion all the same.[88] Evangelicals in their turn participated in mainstream Anglican initiatives, such as the National Society (1811), whose rapid expansion testifies to the broad support it received across the spectrum of churchmen. There were also potential confluences between Evangelicals and the diffuse, rather diminished portion of their brethren who might be labelled latitudinarian or liberal. The independent-minded Bishop of Norwich, Henry Bathurst (bap. 1744, d. 1837), could usually be counted upon to ordain Evangelical missionaries, and was also a vice-president of the CMS. There were, it should be remembered, few visible or tangible distinctions in the pre-Tractarian Church of England between different groups.

[84] Charles Ignatius La Trobe, *Letters to My Children* (London, 1851), 14.

[85] Stott, *Hannah More.*

[86] Mark Smith, 'Thomas Burgess, Churchman and Reformer', in Nigel Yates (ed.), *Bishop Burgess and his World: Culture, Religion and Society in Britain, Europe and North America in the Eighteenth and Nineteenth Centuries* (Cardiff, 2007), 5–40.

[87] Amelia Heber, *The Life of Reginald Heber*, 2 vols (London, 1830), I: 39, 401–2, 492–8.

[88] Peter B. Nockles, *The Oxford Movement in Context: Anglican High Churchmanship, 1860–1857* (Cambridge, 1994), 194–7.

Worship was regulated by the Book of Common Prayer, and even if some gospel ministers thought sections of it unclear or unhelpful, most revered it. Partisan divides were hardening by the 1820s, but social, educational and familial links, friendships and collaborations continued to cut across them and in many respects to matter more.

It remains to explain why the subject of this book is British (rather than English) public life. For although it touches on Ireland, Scotland and Wales, *Converting Britannia* does not pretend to be a 'four-nations' history. Unless otherwise qualified, 'Evangelical' refers here to networks in and around the Church of England and the political establishment. Yet it still makes sense to think in terms of Britishness, albeit a London-centred Anglo-Britishness. For one thing, representatives of the constituent nations of Britain were undoubtedly represented within that world. The Evangelical metropolis was a multi-cultural melting-pot in which denominational identity could be fluid. Many brought up in Presbyterian Scotland or dissenting Wales found congenial homes in Evangelical Anglican congregations. Tactical considerations and careerism also encouraged them to toe the line in a political and ecclesiastical establishment in which 'Protestant' was often read as 'Anglican', although this did not prevent them from acting as go-betweens on behalf of those who worshipped outside it. There were other connections too, not least with Irish Anglicanism. As others have eloquently shown, there was a burgeoning Evangelical movement in Dublin and further afield from the 1780s onwards.[89] Both before and after the creation of the United Church of England and Ireland in 1800, the road to and from Holyhead buzzed with preachers, publications and shared beliefs.[90] This raises an important point, in that I do not want to claim that the networks surveyed here were the only evangelical connections in Britain or the wider British world. They overlapped with parallel networks in the Presbyterian Church of Scotland, and among Methodists and dissenters, none of which are examined here in detail.[91] Nor do our subjects represent the only strand of evangelicalism concerned with nation or empire.[92] Nevertheless, the chapters that follow explore what was in our period probably

---

[89]   Alan R. Acheson, *A History of the Church of Ireland 1691–1996* (Dublin, 1997), 66–168.

[90]   Thomas P. Power (ed.), *A Flight of Parsons: the Divinity Diaspora of Trinity College, Dublin* (Eugene, OR, 2018).

[91]   For a useful summary, see G. M. Ditchfield, *The Evangelical Revival* (London, 1998), 39–56, 78–97.

[92]   See e.g. Susan Thorne, *Congregational Missions and the Making of an Imperial Culture in Nineteenth-Century England* (Stanford, CA, 1999); Michael A. Rutz, *The British Zion: Congregationalism, Politics, and Empire, 1790–1850* (Baylor, TX, 2011).

the most prominent and certainly the most politically significant expression of that piety: a movement whose strength lay in its purchase on the great power-broking institutions of metropolitan and imperial Britain.

The Structure of the Book

Converting Britannia divides roughly into two parts. Chapters 1, 2 and 3 deal with the clergy and the laity in metropolitan Britain, focusing on the patronage networks and associations through which Evangelicals cemented their place in public life. Chapters 4, 5 and 6 examine how Evangelicals penetrated officialdom and institutions in Britain and in the wider British world, focusing in turn on the Sierra Leone Company, the Navy and the East India Company. The date ranges of individual chapters vary, reflecting the fact that Evangelical influence in these settings developed at different rates, and sometimes declined. The Conclusion gives an assessment of the significance of the movement, reflecting on the reasons for its success and asking why and when its influence waned.

Plate 2: John Russell, *Revd John Newton, late Rector of the United Parishes of St Mary Woolnoth and St Mary Woolchurch Haw*. Line Engraving by Joseph Collyer the Younger, 1808.

Chapter 1
'Spheres of Influence': the Evangelical Clergy, c. 1770–1830

In January 1780, the Reverend John Newton accepted the benefice of St Mary Woolnoth with St Mary Woolchurch, an elegant church designed by Nicholas Hawksmoor (1662?–1736), and situated on Lombard Street in the heart of the City of London. It was a far cry from Olney, the lace-making market town in rural Buckinghamshire where he had ministered for the previous sixteen years. And it was worlds away from his early employment in the transatlantic slave trade. For Newton's had not been a conventional career. After almost a decade serving in slave ships, and a vivid conversion experience during a period of fever, he spent several years as a tide surveyor at Liverpool. He was denied ordination in the 1750s, not owing to his former occupation but to his flirtations with 'Methodism', i.e. the early evangelical movement, which spanned Church and dissent and paid little heed to the divisions between them. Being well known in that intimate milieu, his reputation was cemented by his spiritual autobiography, *An Authentic Narrative of some Remarkable and Interesting Particulars in the Life of –* (1764), which brought him to the notice of a young Evangelical nobleman, the Earl of Dartmouth (1731–1801). Dartmouth secured him Anglican orders and the role of curate-in-charge at Olney, while another Evangelical layman, the merchant philanthropist John Thornton (1720–1790), supplemented his stipend and in 1780 orchestrated his move to London. Newton emblematizes the earthiness and ecumenism of early evangelicalism, which valorized emotional religious experiences, had relatively little regard for ecclesiastical and sometimes social niceties and depended on a handful of prominent patrons. Yet Newton's change of scene also serves to underline the growing ambition of Evangelicals by that point. Having previously ministered among the 'half-starved and ragged of the Earth' for only £60 a year, Newton now rejoiced in a cosmopolitan congregation which, as his reputation grew, travelled across London to hear him.[1] He was alive to the benefits of such a prominent post. 'It would be a pretty exploit if the Lord

---

[1]   See [Richard Cecil, ed.], *Memoirs of the Rev. John Newton* (London, 1808).

should enable you to catch a Lord Mayor, & a Sheriff or two in the Gospel net,' he chuckled to a friend in 1783.[2]

Newton's optimism was understandable. 'Gospel ministers' or 'vital religionists', as Anglican Evangelical clergymen called themselves, had remained a tiny, vilified minority for many years. Aside from a few relatively secure pioneers such as William Grimshaw of Haworth (1708–1763), Samuel Walker of Truro (bap. 1713, d. 1761) and Thomas Adam of Wintringham (1701–1784), they had generally been content to gather up crumbs under the establishment table.[3] The boundaries between Church and dissent remained permeable, and numbers small. When John Wesley wrote in 1764 to all the 'serious' clergy he could think of, he could name thirty-four. Their refusal to accede to his proposed union, however, signalled a growing awareness of their distance from him. Not only did Wesley's Arminian focus on human perfectibility sit uneasily with their predestinarian stress on Original Sin; his treatment of the world as his parish was also a sticking point given their inclination to work within the disciplines of the national Church.[4] 'They are a rope of sand,' Wesley dismissively told the Methodist Conference in 1769, 'and such they will continue.'[5] After his death in 1791, the Wesleyan Connexion came more and more to resemble a *de facto* denomination. Similarly, when legal proceedings in the early 1780s forced the Countess of Huntingdon (1707–1791) to register her chapels under the Toleration Act, she lost several leading clergymen who had in the 1760s and 70s been only too glad to accept her scarf of office as chaplains.[6] She denounced them as 'plausible leaders for Satan only': 'half hearted interested creatures' that sought only to 'eat, drink and be merry' in plump establishment livings.[7]

If her comments were overblown, there was truth in them. Many who had flirted with irregularity now set their faces against it: Newton, his friend

---

[2] John Newton to Henry Venn, 15 Mar. 1783, Cadbury Research Library, University of Birmingham, Church Missionary Society Unofficial Papers, Venn Papers, XCM-SACC/ACC/81/C66.

[3] John D. Walsh, 'The Yorkshire Evangelicals in the Eighteenth Century, with Especial Reference to Methodism' (unpublished Ph.D. thesis, University of Cambridge, 1956).

[4] For more on this subject, see Ryan Danker, *Wesley and the Anglicans: Political Division in Early Evangelicalism* (Downers Grove, IL, 2016).

[5] Joseph Benson (ed.), *The Works of the Rev. John Wesley*, 17 vols (London, 1809–13), VI: 382–3.

[6] Alan Harding, *The Countess of Huntingdon's Connexion: a Sect in Action in Eighteenth-Century England* (Oxford, 2003), 296–357.

[7] Lady Huntingdon to Mr Evans, 10 Jun. 1782, cited in John R. Tyson and Boyd Stanley Schlenther (eds), *In the Midst of Early Methodism: Lady Huntingdon and her Correspondence* (Lanham, MD, 2006), 152.

William Romaine (1714–1795), Rector of St Andrew-by-the-Wardrobe with St Ann Blackfriars, in London, and Henry Venn (1725–1797), former Vicar of Huddersfield and now incumbent of Yelling in Huntingdonshire.[8] Their protégés, coming men such as Charles Simeon of Cambridge, Thomas Robinson of Leicester and John Venn of Clapham, further distanced themselves from irregularity, loudly proclaiming the excellence of the Anglican formularies and their allegiance to the national Church.[9] They did so, as the Countess hinted darkly, because they could afford to. Hitherto, revival had spread piecemeal, protected and patronized by a handful of aristocratic sympathizers.[10] It overtopped denominational boundaries, producing an ecumenical culture that in some places died hard.

Now, with the spread of the new piety among the upper middle classes, a generation of confident, charismatic lay leaders, many of them businessmen, was beginning to explore how evangelization might be pursued more systematically and in a more ecclesiastically orderly fashion. One outgrowth of this, as Joseph Stubenrauch has shown, was philanthropy on an industrial scale.[11] Underpinning it, however, and in many places preceding it chronologically, were efforts to exploit existing structures. Nowhere was this truer than in the Church of England, whose system of presentation to livings meant that the manipulation of patronage was vital. This was not a new issue: the 'problem of continuity' had long dogged Evangelicals, who were keenly aware that years of parochial toil could swiftly be unravelled by the appointment of an 'unregenerate' successor, and who had therefore felt justified in sidestepping that system.[12] Now, though, there was growing excitement about their ability to work within it.

Thanks, perhaps, to Anthony Trollope's Barchester novels, clerical place-finding has often been laughed off as harmless fun. In fact the purchase of advowsons – the right, or a share in the right, to present to a benefice – was a serious business: they changed hands for large sums of money. Evangelicals could be as hard-nosed about this as any of their

[8]   D. Bruce Hindmarsh, *John Newton and the English Evangelical Tradition: Between the Conversions of Wesley and Wilberforce* (Oxford, 1996), 289–324.

[9]   See Charles Smyth, *Simeon & Church Order: A Study of the Origins of the Evangelical Revival in Cambridge in the Eighteenth Century* (Cambridge, 1940); Michael M. Hennell, *John Venn and the Clapham Sect* (London, 1958); Gerald T. Rimmington, 'Thomas Robinson: Evangelical Clergyman in Leicester, 1774–1813', *Transactions of the Leicestershire Archaeological and Historical Society*, 75 (2001), 105–17.

[10]   See G.C.B. Davies, *The Early Cornish Evangelicals, 1735–1760* (London, 1951), 178; A. Skevington Wood, *Thomas Haweis, 1734–1820* (London, 1957), 149, 156.

[11]   Joseph Stubenrauch, *The Evangelical Age of Ingenuity in Industrial Britain* (Oxford, 2016).

[12]   Smyth, *Simeon*, 246–50.

contemporaries.[13] 'If you hear of any Advowsons or Presentations to be sold in useful spots with Incumbents above fifty or sickly, I should be glad to lay out a few Thousands that way,' wrote John Thornton slightly callously to a friend in 1787. Money was no object when souls were at stake: 'I don't care how small if there are many Hearers as one may provide against necessity.'[14] Clerical correspondence, too, evinces a near obsession with place and preferment. 'I beg leave to congratulate you upon your success in obtaining the Living of St. Ann's,' enthused John Venn to William Goode (1762–1816). 'And it will give you pleasure to hear that the Chancellor preferred the application on your account to upwards of 40 others ... This I was told by a lady who was in his house at the time.'[15] None of this should be surprising, but it serves to emphasize the problem with assuming anachronistically that Evangelicals were opponents of a 'corrupt' system. Patronage could be used for the wrong purposes, but most contemporary churchmen did not regard it as an ill in itself. It was the accepted way of identifying talent and recognizing mutual ties of obligation, not just within the church but across a wide range of institutions.[16] It linked the church with the aristocracy, the gentry and other bodies, both locally and nationally: some 48 per cent of advowsons were in private hands, while 24 per cent were held by the capitular and parochial clergy, 12 per cent by the episcopal bench, 9 per cent by the Crown and 7 per cent by Oxford and Cambridge colleges, schools, town corporations and other corporate bodies.[17] It was natural for Evangelicals to participate in this. William Wilberforce's *Practical View* was explicit: 'the duty of encouraging vital religion in the Church particularly devolves on all who have the disposal of ecclesiastical preferment'.[18]

Beneficed opponents of Evangelicalism could hardly disapprove. Yet they deplored the fact that patronage seemed to be falling into the wrong hands. 'We know that they do take uncommon pains and spare no expence [*sic*] ... in purchasing presentations and advowsons, for the accommodation of

[13]   Clive Dewey, *The Passing of Barchester* (London, 1991).

[14]   John Thornton to William Richardson, 17 Oct. 1787, CUL, Thornton Family Letters and Papers, MS Add.7674/1/C18.

[15]   William Goode, *A Memoir of the Late Rev. William Goode* (2nd edn: London, 1828), 34.

[16]   W.M. Jacob, *The Clerical Profession in the Long Eighteenth Century, 1680–1840* (Oxford, 2007), 74–94.

[17]   For a useful survey of this, see Peter Virgin, *The Church in an Age of Negligence: Ecclesiastical Structure and Problems of Church Reform, 1700–1840* (Cambridge, 1989), 173–90.

[18]   William Wilberforce, *A Practical view of the Prevailing Religious System of Professed Christians, in the Higher and Middle Classes in this Country, Contrasted with Real Christianity* (London, 1797), 303–4.

what they call Gospel Ministers', commented 'J.W' acerbically in the *Ortho-dox Churchman's Magazine*.[19] In particular they objected to the Evangelical propensity for buying it up systematically. Such criticisms serve to underline another crucial shift in Evangelical priorities in the final decades of the century. While 'means' had usually been taken hitherto to refer to the prescribed ways in which individuals might seek the good of their souls, such as prayer, hearing a sermon or taking communion, entrepreneurial evangelicals now began to use it as shorthand for any tool that might allow them to reshape society more broadly.[20] Questions of patronage thus took on strategic significance. Instead of simply hoping to preach the Word faithfully – irrespective of how people reacted – gospel ministers now talked increasingly of 'spheres of influence', judging success by the number of souls saved.[21] 'The Gospel of Christ', wrote one future cleric earnestly, 'must always when preached in sincerity, produce ... *crowded churches*'.[22] Still more important than a populous 'sphere' was an influential one. Just as the writings of Hannah More and William Wilberforce sought to induce a moral trickle-down effect by tackling the great and good, so too Evangelical preachers prized opportunities to address important hearers. It is important to be clear about what all this was designed to achieve. The conversion imperative was as overwhelming as it had ever been. In applying the laws of cause and effect, however, Evangelical churchmen naturally came to regard adherence to ecclesiastical and social norms as essential. While there were aspects of the Church that they would gladly have reformed, on the whole Evangelicals now sought to work with the grain of it, convincing each other that they, and not the Orthodox, were its staunchest defenders and truest embodiment. Most would have echoed Robinson's exhortation to 'be more than ever circumspect, maintain a perfect consistency of character, show yourselves the true friends of the Church by avoiding everything which might weaken her interests, and then abide all consequences'.[23]

By 1795 Newton was in raptures regarding the advances of the preceding fifty years. 'The gospel is preached in many parts', he rejoiced.

---

[19] 'The Bishop of Rochester.– Evangelical Criticism, Magazine, &c', *Orthodox Churchman's Magazine; or, a Treasury of Divine and Useful Knowledge*, 1 (1801), 241.

[20] Stubenrauch, *Evangelical Age of Ingenuity*, 29–40.

[21] Wesley D. Balda, '"Spheres of Influence": Simeon's Trust and its Implications for Evangelical Patronage' (unpublished Ph.D. thesis, University of Cambridge, 1981).

[22] Charles Hoare to J.W. Cunningham, 6 Oct. 1803, Dorset Record Office, Williams of Bridehead, Littlebredy, Archive, D-WIB /C87, 7.

[23] Charles Hole, *The Early History of the Church Missionary Society for Africa and the East* (London, 1896), 54.

We have it plentifully in London; and many of our great towns, which were once sitting in darkness, have now the true light ... And every year the gospel is planted in new places – ministers are still raising up – the work is still spreading. I am not sure that in the year 1740, there was a single parochial minister, who was publicly known as a gospel minister, in the whole kingdom. Now we have, I know not how many, but I think not fewer than four hundred.[24]

Others were similarly upbeat. William Romaine noted in the mid 1790s how the fifty or so like-minded clergymen active when he began his ministry had swelled to more like 500.[25] This still left them a minority among the 12,000 clergymen of the Church of England, but it also heralded a period of rapid growth. Gladstone, an informed analyst when it came to the Evangelicalism of his youth, reckoned that by the decease of George III in 1820 they made up one in twenty (i.e. about 600) of the established clergy, rising to some one in eight (about 1,500) by the decease of his son ten years later.[26] Charles Jerram (1770–1853) might have put the figure higher, noting in 1823 that the Church Missionary Society had around 1,600 clerical members, although the idea that such societies were composed entirely of Evangelicals should be treated with caution.[27] Kenneth Hylson-Smith suggests perhaps over-optimistically that by 1835 vital religion had a hold on a quarter of all Anglicans.[28]

What follows lays out the emerging national geography of this movement in the closing decades of the eighteenth century and the opening decades of the nineteenth. Basing its findings on a prosopographical database of some 1,000 clergymen active between 1780 and 1830, it delineates a world defined by networking, preferment and common endeavour.[29] On one level it will tell a story of continuity: of the intensification of older networks of

[24]   Newton to correspondent, 1795, cited in John Campbell (ed.), *Letters and Conversational Remarks, by the Late Rev. John Newton* (New York, 1811), 75–6.

[25]   George Redford and John Angell James, *The Autobiography of the Rev. William Jay* (2nd edn: London, 1855), 172, 228n.

[26]   W.E. Gladstone, 'The Evangelical Movement, its Parentage, Progress, and Issue', in Gladstone, *Gleanings of past years*, 7 vols (London, 1879), VII: 210.

[27]   James Jerram, *The Memoirs and a Selection from the Letters of the Late Reverend Charles Jerram* (London, 1855), 295.

[28]   Kenneth Hylson-Smith, *Evangelicals in the Church of England, 1734–1984* (Edinburgh, 1988), 68.

[29]   This database draws on Cambridge and Oxford alumni publications, the *Clerical Guide* for 1817 and 1821, memoirs, unpublished correspondence, the records of the CMS and BFBS, the *BDEB* and the *ODNB*. It represents roughly 50 per cent of the active clergy who can be identified as 'evangelical' during the period in question.

correspondence, intermarriage and sociability. On another it will empha-size institutionalization, as informal connections developed into formal-ized societies with clearly defined objectives: clerical education, missions, fundraising. Contrary to what many Evangelicals thought, none of this was entirely new: earlier reforming movements displayed similar characteris-tics. Nor were any of these techniques or impulses an Evangelical preserve. What was unprecedented, however – and potentially threatening to many contemporaries – was the developing symbiosis of lay resources, clerical associationalism and the systematic exploitation of patronage. By the first decade of the nineteenth century, as we shall see, there was a growing sense among their friends and their enemies alike that the Evangelicals were effectively creating a church of their own within the establishment.

The Gospel Clergy in the Late Eighteenth Century

Ever since the earliest days of revival, clergymen who came out as Evangeli-cals risked isolating themselves professionally, whether they liked it or not. Separatism became a self-fulfilling prophecy and a survival mechanism, as those touched by the new piety shunned or were shunned by 'unregenerate' colleagues. This generated a deep-seated associational culture, connected by correspondence and, as time went on, regular meetings. The clerical club established by Samuel Walker at Truro in the 1750s was a key early exemplar, and by the end of the century gospel ministers had become noto-rious for meeting to exchange prayers, pastoral tips and gossip.[30] While their opponents flayed them for this, they defended themselves stoutly.

> Why may we not meet to pray when others meet to play at bowls? Why may we not have our deliberative assemblies, when others of our brethren have their dancing and drinking assemblies? Why may we not seek to edify one another, whilst they care not if they corrupt one another?[31]

asked Robinson of Leicester. There was more than a little rhetorical exag-geration in this: deanery meetings of clergy and local clerical associations had in fact been widely encouraged by the bishops at the turn of the

---

[30] Davies, *Cornish Evangelicals*, 74.
[31] Edward T. Vaughan, *Some Account of the Life, Ministry, Character, and Writings of the late Rev. T. Robinson* (London, 1815), 266.

eighteenth century.[32] But it is easy to see why Evangelicals, who gathered from further afield and so ostentatiously sought out their own kind, might attract accusations of spiritual snobbery or puritan separatism. Where like-minded figures were thinly spread, such clubs brought together attenders from far and wide. At Little Dunham in the early 1790s, for example, John Venn's meeting included clergymen from across Suffolk and Norfolk: a symptom of the weakness of Evangelicalism in East Anglia.[33] Attendance at such meetings became a badge of churchmanship. 'Have you any meeting of Gospel Ministers in Kent?' Venn asked John Brock (c. 1749–1830), Rector of Bidborough. 'I think such a meeting as they have in Yorkshire and other places would strengthen your hands and be a means of much good.'[34]

In the 1780s and 90s, clerical gatherings burgeoned in scale and frequency. By around 1800, societies such as those at Elland, Hotham and York in Yorkshire, the Eclectic Society in London and the societies at Bristol, Creaton, Rauceby, Aldwinkle and Birmingham gave Evangelicals something approaching a corporate voice nationally.[35] Leading clerics often attended meetings across the country. Robinson managed, for instance, to fit in appearances at Birmingham (Warwickshire), Rauceby (Lincolnshire), Aldwinkle and Creaton (both in Northamptonshire), as well as hosting his own gathering as Vicar of St Mary's, Leicester.[36] Such societies continued to mushroom in the nineteenth century.[37] The most famous, the Islington Clerical Meeting, was founded in 1827, becoming a national hub at which strategic priorities were hammered out.[38] Education also tied together far-flung clerics. As Sara Slinn has shown, clerical tutors such as Thomas Clarke (1719–1793) of Chesham Bois or Samuel Knight (1759–1827) at Wintringham and then Halifax operated 'domestic seminaries', preparing scores of students for ordination and, increasingly, university.[39]

---

[32] Jacob, *Clerical Profession*, 277–81.

[33] Hennell, *John Venn*, 83–8.

[34] *Ibid.*, 84.

[35] Walsh, 'Yorkshire Evangelicals', 262–4.

[36] Vaughan, *Account of Robinson*, 265. See also [Lucy Frances March Phillipps], *Records of the Ministry of the Rev. E.T. March Phillipps* (London, 1862), 19–36.

[37] For a vivid memory of the Dorset Clerical Meeting, see H.C.G. Moule, *Memories of a Vicarage* (London, 1913), 40–4, 76–7. For the Matlock Bath Clerical Society, see Arthur Pollard, 'Evangelical Parish Clergy, 1820–40', *Church Quarterly Review*, 159 (1958), 387–95.

[38] David Bebbington, 'The Islington Conference', in John Maiden and Andrew Atherstone (eds), *Evangelicalism and the Church of England in the Twentieth Century* (Woodbridge, 2014), 48–67.

[39] Sara Slinn, *The Education of the Anglican Clergy, 1780–1839* (Woodbridge, 2017), 170–97.

Yet in the late eighteenth century the distribution of gospel ministers across the country remained far from even. 'I know but of one Clergyman from Bristol to Wellington (50 miles) who preaches or knows of anything of vital Christianity,' lamented Hannah More in 1793.[40] Parts of the Home Counties, the East Midlands and Yorkshire were areas of strength, as was Bristol and its locality. Kent, Sussex and Hampshire, by contrast, contained only a scattering of Evangelical incumbents. Wales had almost none. Cumberland, Westmorland, Northumberland and Durham were also areas of weakness. It is interesting to speculate on the reasons for these disparities. The situation in Wales is most easily accounted for. What became known as Calvinistic Methodism formally separated from the establishment only in 1811, but long before that the popular Welsh-language preaching of Daniel Rowland (1711?–1790), Howel Harris (1714–1773) and William Williams (1717–1791) meant that evangelicalism matured outside or on the fringes of the established Church. The story was similar in other places where Anglican coverage was patchy, such as Cornwall, a hotbed of Methodism. Around Bristol, on the other hand, Evangelical strength owed much to the earlier success of Wesley and Whitefield. There many of the clergy were former Methodists who opted to remain within the Church of England as denominational boundaries solidified from the 1770s onwards.[41] In Yorkshire, Evangelicalism built on the more decidedly Anglican foundations laid by Venn, Grimshaw and others in the 1750s and 60s. Local demographics, too, shaped the character of serious religion. Evangelicalism was a prominent feature in mercantile communities at London, Hull and Bristol from a comparatively early date. But, bearing in mind that patronage and personal influence could promote or block appointments, it is difficult to generalize regarding the presence of the new piety in particular places. Episcopal disapproval, too, could be a major obstruction. 'It is ... notorious', complained one sympathizer, 'that in one or two dioceses, at least, nothing would tend more to ruin the reputation of a Clergyman with his Bishop, than to shew that he is an evangelical preacher.'[42] The associational web that defined the Evangelical clerical world, then, still contained large gaps. As late as 1788 Newton saw

[40]   Hannah More to John Venn, 5 Dec. 1793, CRL, XCMSACC/ACC/81/C19.
[41]   L.E. Elliott-Binns, *The Early Evangelicals: a Religious and Social Study* (London, 1953), 330–52.
[42]   John Pearson, *The Life of William Hey, Esq.*, 2 vols (London, 1822), II: 153n. See 'A Clergyman of the Diocese' [Charles Thomas Longley], *The Lord Bishop of Ripon's Cobwebs to Catch Calvinists* (London, 1838).

the foundation of the Society for the Relief of Poor Pious Clergymen as a chance to flush out fellow believers as yet unknown.[43]

Nor were the gospel clergy socially homogeneous. While accusations of 'Methodism' usually evoked poverty, lack of education and 'enthusiasm', the spread of vital religion in the upper echelons of society made such charges hard to sustain. It opened fresh routes for preferment: aristocratic or gentry sons such as William Cadogan (1751–1797) and Philip Gurdon (1746–1817) could look forward to advancement as soon as they received their orders.[44] Many others, though, moved from curacy to curacy with little hope of ever scraping much more than a pittance. Some, like the Cambridge graduate Samuel Settle (c. 1771–c. 1847), might be forced into pious pluralism, taking several neighbouring cures in order to make ends meet. 'I have gone the road – long and dreary, and without a flower to regale my senses; and I have found at the end of it poverty, contempt, and almost universal neglect,' he sighed.[45] Church Evangelicals were, then, a disparate set, ranging from upper-class heirs to pauper clergy with only a smattering of education, ministering in rural Cumberland or Cornwall, or in the teeming new industrial centres of Lancashire and the Pennines.

Doctrinally, too, the gospel clergy occupied a range of positions. References to the Evangelical 'mainstream', the 'regulars' or the 'Christian Observer school' should be tempered by an awareness that vital believers differed on numerous issues, from eschatology, baptism and scriptural inspiration to more esoteric questions, such as prayers for the dead.[46] One area of broad consensus was soteriology: the vicious predestinarian controversies that had wracked the evangelical world in the 1760s and 70s were for the most part an unpleasant memory. Nearly all of them espoused some form of 'Moderate Calvinism', believing in the sovereignty of God but also holding that humans had moral agency.[47] In any case, Arminians and Calvinists concurred on the cardinal doctrine of justification by faith alone, and the growth in holiness that ought to characterize the Christian life. There was also general agreement on the importance of remaining within

---

[43]   John Newton to William Wilberforce, 5 Jul. 1788, Bodleian Library, Wilberforce Family Papers, MSS Wilberforce, c.49, 23/14, fo. 17.

[44]   See Richard Cecil, *Memoirs of the Rev. William Bromley Cadogan* (London, 1798).

[45]   Thomas Hervey, *Life of the Rev. Samuel Settle* (Colmer, 1881), 63.

[46]   W.J.C. Ervine, 'Doctrine and Diplomacy: some Aspects of the Thought of the Anglican Evangelical Clergy, 1797 to 1837' (unpublished Ph.D. thesis, University of Cambridge, 1979); Grayson Carter, *Anglican Evangelicals: Protestant Secessions from the Via Media, c. 1800–1850* (Oxford, 2001), 3–5.

[47]   Although see Ian J. Shaw, *High Calvinists in Action: Calvinism and the City, Manchester and London, 1810–1860* (Oxford, 2002).

the bounds of the Church of England.[48] No doubt for some this was purely pragmatic, but for many – most famously the Bible commentator Thomas Scott – it was heartfelt, being the result of a bruising process involving intensive reading, inward agitation and debate with other clerics.[49] 'I have thought deeply on every point that seemed to me to accompany salvation;' declared William Richardson of York (1745–1821), 'and I have determined to live and die in the bosom of the Established Church.'[50] Nevertheless, as surviving minutes of the Eclectic and Elland societies make clear, there remained a spectrum of views on this as on most other points.[51] While the majority looked askance at the few itinerating throwbacks who still swapped pulpits with evangelical dissenters – John Berridge (1716–1793) of Everton in Bedfordshire,[52] Thomas Haweis (1734–1820) of Aldwincle in Northamptonshire[53] and Rowland Hill of Surrey Chapel in London – plenty maintained cordial relationships across denominational divides locally, and were prepared to co-operate on non-ecclesiastical and therefore less controversial endeavours, such as the distribution of books and tracts.[54] Even Charles Simeon, that ardent champion of regular churchmanship, was prepared to create private assemblies within his parish, while Thomas Scott deplored the Conventicle Act (which effectively prevented such meetings) as 'a direct opposition of human authority to the word of God', which Christians were duty bound to disobey.[55]

It would thus be premature at this stage to label Evangelicals as a 'party'. A growing patchwork of associations and incumbents meant that by around 1800 there was a growing sense of *esprit de corps* among gospel clergymen. Defined less by the uniformity of their theological views than by the company they kept, many of them readily identified themselves as 'serious', 'vital',

[48] Carter, *Anglican Evangelicals*, 7–30. G.F.A. Best, 'The Evangelicals and the Established Church in the Early Nineteenth Century', *Journal of Theological Studies*, n.s., 10 (1959), 63–78, underestimates the affection of evangelicals for their Church.

[49] See Thomas Scott, *The Force of Truth: an Authentic Narrative* (London, 1779).

[50] Pearson, *William Hey*, 152n.

[51] John H. Pratt (ed.), *Eclectic Notes* (London, 1856); John Walsh and Stephen Taylor (eds), *The Papers of the Elland Society, 1769–1828* (forthcoming).

[52] See Smyth, *Simeon*, 149–200.

[53] Skevington Wood, *Thomas Haweis*.

[54] Isabel Rivers, 'The First Evangelical Tract Society', *Historical Journal*, 50 (2007), 1–22. Although much has been written on pan-evangelical endeavour at the national level, the history of social relations between churchmen and dissenters at a local level has yet to find its historian.

[55] Andrew Atherstone, *Evangelical Mission and Anglican Church Order: Charles Simeon Reconsidered* (London, 2009); John Scott, *The Life of the Rev. Thomas Scott* (4th edn: London, 1822), 332.

'awakened' or 'real Christians', while their opponents responded with a variety of epithets less flattering. Nevertheless, such labels are at best an imperfect guide given how cavalier polemicists could be. This raises an important point about partisan divisions in the late-Hanoverian Church of England. As has long been recognized, Evangelical regularity and conservative mainstream churchmanship were both rooted in reactions against latitudinarian attempts to relax subscription to the Thirty-Nine Articles in the 1770s.[56] The attachment of the Orthodox to the sacraments, to patristic tradition and to the English Reformation as a rediscovery of that inheritance was generally compatible with the Evangelical stress on Scripture and personal conversion, an emphasis which they too traced back to the early Church via the reformers.[57] Even the 'High Church' – a similarly broad term which generally refers to those whose spirituality, sacramentality and ecclesiology was markedly 'advanced' – were somewhere on the same spectrum. On many subjects, common churchmanship trumped other differences. Yet there was a widespread suspicion regarding Evangelical separatism. As one exasperated commentator pointed out, this was often a self-perpetuating process:

> The Evangelical Clergy, it is true, have become a sort of party in the Church … We are jealous of them, we are suspicious, we shun their society, and we refuse to assist in those labours in which they have a share; they, of course, remain a separate body; and we then object to a distinction which we ourselves have contributed to make.[58]

Yet it took time for informal affiliations to become entrenched positions. As the next section will make clear, it was the maturation of earlier initiatives to ensure a supply of well-qualified new clergy that began to weld those associations into a national network.

---

[56] Gareth Atkins, '"True Churchmen?" Anglican Evangelicals and History, c. 1770–1850', *Theology*, 115 (2014), 339–49.

[57] Peter B. Nockles, 'Church Parties in the Pre-Tractarian Church of England 1750–1833: The "Orthodox" – Some Problems of Definition and Identity', in John Walsh, Colin Haydon and Stephen Taylor (eds), *The Church of England, c. 1689–c. 1833: from Toleration to Tractarianism* (Cambridge, 1993), 334–59; Nockles, *The Oxford Movement in Context: Anglican High Churchmanship, 1760–1857* (Cambridge, 1994), 228–69.

[58] [An Orthodox Clergyman], *Considerations on the Probable Effects of the Opposition of the Orthodox Clergy to their Evangelical brethren* (London, 1819), 17.

The Universities

Yorkshire had long been known among Evangelicals as an earthly paradise, 'the Goshen of our land'.[59] As Vicar of Huddersfield from 1759 until 1771, Henry Venn had been immensely influential, controlling appointments to the thirteen chapels-of-ease that made up his immense parish, as well as corresponding with fellow clergymen such as William Grimshaw, Henry Crook (1708–1770) and James Stillingfleet (1741–1826).[60] The greatest legacy of Venn and his generation was the foundation of a Yorkshire clerical club in 1767, later known as the Elland Society.[61] By the end of the century, Leeds, Huddersfield, Halifax, Dewsbury and Haworth in the West Riding, as well as Hull and Hotham in the East, were areas of strength, with gospel ministers in possession of dozens of livings and curacies, in addition to controlling the Grammar Schools at Leeds, Hipperholme, Halifax and Hull.[62] This position of power owed much to the decision in 1777 to address two long-running problems. One was the growing difficulty of securing ordination without a college testimonial.[63] The other was the comparative ease with which awakened young men might be lured away from the Church of England. Accordingly, the Ellanders founded 'a fund for the purpose of educating poor pious young men for the ministry', which quickly attracted attention, both in Yorkshire and beyond.[64] One of its most generous donors was Wilberforce, who eventually gave a total of £2,465, writing to the Leeds surgeon William Hey in 1789 asking after 'the funds of your West Riding Charity for catching the colts running wild on Halifax Moor, and cutting their manes and tails, and sending them to college'.[65] Other sources of income included Henry Thornton (£3,880) and Lord Dartmouth, as well as clergymen such as Romaine in London and Simeon in Cambridge, in addition to subscriptions from the Yorkshire clergy themselves.[66] In the

---

[59]   Walsh, 'Yorkshire Evangelicals', 86–7.
[60]   Henry Venn junior (ed.), *The Life and a Selection from the Letters of the Late Rev. Henry Venn* (London, 1834), 41.
[61]   See Taylor and Walsh, *Elland Society*.
[62]   A.C. Price, *A History of the Leeds Grammar School* (Leeds, 1919), 117–36; John Lawson, *A Town Grammar School through Six Centuries: a History of Hull Grammar School against its Local Background* (Oxford, 1963), 163–91.
[63]   John Newton, *Memoirs of the Life of William Grimshaw* (London, 1799), 105–6.
[64]   John D. Walsh, 'The Magdalene Evangelicals', *Church Quarterly Review*, 159 (1958), 499–511.
[65]   Wilberforce, *Life*, I: 252.
[66]   Hervey, *Samuel Settle*, 21.

first year, the Ellanders received only £88. 10s., but by 1796-7 their income had soared to £1,225. 19s. 6d.

Since 1768, when six students were expelled from St Edmund Hall, Oxford, as 'Methodists', Evangelicals had felt unwelcome at the universities. In 1776, for example, John Venn was refused entry at Trinity College, Cambridge, because of his father Henry's Evangelical notoriety.[67] The new scheme capitalized on an opening at another Cambridge college, Magdalene. Three serious fellows – Samuel Hey (1745–1828), William Farish (1759–1837) and Henry Jowett (1756–1830) – were elected in the 1770s, and in the absence of the non-resident Master, Barton Wallop (1744–1781), gained ascendancy over college affairs.[68] Hey and Jowett hailed from Leeds and were members of the Elland Society: the first pensioner was sent to Magdalene in 1778, the year Hey was elected President.[69] 'We have not any rule against sending [trainees] to Oxford,' explained George Burnet (1734–1793), the Elland Secretary, 'but the advantage they have at Cambridge has prevailed in their favour.'[70] Magdalene was not a large college, with only about fifteen freshmen each year, and so the arrival of fifty-six Elland pensioners between 1778 and 1800 made a significant difference to the tenor of life there. Peter Peckard (bap. 1717, d. 1797), who became Master in 1781, was no Evangelical, but he was an ardent abolitionist, and was impressed by the industry and moral seriousness of the student body. The college flourished, attracting the sons of prosperous Evangelicals – the future politicians Charles and Robert Grant (1780–1838) the most prominent – as well as a continuing stream of indigent northerners, rendering it 'the general resort of young men seriously impressed with a sense of religion.'[71] One representative example is Samuel Settle, who became a scholar in 1794. Settle first came to the notice of the Society through the curate of Barwick-in-Elmet, Thomas Dikes (1761–1847) – a onetime Magdalene student himself.[72] Drawn out of the embrace of the Methodists, Settle was pushed forward by Dikes's successor, John Graham (1765–1844), and proposed by

---

[67]   Hennell, *John Venn*, 39.

[68]   Walsh, 'Magdalene Evangelicals', 500–3.

[69]   Peter Cunich and others, *A History of Magdalene College Cambridge 1428–1988* (Cambridge, 1994), 182. For a detailed account of the Jowett family, see Evelyn Abbott and Lewis Campbell (eds), *The Life and Letters of Benjamin Jowett*, 2 vols (London, 1897), I: 1–28.

[70]   Cited in Walsh, 'Magdalene Evangelicals', 502.

[71]   John King, *Memoir of the Rev. Thomas Dykes* (London, 1849), 6.

[72]   See also Andrew Sharp, *The World, the Flesh and the Devil: the Life and Opinions of Samuel Marsden in England and the Antipodes, 1765–1838* (Auckland, 2016), 23–84.

Miles Atkinson (1741–1811), the Vicar of Leeds.[73] Like most candidates on the Elland conveyor belt, Settle was passed between several tutors, including Thomas Dunham Whitaker (1759–1821) of Whalley in Lancashire and Joseph Milner (1745–1797), Master of Hull Grammar School, before being deemed ready for the academic and social challenges of university life.[74] The Society expected its money to be well spent: Settle was required to live and dress frugally; to attend only the established Church during vacations; and report regularly on his progress. As a 'sizar' he would pay reduced fees, but could expect in return to be placed in the least comfortable rooms and to perform domestic duties.[75] Like many Ellanders he saved hard once employed to repay the costs of his education so that others could tread the same path.[76]

By 1786 the aged Henry Venn could marvel that at Cambridge, 'the professor of law (Dr. Jowett) and the three first mathematicians of the university confessedly, Milner, Coulthurst and Farish, are all on the side of the truth'.[77] Finding suitable places for pious youths was, however, contingent upon the vagaries of college politics. Farish's tutorship at Magdalene was eventually curtailed by the responsibilities of a professorial chair; Hey departed Cambridge in 1787 for marriage and a college living; Jowett replaced Venn at Little Dunham in 1792. Hey's successor as President, Thomas Kerrich (1748–1828), was not favourable to serious religion, having the 'impudence' to interrogate undergraduates as to which of them attended 'Simeon's Church', and when Peckard died in 1797 he was followed as Master by a succession of unsympathetic figures.[78]

By this time, though, there were other potential destinations for serious students. One was St Edmund Hall, Oxford, which became an Evangelical haunt after the appointment of Isaac Crouch (1756–1835) as Vice-Principal in 1783. It attracted a few Ellanders, but the trickle became a stream in 1795 with the foundation of the Bristol Clerical Education Society. This, too, flourished, thanks to strength of Bristol Evangelicalism under the leadership of Thomas Tregenna Biddulph (1763–1838).[79] By 1826 it had assisted

---

[73] Hervey, *Samuel Settle*, 21.
[74] Cunich, *Magdalene College*, 189; see also Lawson, *Hull Grammar School*, 170–5.
[75] Cunich, *Magdalene College*, 145.
[76] Hervey, *Samuel Settle*, 89.
[77] Henry Venn to Rowland Hill, 31 Jan. 1786, cited in Edwin Sidney, *The Life of the Rev. Rowland Hill* (London, 1834), 160.
[78] Cunich, *Magdalene College*, 193–6; Hervey, *Samuel Settle*, 52.
[79] See L.P. Fox, 'The Work of the Reverend Thomas Tregenna Biddulph' (unpublished Ph.D. thesis, University of Cambridge, 1953).

more than a hundred candidates, most of whom attended Oxford.[80] Many of them returned to the West Country, but, as one contemporary observed admiringly, 'there are few parts of the kingdom where one or more of [Crouch's] pupils did not carry the impression of his kindness, piety, truly evangelical doctrines, ecclesiastical knowledge and attachment to the Church of England.'[81] The Creaton Society soon followed, and Elland income dropped to a steady £300–400 a year as a result. By the early nineteenth century clerical education societies were part of the Evangelical landscape. Demand outstripped supply, such that in 1814–15 Simeon helped to found a London Clerical Education Society.[82] This was a refined scheme, the London trustees being 'noblemen and gentlemen of high reputation and proved piety.'[83] Other, humbler associations were formed locally, such as the group of Sunderland clergy who assisted John Hampson (bap. 1753, d. 1819) through St Edmund Hall, where he graduated in 1791.[84] *Ad hoc* arrangements might be made for others who fell through the safety net provided by the clerical societies. The gentleman-scholar and future EIC chaplain Claudius Buchanan (1766–1815) was sponsored through Queens' College, Cambridge, by Henry Thornton, later repaying the money and remitting funds to support others in similar positions.[85]

Critics of Evangelicalism were keenly aware of the Trojan horses being constructed within the establishment. 'That the seeds of sectarianism are sown even in our universities, is a notorious fact,' warned the abrasive anti-Evangelical polemicist Richard Polwhele (1760–1838). 'In Cambridge, Magdalen-college is reported to pour forth Evangelical students more copiously than Edmund-hall in Oxford. It is highly necessary, therefore, that the heads of the universities watch over such societies, and that they check the slightest tendency in their youth to Evangelical irregularities.'[86] In response Evangelicals were more anxious than ever to prove themselves loyal churchmen. The rules of the Bristol Society stipulated that candidates

---

[80] *Ibid.*, 266–7.

[81] 'Recollections of Isaac Crouch', *Christian Observer*, 36 (1837), 411.

[82] Charles Simeon to Thomas Truebody Thomason, 29 Dec. 1814, cited in William Carus, *Memoirs of the Life of the Rev. Charles Simeon* (London, 1847), 218.

[83] William Goode, *A Memoir of the Late Rev. William Goode* (2nd edn: London, 1828), 58; Josiah Bateman, *The Life of the Right Rev. Daniel Wilson*, 2 vols (London, 1860), I: 216–7.

[84] Hampson, a reclaimed Methodist, was in 1791 to become John Wesley's first biographer.

[85] H.N. Pearson, *Life and Writings of the Rev. Claudius Buchanan* (3rd edn: London, 1819), 242–3.

[86] George Lavington, *The Enthusiasm of Methodists and Papists Considered*, ed. Richard Polwhele (London, 1820), cclxxxviii.

must have 'a cordial persuasion of the Truth and Importance of the great principles of the Gospel, as expressed in the Liturgy, thirty-nine Articles, and Homilies', adding that potential recruits were to be 'truly attached to Episcopacy, and the discipline of the Church of England'.[87] One who was certainly beyond reproach was Isaac Milner (1750–1820), who became President (i.e. head of house) of Queens' College, Cambridge, in 1788 and rapidly established it as a destination for would-be gospel clergymen, aided by his Yorkshire connections.[88] A close friend of Wilberforce and a proponent of the supposedly subversive tenet of justification by faith alone, Milner was in other respects a pillar of the Cambridge establishment. First Jacksonian then Lucasian Professor, he was personally known to William Pitt the Younger (1759–1806), being an old friend of Pitt's ecclesiastical advisor Bishop Pretyman of Lincoln (1750–1827), who helped to make him Dean of Carlisle in 1791.[89] Milner was determined to show that political and theological orthodoxy were central tenets for the true Christian. Being 'positively determined to have nothing to do with Jacobins or infidels', on his appointment in 1788 he swept away the fellows who had given Queens' a name for latitudinarian freethinking, bringing in new tutors who included Thomas Thomason (1774–1829) and Thomas Sowerby (c. 1774–1808), both curates to Simeon at Trinity Church.[90] No surprise that the 'very best men' Milner could find were also Evangelicals: snide observers hinted that Milner favoured men of his own college or Magdalene in examinations.[91] Whatever the truth of this, in the following years Queens' played host to numerous pious fellows who would go on to prominence, including the baptismal controversialist G.C. Gorham (1787–1857), the Church Missionary Society leader Henry Venn junior (1796–1873) and another future President of Queens', Henry Godfrey (1781–1832).

Henry Gunning (1768–1854), Milner's gossipy Cambridge contemporary, described him as 'completely despotic'.[92] That despotism was, however, calculated. As Vice-Chancellor, Milner played a leading part in the expulsion

---

87 Fox, 'Thomas Tregenna Biddulph', 264.
88 John Twigg, *A History of Queens' College, Cambridge 1448–1986* (Woodbridge, 1987), 173.
89 Reider Payne, *Ecclesiastical Patronage in England, 1770–1801: a Study of Four Family and Political Networks* (Lewiston, ME, Queenston, ON, and Lampeter, 2010), 255–61.
90 Milner to Wilberforce, Mar. 1801, cited in Mary Milner, *The Life of Isaac Milner* (London, 1842), 243.
91 Henry Gunning, *Reminiscences of the University, Town, and County of Cambridge from the year 1780*, 2 vols (London, 1854), I: 263-4, 92.
92 *Ibid.*, 263–4.

of William Frend (1757–1841) from Jesus College in 1793–4 for theological and political heterodoxy, again broadcasting to the Pitt administration his loyalty in expunging Jacobinism from the university.[93] A similar point can be made about Milner's interference in the election of a new fellow at Trinity Hall at around the same time. There the Senior Tutor, the Professor of Civil Law Joseph Jowett (1756–1830), was another Yorkshire Evangelical, and his initial choice, Francis Wrangham (1769–1842), an erstwhile Magdalene undergraduate 'much distinguished for his talents and attainments' and a product of Hull Grammar School, where Isaac Milner's brother was Master, might have been expected to be a good fit.[94] Yet the President of Queens' had other ideas. One of his own Evangelical fellows was elected instead, amid rumours about Wrangham's republicanism. According to Gunning this left Trinity Hall 'a *Fief of Queens*'.[95] This may well have been the case, but it seems likely that in acting against Wrangham, a Foxite sympathizer at a time of McCarthyite suspicion of anyone on the political 'left', Milner sought also to protect the reputation of Evangelicalism in the university.[96] Likewise, when a British and Foreign Bible Society Auxiliary was mooted at Cambridge in 1811, Milner, like Simeon, prevaricated, being fearful of being 'pointed at as the only Governor in the University who had thought proper to join turbulent pupils'.[97] Opposition to the venture was co-ordinated by the Lady Margaret Professor, Herbert Marsh (1757–1839), who derided the Society for jumbling together churchmen and dissenters and distributing Bibles without the Prayer Book to guide its interpretation. In the event it was Farish who organized a meeting, on 12 December, and spoke decisively on behalf of the Bible Society, but by this time Wilberforce had convinced Milner to attend, and, with Simeon, helped to ensure the backing of the Chancellor, the Duke of Gloucester (1776–1834), the Earl of Hardwicke (1757–1834) and the Master of Trinity and Bishop of Bristol W.L. Mansel (1753–1820).[98] The support of William Otter (1768–1840), a

[93] John Gascoigne, *Cambridge in the Age of the Enlightenment: Science, Religion and Politics from the Restoration to the French Revolution* (Cambridge, 1988), 231–4.

[94] Gunning, *Reminiscences*, II: 16.

[95] *Ibid.*, 32.

[96] See Michael Sadleir, *Archdeacon Francis Wrangham, 1769–1842* (Oxford, 1937), 3–9; 53–7. Later Archdeacon of the East Riding, Wrangham was a regular correspondent of William Wilberforce. One daughter married the son of Henry Raikes, evangelical Chancellor of the diocese of Chester, while another was wife to Robert Wilberforce. David Newsome, *The Parting of Friends: a Study of the Wilberforces and Henry Manning* (London, 1966), 138–9.

[97] Milner to Joseph Jowett, 7 Dec 1811, cited in Milner, *Isaac Milner*, 465–9.

[98] William Otter, *The Life and Remains of the Rev. Edward Daniel Clarke* (London, 1824), 575–7; Milner, *Isaac Milner*, 469–82. For a full summary of the affair, see Ford

future bishop and first Principal of King's College London, and of his friend Edward Daniel Clarke (1769–1822) – often assumed to be an Evangelical solely on the basis of his participation in the Bible Society – underline that this was a rainbow coalition rather than a partisan venture. The inception of the Oxford Auxiliary in June 1813 was even more successful. 'In point of effect, the Meeting was very, very far below that of Cambridge,' explained Simeon, 'but upon paper it is far, very far above us: for even at the first, they had six Masters and four Professors to countenance them, and several of the nobility; and now they have the Duke of Marlborough (Lord Lieutenant) and Lord Grenville (the Chancellor) with a host of others.'[99]

Although Evangelical influence was concentrated at a few powerhouses, it was becoming difficult to ignore their presence in most colleges. It is striking that out of a sample of some 1,000 Evangelical clergymen active during this period, no fewer than 167 were college fellows at some point. At St John's College, Cambridge, a succession of serious men – the future missionary Henry Martyn (1781–1812) the most famous – may have contributed to an upsurge in the number of pious undergraduates there in the early 1800s.[100] At Lincoln College, Oxford, the Hipperholme Grammar School boy and future Bampton Lecturer George Stanley Faber (1773–1854) was elected fellow and tutor in 1793, followed by Thomas Fry (1774–1860) in 1796, William Yeadon (c. 1775–1848) in 1797, Edward William Stillingfleet (1782–1866) in 1812 and George Cracroft (1795–1845) in 1820.[101] Lincoln, too, produced a number of future Evangelical clergymen in this period, including a future CMS missionary, James Connor (c. 1792–1864), despite the choleric opposition of the Rector, Edward Tatham (bap. 1749, d. 1834), 'a blind and furious stickler for Aristocracy' who solemnly got drunk at one college gaudy in order to prove that Lincoln was 'no damned Methodist society'. In 1796, Tatham thwarted efforts by Hannah More and Wilberforce to exploit the position of their friend Fry to make further like-minded fellows, while in 1816 he blocked the elevation of a student, the Yorkshireman James Knight (bap. 1793, d. 1863) in the face of a majority among the fellowship.[102] Once in place, though, Evangelicals were difficult to shift. Hey

K. Brown, *Fathers of the Victorians: the Age of Wilberforce* (Cambridge, 1961), 285–316.

[99] Carus, *Charles Simeon*, 370; Bateman, *Daniel Wilson*, I: 185.

[100] Boyd Hilton, 'The Nineteenth Century', in Peter Linehan (ed.), *St John's College, Cambridge: a History* (Woodbridge, 2011), 245–6.

[101] See Arthur Pollard, 'James Stillingfleet', in *BDEB*, II: 1056–7. V.H.H. Green, *The Commonwealth of Lincoln College, 1427–1977* (Oxford, 1979), 382, 390, 623.

[102] More to Wilberforce, 22 Jul. n.y. [1796]; More to Wilberforce, 3 Aug 1796 [wrongly catalogued 1799], Rubinstein Library, Duke University, Wilberforce Papers, Box 1,

at Magdalene voiced the fear that if he married, his place might be given over to a 'person not serious', while Simeon refused the rich King's living of Greenford in 1804, informing Wilberforce that the 'retaining of Trinity [Church] and residing at Cambridge during terms was a *sine qua non* from the beginning'.[103] Fry only resigned his Lincoln fellowship once the able Daniel Wilson had returned to St Edmund Hall in 1803–4 as assistant tutor.[104] Yeadon remained a fellow until 1823, maintaining an important ministry as curate of All Saints'. Another key Oxford figure was John Natt (1778–1843), who presided over a coterie of pious dons at St John's College, and whose influence was heightened when he accepted the college living of St Giles, in central Oxford, in 1809.[105] After Natt's death Daniel Wilson (1778–1858) saluted his 'firm stand' as Oxford's sole Evangelical incumbent, reckoning this to be 'entirely contrary to his natural tendencies'.[106]

If Simeon's Friday evening discussions in King's College provide the warmest and most enduring image of university Evangelicalism, the foregoing serves to underline that serious religion at both Cambridge and Oxford rested on broader foundations.[107] By the 1820s Evangelicals were well established at Cambridge, while at Oxford Magdalen Hall under J.D. Macbride (1778–1868) was gaining a reputation for seriousness, being joined in the 1830s by Wadham, whose Warden, Benjamin Symons (1785–1878), drove it in the same direction. St Edmund Hall remained a stronghold up until at least the 1850s.[108] Evangelicals were, moreover, seldom as persecuted or peculiar as they imagined themselves to be: by the 1820s there was considerable consensus between different strands of churchmanship on the need for pastoral and theological renovation. 'He accords more with my views of Scripture than almost any other person I am acquainted with,' declared Simeon delightedly of the Provost of Oriel, Edward Copleston

---

Folder 4. James Knight (ed.), *Sermons and Miscellaneous Works of the Rev. Samuel Knight*, 2 vols (Halifax, 1828), I: xlvii–xlix.

[103] Walsh, 'Magdalene Evangelicals', 504; Charles Simeon to William Wilberforce, 14 Nov. 1804, Rubinstein Library, Duke University, Wilberforce Papers, Box 2, Folder 2. See also Henry Martyn to John Hensman, 20 Nov. 1804, CRL, Church Missionary Society Unofficial Papers, XCMSACC/ACC/55/C1.

[104] J.S. Reynolds, *The Evangelicals at Oxford, 1735–1871* (2nd edn: Abingdon, 1975), 73.

[105] John Natt, *Posthumous Sermons* (2nd edn: London, 1855), xx–xv.

[106] *Ibid.*, xxiv.

[107] Abner William Brown, *Recollections of the Conversation Parties of the Rev. Charles Simeon* (London, 1863), 191.

[108] Reynolds, *Evangelicals at Oxford*, 84–94. See also Thomas Mozley, *Reminiscences Chiefly of Oriel College and the Oxford Movement*, 2 vols (London, 1882), I: 24, 242–3.

(1776–1849).[109] Indeed, such was the success of Evangelicals socially that some worried that they had become too fashionable. Thomas Fry warned one student acquaintance against associating too closely with *'the saints'*, because 'there is always reason to fear that when credit and interest are promoted by a profession of religion, some will consent to wear our badge, who are strangers to our principles'.[110]

All these developments did not, it should be noted, mark an educational revolution. They were not intended to. Like most of their contemporaries, Evangelicals were on the whole content, as they always had been, to regard clerical training in fairly minimal terms, as a matter of biblical knowledge, pastoralia and homiletics, and to see this as best provided in parishes by clerical tutors before or after university. They saw little need to involve themselves in the diocesan theological colleges founded from the late 1830s onwards, which were in any case dominated by High Churchmen and Tractarians, instead starting their own institutions, such as St Aidan's College, Birkenhead (1847), the short-lived Litton Hall, Oxford (1855) and St John's Hall, Highbury (1863).[111] All the while, the footholds Evangelicals carved out at the ancient universities served their purpose: to secure their place in the Church of England by producing pious gentlemen with a broad education, sufficient social polish and – crucially – the right sort of connections. Their relative complacency was a sign of their success.

Evangelicalism in c. 1799: the Church Missionary Society

The institutional framework that clerical and educational societies provided for the Evangelical movement became especially important in the 1790s. The fallout of the revolution in France sparked a major upsurge in prophetic speculation, as well as waves of potentially unruly revivalism that affected all of the major denominations.[112] Religious publishing

---

[109] Carus, *Charles Simeon*, 396.

[110] [Thomas Fry], *Domestic Portraiture; or, the Successful Application of Religious Principle in the Education of a Family* (London, 1833), 119.

[111] David A. Dowland, *Nineteenth-Century Anglican Theological Training: the Redbrick Challenge* (Clarendon, 1997), 64–106.

[112] The literature on this is vast. See W.R. Ward, *Religion and Society in England, 1790–1850* (London, 1972); Deryck W. Lovegrove, *Established Church, Sectarian People: Itinerancy and the Transformation of English Dissent, 1780–1830* (Cambridge, 1988); Deborah Madden, *The Paddington Prophet: Richard Brothers's Journey to Jerusalem* (Manchester, 2010); Philip Lockley, *Visionary Religion and Radicalism in Early Industrial England: from Southcott to Socialism* (Oxford, 2013).

exploded, with the number of firms growing fourfold between 1790 and 1825.[113] Evangelicals shared some of this temper, preaching not just the importance of personal repentance but of combating public immorality and national sins.[114] More than ever, though, they saw the need to tread a fine line between 'enthusiastic' popular preaching, on the one hand, and dry formalism, on the other. Against dissenters who denounced the Liturgy as soulless or semi-papistical, figures like Biddulph and Simeon vociferously maintained that the words were spiritual, not to mention acting as a prophylactic against error; against stiff churchmen they insisted that they ought to be fervent and heartfelt.[115] This synthesis came more and more to resemble a defining party line, being policed in periodical publications such as *Zion's Trumpet* (later the *Christian Guardian*), begun by Biddulph and his Bristol colleagues in 1795, and the more mellow and urbane *Christian Observer*, founded in London in 1802 under the aegis of Zachary Macaulay (1768–1838) and a consortium of metropolitan Evangelicals, many of them laymen.[116] The *Christian Observer* in particular was influential in the development and dissemination of an eirenic, activist and above all churchman-like brand of Evangelical thought among the upper echelons of society. Its inaugural editorial deliberately faced in two directions, following the desire originally expressed at an Eclectic meeting in February 1799: 'to correct the false sentiments of the religious world' and 'to explain the principles *of the Church*'.[117] Here again was evidence of Evangelical priorities: eternal salvation was of overriding importance, but the Church of England was the means through which it was to be pursued.

Yet this sat uneasily with a growing sense of urgency regarding overseas mission. William Carey's *Enquiry into the Obligations of Christians to use Means for the Conversion of the Heathens* (1792) drew on imperial ethnographical and geographical knowledge to hammer home the magnitude of the task. It heralded a wave of new foundations: the Baptist Missionary Society (BMS) in 1792; what was to become known as the London Missionary Society (LMS) in 1795; the Edinburgh and Glasgow Missionary Societies in 1796.[118] Henry Thornton, Wilberforce and Newton all supported

---

[113] Josef L. Altholz, *The Religious Press in Britain, 1760–1900* (Westport, CT, 1989), 10.

[114] M.J.D. Roberts, *Making English Morals: Voluntary Association and Moral Reform in England, 1787–1886* (Cambridge, 2004), 59–95.

[115] T.T. Biddulph, *Practical Essays on the Morning and Evening Services of the Church of England* (4th edn: London, 1809), 1–14.

[116] Fox, 'Thomas Tregenna Biddulph', 276–84.

[117] Pratt, *Eclectic Notes*, 92.

[118] Andrew Porter, *Religion versus Empire? British Protestant Missionaries and Overseas Expansion, 1700–1914* (Manchester, 2004), 40–2.

the Baptist scheme, albeit in a low-key way; but for many conscientious clergymen this was impossible.[119] Many Evangelicals instead supported the existing Anglican bodies, the Society for Promoting Christian Knowledge (SPCK) and the Society for the Propagation of the Gospel in Foreign Parts (SPG). Yet they also realized that those bodies had limited capacity: the latter had been hit hard by the loss of its main American mission field, and between 1783 and 1819 its annual voluntary income rarely struggled above £500 a year.[120] For Thomas Haweis, by this time a member of the Countess of Huntingdon's Connexion, the travails of the existing societies was a clear sign of the need for pan-evangelical co-operation on a 'broad basis'.[121] While such arguments could not convince the regular majority, the swift success of the LMS plan was undeniable. '£10,000 is said by Mr Haweis to be already collected for the Missionary Society,' reported Henry Thornton in 1795.

> What a striking thing it is that the Bishop of London is hardly able (as I suspect) to scrape a few hundred pounds together for the Missionary Plans in his hands among all the people of the Church Establishment and that £10,000 should be raised in such a few days by the Irregulars who are also so much poorer a Class of People than the others.[122]

Striking, perhaps, but not surprising given that the 'Irregulars' were necessarily voluntarists accustomed to dipping into their own pockets to support ministers or building appeals, unlike Anglicans with their inherited buildings and social cachet. Already in 1796, the new society sent a missionary party to Tahiti, and between then and 1812 collections averaged an impressive £6,795 a year.[123]

In the Church of England matters proceeded more slowly. Discussions about a Missionary Society 'under the sanction of the Established Church' took place at Rauceby in Leicestershire in 1795 and among the Eclectics in early 1796, but it took much longer for plans to be made in earnest.[124] 'I rejoice to hear that the Mission business succeeds so well,' wrote Henry William Coulthurst of Halifax (1753–1817) to Simeon in around 1797, 'and if my poor endeavours can be of any avail, you are most sincerely welcome to them.'[125] Simeon seems to have been a key go-between, co-ordinating the

[119] Brian Stanley, *The History of the Baptist Missionary Society* (Edinburgh, 1992), 21.
[120] Porter, *Religion versus Empire*, 55.
[121] Cited in Wood, *Thomas Haweis*, 192.
[122] Henry Thornton to John Venn, 25 Sep. 1795, CRL, XCMSACC/ACC/81/C68.
[123] Porter, *Religion versus Empire*, 55–8.
[124] Hole, *Church Missionary Society*, 24–6; see also Pratt (ed.), *Eclectic Notes*, 102–3.
[125] Coulthurst to Simeon, c. 1797, cited in Hole, *Church Missionary Society*, 29.

clerical societies with wealthy backers in the capital. Tensions remained, however, and were much in evidence at the Eclectic Society when it met on 18 March 1799. 'We cannot join the [London] Missionary Society,' declared Simeon, 'yet I bless God that they have stood forth.' 'We require something more than resolutions,' he urged, warning that 'Many draw back because we do not stand forward … We have been dreaming these four years, while all England, all Europe, has been awake.'[126] 'It should be known that there is such a design,' exhorted the London clergyman Josiah Pratt (1768–1844). 'Fix upon persons to write to. It must be kept in evangelical hands.'[127] The upshot was an assembly at the Castle and Falcon Inn, in Aldersgate Street in London, on 12 April. Sixteen clergy were present, as well as a number of prominent London laymen.[128] The 'Society for missions to Africa and the East instituted by members of the Established Church' was presented to the public in May. There was no shortage of prominent supporters: Vice-Admiral James Gambier (1756–1833) was President, while Charles Grant senior (1746–1833) and Edward Parry (1750–1827) of the EIC, the banker Henry Hoare (1750–1828) and the MPs William Wilberforce, Sir Richard Hill and Samuel Thornton (1754–1838) were governors. Suitably 'serious' banking firms – Messrs. Down, Thornton and Co. and Messrs. Dorien, Martin and Co. – were appointed to receive subscriptions. Everything was done to make the new Society appear respectable, including an approach to the Archbishop of Canterbury.[129] In targeting Africa and India, its manifesto deliberately avoided trampling Orthodox sensibilities, sidestepping areas of SPG strength and noting carefully that 'the world is an extensive field, and in the Church of Christ there is no competition of interests.'[130] The *Missionary Magazine* for 20 May optimistically opined that the new Society would attract the contributions of those 'whose predilection for the Church and dislike to Methodists and Dissenters, would have effectively kept them from aiding the [London Missionary Society].'[131]

This was wishful thinking. In its first decade the CMS stagnated. Subscriptions grew slowly, confidence was low and no flood of volunteers for overseas work materialized. While poverty was frequently pleaded as an excuse, it is difficult to escape the impression that the gospel clergy were

---

[126]   Pratt, *Eclectic Notes*, 98.

[127]   *Ibid.*, 98.

[128]   For details, see John H. Pratt and Josiah Pratt jun., *Memoir of the Rev. Josiah Pratt* (London, 1849), 13–15.

[129]   *Ibid.*, 15–17.

[130]   *Proceedings of the Church Missionary Society for Africa and the East*, 1 (1801), 8–9, 11.

[131]   'New Missionary Society', *Missionary Magazine*, 4 (1799), 236.

less than zealous about the venture. From 1799–1802 the vast majority of income came from lay subscriptions and benefactions. The banker Ambrose Martin (c. 1744–1826), the pious Danish Consul-General George Wolff (1736–1828) and the porcelain manufacturer James Neale (d. 1814) each gave £100; the three Thornton brothers contributed fifty guineas apiece; Wilberforce gave £50.[132] Receipts of £2958 8s. 7¼d. in 1811 remained a fraction of those of the LMS. Yet for our purposes this is beside the point. As Charles Hole (1823–1906) recognized long ago in his monumental 677-page history of the CMS up to 1814, the first decade or so of its existence is central to understanding a crucial period in the development of Evangelicalism. Although woefully unsuccessful at first as a missionary society, it provided a cause and a framework around which local networks and isolated individuals coalesced. This at once reinforced the ecclesiastical identity of the gospel clergy and pushed them in more radical directions, towards organizing themselves. 'I would do a great deal to keep up the Establishment,' commented John Venn, 'but not to sacrifice the good of souls.'[133] To suggest, as Elizabeth Elbourne does, that the CMS was the brainchild of the Eclectic Society and the Clapham Sect, and that it created 'a network of self-defining Evangelicals' is to ignore discussions that had been taking place in clerical societies more generally for several years.[134] Granted, the immediate impetus in 1799 came from the capital: most of the clergy involved were based there. But Simeon, too, was a leading light, while two more of the first committee were Oxford men, Thomas Fry and John Witherington Peers (1745–1835). At the inaugural meeting there were also clergymen from Cornwall and Scotland.[135] Connections between the metropolitan and provincial clergy were deep-rooted, moreover. Most of those involved in the foundation of the CMS had previously held livings or curacies outside London. Far from merely creating networks, then, the Society both connected and reinforced pre-existing linkages.

Its first secretary was the biblical commentator and Lock Hospital chaplain Thomas Scott. Initial replies to his circulars manifested guarded approval but a distinct lack of material support. Poverty, isolation and the burdens of day-to-day ministry were all given as reasons for proffering

---

[132] Hole, *Church Missionary Society*, 45. For Wolff, see Peder Borgen, 'George Wolff (1736–1828): Norwegian-born Merchant, Consul, Benevolent Methodist Layman, Close Friend of John Wesley', *Methodist History*, 40 (2001), 17–28.

[133] Pratt, *Eclectic Notes*, 97.

[134] Elizabeth Elbourne, 'The Foundation of the Church Missionary Society: the Anglican Missionary Impulse', in Walsh, Haydon and Taylor (eds), *Church of England, c. 1689–c. 1833*, 249.

[135] Pratt, *Josiah Pratt*, 13–15.

goodwill instead of guineas.¹³⁶ Several cited age, lamenting as they did so the lukewarmness of younger colleagues. 'I put the circular address into the hands of two young Clergymen of whom I wish'd to hope well,' snorted one correspondent, 'but for any thing [*sic*] which they will do for the poor per-ishing Heathens, I believe that I might as well have shown it to two dancing masters.'¹³⁷ The initial lack of episcopal enthusiasm also proved a potential sticking point.¹³⁸ For some correspondents the force of habit was evidently difficult to break: Thomas Jones of Creaton (1752–1845) rambled content-edly about the strength of his local meeting, neglecting even to mention the subject of missions: 'Simeon gave us a very great sermon. I wish we had you amongst us, pray come next Easter if practicable.'¹³⁹ Elsewhere, however, correspondents grasped more readily what the Corresponding Committee required. Matthew Powley (1740–1806) wrote from Dewsbury in August in businesslike vein on behalf of the Elland Society, asking for a hundred copies of the pamphlet to be sent in advance of their meeting in October.¹⁴⁰ From Leicester, the well-connected Robinson listed the exhibi-tions available to send putative missionaries to university.¹⁴¹ From Oxford, Isaac Crouch and Thomas Fry compiled an immense list of 104 potential allies, categorized by county. 'London, Bristol and Cambridge are not included in this list,' they noted, probably because the committee already had contacts there.¹⁴²

If early CMS support followed the contours of existing societies, its ter-minology also mirrored their usages: 'committees of correspondence' and 'country members', such as at Elland and Hotham. As early as 27 May they had drawn up a list of fourteen potential 'country members': Edward Burn of Birmingham (1762–1837), Thomas Dikes of Hull, James Stillingfleet of Hotham, Richardson of York, Robinson of Leicester and Simeon of Cam-bridge, among others. Yorkshire had four. The choice of Biddulph as puta-tive representative for Bristol and Robert Hawker for Plymouth serves to underline the Society's hopes for support from Wiltshire, Somerset, Devon and Cornwall, while the absence of members for Kent, Sussex, Hamp-shire and the North West suggest that these were still areas of Evangelical

¹³⁶ This correspondence is preserved at the CRL in Church Missionary Archive, Incom-ing Home Correspondence, Papers, Home Correspondence, XCMS/G/AC/3.
¹³⁷ William Pinnock to Josiah Pratt, 27 Feb. 1806, CMS Papers, Home Correspondence, XCMS/G/AC/3/3/4.
¹³⁸ Hole, *Church Missionary Society*, 57.
¹³⁹ Thomas Jones to Thomas Scott, 13 Aug. 1800, XCMS/G/AC/3/1/27.
¹⁴⁰ Matthew Powley to Thomas Scott, 16 Aug. 1800, XCMS/G/AC/3/1/30.
¹⁴¹ Thomas Robinson to Thomas Scott, 15 Aug. 1800, XCMS/G/AC/3/1/29.
¹⁴² Isaac Crouch to Thomas Scott, 1 Feb. 1801, XCMS/G/AC/3/1/48.

weakness. Further names were added in 1800, most notably John Fawcett (1769–1851) at Carlisle and Robert Jarratt (1765–1843) at Wellington in Somerset. The astute use of regional leaders meant that word about the new society spread rapidly. Long-distance cross-connections were also evident. Fawcett of Carlisle sent a pamphlet to his friend 'Mr Grainger Curate of Wintringham', i.e. Lorenzo Grainger (c. 1769–1839), a fellow Hull Grammar School attender with whom he had served in curacies around Hull in the early 1790s.[143] By the end of the decade, clerical membership of the CMS had become a marker of identity: most correspondents assumed the link between Evangelical opinions and likely support for the CMS.[144] Numbers of ordained supporters rose steadily, from some 85 in 1802, to 233 in 1807, 237 in 1808 and 257 in 1811, the vast majority of whom were part of at least one clerical network. At a conservative estimate this latter figure represented between a third and half of the gospel clergy. Even so, belated letters continued to trickle in, informing the Secretary of Irish interest and of isolated pockets of would-be supporters, such as in North-East England.[145]

Nevertheless, the horizons of the CMS remained limited and its operations amateurish. Scott resigned in December 1802 and was replaced by the more dynamic Josiah Pratt, who remained until 1824. Yet its correspondence suggests that many clergymen still treated it as a glorified parsons' club. None volunteered for overseas service: that gap was filled from 1804 by Lutherans, sent from the Missionary College recently founded in Berlin by Johannes Jänicke (1748–1827), and later by recruits from the Basel *Evangelische Missionsgesellschaft*.[146] Most of the early missionaries were gradually dribbled out to the unhealthy settlement at Sierra Leone, while a slightly better-fated small contingent was sent to New Zealand under Samuel Marsden (1765–1838) in 1814.[147] It was only in 1817 that British volunteers began to outnumber those from continental Europe. For the time being, rhetoric outweighed action. The annual May sermons preached at St Ann Blackfriars attracted leading preachers. But while these raised the profile of the Society, and brought in some money, the sums were paltry

---

[143] John Fawcett to Thomas Scott, 28 Feb. 1801, XCMS/G/AC/3/1/53. *Alum. Cantab.*, part 2, II: 469; Arthur Pollard, 'Thomas Dykes' in *BDEB*, II: 338–9; *idem*, 'John Fawcett', in *ibid.*, II: 381–2.

[144] Matthew Powley to Thomas Scott, 18 Feb. 1801, XCMS/G/AC/3/1/52; John Fawcett to Thomas Scott, 28 Feb. 1801, XCMS/G/AC/3/1/53; J. Brock to Thomas Scott, 23 Mar. 1801, XCMS/G/AC/3/1/58.

[145] George Carr to Secretary, 18 Apr. 1804, XCMS/G/AC/3/1/151; N. Hollingsworth to Josiah Pratt, 2 Mar. 1807, XCMS/G/AC/3/3/52.

[146] Hole, *Church Missionary Society*, 115–26.

[147] Porter, *Religion versus Empire*, 57.

by comparison with those of the LMS. More significant, as Bob Tennant has argued, was how these occasions became a proving ground for Anglican Evangelical missionary doctrine, which as Britain's military fortunes improved conjoined postmillennial optimism and patriotism to place Evangelical endeavour at the centre of the divine plan.[148] 'The ardent zeal which hath, especially in late years, been excited to diffuse the knowledge of the Christian religion may surely be considered as a symptom of the approach of its glory,' claimed Basil Woodd with excitement in 1807, revelling in the hope that England could become 'a House of Prayer for all nations'.[149] Yet for all the preachers' valorization of missionary courage – in terms that placed them above mere military or naval heroes – volunteers were conspicuous by their absence.[150] Melville Horne (c. 1761–1841), a former Sierra Leone chaplain, found the situation intolerable and he used his 1811 sermon to excoriate his brethren in scorching terms. 'Serious Christians of all denominations are espousing the cause of Missions, and anxious to prepare the way of the Lord,' he thundered, '… but sorry am I to say that the clergy, and the clergy alone, decline the Cross.'[151]

Clerical Careers

One of the chief reasons for this, as has been suggested, was the priority Evangelicals gave to securing their position in England. This final section, then, turns away from the national movement to examine the careers of some clergymen in detail. It focuses on three: Patrick Brontë (St John's, Cambridge, B.A. 1806), Charles Jerram (Magdalene, Cambridge, B.A. 1797) and William Henry Havergal (St Edmund Hall, Oxford, B.A. 1816), using them to show how Evangelical connections operated on a local level. It then examines this issue from a lay perspective, considering the activities of William Wilberforce as an ecclesiastical patron in his native Yorkshire.

Patrick Brunty or Brontë (1777–1861) was a native of County Down, who arrived in Cambridge in October 1802, armed with little more than the advice of Thomas Tighe (1750–1821), the Evangelical rector of

---

[148] Bob Tennant, *Corporate Holiness: Pulpit Preaching and the Church of England Missionary Societies, 1760–1870* (Oxford, 2013), 92–135.

[149] *Proceedings of the Church Missionary Society for Africa and the East*, 7 (1807), 151–2.

[150] Gareth Atkins, 'Christian heroes, providence and patriotism in wartime Britain, 1793–1815', *Historical Journal*, 58 (2014), 400, 413.

[151] *Proceedings of the Church Missionary Society for Africa and the East*, 11 (1811), 206–7.

Drumballyroney and himself a graduate of St John's.[152] Brontë was initially befriended by James Wood (1760–1839), the President, but then came to the notice of a more decidedly Evangelical figure, Henry Martyn, the 1801 Senior Wrangler and soon to be Simeon's curate. Martyn took up his case among the Evangelical great and good. 'An Irishman, of the name of Bronte entered at St John's a year and a half ago as a sizar,' Martyn reported.

> During this time he has received *no* assistance from his friends who are incapable of affording him any – Yet he has been able to get on in general pretty well by help of Exhibitions &c which are given to our sizars. Now however, he finds himself reduced to great straits and applied to me just before I left Cambridge to know if assistance could be procured for him from any of those societies, whose object is to maintain pious young men designed for the ministry.

'For the character of the man I can safely vouch as I know him to be studious, clever, and pious,' he added.[153] Wilberforce and Thornton each agreed to sponsor him '10L. each anny' through university.[154] Graduating in 1806, Brontë took up a curacy on behalf of Joseph Jowett (1752–1813) at Wethersfield, Essex, where he also met Robert Storry (1751–1814), incumbent of St Peter's, Colchester. Both men signed his letters testimonial for a new post, the curacy of Glenfield in the parish of Broughton Astley in Leicestershire, whose Vicar, Robert Cox (fl. 1803–24), had been a near-contemporary of Brontë at St John's.[155] In the event, however, he went to Shrewsbury in 1809, where John Nunn (1782–1861), a native of Colchester and another Johnian friend, helped to secured a curacy for him under John Eyton (c. 1779–1823) at All Saints', Wellington.[156] Eyton, in turn, was yet another Johnian (B.A. 1799), one who at Cambridge abandoned dissipated habits for a life of religious zeal. Before the end of the year Brontë was again on the move, this time to Yorkshire. After a two-year curacy with John Buckworth of Dewsbury (1779–1835),[157] and four years as Vicar of Hartshead, he finally settled down in 1820 as Perpetual Curate of Haworth.[158] Notwithstanding the later fame of his daughters, in many respects Brontë was typical of older models of Evangelical ministry: of the many clergy who were content to teach,

[152] Juliet Barker, *The Brontës* (London, 1994), 1–14.
[153] Martyn to John Sargent, Jan.–Feb. 1804, Bodl., MSS Wilberforce, d.14, fo. 16.
[154] Martyn to Wilberforce, 14 Feb. 1804, MSS Wilberforce, d.14, fo. 17.
[155] Barker, *Brontës*, 21.
[156] For the Nunn family, see Shaw, *High Calvinists*, 69–110.
[157] St Edmund Hall BA 1805.
[158] *Alum. Cantab.*, part 2, I: 392.

preach and pastor a flock wherever they could find an opening, and were shuffled from curacy to curacy in the process. What is striking, though, is the extent to which by the early nineteenth century even a poverty-stricken young curate like Brontë could be introduced at college into a well-functioning world of multiple interconnections.

Brontë's near-contemporary Charles Jerram was from a similarly humble background. The son of a Nottinghamshire farmer, he was groomed for Presbyterian ministry by his devout mother, in around 1790 becoming assistant at a 'Socinian' school in Highgate: a plum situation for a youth who sought a salary and 'literary improvement'. The sermons of Richard Cecil (1748–1810), the renowned minister of St John's Chapel, Bedford Row, gradually convinced him that the opinions of his employers were unscriptural and tended towards moral laxity.[159] At the behest of Thomas Cursham (d. 1805), the Evangelical curate of his home parish of Blidworth, he became instead an Elland pensioner, being sent – like many others – to Thomas Clarke of Chesham Bois in Buckinghamshire (hailed by Romaine as the 'Solomon of the age') to prepare for university.[160] Jerram thrived academically: he graduated Seventeenth Wrangler in 1797 with a Norrisian Prize for Divinity to his name (1796). A putative curacy at Wigston Magna near Leicester via Thomas Robinson fell through, so with no money to remain at Magdalene he wrote to 'my excellent friend the Rev. J. Pugh, Vicar of Rauceby'. This letter elicited two or three offers, and Jerram accepted that of Long Sutton in Lincolnshire, whose absentee incumbent had asked Pugh (1744–1799) to find him a curate of 'his own sort'.[161] The importance of clerical 'fixers' like Robinson and Pugh is immediately evident. His next move came courtesy of Cecil, who was on the lookout for curates for his two Surrey livings, Chobham and Bisley.[162] Evangelicals, it should be emphasized, had no problems whatsoever with pious pluralism, which allowed them to use curates to occupy several useful spheres at once. Moving to Chobham in 1805, Jerram was initially regarded as an exotic by neighbouring clergy, but as time passed their hostility waned, helped perhaps by the arrival of John King (c. 1765–1845) at Bisley in 1810, and the 'condescending kindness and attention' of the Duke of Gloucester (1776–1834), whose seat at Bagshot Park was nearby.[163] The Duke, it will be remembered, was

[159] Jerram, *Memoirs*, 38, 43–4.
[160] *Ibid.*, 67–80. For Romaine, see John Venn, *Annals of a Clerical Family* (London, 1904), 90n. For details of Clarke's life, see Erasmus Middleton, *Evangelical Biography*, 4 vols (London, 1807), I: 541–3.
[161] Jerram, *Memoirs*, 136.
[162] *Ibid.*, 236–7.
[163] *Ibid.*, 262, 278.

President of the Cambridge Bible Society, and the growing social acceptability of such endeavours was underlined by the formation of a Bible Society auxiliary for Surrey at Guildford in 1813, supported by the Lord Lieutenant, Lord Onslow (1731–1814). In 1824 Jerram took up St John's, Bedford Row, in London, but returned to Chobham in 1826. The accession of the Evangelical C.R. Sumner (1790–1874) as Bishop of Winchester in 1827, however, opened up fresh avenues: Jerram was made Rural Dean and then in 1834 preferred to the rich living of Witney in Oxfordshire, where he spent the remainder of his life as an active pastor and prolific writer.

Jerram's career hints at the growing national co-ordination of the gospel clergy. Chobham was a living administered by the nascent Simeon Trust, originally set up on the death of John Thornton in 1790 in order to keep together the livings he had purchased.[164] Now, Evangelical success at the universities meant that such openings were at a premium. One vacancy at Darlaston, Staffordshire, in 1814 attracted seven candidates, with Lord Calthorpe (1787–1851), Thomas Gisborne (1758–1846), Henry Thornton, William Wilberforce, John King and Simeon vying to present their protégés. Predictably, Simeon had his way. 'To obtain a fit person will not satisfy my conscience,' he stated firmly. 'I must, in order to approve myself to God, have the fittest person I can possibly find.'[165] While Simeon and his fellow trustees eventually administered patronage on a grand scale, controlling ten livings in 1814 and thirty by 1836, elsewhere patrons gained control of single churches through self-perpetuating patronage trusts, or through the construction of new chapels with presentation rights vested in their backers.[166] These, too, called upon wide-ranging connections. St Anne's Church, Lancaster, for example, was built by Robert Housman (1759–1838), a former curate to Robinson at Leicester, and attracted donations from his Cambridge mentor, Simeon, as well as Wilberforce and a local landowner, William Carus Wilson (1764–1851).[167] In Birmingham a commanding position developed around Edward Burn. Already incumbent of St Mary's, St James's Chapel, Ashted, was purchased for him in 1810. Vital religion was even fashionable by the 1820s, owing to the aristocratic Calthorpe interest in the growing suburb of Edgbaston and the influence of the Spooner family at Elmdon.[168] In 1825 a Birmingham Clerical Society was founded,

---

[164] Balda, '"Spheres of Influence"', 25–35.
[165] Simeon to trustees, 14 Jul. 1814, cited in *ibid.*, 64.
[166] *Ibid.*, 35–6; 130–1
[167] R.F. Housman, *The Life and Remains of the Rev. Robert Housman* (London, 1841), xc–xci.
[168] William Wilberforce married Barbara Spooner (1777–1847) at Bath in 1797. For the Calthorpes, see David Cannadine, *Lords and Landlords: the Aristocracy and the*

which took control of the main parish church, St Martin-in-the-Bullring, in 1829. Like the Simeon Trust, the living was placed in the hands of four trustees, eminent clergymen of national stature. Some of these purchases were personal or opportunistic, such as when the wealthy Holborn iron-monger and Middlesex magistrate James Oldham (1750–1822) procured Great Missenden in Buckinghamshire 'for the purpose of perpetuating a gospel ministry in that place'.[169] Increasingly, though, Evangelicals operated strategically. As Simeon told Isaac Milner in 1816:

> Cheltenham, where there are ten thousand souls, besides ten thou-sand visitors, or nearly so, is mine. It was to be sold for three thousand pounds, and I instantly secured it: and the Lord has raised up friends to concur with me; so that the burthen is light.[170]

It was no accident that livings in mercantile centres including Hull,[171] Newcastle,[172] Manchester,[173] Macclesfield[174] and Liverpool[175] were all created or snapped up by serious patrons in our period; nor that watering places like Cheltenham, Clifton, Bath, Buxton and Tunbridge Wells were also sought after and gradually bought up.[176] The desire to secure a significant 'sphere' was strong.

Like many educated at St Edmund Hall, William Henry Havergal (1793–1870) gravitated towards Bristol. It was an attractive proposition. 'I could not but admire the efficiency of the Evangelical body,' commented one observer. 'Every man seemed to do his duty under Biddulph as their leader, and I could not help considering him as virtually Bishop of Bristol.'[177] Lay influence played a key part in maintaining this hegemony: the Harford family were local figures of pious repute, while the Irish Evangelicals Lord

---

Towns, *1774–1967* (Leicester, 1980). For evangelical culture in Birmingham more generally, see Leonore Davidoff and Catherine Hall, *Family Fortunes: Men and Women of the English Middle Class, 1780–1850* (London, 1987).

[169] 'Obituary. J.O. Oldham, Esq.' *Monthly Repository*, 17 (1822), 511.

[170] Milner, *Isaac Milner*, 635.

[171] King, *Thomas Dykes*, 152–3.

[172] Alan F. Munden, 'The Origin of Evangelical Anglicanism in Newcastle-upon-Tyne', *Archaeologia Aeliana*, 5th ser., 11 (1983), 301–7.

[173] See Arthur Pollard, 'Cornelius Bayley', in *BDEB*, I: 70; Henry D. Rack, 'Edward Smyth', in *ibid.*, II: 1031–2.

[174] See Arthur Pollard, 'David Simpson', in *BDEB*, II: 1015–16.

[175] See D.W. Bebbington, 'Sir John Gladstone', in *BDEB*, II: 446–7.

[176] See Balda, '"Spheres of Influence"', 130–1; Kenneth Hylson-Smith, *Bath Abbey* (Bath, 2003), 169–73.

[177] Henry Budd, *A Memoir of the Rev. Henry Budd* (London, 1855), 267.

and Lady Lifford stayed regularly at Clifton. To these aristocratic friends could be added the majority of the Corporation. Supporters included the attorney John Vowles (fl. 1790s), the merchant gentlemen James Ireland of Brislington Hall (fl. 1770s–90s) and John Fisher Weare (c. 1747–1816), and James George (probably c. 1789–1858), a brewer and merchant who served as Sheriff and Mayor.[178] The Corporation controlled nine Bristol livings: out of thirteen presentations made between 1799 and 1838, at least ten were CMS supporters.[179] Evangelicals were also influential in Bristol's hinterland. In 1816 Biddulph advertised for a curate to assist him at St James's Church in the city, and to share his duties at Durston and Lyng, some forty miles away. 'So desirable is the position', reported Havergal, 'that Mr Biddulph has had no less than six applications.'[180] Havergal was the successful candidate, and was immediately thrown into the pastoral aftermath of the 'Western Schism', the previous curate being the Honourable and Reverend George Baring (1781–1854), one of a group of prominent high Calvinist seceders.[181] The arrival of Henry Ryder (1777–1836) as Bishop of Gloucester brought further opportunities. In 1820, Havergal moved again to the industrializing market town of Dursley, 'an important sphere ... [the Bishop] longs to get the truth preached in it'.[182] By this time there was growing excitement among Evangelicals about the national momentum of their cause, and when a group of celebrity preachers including Josiah Pratt (1768–1844) and Edward Bickersteth (1786–1850) descended on Bristol in 1820 for the anniversary celebrations of its CMS Association, Havergal could boast to a friend about his acquaintance with them.[183] Later Havergal became renowned in the Midlands and South West as a preacher for the CMS, being also a musician and father to the famous Victorian hymn-writer Frances Ridley Havergal (1836–1879).[184]

The role of William Wilberforce as an ecclesiastical patron in Yorkshire has seldom received sustained attention. But it serves to highlight how civic and philanthropic politics might be exploited to cement pious influence in particular regions. If the West Riding was the Elland Society heartland, gospel ministers in the East Riding came together in the Hotham Clerical

---

[178] Fox, 'Thomas Tregenna Biddulph', 45–6; 307–8.

[179] *Ibid.*, 307–8.

[180] Jane Miriam Crane, *Records of the Life of the Rev. William H. Havergal* (London, 1883), 9–10.

[181] *Ibid.*, 16–17; see also Grayson Carter, *Anglican Evangelicals*, 105–51.

[182] Crane, *Havergal*, 24–5.

[183] *Ibid.*, 24.

[184] For Havergal's missionary preaching tours, see CRL, Church Missionary Society Unofficial Papers, Papers of the Havergal Family, XCMSACC/ACC/81/C95.

Society. Established at the home of James Stillingfleet, it included the venerable Thomas Adam of Wintringham (1701–1784) and William Richardson of York, as well as three eminent Hull names: Joseph Milner, Thomas Dikes and John Scott. Hull had long been a hotbed of serious religion: although opposed at first, Milner's long Mastership of Hull Grammar School (1767–1797) and his curacy at North Ferriby, where many of the merchants had their country seats, and as lecturer at Holy Trinity ('The High Church'), secured him a hearing among the city's elite.[185] The foundation of a Bible Society Auxiliary in 1811 and a Hull and East Riding Church Missionary Association in 1814 were posthumous testimony to his success.[186] Financial substance was provided by merchant families such as Richard (d. 1804) and Avison Terry (c. 1774–1866), the Wesleyan banker and MP Thomas Thompson (1754–1828) and the strong Wilberforce family interest.[187] Those same families took the lead in providing new church accommodation in the burgeoning city – St John's Church in 1790–2 and Sculcoates in 1821 – as well as the purchase of Holy Trinity in 1836.[188] Wilberforce himself was instrumental in Dikes's appointment to St John's,[189] also buying North Ferriby in 1787 to make Milner its incumbent and supplement his income,[190] and in 1826 giving Henry Venn junior (1796–1823) his first incumbency. 'There is a little living of which I have the disposal during my life,' wrote the recently retired MP, 'tho rather on sufferance than of right – It is that of Drypool a populous village at abt a quarter of a mile from Hull, close to the Garrison. The Value of it is about 200 or rather more, with I believe a tolerable House.'[191]

As MP for Yorkshire from 1784 to 1812, Wilberforce could also deploy significant weight in the affairs of the county capital. Since 1771 a pivotal figure in York had been William Richardson, incumbent of St Michael-le-Belfry, in the shadow of the Minster, and St Sampson's Church, and a member both of the Hotham and Elland societies.[192] Richardson's congregation included William Gray (1751–1845), a Hull-born lawyer whose work as clerk for the

[185] I. Milner, *An Account of the Life and Character of the Late Rev. Joseph Milner* (London, 1804).

[186] King, *Thomas Dykes*, 80, 85–6.

[187] For Thompson see J.A.S.L. Leighton-Boyce, *Smiths the Bankers 1658–1958* (London, 1958), esp. 183–242; Arthur R.B. Robinson, *The Counting House: Thomas Thompson of Hull 1754–1828 and his Family* (York, 1992).

[188] King, *Thomas Dykes*, 21–6; 115; 152–3.

[189] Thomas Dikes to John Scott, n.d., 1833, cited in King, *Thomas Dykes*, 144.

[190] John Thornton to William Richardson, 13 Apr. 1787, CUL, MS Add.7674/1/C17.

[191] William Wilberforce to Henry Venn, 26 Oct. 1826, CRL, XCMSACC/ACC/81/C35.

[192] Gray, *York family*, 16–17

Yorkshire Association brought him into contact with Wilberforce during the 1784 election. The two became friends, and Gray became almoner for Wilberforce's charities in the county, being appointed Distributor of Stamps for York and the West Riding in 1790 through the offices of Wilberforce and the other knight of the shire, Henry Duncombe (1728–1818). Duncombe was a prominent abolitionist, but there are hints that his religious sympathies may also have matched those of his co-adjutors. He was well known to Richardson and, like Wilberforce, was a friend of Lord Muncaster (bap. 1741, d. 1813) and the Leeds surgeon William Hey.[193] Wilberforce was again at work in 1796, when John Graham, erstwhile curate of Barwick-in-Elmet, accepted the twin livings of St Saviour and St Mary, Bishophill Senior, both in the gift of the Lord Chancellor, which he held until 1844. Next in line was Richardson's curate, John Overton (1763–1838), another Magdalene man, who was presented in 1802 to two more Lord Chancellor's livings, St Crux and St Margaret's, again through Wilberforce's intervention. Thanks to this largesse and to the energy of the Gray family, the Evangelical clique gained a leading role in city affairs, playing a part in the York Dispensary and the County Hospital, as well as founding Sunday Schools, a Female Friendly Society, the local Anti-Slavery Society, a Church Missionary Association and a Bible Society Auxiliary.[194] All this brought political as well as religious benefits. The importance of 'Methodists' in Wilberforce's re-election campaigns has often been noted, and while it is undoubtedly true that Wesleyans cheered his anti-slavery campaigning, it seems more likely that this stems from the wry contemporary nickname for Evangelicals, who canvassed actively on his behalf. When Wilberforce visited York for elections or on other business he frequently stayed at Gray's Court, the family's comfortable townhouse.

Success

By the early 1800s gospel ministers were in a far stronger position than their forebears. There were well-mapped routes to take through grammar school or a private clerical tutor to university, and from there curacies and perhaps a living, through one or another of the patronage trusts, or through a lay patron. For patrons the situation was also more straightforward, since

---

[193] John Thornton to William Richardson, 15 Sep. 1775, CUL, MS Add.7674/1/C5.

[194] Gray, *York family*; Linda Perriton, 'The Parochial Realm, Social Enterprise and Gender: the Work of Catharine Cappe and Faith Gray and others in York, 1780–1820', *Business History*, 59 (2017), 202–30. See also York Libraries and Archives, Gray Family of Gray's Court Papers, GRF/3–5.

recipients had often been noticed, vetted and assessed years in advance of any presentation. If anything this served to intensify the Evangelical fixation with 'spheres of influence'. Indeed, the struggle to capture such spheres could take on local and even national significance as anxious onlookers awaited the result of financial and political manoeuvrings. With growing influence in the capital and the provinces, a web of local clerical groups and the national framework provided by the CMS, Evangelicals were coming to see themselves as part of a national movement.

Chapter Two

Business, Banking and Bibles in Late-Hanoverian London

Bad news always unsettles the financial markets. 'Yesterday morning,' reported the *Morning Chronicle* on Friday 19 August 1814, 'the Stock Exchange was thrown into a state of dismay by the declaration, that a person of some consideration in the City had confessed himself unable or unwilling to pay his differences, to the amount of £45,000.'[1] Details emerged over the next few days. This was no ordinary bankruptcy. The subject of the scandal was Robert Thornton (1759–1826), an intimate of the Prince Regent and a leading London businessman who at the time of his disgrace was Chairman of the East India Company, Marshal of the Court of Admiralty and MP for Colchester. Finding himself in difficulties, Thornton had resorted to speculation in order to maintain a lavish lifestyle at his townhouse in Grafton Street and his elegant Clapham villa. 'At first he was very successful and gained £30,000 or £40,000,' his sister-in-law told a friend.

> This very success proved fatal, for enamoured of his own sagacity he went on venturing more and more, till the depression in the stocks annihilated all his gains and in the true spirit of a gambler he attempted to retrieve this loss by desperate efforts and at last foiled and disappointed in every effort he became a defaulter to the amount of £45,000.[2]

This was an immense sum – worth perhaps £33 million today – and the sale of his library, his collection of prints and other property failed to satisfy Thornton's creditors.[3] As newspaper interest built to a crescendo, his nerve broke. By September he had left his wife and fled to France under

---

[1]   *Morning Chronicle*, 19 Aug. 1814, 2.
[2]   Mrs Henry Thornton to Patty Smith, [n.d.] 1814, cited in E.M. Forster, *Marianne Thornton, 1797–1887: a Domestic Biography* (London, 1956), 36.
[3]   https://www.measuringworth.com/calculators/ppoweruk/, last accessed 7 Sep. 2017.

an assumed name, and in the turmoil surrounding the return of Napoleon in early 1815 'Richard Tyler' emigrated to the United States, where he died in 1826. Though they had long pursued different ends, mused his brother Henry sadly, 'I had never till now had to contemplate him as a Prodigal who had literally wandered from home.'[4]

Robert's fall was all the more shocking because this was not the behaviour expected of a Thornton. According to the *Gentleman's Magazine* his father, John (1720–1790), had been 'the greatest merchant in Europe, except Mr. Hope, of Amsterdam', an Evangelical philanthropist who, despite giving to charity between £100,000 and £150,000 during his lifetime, had left an estate valued at £600,000.[5] Robert's older brother Samuel (1754–1838) inherited both his father's beliefs and his commercial empire, a vast concern stretching from Hull and London to St Petersburg and the Baltic, which dealt in everything from sugar and soap refining to shipping, tar, timber and cordage. Samuel was also a Director of the Russia Company and the Bank of England, as well as being MP for Hull and then Surrey. The other brother, Henry (1760–1815), was similarly pious: a banker, MP for Southwark and a leading figure among the Saints. Small wonder, then, that Robert's disgrace caused such a stir. Disappointment and disapproval echo through the pages of *Marianne Thornton*, E.M. Forster's famous memoir of his great aunt, published over a hundred years later in 1956.[6] Dealing with bankruptcy badly was, as Boyd Hilton has pointed out, an unforgivable sin for Evangelical businessmen, for whom failure represented providential chastisement.[7] Yet to wall Robert off from his brothers is misleading.[8] Granted, Henry disapproved of his high living, and thought that he had departed from his pious upbringing.[9] But Samuel, too, was known for keeping a comfortable establishment and he, too, experienced financial difficulties during the continental blockade.[10] Robert's activities as a charitable patron and parliamentarian, moreover, resemble those of his brothers. Like them he was active philanthropically.[11] In the Commons he frequently

---

[4] Diary, 6 Nov. 1814, CUL, Thornton Family Letters and Papers, Ms. Add.7674/1/R, fos. 176–8.

[5] 'Obituary of Considerable Persons; with Biographical Anecdotes: 7', *Gentleman's Magazine*, 60 (Nov. 1790), 1056.

[6] Forster, *Marianne Thornton*, 36–8.

[7] Boyd Hilton, *The Age of Atonement: the Influence of Evangelicalism on Social and Economic Thought, 1785–1865* (Oxford, 1988), 136–47.

[8] He is omitted, for instance, from the *BDEB*.

[9] Diary, 6 Nov. 1814, CUL, MS Add.7674/1/R, fos. 176–8.

[10] Forster, *Marianne Thornton*, 35.

[11] Ford K. Brown, *Fathers of the Victorians: the Age of Wilberforce* (Cambridge, 1961), 358, calculates that the brothers, along with Samuel's son John, had between them

voted with the Saints, supporting the Sierra Leone settlement, slave trade abolition and Wilberforce's call for peace negotiations with France in the 1790s, speaking in 1803 against militia drilling on Sundays and favouring the censure of Melville in 1805. Ironically, he also contributed to the Society for the Discharge and Relief of Persons Imprisoned for Small Debts.[12]

If Robert Thornton's omission from the history of Evangelicalism highlights the danger of inferring the wrong thing from contemporary equations of religiosity with financial rectitude, it simultaneously underlines how the new piety infused the world of the London merchantocracy in our period: a world where trust was paramount and sobriety a cardinal virtue. As Boyd Hilton has brilliantly shown, the financial crises that punctuated our period (1788, 1793, 1797, 1803, 1807–8, 1810–11, 1816, 1819, 1826) were conducive to an ethic that saw economic malfunctions as periods of salutary chastisement for over-speculation. But although the influence of Evangelicalism on social and economic thought is well known, the networks through which it penetrated this world are not.[13] This chapter, then, examines that milieu from different angles. First, it considers the developing symbiosis between the Evangelical clergy and their patrons from the late eighteenth century onwards. Next, it shows how the growth of affluent congregations was driven by and in turn encouraged the development of an Evangelical culture among merchants, bankers, professionals and prosperous laypeople. It then explores the effects of this, tracing the spread of Evangelical business networks in the City of London and suggesting that in the process the more focused vital religion of earlier generations broadened into a creed that valued 'practical Christianity' above doctrinal details. Finally, and following on from this, it shows how lay money, organizational skills and marketing expertise were deployed to make Evangelical philanthropy fashionable. As will be shown, this was a world whose boundaries were never sharp and which, as a consequence of its success, became ever more blurred around the edges.

Pious Patrons

John Thornton's lasting legacy to his co-religionists was the ecclesiastical patronage he bequeathed to them on his death in 1790. It helped to ensure that Evangelicalism in London was growing in momentum long before his son Henry, John Venn and William Wilberforce moved to Clapham in

---

173 subscriptions to philanthropic organizations.
[12]   Brown, *Fathers of the Victorians*, 349.
[13]   Hilton, *Age of Atonement*.

1792. What became known as the Thornton Trust – later the nucleus of the Simeon Trust – ensured that Evangelicals held nine livings and one next presentation: Clapham was one and St Dunstan's-in-the-West another.[14] But Thornton had already preferred gospel ministers to two of the suburbs and villages surrounding the capital: Roger Bentley (c. 1734–1795) at St Giles's, Camberwell, where he served between 1769 and 1789, and Richard Conyers (1725–1786), at St Paul's, Deptford from 1775–86. Other pious incumbents included John Simons (bap. 1755, d. 1836, at St Paul's Cray near Bromley from 1781 until his death,[15] William Bromley Cadogan, at the family living of St Luke's, Chelsea from 1775–97, William Jarvis Abdy (1755–1823) at St John's, Horsleydown, where he was curate-in-charge from 1782–1805, then Rector from 1805–23,[16] and Robert Myddelton (1751–1815), at St Mary's, Rotherhithe from 1792–1815. In the City itself William Romaine, Rector of St Anne Blackfriars since 1766, had for many years been the sole beneficed Evangelical, but was joined in 1780 by Newton at St Mary Woolnoth, again thanks in large part to Thornton.

It must not be supposed, however, that incumbents were the only Evangelicals in the capital. The 'ecclesiastical underworld' of preacher-ships and lectureships endowed by puritans in the sixteenth and seventeenth centuries contained numerous potential openings.[17] The 'brilliant and meteor-like' George Pattrick (1746–1800), for example, reputedly attracted average congregations of 1,500 – more than any other London church – and was elected to St Leonard's in 1796 by the immense margin of 947 to 357 votes.[18] Once chosen, usually by the parish vestry, which might include dissenters, such officeholders operated outside the effective sanction of their parish incumbents.[19] 'We have about ten clergymen,' Newton informed one correspondent in 1781, 'who, either as morning preachers or lecturers, preach either on the Lord's day, or at different times of the week,

---

[14] Wesley D. Balda, '"Spheres of Influence": Simeon's Trust and its Implications for Evangelical Patronage' (unpublished Ph.D. thesis, University of Cambridge, 1981), 35–6.

[15] Charles Hole, *The Early History of the Church Missionary Society for Africa and the East* (London, 1896), 640.

[16] Made curate through the influence of John Jowett of Newington Butts, and Rector through Henry Thornton. Hole, *Church Missionary Society*, 621.

[17] D. Bruce Hindmarsh, *John Newton and the English Evangelical Tradition: Between the Conversions of Wesley and Wilberforce* (Oxford, 1996), 291–3.

[18] Hole, *Church Missionary Society*, 635–6.

[19] Although see E.A. Varley, *The Last of the Prince Bishops: William Van Mildert and the High Church Movement of the Early Nineteenth Century* (Cambridge, 1992), 34, for the removal of Abdy from the Bow lectureship in 1796.

in perhaps fifteen or sixteen churches.'[20] Newton's ten may have included George Dyer (fl. 1759–?1780s) at St George-the-Martyr, Southwark; Henry Foster (1745–1814) at St Antholin's, Watts Wilkinson (1755–1840) at St Mary Aldermary and William Goode at St Lawrence Jewry, all in the City; Pattrick at St Leonard's, Shoreditch and St Bride's, Fleet Street; and William Winkworth (1750–1804) at St Paul's, Shadwell, who was also Chaplain of St Saviour's, Southwark and Chaplain to Surrey County Gaol.[21] There were also Evangelical lecturers at St Alban's, Wood Street; St Swithin's, London Stone; St Mary Somerset; St Margaret's, Lothbury; Bow Church; All Hallows; St Peter's, Cornhill; and St Bartholomew the Great.[22]

Evangelicals with the ability to command a crowd were also drawn towards London's proprietary chapels. Like lectureships, these stood outside parochial discipline. Being erected at private expense and supported by pew-rents, they were dependent upon their ministers' ability to bring in well-to-do hearers. At the Lock Hospital Chapel near Hyde Park Corner, for instance, the cultivated Calvinist Martin Madan (1726–1790) had from the 1750s attracted a prosperous congregation with his electrifying preaching and promotion of oratorios and hymn-singing, all of which financed its rebuilding in 1762.[23] Following his resignation in 1780 after the furore surrounding *Thelyptora*, his book recommending polygamy, the upward trend continued under his successors, C.E. de Coetlogon (1746–1820) and Thomas Scott. In the 1780s and 90s worshippers there included Lord Dartmouth, Sir Charles Middleton (1726–1813), Wilberforce, Henry Thornton and Edward Eliot (1758-97) – all MPs – the agriculturalist Arthur Young and the civil servant and devotional writer Ambrose Serle (1742–1812). 'We shall soon have gout numbered among the privileges of the gospel!' chuckled one member.[24] Elsewhere, the 1780s witnessed the commencement of other important ministries, including those of Richard Cecil at St John's Chapel, Bedford Row (1780–1810), Henry Foster at Long Acre (1784?–1804) and Basil Woodd at Bentinck Chapel, Marylebone (1785–1831).

[20]   Newton to William Barlass, 23 Feb. 1781, in *The Original Letters of the Rev. John Newton, A.M., to the Rev. W. Barlass* (London, 1819), 129.

[21]   L.E. Elliott-Binns, *The Early Evangelicals: a Religious and Social Study* (London, 1953), 241–7; George R. Balleine, *A History of the Evangelical Party in the Church of England* (2nd edn: London, 1951), 48–51; Margaret J. Shaen, *Memorials of Two Sisters: Susanna and Catherine Winkworth* (London, 1908), 1–3.

[22]   Hindmarsh, *John Newton*, 292n.

[23]   Nicholas Temperley, 'The Lock Hospital Chapel and its Music', *Journal of the Royal Musical Association*, 118 (1993), 44–72.

[24]   John Scott, *The Life of the Rev. Thomas Scott* (4th edn: London, 1822), 243.

Yet proprietary chapels were not without drawbacks. 'In London', Scott opined, 'almost all are either *hugged* or *kicked* to death, according as they are popular or unpopular.'[25] He was well-placed to judge: in the 1790s, Wilberforce, Thornton and Eliot often followed him from the Lock in the morning to hear his afternoon lecture at St Mildred's, Bread Street.[26] While most clergymen acknowledged the need to cater for their hearers' tastes, many also feared that ministerial independence might be compromised by religious consumerism. For Cecil's assistant Charles Jerram, the congregation at Bedford Row 'was not altogether of the character I liked':

> It was not parochial, and such as I could consider as peculiarly my own; but collected from various parts of the metropolis, the large portion of whom were entire strangers to me ... As, moreover, a congregation of this description is usually of a more fluctuating character than a parochial charge ... the comfort of the minister, and that independence which he ought to feel, are liable to be more or less affected by the caprice and humours of his hearers.[27]

This last point echoed criticisms more usually levelled at nonconformity. How could a minister fearlessly declare God's Word to the congregational 'customers' who funded his stipend?[28] What if he needed to seek re-election?[29] Was it wrong to poach hearers from other parishes? 'The whole affair', Jerram concluded, 'had too much of the voluntary system in it to suit my taste.'[30] This too was an acute comment. With denominational boundaries hardening in the 1780s and 90s, many erstwhile followers of Whitefield opted to remain within the Established Church, and it seems likely that they found the quasi-Methodist proprietorial chapels congenial. Still, it is important not to overstate this. Even a secure incumbent like Newton might modify his sermons, being sensible that although many parishioners disparaged his 'Methodism' he might yet win their favour.[31]

25   *Ibid.*, 394.
26   *Ibid.*, 617.
27   James Jerram, *The Memoirs and a Selection from the Letters of the Late Reverend Charles Jerram* (London, 1855), 305.
28   See e.g. John Pearson, *The Life of William Hey*, 2 vols (London, 1822), I: 85–7.
29   Requests for the recipient's 'vote and interest' are scattered through archives of evangelical correspondence. See e.g. Thomas Scott to Arthur Young, 20 Feb. 1802, 31 Jan. 1808, Arthur Young Letters, BL Add. MS 35128, fo. 295; 35129, fo. 7.
30   Jerram, *Charles Jerram*, 305.
31   Hindmarsh, *John Newton*, 307.

Few careers better illustrate the workings of metropolitan Evangelicalism at the turn of the century than that of Daniel Wilson. The son of a Spitalfields silk manufacturer, Wilson was apprenticed to his maternal uncle, William Wilson (1756–1821) of Milk Street, Cheapside, 'an extensive silk manufacturer and merchant', in 1792, aged fourteen. Daniel's parents were 'a kind of loose church people', first attending Romaine on Sunday mornings and Whitefield's Tabernacle in the afternoons, and later attending dissenting chapels when they moved house, a common predicament for those who preferred a pious minister without the Church over an unregenerate one within it. His uncle, by contrast, was 'a strict and conscientious' though choosy Evangelical churchman, attending Romaine, Cecil, Scott, Woodd and Samuel Crowther (1769–1829), the latter at Christ Church, Newgate Street.[32] Many among the new generation of pious clergy were drawn from the upper end of the London mercantile classes, and Wilson junior entered St Edmund Hall in 1798 to train for ordination. Already marked as a future leader, he was curate to Cecil at Chobham in Surrey from 1801–3 before returning to St Edmund Hall as Assistant Tutor in 1804, then sole tutor and vice-president in 1807, which positions he combined with the curacy of Over and Nether Worton, where his uncle owned land. Having been groomed for ministerial greatness, he began assisting Cecil at St John's, Bedford Row in 1808 or 1809, resigning his academic posts and taking full charge in 1812.[33]

While his new situation entailed a significant cut in income, it could be regarded as the hub of the Evangelical movement in the capital. It was the home of the Eclectic Society, which met in the vestry.[34] Situated in the shadow of Gray's Inn in the legal district of Holborn and Fleet Street, it drew in lawyers and solicitors like Thomas Bainbridge (c. 1750–1830),[35] William Cardale (1777–1826)[36] and William Roberts (1767–1849), Hannah More's biographer and the editor of the Tory Evangelical *British Review* (1811–22), all of whom worked for and contributed lavishly to philanthropic causes. Another worshipper, the banker Ambrose Martin, was a leading member of the early CMS.[37] Wilson's congregation also incubated a circle of younger lawyers, including William Albin Garratt (1780–1858), Nadir Baxter (c. 1800–c. 1850) and John Bridges (1787–1865), who would in the

---

[32] Josiah Bateman, *The Life of the Right Rev. Daniel Wilson*, 2 vols. (London, 1860), I: 4–5.
[33] *Ibid.*, I: 130.
[34] John H. Pratt (ed.), *Eclectic Notes* (London, 1856), 2.
[35] Hole, *Church Missionary Society*, 621–2.
[36] *Ibid.*, 624.
[37] *Ibid.*, 634.

1820s and 30s become leading Evangelical committee men, championing harder-edged sabbatarianism, Irish missions and anti-Catholicism.[38] In the 1810s, however, it was more significant that St John's Bedford Row became the preferred worshipping place for many of the Saints, who by this time were moving away from Clapham, the Wilberforces to Knightsbridge and the Macaulays and Grants to Bloomsbury. They were joined as regular attenders by the Stephens, Lord Calthorpe, John Bowdler junior (1783–1815), Sir Digby Mackworth (1766–1838) and the Duchess of Beaufort (1771–1854). The genteel support base of the London Clerical Education Society (1816), whose first secretary Wilson was, further underlines the strategic importance of his post.[39]

> Thirty or forty carriages might often be counted during the London season, standing in triple rows about the doors; and though there was, as is too often unhappily the case in proprietary chapels, but scant accommodation for the poor, yet they loved to attend, and every vacant sitting-place was filled by them, the moment the doors were opened ... The importance of such a congregation is obvious at a glance; and the minister himself was quite sensible of it.[40]

That this was the case in 'the London season' comes as a reminder that such churches were nodes not just locally but for visitors and for those with connections or country seats elsewhere.

Wilson was not the only minister who could boast a well-heeled congregation. At Bentinck Chapel, in Paddington, whose lease he bought in 1793, Woodd preached to the illustrious Bond Street upholsterer and Clapham resident Charles Elliott (1751–1832), the London and Staffordshire porcelain manufacturer John Mortlock (1776–1837) and the American loyalist and onetime Governor of the New England Company Sir William Pepperell (1746–1816).[41] Another attender, Lady Mary Manners (1737–1829), presented Woodd to the living of Drayton Beauchamp in 1808.[42] By the 1810s there were ministers in many such pulpits: Thomas White (c. 1777–1849) at Welbeck Chapel, Marylebone from 1802–49, Josiah Pratt at Wheler Chapel, Spitalfields from 1810–26, J.H. Stewart (1776–1854) at Percy Chapel in Fitzrovia from 1812–28 and William Howels (1778–1832)

---

[38] Their number also included Robert Dudley Baxter, Charles Brodrick, William Dugmore, William Grane, E.V. Sidebottom and J.M. Strachan.
[39] *Bateman, Daniel Wilson*, I: 216–17, 256.
[40] *Ibid.*, I: 178.
[41] See Hole, *Church Missionary Society*, 646, 635, 444.
[42] *Ibid.*, 646.

at Long Acre Chapel in Covent Garden from 1817–32 as well as others at Tavistock Chapel, Drury Lane; Ely Chapel, Holborn; Broadway Chapel, Westminster and elsewhere. Like their congregations, they often remained in London only during the 'season', entrusting their chapels to curates and visiting preachers for the summer and removing to country parishes. Several balanced ministerial commitments with other responsibilities: Pratt was Secretary of the CMS, Thomas Webster (c. 1783–1840) editor of the *Christian Guardian*, Stewart a travelling preacher for the CMS and LSPCJ and Thomas Hartwell Horne (1780–1852) assistant minister at Welbeck from 1825–33 and Senior Assistant Librarian at the British Museum.[43] To a movement thirsty for numbers and influence, this was success indeed. But to Bishop Randolph (1749–1813) of London, proprietary chapels formed a dangerously self-sufficient sphere: his 1810 Primary Visitation Charge blamed the want of adequate parish provision and the increase of dissent in the capital on their proliferation.[44]

Mapping Metropolitan Evangelicalism

To survey the worshipping places of London and its environs is to mirror one way that Evangelicals and their contemporaries conceived of the pious world. It was natural, as one critic did, to sneer at the 'Christian Ladies Diary and Pocket Companion!', which listed only thirty-five '*Churches, Chapels, and Meeting Houses* where the Gospel is reputed to be preached every *Lord's Day*, in and near London', and differentiated even between lecturers and their unawakened incumbents.[45] His comments were spiced with resentment at those who proclaimed themselves to be more spiritual than their brethren. For serious readers, though, almanacs were important guides to where they might meet the like-minded. Evangelical congregations were spiritual and social magnets for newcomers and for those visiting London socially or on business. Their members were linked by multiple interconnections: marriage, business partnerships, shared endeavour. Any of the congregations detailed above would provide fascinating material for more detailed study. They are not, though, the only way in which this milieu can be mapped.

[43]   Sarah Anne Cheyne, *Reminiscences, Personal and Biographical, of Thomas Hartwell Horne* (London, 1862).

[44]   John Randolph, *A* Charge *Delivered to the Clergy of the Diocese of* London, *at his Primary Visitation* (Oxford, 1810), 25–7.

[45]   E.J. Burrow, *A Second Letter Addressed to the Rev. William Marsh* (2nd edn: London, 1819), 79.

The bookshop established by John Hatchard (1768–1849) in Piccadilly in 1797, for instance, became 'a kind of club' for Evangelical readers and writers, luring them away from the long-established Bible shop belonging to the Rivington family in St Paul's Churchyard.[46] Hatchard's was at once a social and a business space, publishing the *Christian Observer* and the writings of Hannah More, receiving donations and subscriptions on behalf of philanthropic societies and, as Sydney Smith jibed, providing a venue for smug Evangelicals to congratulate one another on their latest publications.[47] On Fleet Street, Leonard Benton Seeley (1766–1834) was official bookseller for the Bible Society, while Joseph Butterworth (1770–1826) published and sold law books, his business serving as another meeting-place for philanthropic committees.[48] The Baptist publisher Samuel Bagster (1772–1851) occupied premises on the Strand and then in Paternoster Row, and was integral to a broad milieu of Evangelical and dissenting biblical scholars, including Josiah Conder (1789–1855), Adam Clarke (c. 1760–1832) and Samuel Lee (1783–1852).[49] Within the professions, too, there were religious connections that remain mostly unexplored, and at which it is only possible to hint here. John Pearson (1758–1826) of Golden Square, Soho, for instance, was surgeon to the Lock from 1781–1818. A Yorkshireman who trained with William Hey at the Leeds Infirmary in the late 1770s, he was a Fellow of the Royal Society and of the Linnaean Society.[50] Pearson's pupil, William Blair (1766–1822), was Assistant Surgeon to the Lock from 1802, being also linked with the Bloomsbury and Finsbury Dispensaries and the Female Penitentiary at Pentonville, writing on prostitution and venereal disease and serving on the committee of the Bible Society.[51] Dr Devey Fearon (c. 1769–1847) of the Middlesex Hospital

[46] A.L. Humphreys, *Piccadilly Bookmen: Memorials of the House of Hatchard* (London, 1893), 33–49; James Raven, *The Business of Books: Booksellers and the English Book Trade, 1450–1850* (New Haven, CT, 2007), 181–2, 313, 374.

[47] [Sydney Smith], 'Remarks on the System of Education in Public Schools', *Edinburgh Review*, 16, 32 (1810), 326–33.

[48] Leslie Howsam, *Cheap Bibles: Nineteenth-Century Publishing and the British and Foreign Bible Society* (Cambridge, 1991), 10, 154–6; H. K. Jones, *Butterworths: History of a Publishing House* (1980).

[49] Samuel Bagster, *Samuel Bagster of London, 1772–1851* (London, 1972). Michael Ledger-Lomas, 'Conder and Sons: Dissent and the Oriental Bible in Nineteenth-Century Britain', in Scott Mandelbrote and Michael Ledger-Lomas (eds), *Dissent and the Bible in Britain, c. 1650–1950* (Oxford, 2013), 205–32.

[50] Hole, *Church Missionary Society*, 636.

[51] Howsam, *Cheap Bibles*, 25.

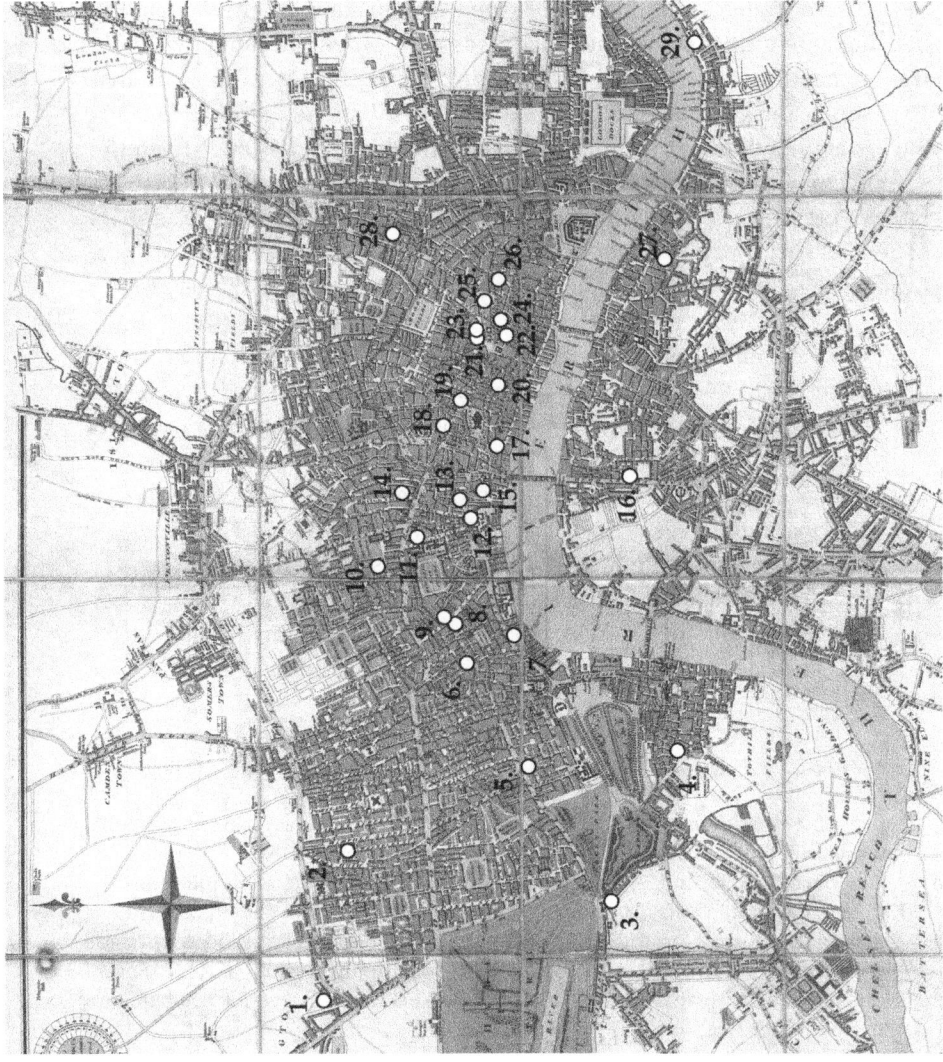

1. Bentinck Chapel, Paddington
2. Welbeck Chapel, Marylebone
3. Lock Hospital and Chapel
4. Broadway Chapel, Westminster
5. Hatchard's bookshop, Piccadilly
6. Long Acre Episcopal Chapel, Covent Garden
7. Samuel Bagster, publisher, 81 The Strand
8. Freemasons' Hall
9. Tavistock Chapel, Drury Lane
10. St John's Chapel, Bedford Row
11. Society for Promoting Christian Knowledge, Bartlett's Buildings
12. Joseph Butterworth, publisher, 43 Fleet Street
13. Leonard Benton Seeley, publisher, 169 Fleet Street
14. Ely Chapel, Holborn
15. Salisbury Square [Church Missionary House from 1813]
16. Surrey Chapel, Blackfriars Road
17. St Andrew-by-the-Wardrobe
18. Christ Church, Newgate Street
19. New London Tavern, Cheapside
20. St Antholin, Budge Row; St Mary Aldermary
21. Bank of England, Threadneedle Street
22. St Mary Woolnoth, Lombard Street
23. Down, Thornton and Free, bankers, Bartholomew Lane
24. African Institution Office, Birchin Lane
25. London Tavern, Bishopsgate
26. East India House, Leadenhall Street
27. St John's Horsleydown
28. Wheler Chapel, Spitalfields
29. St Mary's, Rotherhithe

Map 1: Evangelical London, c. 1810

in Fitzrovia was another intimate of the Evangelical inner circle, and was ordained in 1807 after the death of his wife.[52]

These networks and the wider Evangelical world of provincial Britain were tied together by shared reading, most notably the *Christian Observer*, founded in 1802. The projectors' choice of the polished lay businessman Zachary Macaulay over Thomas Scott to be its first editor was a statement of their intent. Scott was a diamond, Wilberforce told Hey, but 'a *rough* diamond.' 'He has not general knowledge nor taste sufficient for such an office.'[53] It was significant that when the 1810 preface to the *Christian Observer* enumerated the triumphs of the preceding decade, the correction of common prejudices against Evangelicalism was listed above the abolition of the slave trade. 'The influence of true Religion', claimed the writer, 'has become much more prevalent': and it was now widely accepted that there was 'no hostility between serious Religion and Elegant Literature; and that Philosophy and Genius rejoice to take up their Cross and follow CHRIST'.[54] Such statements might sound like wishful thinking, but a letter from the seventeen-year-old Hon. Baptist Noel (1798–1873) protesting against his father's prejudices eloquently demonstrates the effect of pious exemplars in genteel society. He was not unaware, he admitted, that 'Methodists' (i.e. Evangelicals) were reputed to be uncouth, as well as religiously suspect.

> But what am I saying [is:] are all Methodists so[?] If they are not I need not be[. I]s Mr Wilberforce gluttonous ... sulky, selfish? Is Lady Olivia Sparrow that pattern of Elegance and model of high Manners, is Lady Olivia Sparrow clumsy, awkward, unsociable, greedy? Is the Bishop of Gloucester, is Sir Charles Grey, is Charles and Gerard Noel was Mrs Hoare disagreeable and ill mannered? The answer is and must be in the negative. Surely then if they are thus not horrible, and yet are (what are called) Methodists, I who am a Methodist also may be exempt also from the like Evils; but if they are not Methodists I will not be. I conclude then that I may be Religious, and yet of good manners.[55]

---

[52]   Hole, *Church Missionary Society*, 627; Zachary to Colin Macaulay, 2 Apr. 1808, Senate House Library Archives, Booth Family Papers, MS 797/I/5618.

[53]   Wilberforce to William Hey, 28 Jul. 1798, cited in Wilberforce, *Life*, II: 308.

[54]   'Preface', *Christian Observer*, 9 (1810), iv–vi.

[55]   Baptist Wriothesley Noel to Gerard Noel Noel, 6 Aug. 1816, Record Office for Leicestershire, Leicester and Rutland, Records of the Noel Family, DE3214/302/82/2. Seven years later, and against the wishes of his family, Noel was ordained in the Church of England.

He was ordained in 1824 and placed in charge of St John's Bedford Row – an important post for one still only in his twenties – only three years later.

Artistic patronage throws further light on circles of acquaintance. Notwithstanding the work of Doreen Rosman, there remains a lazy assumption that Evangelicals were philistines or even actively hostile to the arts.[56] In reality, polite piety generated plenty of custom for artists, several of whom were serious themselves. Foremost among them was the pastellist John Russell (1745–1806). 'Called out of darkness into God's marvellous light, under the ministry of dear Mr. Madan at the Lock' in 1764, Russell became a fervent follower of Whitefield and Romaine, although in the 1790s he came to affirm the importance of remaining within the establishment.[57] Historians have sometimes struggled to comprehend how Russell's beliefs related to a successful career as a member of the Royal Academy and an intimate of Sir Joshua Reynolds (1723–1792); one, moreover, who could charge as much as £150 for a full-length group portrait. According to Martin Postle, for example, Russell was 'an absolute pain, inflicting his religious mania on his master and upon his sitters alike'. 'Yet', Postle adds, 'he attracted numerous patrons.'[58] In reality, there is no conundrum to explain. Russell's catalogue is a roll-call of religious revival, ranging from the Wesleys, Whitefield and the Countess of Huntingdon to Wilberforce, whom he painted both as an eleven-year-old boy and as a fully fledged abolitionist, leading London gospel ministers and families from the Lock congregation.[59] Thanks to his friend William Hey, he was also a favourite with textile merchants, clergymen and their families in the Evangelical strongholds of Yorkshire, as well as portraying the poet William Cowper (1731–1800) and the pious Hill family of Hawkstone Court in Shropshire and scores of others.[60]

Although their religiosity was a selling point for many of their clients, Russell and his pious friends, the painter John Francis Rigaud (1742–1810) and the sculptors John Bacon, father (1740–1799) and son (1777–1859), were widely admired outside Evangelical circles.[61] Bacon senior was a sculptor

[56] Deborah Cohen, *Household Gods: the British and their Possessions* (New Haven, CT, 2006), 3–13.

[57] Antje Steinhöfel, 'John Russell and the Impact of Evangelicalism and Natural Theology on Artistic Practice' (unpublished Ph.D. thesis, University of Leicester, 2005), 24, 45. Steinhöfel slightly misleadingly refers to Russell and his circle as 'Methodists'.

[58] Martin Postle, *Angels and Urchins: the Fancy Picture in Eighteenth-Century British Art* (Nottingham, 1998), 89.

[59] See Neil Jeffares, 'Pastels and Pastellists', online database, http://www.pastellists. com/Articles/Russell.pdf, last accessed 7 Sept. 2017.

[60] Steinhöfel, 'John Russell', 8–11, 39–40.

[61] Doreen M. Rosman, *Evangelicals and Culture* (London, 1984), 154–62.

of national repute, whose expressive sentimentalism set him against the sparseness of the neoclassicism that was coming into vogue and made his works some of the most recognizable of their time. He was also a member of the early CMS and one of the few lay attenders of the Eclectic Society.[62] As Sarah Burnage has recently shown, he pursued an aesthetic that was overtly pious, being packed with allegorical references to the Bible and to the consolations of faith.[63] Aside from figures for Somerset House and the pediment for East India House on Leadenhall Street, some of his major commissions were monuments for religious luminaries: Samuel Johnson (1709–1784) and the prison reformer John Howard (1726–1790), both for St Paul's Cathedral, and Thomas Guy (1644–1724) at Guy's Hospital Chapel. His son continued in a similar vein, filling Indian cathedrals with marbles of missionaries, military heroes and pioneer bishops, and supplying civic and funerary commissions across the Anglo-world.[64] The Bacons provide a tantalizing glimpse of how Evangelicalism shaped contemporary art and iconography: a subject that is yet to find its historian.

There have been several glimpses in the foregoing of Evangelical net-works beyond London and its environs. The clerical connections dis-cussed in the preceding chapter provide one perspective on this. Yet the gravitational pull exerted by the capital as a centre of business, fashion and sociability was conducive to other forms of connectivity. In the West Riding of Yorkshire, for instance, figures like William Hey were impor-tant middle-men, corresponding with Wilberforce and with expatriate Yorkshire businessmen such as his friend John Jowett (1745–1800) of Leeds and Newington Butts, whose extended family became academics, clergymen, missionaries and merchants.[65] Vital religion also found fertile soil in other mercantile centres such as Hull, Newcastle, King's Lynn and Bristol. County towns, too, such as York, Carlisle, Shrewsbury, Colchester and Norwich, witnessed the growth of prominent congregations around charismatic ministers, while watering places such as Bath were also sites for pious sociability and connection-making. 'Much invited out now by

---

[62] Hole, *Church Missionary Society*, 621; Richard Cecil, *Memoirs of John Bacon* (London, 1801).

[63] Sarah Burnage, 'The Works of John Bacon R.A. (1766–1799)' (unpublished Ph.D. thesis, University of York, 2007), 14–27.

[64] Barbara Groseclose, *British Sculpture and the Company Raj: Church Monuments and Public Statuary in Madras, Calcutta, and Bombay to 1858* (Cranbury, NJ, 1995), 77–99.

[65] Evelyn Abbott and Lewis Campbell, *The Life and Letters of Benjamin Jowett*, 2 vols (London, 1897), I: 1–12.

some in higher circumstances, and much attended to', enthused the Vicar of Leeds, Miles Atkinson, in 1799.[66]

In the Church of Ireland, Dublin became a centre for Evangelicalism in much the same way that London was in England. Bethesda Chapel, founded in 1784 by the merchant and nephew of the Archbishop of Dublin William Smyth (fl. 1780s), in conjunction with a female orphanage and Lock penitentiary, formed the base for an influential philanthropic circle that conjoined the professions, the business world and Trinity College. Although it was initially viewed with suspicion by the ecclesiastical establishment, the Bethesda congregation came to include a founder of the Royal Irish Academy, Dr Robert Perceval (1756–1839); the Guinness brewing family; and the La Touche banking dynasty, who were instrumental in the formation of the Bank of Ireland.[67] The mood of postmillennial optimism that attended the end of war with Napoleon in 1815 was the catalyst for further expansion, and the rapid spread of Evangelicalism among the Irish Protestant gentry and aristocracy in turn opened up ecclesiastical patronage to like-minded clergymen.[68] The 'Second Reformation' – the attempt to convert the Catholic peasantry to Protestantism in the 1820s – was incubated in the Hibernian Bible Society and various Dublin-based educational charities. 'You who know the precise line in which I walk at Cambridge would be astonished as I myself was,' reported Charles Simeon in 1822, 'to find Earls and Viscounts, Deans and Dignitaries, Judges, etc. calling upon me, and Bishops desirous to see me ... I dined at the Countess of Westmeath's and met Judge Daly and many other characters of the highest respectability.'[69] The success of the Evangelical painter Maria Spilsbury (1776–1820) suggests that in Dublin, as in London, the conjunction of piety and prosperity provided ample opportunities for artistic as well as ecclesiastical patronage.[70] The Evangelical 'season' of April meetings, devised to resemble but not to clash

---

[66] Cited in John D. Walsh, 'Evangelicals and Predestination, 1730–1830' (unpublished essay, n.d.), 60.

[67] M.C. Motherwell, *A Memoir of the Late Albert Blest* (Dublin, 1843); W. Urwick, *Biographic Sketches of James Digges La Touche* (Dublin, 1868); Alan R. Acheson, *A History of the Church of Ireland 1691–1996* (Dublin, 1997), 66–168; Nigel Yates, *The Religious Condition of Ireland, 1780–1850* (Oxford, 2006), 250–81.

[68] Irene Whelan, 'The Bible Gentry: Evangelical Religion, Aristocracy, and the New Moral Order in the Early Nineteenth Century', in Crawford Gribben and Andrew R. Holmes (eds), *Protestant Millennialism, Evangelicalism and Irish Society, 1790–2005* (Basingstoke, 2006), 52–82.

[69] William Carus, *Memoirs of the Life of the Rev. Charles Simeon* (London, 1847), 564.

[70] Charlotte Yeldham, *Maria Spilsbury (1776–1820): Artist and Evangelical* (Farnham, 2010), 123–64.

with the May meetings of the metropolitan societies in London, further underlines the resemblance.[71]

While it is impossible to demonstrate this with any certainty, it seems likely that Evangelicalism was often spread and diffused in the same manner and along much the same routes as other intellectual and social trends. What is certain is that with the growth of London-based national societies in the 1800s, 1810s and 1820s the capital became the *de facto* hub of the Evangelical world, not just in Britain, but increasingly in the empire too. Correspondence flowed to and from society headquarters, while the May meetings and printed accounts of them allowed people to see themselves as part of an imagined community of shared belief and action with an increasingly global purview.

Saints and the City

While the activities of the Saints at Westminster are well known, it is often forgotten that their real power base lay at the other end of London, in the narrow streets of the financial Square Mile. Henry Thornton is a case in point.[72] His firm was based at Bartholomew Lane, in the shadow of the Bank of England, and when he spoke at Westminster, he often did so on behalf of the City, also collaborating closely with Francis Horner (1778–1817) and William Huskisson (1770–1830) in the preparation of the 1810 Bullion Report.[73] His election as member for Southwark owed much to the influence he could command north of the Thames. 'I think he must have been thrown out but for the exertions of his friends in the City ... in the India House etc.', his wife told a friend in 1807.[74] (His successor, the Quaker abolitionist Charles Barclay [1780–1855], was, similarly, a banking MP with a pious bent.) Samuel, meanwhile, was a high-profile defender of the Bank of England, as well as a close friend and adviser to Nicholas Vansittart (1766–1851), the Chancellor of the Exchequer, another man of Evangelical

[71] Alan R. Acheson, 'Trinity College, Dublin, and the Making of Irish Evangelicalism, 1790–1850', in Thomas P. Power (ed.), *A Flight of Parsons: the Divinity Diaspora of Trinity College Dublin* (Eugene, OR, 2018), 22.

[72] Standish Meacham, *Henry Thornton of Clapham, 1760–1815* (Cambridge, 1964).

[73] Henry Thornton, *An Enquiry into the Nature and Effects of the Paper Credit of Great Britain*, ed. F.A. van Hayek (London, 1939); Charles F. Peake, 'Henry Thornton in the History of Economics: Confusions and Contributions', *Manchester School*, 63 (1995), 283–96.

[74] Mrs Henry Thornton to Hannah More, 11 May 1807, 'Family Letterbook and Recollections', CUL, MS Add.7674/1/N, fo. 229.

piety but too much of a ministerialist to be counted among the Saints.[75] Ian Bradley suggests that Commons finance and commerce committees often took on a 'distinct Saintish bias', with Thomas Babington (1758–1837) and the La Touches, John (?1774–1820) and his brother Robert (?1773–1844), and their cousin David (1769–1816), as well as other relatives who served as MPs more briefly, boasting considerable professional expertise.[76] Another pious member with a banking background was Sir Thomas Baring (1772–1848), although like Wilberforce he did not play an active part in the family business, preferring – to his father's disgust – 'to tend his estates, collect pictures, sit in the House of Commons, and generally behave in a gentlemanly way'.[77] While Ian Rennie suggests that mighty Barings Bank, the 'sixth great power' in Europe, was an Evangelical concern, it was not run by pious partners until later in the century. 'The two things I hate most are Saints and Abolitionists', growled Thomas's more businesslike brother Alexander (1773–1848) in 1826.[78] More significant was a web of family firms – the Deacons, Dorriens, Drummonds, Grotes, Hoares, Mannings, Martins, Neales, Raikeses and Williamses, as well as Quaker concerns such as the Barclays, Lloyds, Gurneys and Hanburys – whose business alliances and social connections pulsed with serious religion.[79]

Consequently, Evangelicals were well represented in City institutions. According to one contemporary, the twenty-four Bank of England directorships formed 'a sort of COMMERCIAL PEERAGE in the City', and while it is often difficult to discern more than the bare biographical details of its members, there is plenty of circumstantial evidence to suggest that Evangelicals played an important and periodically dominant role within it.[80] Henry, Robert and Samuel's uncle, Godfrey Thornton of Moggerhanger

---

[75] Information on Bank officials is taken from Richard Roberts and David Kynaston (eds), *The Bank of England: Money, Power and Influence 1694–1994* (Oxford, 1995), Appendix 2.

[76] Ian Bradley, 'The Politics of Godliness: Evangelicals in Parliament, 1784–1832' (unpublished D.Phil. thesis, University of Oxford, 1974), 276–8, 283, 142–3.

[77] Philip Ziegler, *The Sixth Great Power: Barings 1762–1929* (London, 1988), 45.

[78] Alice Harford, *Annals of the Harford Family* (privately printed, 1909), 104.

[79] Ian S. Rennie, 'Evangelicalism and English Public Life, 1823–1850' (unpublished Ph.D. thesis, University of Toronto, 1962), 11; Hector Bolitho and Derek Peel, *The Drummonds of Charing Cross* (London, 1967), 137–44; *Williams Deacons, 1771–1970* (Manchester, 1970); Jacob M. Price, 'The Great Quaker Business Families of Eighteenth-Century London: the Rise and Fall of a Secular Patriciate', in Richard S. Dunn and Mary Maples Dunn (eds), *The World of William Penn* (Philadelphia, PA, 1986), 363–99.

[80] Joseph Hume, *The Substance of the Speech of Mr Joseph Hume at the East India House on the 6th October 1813 ...* (London, 1814), 46.

Park (1737–1805), was a Director from 1772–1801, being Deputy Governor from 1791–3 then Governor from 1793–5.[81] Thomas Raikes (1741–1813), brother of Robert (1725–1811), the Sunday School pioneer, was another Hull merchant and distant relation of the Thorntons, as well as being a close friend and confidant of Wilberforce and Grant: he was Governor from 1797–9, playing a key role in the suspension of cash payments in 1797. Most influential was Samuel Thornton, who succeeded Raikes as Governor from 1799–1801, but held a directorship for fifty-three years, from 1780–1833. Upon Samuel devolved the management of his father's patronage trust, and it was probably with this in mind that 'A Constant Reader' wrote to the *Morning Chronicle* in 1822 to complain about the spread of seriousness in the Bank of England:

> Mr Wilberforce ... and sundry of the Bank Directors (who delight in staid conversation, lively faith, and forgery executions), together with other opulent persons of less notoriety, have constituted themselves Protectors of the Evangelical Clergy, for whom they purchase livings, provide Curacies – in short, exercise all the ... acts of Ecclesiastical Patronage.[82]

There were plenty of others at Threadneedle Street whom contemporaries might have regarded as pious. Edward Simeon (c. 1755–1812), Director 1792–1811, was Charles Simeon's brother; William Manning (1763–1835), Governor 1812–14 married Elizabeth (d. 1789), the daughter of Abel Smith (1717–1788); William Mellish (c. 1764–1838), Governor 1814–16, was a subscriber, governor or vice-president of some thirty-three philanthropic societies.[83] J.J.W. Freshfield (1774–1864), one of the senior partners in the Bank's firm of solicitors, was an outspoken defender of the Bible Society: the future abolitionist leader and second-generation Claphamite, George Stephen (1794–1879), was first his pupil and then his partner.[84]

---

[81]   Gareth Atkins, 'Piety and Plutocracy: the Social and Business World of the Thorntons', in Jane Brown and Jeremy Musson (eds), *Moggerhanger Park: an Architectural and Social History* (Ipswich, 2012), 183–99.
[82]   *Morning Chronicle*, 25 Nov. 1822, 3.
[83]   Brown, *Fathers of the Victorians*, 357.
[84]   For Freshfield, see John Clapham, *The Bank of England: a History*, 2 vols (Cambridge, 1944), II: 83; J.W. Freshfield, *Remarks on the 'Counter-Address' to the Inhabitants of Hackney, on the Proposed Formation of an Auxiliary Bible Society* (London, 1812). See also Sir George Stephen, *A Memoir of the Late James Stephen, one of the Masters in the High Court of Chancery, in relation to Slave Emancipation* (Brighton, 1875), 57–8.

Evangelical influence was even more pronounced at the East India Company in nearby Leadenhall Street. In the late 1800s and 10s Charles Grant, Edward Parry and their allies, George Smith (1765–1838), Robert Thornton and William Thornton Astell (1774–1847), dominated elections to the Chairmanship and Deputy-Chairmanship. Between 1804 and 1815 there were only two years in which they did not hold one or both of these posts. Its twenty-four directors were, according to one MP, 'the monarchs of an empire, greater in extent and population, if he excepted China, than any other in the world', and so it was hardly surprising that developments within the Company were keenly followed.[85] In the aftermath of the Vellore Mutiny of 1806, critics were quick to accuse Evangelicals of endangering its stability.[86] 'The civil servant in India will not only not dare to exercise his own judgement in checking the indiscretions of ignorant missionaries;' warned Sydney Smith, 'but he will strive to recommend himself to his holy masters in Leadenhall Street, by imitating Brother Cran and Brother Ringletaube [LMS missionaries], and by every species of fanatical excess.' 'Methodism at home is no unprofitable game to play,' he concluded. 'In the East it will soon be the infallible road to promotion.'[87] The controversy polarized the Court of Directors. 'The present attempt ... is to recall Buchanan and discountenance missions,' Henry Thornton fretted. 'Parry, the Chairman, and Mr. Grant, Deputy, head one army, Sir F[rancis] Baring the other.'[88] Grant's position was pivotal, owing both to the position of strength he had built within the Company over many years and, it seems, his influence over weaker directors. Astell, for example, another son of Godfrey Thornton, was sourly described as a 'vain empty blockhead totally unequal to the situation where he has to sit alone and when he has time to consult, wholly in the hands of Charles Grant'.[89] Detailed voting lists do not survive, but the elections and re-elections of such men undoubtedly demonstrate the purchase of the new piety among the shareholding classes. The chairman and deputy chairman were chosen from among the directors, who were in turn elected by the Court of Proprietors, i.e. all holders of £1,000 of stock.[90] Almost all

[85]   Hume, *Substance of the Speech*, 10.

[86]   Jörg Fisch, 'A Pamphlet War on Christian Missions in India 1807–1809', *Journal of Asian History*, 19 (1985), 22–70.

[87]   [Sydney Smith], 'Indian Missions', *Edinburgh Review*, 12, 23 (1808), 173.

[88]   Henry Thornton to Hannah More, 20 Jan. 1808, 'Family Letterbook and Recollections', CUL, MS. Add. 7674/1/N, fo. 250.

[89]   Cited in Thorne, *HoP*, V: 380. Astell adopted his maternal grandmother's surname in 1807 in order to inherit her estates.

[90]   H.V. Bowen, *The Business of Empire: The East India Company and Imperial Britain, 1756–1833* (Cambridge, 2006), 93.

of the leading Claphamites qualified for this in this period: Thompson and the Thorntons had appreciable holdings, while in 1810 Zachary Macaulay could inform his brother Colin (1760–1836), an officer in the East India Company army, that he had helped to secure the election of the latter's friend, Colonel John Bladen Taylor (1764–1820), as a Director.[91] Abel Smith senior cannily ensured that each of his sons inherited sufficient stock to confer a vote.[92] The sculptor John Bacon senior, likewise, bequeathed his shares to his family when he died in 1799. It was no coincidence that during the 1790s Bacon had executed all the major sculptural commissions for the Company, including the pediment of the new East India House, which was completed by his son.[93]

Table 1: Chairmen and Deputy Chairmen of the East India Company, 1804–15[94]

Year	Chairman	Deputy Chairman
1804	William Elphinstone	Charles Grant
1805	Charles Grant	George Smith
1806	William Elphinstone	Edward Parry
1807	Edward Parry	Charles Grant
1808	Edward Parry	Charles Grant
1809	Charles Grant	W.T. Astell
1810	W.T. Astell	Jacob Bosanquet
1811	Jacob Bosanquet	Hugh Inglis
1812	Hugh Inglis	Robert Thornton
1813	Robert Thornton	William Elphinstone
1814	William Elphinstone	John Inglis
1815	Charles Grant	Thomas Reid

Nevertheless, Evangelical strength in City institutions bespeaks not so much a concerted takeover bid as the spread of the new piety in a culture that had always been religious as well as commercial.[95] Livery companies

91   Capital Investments, 1601–1943, BL, India Office Records, L/AG/14/5/25-35; Zachary to Colin Macaulay, 6 Apr. 1810, Senate House Library, Booth MS 797, I/5622.

92   J.A.S.L. Leighton-Boyce, *Smiths the Bankers 1658–1958* (London, 1958), 80.

93   Mary Ann Steggles, 'The Empire Aggrandized: a Study in Commemorative Portrait Statuary exported from Britain to her Colonies in South Asia, 1800–1939', 2 vols (unpublished Ph.D. thesis, University of Leicester, 1993), I: 13–18.

94   Based on C.H. and D. Philips, 'Alphabetical List of Directors of the East India Company from 1758 to 1858', *Journal of the Royal Asiatic Society*, 73 (1941), 338.

95   From a considerable literature on Puritan London, see Patrick Collinson, *The Elizabethan Puritan Movement* (2nd edn: Oxford, 1990), esp. 84–91; see also Jennifer Farooq, *Preaching in Eighteenth-Century London* (Woodbridge, 2013).

and guilds, for example, were philanthropic concerns; they inhabited spheres of parish and civic benevolence and had close links to charity schools and particular city churches.[96] The activities of the High Church Hackney Phalanx, too, depended on business connections: Joshua Watson (1771–1855), as a wine merchant, and the Sikeses, as bankers.[97] Such men, like their Evangelical contemporaries, undoubtedly identified with particular institutions and causes, but it would be misleading to assume that controversialists on either side represented the views of a well-defined party.[98] There were plenty of spheres in which churchmanship was subordinated to broader aims. Asylums and hospitals, for instance, attracted support from across the religious spectrum: from Quakers and Quaker-turned-Evangelicals, dissenters and radical 'friends of humanity' to the staunchest churchmen.[99] Individual families, too, defy neat categorization: while Samuel Bosanquet (1744–1806), a businessman of Huguenot descent and Bank of England Governor from 1791–3, was a conventional churchman, his sister Mary (1739–1815) married the Methodist John Fletcher and became a celebrated preacher in her own right.[100] That said, there is evidence to suggest that businessmen favoured those who shared their beliefs. Evangelicals certainly regarded religion as a prophylactic against fraud, and heart religion the most effective preventative of all.[101] They also took a keen interest in the careers of like-minded figures. Henry Thornton longed for a more serious business partner, and his diary evinces a morbid fascination with pious bank failures, as well as showing his disillusionment regarding those who ought to have known better. 'Today I fear D & C must stop – I have been deceived again and again by the D's – and have been taught by them not to trust too much to a Calvinistic profession,' he wrote grimly in 1795.[102] Samuel, too, obsessively noted successes, failures and deaths.[103]

[96] Sarah Lloyd, 'Pleasing Spectacles and Elegant Dinners: Conviviality, Benevolence, and Charity Anniversaries in Eighteenth-Century London', *Journal of British Studies*, 41 (2002), 23–57.

[97] For a recent reassessment of this milieu, see Robert M. Andrews, *Lay Activism and the High Church Movement of the Late Eighteenth Century* (Leiden, 2015), 70–99.

[98] See Donna T. Andrew, *Philanthropy and Police: London Charity in the Eighteenth Century* (Princeton, NJ, 1989), 213–24.

[99] Brown, *Fathers of the Victorians*, 351–4.

[100] See David R. Wilson, 'Church and Chapel: Methodism as Church Extension', in Peter Forsaith and Geordan Hammond (eds), *Religion, Gender, and Industry* (Cambridge, 2011), 53–76.

[101] Leighton-Boyce, *Smiths*, 152–5; Victoria Hutchings, *Messrs Hoare Bankers: a History of the Hoare Banking Dynasty* (London, 2005), 107.

[102] Diary, 23 May, 25 Jun. 1795, CUL, MS Add.7674/1/R, fos. 130, 141.

[103] Samuel Thornton, *The Book of Yearly Recollections of Samuel Thornton* (London, 1891).

Among the most prominent and best documented examples of an Evangelical business network is that surrounding the Thornton, Wilberforce, Sykes and Smith families. Although nineteenth-century biographers of the Claphamites were keen to extol the statesmanlike qualities of their subjects, their shared background was mercantile, linking being rooted in east coast shipping, trading and banking concerns. 'We are all City people and connected with merchants, and nothing but merchants on every side,' Henry Thornton once remarked wryly in response to Samuel's pretensions.[104] Here too the gravitational pull of London is evident. John Thornton's wife, Lucy Watson (1722–1785), was part of another Hull merchant dynasty, while Henry's marriage to Marianne Sykes (1765–1815) in 1796 underlined pre-existing connections with Joseph Sykes of West Ella (1723–1805), a respectable Hull inhabitant and Evangelical whose business as a metal merchant was closely concerned with the Thorntons' Baltic trade.[105] Henry's cousin Wilberforce was heir to a mercantile fortune of his own: his election for Hull in 1780 had less to do with charisma than with his family's high commercial standing, and his ability to pay the requisite two guineas per vote.[106] Wilberforce himself was never an active partner: as Anne Stott has recently shown, he gradually ran down the family businesses through a combination of neglect and overspending, some of it philanthropic.[107] But his Hull business was closely tied to that of the Sykeses, as well as to the Smiths, another branch of the extended family nexus. Originally bankers in Nottingham, by the early nineteenth century Smith, Payne & Smiths – now based in London – had branches in Lincoln and Derby, being also partners in Wilberforce, Smith & Company of Hull.[108] Four of the sons of Abel Smith senior moved into politics, thanks in part to the purchase of Wendover and Midhurst as 'family' boroughs. Robert (1752–1838), an intimate of both Wilberforce and Pitt, was ennobled in 1796 as Lord Carrington; the deeply pious Samuel (1754–1834) was one of the staunchest Saints, along with his son Abel (1788–1859); John (1767–1842) was a leading London banker; George, as we have seen, was a longstanding East India director. Another pious connection was the Wesleyan Methodist Thomas Thompson, who had joined the Wilberforce counting house in Hull aged sixteen, and who later became a banker in his own right. In 1787 Abel Smith senior made him a partner, and from 1807–18 he was MP for Midhurst, which seat was

---

[104] MS 'Recollections of Marianne Thornton' [1857], cited in Thornton, *Enquiry*, ed. Hayek, 12.
[105] Leighton-Boyce, *Smiths*, 198, 202–3.
[106] John Pollock, *Wilberforce: God's Statesman* (London, 1977), 3–18.
[107] Anne Stott, *Wilberforce: Family and Friends* (Oxford, 2012), 250–1.
[108] Leighton-Boyce, *Smiths*, 20, 189–240.

Samuel WILBERFORCE b. 1663

William WILBERFORCE 1690–1776 Alderman

John THORNTON d. 1729 = Jane Field

Robert THORNTON Merchant; Bank of England Director

Godfrey THORNTON

William THORNTON

Sarah Thornton

Robert WILBERFORCE 1728–1768 = Elizabeth Bird 1727–1798

Ann Wilberforce

Judith Wilberforce b. 1727

John BIRD d. 1804 Merchant; City Alderman

Mary Bird

Abel SMITH 1717–1788 Banker, merchant

Hannah Bird 1756?–1846 = Rev. Robert SUMNER 1748–1802

Charles Richard SUMNER 1790–1874 Bishop of Winchester

John Bird SUMNER 1780–1862 Archbishop of Canterbury

Abel SMITH d. 1779

Robert SMITH 1752–1838 Lord Carrington MP; banker

Samuel SMITH 1754–1834 MP

George SMITH 1765–1838 MP; East India Company Deputy Chairman

John SMITH 1767–1842 MP

Hannah Thornton d. 1788

John THORNTON 1720–1790 Merchant = Lucy Watson

Henry THORNTON 1760–1815 MP; banker

Robert THORNTON 1759–1826 MP; East India Company Chairman

Samuel THORNTON 1755–1838 MP; Bank of England Governor

William WILBERFORCE 1721–1777

Sarah Wilberforce 1758–1816 (1) Rev. A. CLARKE d. 1797 (2) James STEPHEN 1758–1832 MP

Sir James STEPHEN 1789–1859 = Jane Catherine Venn 1793–1875

William WILBERFORCE 1759–1833 MP = Barbara Ann Spooner 1777–1847

Joseph SYKES c. 1723–1803 Merchant; MP; Mayor of Hull = Dorothy Twigg

Richard SYKES 1755–1832 Rector of Foxholes, E. Yorks.

John SYKES 1763–1813 Merchant; Mayor of Hull

Nicholas SYKES 1765–1827 Merchant; Alderman; Mayor of Hull

Marianne Sykes 1765–1815 =

Daniel SYKES 1766–1832 MP; Recorder of Hull

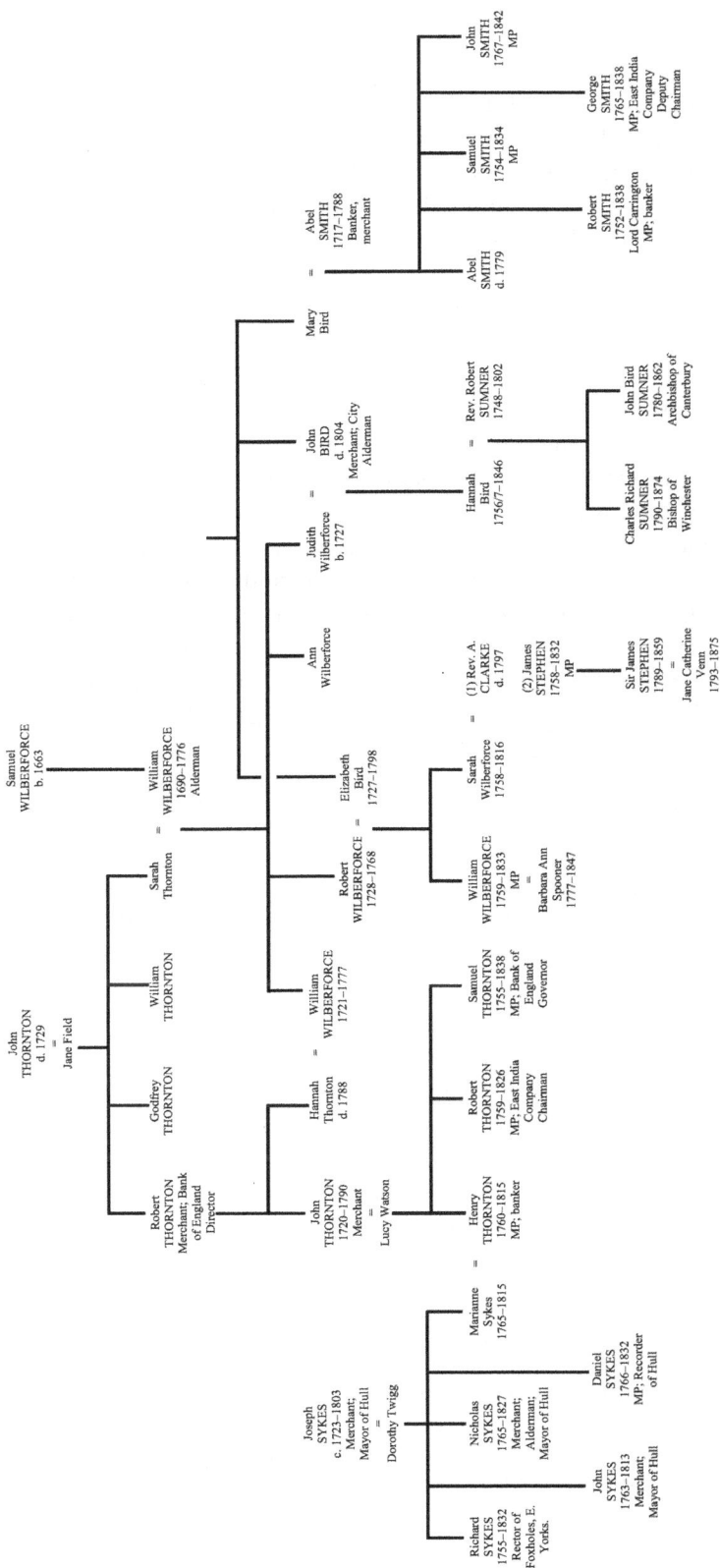

Figure 1: Thornton, Smith, Stephen, Sumner, Sykes and Wilberforce Families

given to him by Carrington. 'From the commencement of my acquaint-ance with him ... he has pressed me forward into notice, and into situations beyond my desires or deserts,' rejoiced Thompson.[109]

In a high-risk, high-profit world, membership of a nexus that combined kinship and shared beliefs conferred advantages. Trust, mutual obligation and the ability to raise credit through extended religious networks were crucial to the business success of Huguenot, Quaker and Jewish firms throughout the eighteenth and nineteenth centuries, and similar points can be made about the Thornton–Wilberforce–Sykes–Smith cousinhood.[110] Their interests were diverse, covering much of the east coast and Midlands, allowing them to transfer capital to take advantage of local openings, and generating reserves to ride out periods of difficulty.[111] The Revolutionary and Napoleonic Wars magnified both the problems and the opportunities. In the trade boom of the 1790s, for example, the Smiths raked in large profits from business transacted in Hull through their stake in Wilberforce, Smith & Co.[112] The continental blockade of the late 1800s and early 1810s severely damaged the group's finances. In 1810, for instance, we find Henry Thornton borrowing stock from 'rich connections and friends' to meet increased liabilities, remarking of Wilberforce that, as Smiths had 'the first claim' on him as their partner, he ought to be careful how much he lent, although 'neither they nor we as I trust shall have any need of our friends [*sic*] kindness'.[113] His nonchalant request in 1814 for '£20 to £25,000 or thereabouts' from Macaulay comes as a further reminder of how business interests underpinned Clapham friendships.[114] The cousinhood's political clout brought it further commercial advantages, such as in the case of the various Hull Dock Bills that the Smith brothers – being bankers to the Dock Company as well as shareholders in it – helped to push through the Commons.[115]

Money and influence could in turn subserve pious political ends. In 1807, the fall of the Talents Ministry prompted a General Election. In Yorkshire

[109] Cited in Arthur R.B. Robinson, *The Counting House: Thomas Thompson of Hull 1754–1828 and his Family* (York, 1992), 28.

[110] David H. Pratt, *English Quakers and the First Industrial Revolution* (London, 1985); Price, 'Quaker Business Families'.

[111] Gordon Jackson, *Hull in the Eighteenth Century: a Study in Economic and Social History* (London, 1972), 109, 218–20.

[112] Leighton-Boyce, *Smiths*, 193, 198–9, 204.

[113] Henry Thornton to Zachary Macaulay, n.d., 1810; 3 Jul. 1810, CUL, MS Add.7674/1/M, fos. 38–9, 40; see also Thornton, *Enquiry*, ed. Hayek, 27.

[114] Henry Thornton to Zachary Macaulay, Oct. 1814, CUL, MS Add.7674/1/M, fo. 40.

[115] Leighton-Boyce, *Smiths*, 239; Jackson, *Hull*, 257–8.

this sparked the first contest since 1741. It was clear that the battle would be an expensive one: it pitted Wilberforce against the Fitzwilliam interest and the fortune of Henry Lascelles (1767–1841). To stand a chance of success Wilberforce needed to raise sufficient funds. The ball was set rolling in London in mid May at a meeting chaired by Lord Teignmouth (1751–1834), which all the Evangelical great and good in the capital attended.[116] The eventual sum raised was nearly £65,000, a total that included subscriptions in Birmingham, Bristol, Colchester, Leicester and Reading, all places with thriving Evangelical congregations.[117] Those who contributed – clergymen, professionals, merchants and their families, as well as Quakers, Methodists and abolitionists more broadly – saw his re-election, as in 1806, as a test of the strength of anti-slavery principles. 'The cause of Mr W. is the cause of justice, humanity, and piety, as well as of Britain,' Scott earnestly told a friend.[118] Most gave only a few pounds. But there were also a great many substantial contributions. Henry Thornton not only pledged £300, but also hastened up the Great North Road to York with other 'Claphamites' – Robert Grant, James Stephen (1758–1832) and his sons – to assist on Wilberforce's election committee, which was based at the house of the York lawyer William Gray.[119] Stephen, Charles Grant senior, Thomas Gisborne and Teignmouth each contributed £100. The Danish Consul-General George Wolff gave £205; Admiral Gambier gave £200; Robert and Samuel Thornton gave £100, as did the Quaker banker Samuel Hoare (1751–1825) and the unrelated banking churchmen Henry (1750–1828) and his son William Henry Hoare (1776–1819); among those who contributed £50 were Babington, Vansittart, Joseph Hardcastle (1752–1819), Sir Richard Hill and William Cardale. One of the handsomest donations came from the fourth Smith brother, George, who gave his cousin 200 guineas, but this was trumped by Thompson, who contributed a huge sum: £500. 'I lived eighteen days at York at my own charge,' he later recalled, 'labouring in Committees, and in every possible way to secure [Wilberforce's] election.'[120]

---

[116] *The Times*, 14 May 1807, 2.

[117] A printed subscription list can be found in London, British Library Add. MS 35129, fos. 411–13. See also William Wilberforce Esquire Committee account, Henry Thornton Esquire Treasurer, Hoares Bank Archive, London, Customer Ledger 98 (1807–8), 353–6.

[118] Scott, *Thomas Scott*, 420.

[119] For scribbled details of Thornton's activities there, see Mrs Henry Thornton to Hannah More, 25 May; Henry Thornton to Mrs Henry Thornton, 27 May, 10 Jun.; Henry Thornton to Marianne Thornton, 28 May 1807, 'Family Letterbook and Recollections', CUL, MS Add.7674/1/N, fos. 230–41.

[120] Cited in Robinson, *Counting House*, 28.

Nevertheless, what became known as the 'Great Yorkshire Election' was a close-run thing. Such was Hannah More's agitation as she followed events from Somerset that her apothecary prescribed double doses of opium.[121] To pious jubilation, Wilberforce eventually headed the poll with 11,808 votes, followed by Viscount Milton (1786–1857) with 11,177 and Lascelles with 10,990. Between them they spent some £250,000, making this the most expensive poll of the pre–1832 era: an 'Austerlitz of Electioneering'.[122]

Not everyone in the Wilberforce–Thornton cousinhood can straightforwardly be identified as Evangelical. Carrington, for instance, remained studiedly impervious to Wilberforce's conversational gambits.[123] 'He knew he could not convert me', he boasted.[124] Curiously, though, Carrington does appear in the *Blackwell Dictionary of National Biography*. More significantly, perhaps, he was immortalized in Cowper's *The Task* (1785), an immensely popular poem among vital religionists, as 'the man who, when the distant poor / Need help, denies them nothing but his name'.[125] With his brother and nephew he provided funds for eight new Hertfordshire churches and the rebuilding of twenty others, while he was also a committed abolitionist, becoming a SLC shareholder, voting in favour of Wilberforce's 1791 anti-slavery motion and acting as teller for later motions.[126] Later on, he was a member of the Bible Society. No doubt Wilberforce was distressed by his cousin's reluctance to toe the line, but to quibble over precise beliefs misses the wider point. Plenty of Carrington's contemporaries shared his combination of moral seriousness and broad-based, active establishment religiosity. While Wilberforce and his closest colleagues among the Saints at Westminster acted tribally on moral and religious issues, they were also part of a fuzzier milieu that was broadly Pittite in politics, professional-minded and tinged with Evangelical earnestness. The mercantile world from which many of them were drawn was connected to

---

[121] Hannah More to William Wilberforce, [15 Jun. 1807], Bodl., MSS Wilberforce, c.3, fo. 89.

[122] E.A. Smith, 'The Yorkshire Elections of 1806 and 1807: a Study in Electoral Management', *Northern History*, 2 (1967), 62–90; Ellen Gibson Wilson, *The Great Yorkshire Election of 1807*, ed. Edward Royle and James Walvin (Lancaster, 2015), 280–6.

[123] Wilberforce, *Life*, III: 114–21.

[124] Pollock, *Wilberforce*, 67. I have not been able to find the source of this quotation.

[125] William Cowper, *The Task: a Poem, in Six Books* (London, 1785), 159. See William Cowper to William Unwin, 10 Oct. 1784, cited in Thomas Wright (ed.), *The Correspondence of William Cowper*, 4 vols (London, 1904), II: 252n.

[126] C.B. Wadström, *An Essay on Civilization*, 2 vols (London, 1794–5), II: 351; Stephen Farrell, 'Contrary to the Principles of Justice, Humanity and Sound Policy': the Slave Trade, Parliamentary Politics and the Abolition Act, 1807', *Parliamentary History*, supplement (2007), 182.

government through the fulfilment of contracts and investment in bonds, heightening the association between fundholders and what Boyd Hilton calls Pitt's 'virtuous economics' of national debt redemption.[127] Denizens of this milieu certainly patronized good causes, including Evangelical societies, but they could be reluctant to identify themselves with a brand of piety that placed a sharp divide between the regenerate and the unregenerate. As the next section will suggest, the triumph of Evangelical philanthropy in the 1800s and 10s stemmed in large part from its ability to bridge that gap.

The Importance of being Practical

'God Almighty has set before me two great objects, the suppression of the slave trade and the reformation of manners.'[128] So, famously, wrote Wilberforce in his diary for 28 October 1787, shortly after his conversion. Perhaps because this has so long been regarded as a watershed moment in the history of Evangelicalism, alliances between the new piety and other groups have been underplayed. Crucially for this book, so too have the networks that placed them at the centre of a much broader set of activist milieux. For a start, it should be stressed that much of the energy that Wilberforce devoted to these twin causes was spent welding broad and sometimes unstable coalitions. For if the national mood of soul-searching following defeat in America created fertile soil for the spread of Evangelicalism, it also prompted others to ponder the effects of urbanization on the poor, of luxury among the rich and of 'old corruption' among the political classes, as well as how to deal with crime and demographic change.[129] Evangelicals were not the only group to prescribe moral reform. The Society for Carrying into effect His Majesty's Proclamation Against Vice and Immorality, commonly known as the Proclamation Society, was a case in point. To be sure, the proclamation in question was Wilberforce's brainchild, and it was his pressure on Archbishop Moore (1730–1805) and Queen Charlotte

---

[127] Boyd Hilton, *A Mad, Bad, and Dangerous People: England, 1783–1846* (Oxford, 2006), 113-18.

[128] Wilberforce, *Life*, I: 149

[129] Hilton, *Age of Atonement*, 3–26; 203–11; Leonore Davidoff and Catherine Hall, *Family Fortunes: Men and Women of the English Middle Class, 1780–1850* (London, 1987), 73–106; Dror Wahrman, 'Percy's Prologue: from Gender Play to Gender Panic in Eighteenth-Century England', *Past and Present*, 159 (1998), 113–160; Philip Harling, *The Waning of 'Old Corruption': Economical Reform, 1779–1846* (Oxford, 1996), 31–55; M.J.D. Roberts, *Making English Morals: Voluntary Association and Moral Reform in England, 1787–1886* (Cambridge, 2004), 24–33; Joanna Innes, *Inferior Politics: Social Problems and Social Policies in Eighteenth-Century Britain* (Oxford, 2009), 109–226.

(1744–1818) that induced the King to issue it. In courting the political and professional establishment, however, Wilberforce sought not to direct a programme of reform, or to create a religious pressure-group, but to lend countenance to an existing groundswell of reformism: the 'respectable inhabitants' of lesser rank in places like Yorkshire and Middlesex who had already begun to lobby the authorities regarding extravagance and dissipation. By early 1788, he had enlisted most of the English bishops and several peers, including Lord Dartmouth, the 3rd Duke of Grafton (1735–1811) – an aristocratic Unitarian and reformed rake – and the ex-Prime Minister, Lord North (1732–1792), alongside prominent county MPs, courtiers, civil servants and crown law officers, only a few of whom can be identified as Evangelical.[130]

To some extent the shape the Proclamation Society took may evince a tactical desire on Wilberforce's part to sidestep the accusations of 'Methodism' that often dogged moral movements. Yet it was also part of a striking expansion of the moral imagination of reformers in the post-war period: one in which Evangelicals played a key part but were not the only actors.[131] Efforts to reprove vice and encourage religious observance were not unprecedented. But the societies for the reform of manners of the late 1690s and the workhouse and charity school movements of the early decades of the eighteenth century were national movements in name only, and flourished only for a generation or so. Anglican societies such as the SPCK (1698) and SPG (1701) were global in their rhetoric, but were peopled by churchmen deeply suspicious of dissent.[132] Schemes for ensuring the health and supply of British manpower flourished only periodically, usually during wartime.[133] By contrast, the interlocking moral causes of the 1780s – prison reform, slave trade abolition, the Association Movement – envisaged change on a national scale and for the good of the whole of society. They spanned denominational, political and class cleavages, melding together existing ideas about civic benevolence and patriotic philanthropy with newer associational models to produce tools for national change. The Sunday School Society, for instance, founded in London in 1785, was deliberately unsectarian, proclaiming that it was 'united to prevent the corruption of morals and advance the peace and morality of the country'.[134] Such

---

[130] Innes, *Inferior Politics*, 197–200.

[131] Roberts, *Making English Morals*, 17–58.

[132] Brent Sirota, *The Christian Monitors: the Church of England and the Age of Benevolence, 1680–1730* (New Haven, CT, 2014), 69–148.

[133] Linda Colley, *Britons: Forging the Nation, 1707–1837* (New Haven, CT, 1992), 91–8.

[134] T.W. Laqueur, *Religion and Respectability: Sunday Schools and Working-Class Culture, 1780–1850* (New Haven, CT, 1976), 21–36; Roberts, *Making English Morals*, 17–24.

concerns became urgent in the context of war with France in the 1790s. The Society for Bettering the Condition and Increasing the Comforts of the Poor (the 'Bettering Society'), founded in 1796 by the conveyancer and philanthropist Sir Thomas Bernard, along with his cousin Bishop Barrington of Durham, Wilberforce and E.J. Eliot, sought to interest 'liberal and benevolent minds' in instilling habits of virtue and self-reliance among the poor, while the Society for the Suppression of Vice (the 'Vice Society'), founded in 1802, was another multi-coloured coalition. Its elite leaders occupied a range of religious and political positions, and the rhetoric surrounding it demonstrates the purchase of providential and patriotic ideas among middling metropolitan businessmen, for whom the prosecution of infidelity, sabbath-breaking, obscene prints, prostitution and short weights became part of the war-effort.[135]

Yet if Wilberforce and his coadjutors were in some ways moving with the times, they also shaped beliefs and behaviour in powerful ways. Seminal texts such as Hannah More's *Thoughts on the Importance of the Manners of the Great to General Society* (1788), Thomas Gisborne's *An Enquiry into the Duties of Men in the Higher and Middle Classes of Society in Great Britain* (1794) and *An Enquiry into the Duties of the Female Sex* (1797), and William Wilberforce's *Practical View of the Prevailing System of Professed Christians in the Higher and Middle Classes of this Country Contrasted with Real Christianity* (1797) were instrumental in pushing the idea that the upper orders were, or ought to be, moral exemplars. 'Reformation must begin with the GREAT, or it will never be effectual,' More declared trenchantly. 'To expect to reform the poor while the opulent are corrupt, is to throw odours into the stream while the springs are poisoned.'[136] These works fostered a growing sense among laypeople that they occupied the front ranks in the struggle against immorality, infidelity and nominal religion. 'Men of authority and influence,' exhorted Wilberforce, ought to use every legitimate means at their disposal to advance moral and religious causes.[137] Undergirding all of this was a call to personal spiritual renovation that also had collective ramifications. The idea that established religion underpinned the stability of the political and social hierarchy was, of course, a

[135] Roberts, *Making English Morals*, 59–95.

[136] Hannah More, *Thoughts on the Importance of the Manners of the Great to General Society* (London, 1788), 117.

[137] William Wilberforce, *A Practical View of the Prevailing Religious System of Professed Christians, in the Higher and Middle Classes in this Country, Contrasted with Real Christianity* (London, 1797), 302–4.

commonplace among Anglican thinkers in the era of counter-revolution.[138] Evangelical writers agreed, but placed a new onus on individual sincerity, worrying that many were Christian in name only.[139] The only firm foundation for public life was, they insisted, heart religion: the truest Christian would also be the truest patriot, the most judicious magistrate, the bravest military officer. The works that promulgated this message achieved vast circulations. More's *Thoughts* was read by bishops, socialites and even Queen Charlotte, going through seven editions within three months. Wilberforce's *Practical View* went through five editions within the year, eight by 1805 and fourteen by 1820, being translated into several languages and endlessly reprinted in the United States.[140] For Daniel Wilson, writing in 1826, it was 'a mighty instrument in carrying forward the great work'; a text that in his judgement had done more to advance the Evangelical cause among the elite than any other.[141]

Evangelicalism and moral reform more generally were thus on converging tracks. After all, the simple piety unfolded by Wilberforce and the rest was concerned more with the heart than the head. 'Real Christianity' bespoke warmth, fervency, sincerity and activity. It did not respect denominational boundaries or theological niceties. Certainly, such writers agreed, it was regrettable when sheep strayed from the Anglican fold, but they wandered only because they were starving for want of spiritual nourishment. 'The religion of Methodists and Dissenters we doubtless think very inferior to that of the Church of England;' conceded the *Christian Observer*, 'but we think it infinitely preferable to no religion, or even ... to those cold, heathen, heartless, barren generalities, but little raised above heathen ethics; which to many in the present day substitute for the true, spiritual, efficacious, life-giving Gospel of Jesus Christ.'[142] Denunciatory episcopal charges against 'schismatics', which multiplied in the first decade of the nineteenth century, Evangelicals declared, were therefore not just uncharitable but unchristian.[143] 'I deeply feel,' wrote the

---

[138] Robert Hole, *Pulpits, Politics and Public Order in England, 1760–1832* (Cambridge, 1989), 127–59.

[139] *Ibid.*, 136–7.

[140] Anne Stott, *Hannah More: the First Victorian* (Oxford, 2003), 97–8; John Wolffe, 'William Wilberforce's *Practical View* (1797) and its Reception', in *Studies in Church History*, 44 (2008), 175–84.

[141] Daniel Wilson, 'Introduction', in William Wilberforce, *A Practical View ...* (Glasgow, 1826), xlv.

[142] 'Review of *Select Homilies of the Church of England*', *Christian Observer*, 10 (1811), 633.

[143] 'Bishop of Durham's Charge to the Clergy', *Christian Observer*, 1 (1802), 29–32.

evangelical Quaker Joseph John Gurney (1788–1847) in 1809, 'that as long as the grand thing – practical Christianity – is kept in view by us all, we have no reason to be discontented and differing from one another on secondary points.'[144] Churchmanship generally mattered more to the clergy than the laity. The *Christian Observer*'s determination to 'be true to moral principles, wherever we find them', made it attractive to cultivated readers, among whom it reached a circulation of between 1,500 and 2,000.[145] Its reception among clergymen was more mixed. 'I send you the last Xtian Observer which excites more and more enmity among the Calvinistic clergy and others,' reported its editor, Zachary Macaulay, in late 1802. 'The High Church Yorkshiremen abuse it as favouring Methodists and dissenters – the Dissenters violently abuse it on the other hand as high Church and intolerant. Even Scott designates it as an Arminian Magazine, while Daubeny and his party [i.e. outspoken High Church controversialists] stigmatize us as Calvinists.'[146]

The idea that Christianity was above all personal and practical undoubtedly appealed to undogmatic laymen with little time for doctrinal logic-chopping. It also made for a productive intermingling with humanistic currents deriving from enlightenment thinkers. The LMS and RTS in the late 1790s had already shown how denominational differences might be set aside in the pursuit of broadly defined causes.[147] This was pushed a step further in the foundation of the BFBS, whose hard-headed aim – to distribute cheap vernacular Bibles in Britain and across the globe – was designed to exclude as few potential supporters as possible. 'The line of business is, with few exceptions, as direct at the Bible Committee as it is at Lloyd's;' one of its spokesmen declared, 'and there is little reason to expect the peculiar tenets of Calvin and Socinus to enter into a debate for dispersing an edition of the Scriptures, as there would be if the same men met to underwrite a policy of insurance,' as well they might on a different day of the week.[148] Such claims

---

[144] Joseph Bevan Braithwaite (ed.), *Memoirs of Joseph John Gurney: with Selections from his Journal and Correspondence*, 2 vols (Norwich, 1854), I: 50.

[145] 'Great Britain. General Reflections on the State of Domestic Politics', *Christian Observer*, 8 (1809), 336; Ian Bradley, 'The Politics of Godliness', 10–11.

[146] Zachary Macaulay to Thomas Gisborne, 1 Nov. 1802, Trinity College, Babington Letters, 26/44. For Daubeny, see Peter B. Nockles, 'The Waning of Protestant Unity and Waxing of Anti-Catholicism? Archdeacon Daubeny and the Reconstruction of "Anglican" Identity in the Later Georgian Church, c. 1780–c. 1830', in William Gibson and Robert G. Ingram (eds), *Religious Identities in Britain, 1660–1832* (Aldershot, 2005), 179–230.

[147] Roger H. Martin, *Evangelicals United: Ecumenical Stirrings in Pre-Victorian Britain, 1795–1830* (Metuchen, NJ, 1983), 28.

[148] John Owen, *A Letter to a Country Clergyman* (London, 1805), 50.

were, of course, intended to avert criticism, but they also serve to highlight two interrelated theological developments. One was the soft-pedalling of Calvinism as a pulpit doctrine, which helped to ensure that evangelicals of every stripe came to regard technology, commerce and the public sphere as potential tools for conversion. Just as important, though, among churchmen in particular, was a radical reorientation of attitudes towards wealth and status. Gospel ministers continued, as they always had done, to warn their congregations that salvation could not be purchased through 'money ... estates ... connexions ... rank and appearance in the world ... riches and consequence'.[149] Simultaneously, though, there was a growing awareness of the opportunities to which these could be turned. It was no longer enough to preach the Gospel and let the Almighty do the rest. 'Christian usefulness ... is a science in itself, as capable of being reduced to fixed principles as Political Economy,' the Dublin banker J.D. La Touche (1788–1826) maintained. 'You have therefore to look around and choose your department, seeking Divine direction in the choice; and having found your post, it will be comparatively easy to discharge its duties well'.[150] Whereas direct proselytization had once been the overmastering priority among evangelicals, they now redefined 'usefulness' as a Christian and social virtue, seeing everything from lying-in and debt-relief societies as aids to individual and national reformation, and pushing the idea that bulging balance sheets were a mark of success.

'A New Aera in the History of Religion'

Such convictions both drove and were driven by a sustained boom in support for Evangelical societies that began relatively suddenly in the late 1800s and peaked in the years after the victory at Waterloo. The scale of this development seems to have taken even the most optimistic pious prognosticators by surprise, and it warrants close examination. For even though there remained many who found Evangelical ideas and politics deplorable, this period marks the moment when influence in high places and pressure-group politics combined to make the new piety impossible to ignore. The geopolitical context is crucial. Between 1804 and 1811 invasion scares, continental defeats, the illness of the king, depressed trade and public unrest gave rise to a sense of gloomy foreboding, lending urgency and

---

[149] Isaac Milner (ed.), *The Works of the Late Rev. Joseph Milner,* 8 vols (London, 1810), VI: 304.
[150] Urwick, *James Digges La Touche,* 232.

Plate 3: Thomas Uwins, *Representation of the Annual Meeting of the British and Foreign Bible Society in Freemasons' Hall*. Etching by J.H. Clark, 1819

credibility to notions of national moral culpability that, as we have seen, already had a broad currency.[151] The abolition of the slave trade in 1807, the Royal Jubilee of 1809 and growing military success were thus cathartic, being read as signs of providential favour. Evangelical philanthropy seems to have represented both an outlet for providential pessimism and then cause for ever-greater optimism as the mood shifted in the early 1810s. Organizational changes acted as a crucial catalyst for this. In 1809 the Bible Society pioneered the adoption of local 'auxiliary' branches, a model adopted with alacrity by other societies when they witnessed its success.[152] The networks thus formed equated piety with patriotism, encouraging supporters

---

[151] Boyd Hilton, '1807 and All That: Why Britain Outlawed Her Slave Trade', in Derek R. Peterson (ed.), *Abolitionism and Imperialism in Britain, Africa, and the Atlantic* (Athens, OH, 2010), 63–83; John Coffey, '"Tremble, Britannia!": Fear, Providence and the Abolition of the Slave Trade, 1758–1807', *English Historical Review*, 127 (2012), 844–81.

[152] Charles Stokes Dudley, *An Analysis of the Bible Society throughout its Various Parts* (London, 1821).

literally to buy into national causes. Auxiliaries tapped into notions of civic pride, too, enlisting leading local citizens as 'vice-presidents', but involving all members in fundraising through a mixture of subscriptions, sales, donations, legacies and congregational collections. All of this was faithfully reported down to the last farthing in the annual 'proceedings' of the parent societies, along with the names of all subscribers, for which the rate was a guinea. It was a successful formula whose appeals to social status, local identity, patriotic feeling and unflashy practical piety attracted not just dyed-in-the-wool partisans but a much broader constituency.

The effects were spectacular. The income of the Bible Society increased steadily from £5,835 in 1808–9 to £14,284 in 1809–10, falling back slightly to £12,117 in 1810–11, probably owing to the financial crash, before soaring exponentially upwards: £34,442 in 1811–12, £54,728 in 1812–13 and a staggering £70,267 in 1814–15, £61,848 of which came from auxiliaries.[153] The 'religious intelligence' section of the *Christian Observer* bulged; but even so, tidings of new auxiliaries poured in so rapidly that it often had to postpone reporting them until there was sufficient space. (By 1816 the total number had ballooned to 541.) As Figure 2 shows, other societies, including SPCK and SPG, enjoyed a parallel surge in income, although with some important structural differences. While all societies invested in stock, using dividends and selling stock where necessary to cover annual shortfalls, the older Anglican societies had much larger stock and property holdings, and so this made up a much larger share of their income.[154] A large proportion of the SPCK's income came from sales of books to its members, while the SPG also received government grants for schools and ecclesiastical provision in British North America, until the early 1830s when this support was phased out. This generally comprised between a half and two thirds of its annual income, but even so – and despite periodic 'King's Letters', circulated to all parishes asking them to hold a collection – it had to sell quantities of stock most years before its own voluntary takeoff in the late 1830s replaced and then rapidly exceeded the withdrawn grant. While fuller analysis of all of these developments would be fascinating, for our purposes several broad observations can be made. Most obviously, Figure 2 serves to underline the vibrancy of the voluntary model. In terms of their voluntary income and the number of their active supporters, Evangelical societies were now by far the biggest voluntary organizations in the country. It also hints at

---

[153] W. Canton, *The History of the British and Foreign Bible Society*, 5 vols (London, 1904–10), I: 50–1.

[154] See Bob Tennant, *Corporate Holiness: Pulpit Preaching and the Church of England Missionary Societies, 1760–1870* (Oxford, 2013), for discussion of the administrative, structural and theological differences between the SPCK, SPG and CMS.

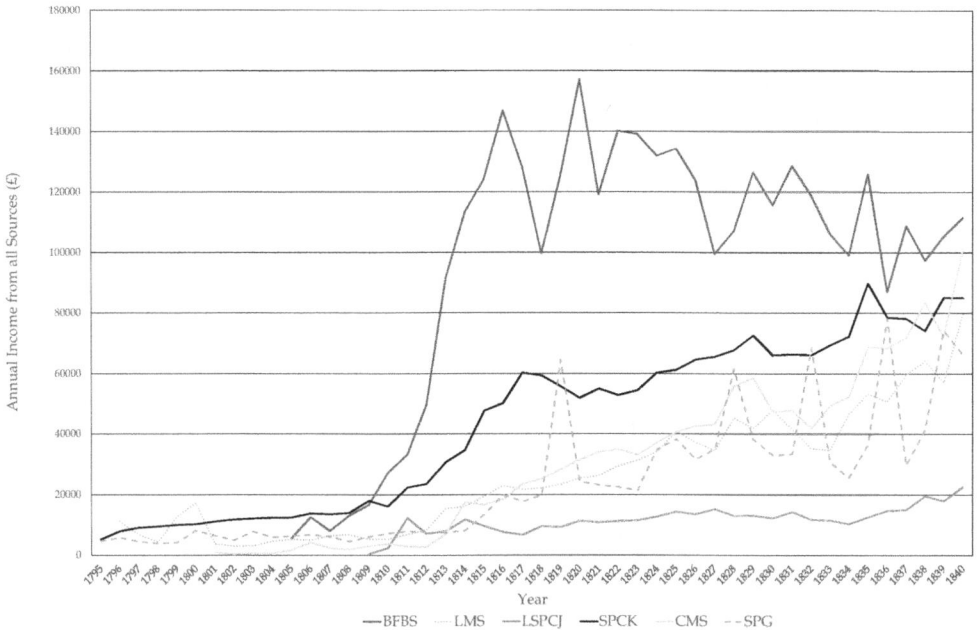

Figure 2: Societies' Income, 1795–1840

Note: Figures are drawn from annual reports published in the years indicated. It should be noted that societies also calculated their income differently, as well as frequently changing their criteria for doing so. Spikes in SPG income are the result of the 'King's Letters' discussed above. Information is drawn from the *Missionary Register*; the *Christian Observer*; Annual Reports of the British and Foreign Bible Society; Annual Reports of the Society for Promoting Christian Knowledge; William Thomas Gidney, *The History of the London Society for Promoting Christianity Amongst the Jews: from 1809–1908* (London, 1908), 638; Richard Lovett, *The History of the London Missionary Society, 1795–1895*, 2 vols (London, 1899), II: 750–3; C.F. Pascoe, *Classified Digest of the Records of the Society for the Propagation of the Gospel in Foreign Parts, 1701–1892* (London, 1898), 831.

how closely such societies were tied to the world of metropolitan finance, through stockholding and through Evangelical-led banks that acted as receivers of funds and held those societies' accounts. It is easy to see why all this was greeted with such euphoria. 'We are persuaded that no ten years, with the exception of the apostolic age, have done more than the first ten years of [the BFBS] towards the promotion of true religion,' trilled the *Christian Observer* in 1816.[155] From 1823 onwards the *Missionary Register* triumphantly lumped together the incomes of all the major national societies, evangelical and otherwise, as well as the biggest American bodies, to

---

[155] 'Review of Owen's History of the Bible Society', *Christian Observer*, 15 (1816), 730.

spin a story of continual growth. By 1830 it could point to annual charitable receipts of £627,382: this at a time when British government spending was only £53.7 million per year.[156]

Especially thrilling in the 1810s, to those as yet unaccustomed to such success, was the surging popularity of Evangelical causes among the rich and titled. The Bible Society seemed to mark a new epoch: 'behold our kings, and our princes, and the nobles of the land, brightening their honours by patronising this divine work!'[157] In a broadly Protestant culture that sloganized about the accessibility of scripture to all believers, its appeal was hard to resist. The patronage of the Royal Dukes of Kent, Sussex, Cambridge, Cumberland and Gloucester was, Evangelicals considered, evidence of a country coming to its senses. That feeling was given gratifying piquancy by memories of the votes of the Duke of Clarence (1765–1837) – the future William IV – against abolition in the House of Lords.[158] By 1814 every English county had its own auxiliary, with the shire aristocracy or gentry standing forward as chairmen: the 4th Duke of Grafton (1760–1844) for Northamptonshire, the Duke of Bedford (1766–1839) for Bedfordshire, Viscount Anson (1767–1818) for Staffordshire and Viscount Hinchingbrooke (1773–1818) for Huntingdonshire. Auxiliaries in the capital had a more mercantile complexion. The Lord Mayor, the solicitor Sir Claudius Hunter (1775–1851), was chair at the establishment of the City of London auxiliary and Grant at the Bloomsbury and 'South Pancras [sic]' branch.[159] At Blackheath, the inaugural meeting was chaired by the maritime insurer and shipping agent J.J. Angerstein (1732–1823), the proximity of Greenwich Naval Hospital and the Royal Arsenal complex at Woolwich being evinced in the election of several naval and military men, including General Anthony Farrington (1742–1823) of the Royal Artillery, Major-General Andrew Burn (1742–1814) of the Royal Marines and Dr Olinthus Gregory (1774–1841), mathematical tutor at the Royal Military Academy.[160] The foundation of the North-East London auxiliary in 1812 was a glittering affair chaired by the Duke of Kent (1767–1820), who was supported by the Earl

---

[156] 'Annual Receipts of Bible, Missionary, Education, and Tract Societies', *Missionary Register*, 18 (1830), 516–17; https://www.ukpublicspending.co.uk/uk_year1830_0. html, last accessed 22 Feb. 2019.

[157] 'Preface', *Christian Observer*, 10 (1811), [n.p.].

[158] Brown, *Fathers of the Victorians*, 256. The support of the Prince Regent's estranged wife, Princess Caroline, might have been less pleasing.

[159] *Report of Proceedings at the Meeting in the Egyptian Hall, in the Mansion House ...* (London, 1812); *Proceedings of the Public Meeting at Freemasons' Hall ...* (London, 1813).

[160] *An Account of the Proceedings at the Green Man Inn, Blackheath ...* (London, 1812).

of Darnley (1767–1831) and Lords Gambier and Holland (1773–1840). The officers chosen included Carrington, Henry Thornton, the Quaker banker Samuel Hoare, the brewers Thomas Fowell Buxton (1786–1845) and Samuel Whitbread (1764–1815), the banker William Mellish and the brewer Sampson Hanbury (1769–1835), and Wilberforce himself.[161] By 1816 the Prime Minister, Lord Liverpool, had been enlisted as a national vice-president, a role that he, like the Duke of Wellington (1769–1852), already performed for the Naval and Military Bible Society. Naturally, such names took pride of place in annual reports and proceedings.

'From this time on', Ford K. Brown comments, 'it was an absurdity to claim that Evangelicals were Methodists or subversive fanatics.'[162] Wilberforce had become keeper of the national conscience.[163] Not everyone shared his convictions. But the success of Evangelicals in enlisting the powerful gave them disproportionate influence. One impressive measure of their reach was the success of the Committees for the Relief of Distress in Germany, revived in early 1814 in the aftermath of the Battle of Leipzig.[164] Germany had long been an evangelical concern: links with missionary institutions and Bible Society agents there meant that the sufferings of German Pietists featured prominently in the *Evangelical Magazine* and its Edinburgh-published counterpart, the *Missionary Magazine*, in the mid 1800s.[165] In 1805, BFBS leading lights joined London-based go-betweens such as the Lutheran minister Karl Friedrich Adolf Steinkopf (1773–1859) and the Moravian Christian Ignatius La Trobe (1758–1836) to form the first Committee, which raised just under £25,000 by the time it was wound up in 1808.[166] In 1814, however, the 'City' Committee was wealthier and more influential: its patron was the Duke of Sussex (1773–1843) and Henry

---

[161] *Report of Proceedings of a Meeting held at the London Tavern …* (London, 1813).

[162] Brown, *Fathers of the Victorians*, 257.

[163] See Roshan Allpress, 'William Wilberforce and "the Saints"', in Gareth Atkins (ed.), *Making and Remaking Saints in Nineteenth-Century Britain* (Manchester, 2016), 209–25.

[164] Andrew Kloes, 'The Committee for the Relief of Distress in Germany: a Case Study of Co-operation and Solidarity between British Evangelicals and German Pietists during the Napoleonic Era', *Pietismus und Neuzeit*, 40 (2014), 163–201; Norbert Götz, 'Rationales of Humanitarianism: the Case of British Relief to Germany, 1805–1815', *Journal of Modern European History*, 12 (2014), 186–99.

[165] For this broad milieu, see Nicholas Railton, *No North Sea: the Anglo-German Evangelical Network in the Middle of the Nineteenth Century* (Leiden, 1999), 71–8. See also Norbert Götz, 'The Good Plumpuddings' Belief: British Voluntary Aid to Sweden during the Napoleonic Wars', *International History Review*, 37 (2015), 519–39.

[166] *Reports of the Committees Formed in London in the Year 1814, for the Relief of the Unparalleled Distresses in Germany* (London, 1814)

Thornton was Treasurer. Most but not all of the metropolitan clergymen and businessmen who sat alongside them were Evangelical churchmen and foreign residents of London.[167] There was also a marked shift in tone. Philanthropy was painted not just in humanitarian terms or as a duty to fellow Protestants, but as a national characteristic. One sermon labelled England 'a land of Bibles', while another spokesman called for action 'worthy of Englishmen, worthy of Christians, worthy of the nation that abolished the slave trade'.[168] In only a year, over £113,000 was raised, which sum included the product of congregational collections from all the major denominations, and from London synagogues, as well – significantly – as institutional donations from the Bank of England and the EIC.

A second, 'Westminster' Committee, formed in April 1814, was more elite in composition, comprising bishops, lords and MPs and including leading Hackney Phalangists alongside prominent Saints. The subscriptions it raised were modest, but it secured a parliamentary grant of £100,000, as well as organizing a grand concert in Whitehall Chapel. Attenders included Field Marshall Blücher (1742–1819), the Duke of Wellington and Prince Leopold of Saxe-Coburg (1790–1865), as well as Queen Charlotte and other royals, bishops, ambassadors and the Speaker of the House of Commons.[169] Displays of glittering military religiosity were by no means a narrowly Evangelical phenomenon. But it is easy to see why Evangelical publicists discerned the hand of God in such developments. 'More than thirty thousand pounds, the produce of one year, and the probability of more than fifty thousand for the next;' trumpeted the Baptist and Bible Society Secretary Joseph Hughes (1769–1833): '... the pleadings of Ministers of the Gospel and Ministers of State; ... the sanction of Magistrates and Judges; ... the patronage of Nobles, and Princes, and Sovereigns; above all ... the clearest symptoms of Divine approbation.'[170] Here was revealed the machinery for making a truly Christian nation and converting the world, a machinery fuelled by money, lubricated by influence and controlled by bankers and businessmen.

It was not just the material success of philanthropy but its ecumenism that was exhilarating. 'Five or six hundred people of all sects and parties, with one heart, and face, and tongue', rhapsodized Wilberforce after one meeting in 1809, while several new auxiliaries – reading, it seems, from a

---

[167] Cited in Götz, 'Rationales of Humanitarianism', 19.

[168] Henry George Watkins, *Distress in Germany: a Sermon* ... (London, 1814), 13.

[169] *A Short Account of Successful Exertions in behalf of the Fatherless and Widows after the War in 1814* (privately printed, 1871), 22; *The Times*, 29 Jun. 1814, 3.

[170] *Proceedings of the Public Meeting for the Purpose of Establishing an Auxiliary Bible Society for Hackney* ... (London, 1812), 12.

text circulated by the parent body – hailed the British and Foreign Bible Society as signalling 'a new æra in the history of Religion, which may be styled the Æra of Unanimity'. The Bible Society was 'a rallying point for the piety of the age'.[171] Events added further layers of significance. Speaking in the Egyptian Hall of the Mansion House, London, on 6 August 1812, at the formation of the City of London Auxiliary, Nicholas Vansittart reflected that 'it appears to be the design of Providence, that the thunder of universal war should be the harbinger of the still small voice of the gospel of peace'.[172] Against a bleak backdrop darkened further by the 'black deed of assassination' that had removed Spencer Perceval only weeks before, what could better promote national interests, he asked, than to advance knowledge of the Gospel? And what could better aid the world than for London to export Bibles alongside commercial goods?[173] By 1815 guarded optimism had broadened into full-blown triumphalism. Preachers and pamphleteers revelled in the blossoming of pious philanthropy, the defeat of Bonaparte and the portended global spread of Christianity alongside British trade.

Opponents of Evangelicalism found much of this nauseating. High Churchmen like J.H. Spry (1777–1854) of Oriel College, Oxford, and Henry Handley Norris (1771–1850), curate of Hackney, railed against lay-led endeavours whose command structures subverted episcopal authority, replaced parishes with collecting districts and jumbled all brands of Christianity together into potentially radical 'combinations'. Instead of seeking to catechize or baptize, one combatant snorted, 'the saints ... [affirmed that] the *press* was ... the blessed instrument ordained in the counsels of Providence for diffusing the knowledge of Christianity to the ends of the earth'.[174] Still more scandalous was their subversion of gender norms. When Elizabeth Fry (1780–1845) prayed publicly at the inception of the Norwich Bible Society Auxiliary in 1811, she was not condemned but commended, in the words of the Apostle Peter, as a sign that the Almighty was working in new ways: '"Now of a truth I perceive that God is no respecter of persons"', marvelled Joseph Hughes.[175] To others this was anathema. 'We now see WOMEN ... placed in situations, not only unbecoming the natural

[171] Wilberforce, *Life*, III: 407; 'Religious Intelligence', *Misionary Magazine*, 15 (1810), 279; 'Dumfries-shire Bible Society', *Christian Observer*, 9 (1810), 326.

[172] *Meeting in the Egyptian Hall*, 28.

[173] *Ibid.*, 29–30.

[174] Andrew O'Callaghan, *The Bible Society against the Church and the State* (London, 1817), 3–5.

[175] Braithwaite, *Joseph John Gurney*, I: 70–1. For the Gurney-Fry circle, see also David E. Swift, *Joseph John Gurney: Banker, Reformer, and Quaker* (Middletown, CT, 1962), 50–3, 109–17, 122–4.

modesty of their sex, but totally foreign to the unobtrusive propriety of the English female character,' ranted one critic. 'We see them sitting, not simply as hearers of the speeches, in Assize halls, and other places of notoriety, but as regular members, as recorded patronesses.'[176] Such foaming prose bespoke more than mere snobbery or sexism. It evinced a broader uneasiness with decoupling the Bible from its lawful interpreters, with transgressing social norms, and with replacing defined Christian virtues with 'usefulness'. This was not a new debate. Brent Sirota has argued that as far back as the 1690s churchmen sought to demarcate and defend 'the sacred' as something set apart from everyday life and commerce.[177] By adapting to new circumstances and touting the gospel among the titled Evangelicals were allowing secular values to pollute the religious sphere: subordinating theological and ecclesiological particularities to a mushy, ill-defined 'usefulness', or so their opponents averred.

To many practical-minded laymen, however, clerical cavils about the perilous 'sin of schism' seemed laughable.[178] Witness the spoof letter published in 1815 ascribing murders in Shadwell and burglaries in Hertfordshire to the formation of BFBS auxiliaries, sentencing the society's vice-presidents to be hanged and its members to transportation.[179] In any case, Evangelicals objected, their brethren were coming to emulate their methods. The *Christian Observer* could not resist congratulating the Bath District Committee of the SPCK for its adoption of Bible Society-style resolutions, reports and advertisements, all of which had been denounced by its secretary, Spry.[180] Voluntary endeavour seemed to be carrying all before it.

Pietas Londinensis

'No capital in the world can vie with our own metropolis in the number, the ample funds, or the excellent regulations of its charitable establishments.'[181] So began an account of *The Annual Subscription Charities and Public*

[176] Josiah Thomas, *Real Charity and Popular Charity: a Discourse* (London, 1819), 18.

[177] Brent S. Sirota, 'Robert Nelson's *Festivals and Fasts* and the Problem of the Sacred in Early Eighteenth-Century England', *Church History*, 84 (2015), 556–84.

[178] John Hume Spry, *An Enquiry into the Claims of the British and Foreign Bible Society, to the Countenance and Support of Members of the Established Church* (London, 1810), 22.

[179] 'Truth of Mr Norris's Demonstrations Demonstrated', *Christian Observer*, 14 (1815), 446–9.

[180] 'Religious Intelligence. Society for Promoting Christian Knowledge', *Ibid.*, 12 (1813), 178–83.

[181] *The Annual Subscription Charities and Public Societies in London* (London, 1823), v.

Societies in London, published by John Murray in 1823, an abridgement of Anthony Highmore's *Pietas Londinensis* (1810) designed for 'all public men who are in the habit of attending the meetings of these several societies'.[182] The section headings alone evince the array of causes jostling for attention: societies for religious instruction, lying-in charities, general hospitals, hospitals for particular complaints, national schools, Sunday schools, charity schools, schools of instruction and industry, societies pertaining to particular professions, philanthropic reform societies, societies for the relief of the distressed, dispensaries, societies for providing for the destitute, benefit societies, local charities and so on. Many of those listed were of considerable vintage, and Evangelicals did not have a monopoly on them. Indeed, voluntary societies had long been a feature of urban Britain.[183] All the same, the ability of Evangelicals to mobilize emphasizes that they were well versed in that associative tradition and thus well placed to appeal to a broad section of middling and elite society. As R.J. Morris pointed out long ago, associations allowed the middle classes both to exert a hold over civic politics and the public sphere and to define what ought to be the targets of that power.[184] The foregoing chapter re-emphasizes the role of Evangelicals in providing the models and the national frameworks for that shift.

Murray's handbook illustrates especially well how Evangelicalism was altering the geography of the charitable world of London. Churches and chapels still mattered, but by the mid 1820s there was also Church Missionary House and the Prayer Book and Homily Society in Salisbury Square, the CMS training college in Islington, Bible House in Blackfriars, and Palestine Place, the LSPCJ complex in Bethnal Green. Evangelicals also had habitual meeting places, chief among them Freemasons' Hall, replaced in the 1830s by the vast purpose-built auditorium on the Strand that gave the movement its mid-Victorian metonym: Exeter Hall.[185] Not just London space but London time, too, was remoulded. Amid the sermons, dinners, concerts, balls and meetings detailed in Murray's calendar, the great anniversary meetings of the Evangelical societies made May by far the busiest month.[186] 'We have had such a week of religious dissipation,' Marianne Thornton

[182] *Ibid.*, vi.
[183] Peter Clark, *British Clubs and Societies, 1580–1800: the Origins of an Associational World* (Oxford, 2000).
[184] R.J. Morris, *Class, Sect and Party. The Making of the British Middle Class: Leeds, 1820–50* (Manchester, 1990), 161–317.
[185] *The Hall in the Garden: the Story of Freemasons' Hall* (London, 2006), 18; *Random Recollections of Exeter Hall, in 1834–1837. By One of the Protestant Party* (London, 1838), 3–20.
[186] *Annual Subscription Charities*, xxi–xxii.

senior told Hannah More in 1813. 'Such sermons for Missions and Jews and Homilies and such meetings after each sermon – such collections and such a parent Bible meeting that I think all the good people look 10 years younger than they did.'[187] Year on year, the reports and proceedings of such societies brought tidings of increased collections, growing subscription lists and new initiatives. Guineas and godliness seemed almost interchangeable.

[187] Mrs Henry Thornton to Hannah More, 6 May 1813, 'Family Letterbook and Recollections', CUL, MS Add.7674/1/N, fo. 363.

Chapter Three
The Development of an Anglican Evangelical Party, c. 1800–35

The inception of a branch of the Church Missionary Society in Bath in late 1817 was not expected to be controversial. By this stage the replication of societies locally was a matter of painting by numbers, a process honed over many years. Events at Bath initially followed the usual pattern. The Bishop of Gloucester, Henry Ryder, the first and at that point the only avowed Evangelical on the episcopal bench, arrived on Sunday, 30 November, and preached on behalf of the society to an enormous congregation at the plush Octagon Chapel. 'You will rejoice to hear that I came out alive,' the ageing socialite Hester Lynch Piozzi (1741–1821) told a friend. 'We were packed like seeds in a sunflower.'[1] At the Guildhall the following evening, Ryder was in the chair for the inauguration of the auxiliary. No sooner had he delivered his opening speech, however, than the meeting was violently interrupted by Josiah Thomas (1760–1820), the Archdeacon of Bath. Amid pandemonium, Thomas delivered a pre-prepared diatribe against the society, its methods and its personnel. Having registered his protest in the name of himself, the rectors of Bath and 'nineteen twentieths' of the local clergy, he stalked out without waiting for a reply.[2] News spread rapidly. The Archdeacon's protest, spattered with multiple exclamation marks and frequent capitalization, went into at least seven editions, and over the next few months at least twenty further pamphlets were produced, stoking controversy in the pages of ecclesiastical journals such as *The British Critic* and the *British Review*.[3]

---

[1] Hester Lynch Piozzi to Sir James Fellowes, 15 Dec. 1817, cited in Edward A. and Lilian D. Bloom (eds), *The Piozzi Letters, Volume VI: 1817–1821* (Newark, NJ, and London, 2010), 149.

[2] Josiah Thomas, *An Address in a Meeting Holden at the Town-Hall, in the City of Bath* … (5th edn: London, 1817), 9. I am indebted here to Mark Smith, 'Henry Ryder and the Bath CMS: Evangelical and High Church Controversy in the Later Hanoverian Church', *Journal of Ecclesiastical History*, 62 (2011), 726–43.

[3] Josiah Bateman, *The Life of the Right Rev. Daniel Wilson*, 2 vols (London, 1860), I: 150–1.

Thomas's speech crystallized what some among the clergy found objectionable about the activities of their Evangelical brethren. It was bad enough, he declared, that the CMS unnecessarily duplicated the function of the existing Society for the Propagation of the Gospel (SPG). But it undermined ecclesiastical order in more drastic respects, not least in placing its operations 'under the MANAGEMENT (that is the word) of A CORRESPONDING COMMITTEE!!!' rather than the ordained clergy. This disregard of properly constituted authority was evident at every level of CMS activity. Was it 'worthy of the Church of England', Thomas spat, to depute 'persons' to take 'pence and farthings from servants, school boys and apprentices' and to allow them the privileges of full society membership on the strength of collecting a shilling a week?[4] Rounding on Ryder, Thomas lambasted him for trespassing outside his diocese against the wishes of its own bishop: 'could he give a more decisive proof of his indifference to the dignity of the high office, to which he has been but a few years consecrated, as well as his contempt of ecclesiastical order?'[5] Perhaps most annoying of all was the way Evangelicals assumed their spiritual superiority. The CMS, he announced, had been set up by a 'NEW SECT' in the Church 'of which the adherents distinguish themselves by the names of SERIOUS CHRISTIANS and EVANGELICAL MINISTERS'.[6] It mattered little that its supporters were respectable: they mixed indiscriminately with dissenters. Their desire to convert the heathen was laudable, but it would be accomplished only by men 'orderly consecrated to their holy office'.[7]

Hannah More thought the contretemps absurd. In a bracing letter to her friend Ryder she exulted in 'the sousing of mitred heads and stalled Theologians, from their long slumber', rightly reckoning that Thomas had unintentionally imparted a 'new impulse' to the CMS cause.[8] Yet he also touched a raw nerve. Evangelicals were still smarting from the 'Western Schism' of 1815, in which aristocratic high Calvinists and clergymen in Hampshire and around Bristol had seceded from the Church. One of the ringleaders, the MP Thomas Read Kemp (1782–1844) had been a national vice-president of the CMS.[9] A reply was called for, and it was produced by

---

[4] Thomas, *Address*, 3.
[5] *Ibid.*, 3–4.
[6] *Ibid.*, 2.
[7] *Ibid.*, 8.
[8] Hannah More to Henry Ryder, n.d., [Dec. 1817], Sandon Hall, Harrowby MSS, 2nd ser., vol. 40, Supplementary Volume, xl, fos. 256–7.
[9] See Grayson Carter, *Anglican Evangelicals: Protestant Secessions from the Via Media, c. 1800–1850* (Oxford, 2001), 105–51.

Daniel Wilson, now Minister of St John's Chapel in London's Bedford Row, whose pamphlet eventually reached seventeen editions.[10] Central to Wilson's argument was the fact that the CMS was, like the existing Anglican flagships, a voluntary society. Although it was run by sincere churchmen, its members were motivated by conscience. The Archdeacon's protest was therefore 'a flagrant departure from the decorum ordinarily observed in civilized society', for the local clergy had no authority to veto an event sanctioned by the Mayor, held in the Guildhall and composed of private individuals.[11] Nor ought they to assume that they knew their diocesan's mind. As Dean of Wells, Wilson pointed out, Ryder had every right to appear in that diocese as patron for the Church Missionary Association, especially when Bishop Beadon (1737–1824) had declined that post 'in terms of courtesy and respect'.[12] Still more damning was the revelation that while Ryder was a public advocate of the SPCK, CMS and BFBS, the Archdeacon did not appear on the books of the SPG, whose cause he had so intemperately broadcast.[13] Notwithstanding Thomas's prim disapproval, Wilson wryly pointed out, there was also significant organizational cross-pollination between the new societies and their older counterparts. The SPCK's 'District Committees' looked suspiciously like the Bible Society and CMS auxiliaries that the Archdeacon so deplored.[14]

It would be a mistake to assume from this that Church of England was polarized into distinct camps. Many Orthodox churchmen seem to have regarded Evangelicals with scepticism rather than hostility, seeing them as well-meaning oddballs whose fervour did them credit, even if it sometimes led them into indiscretions. 'I give [inserted: 'many of'] them full credit for their zeal', wrote Lord Liverpool, 'and believe that good may sometimes arise from their Enthusiasm', even if his insertion betrayed a degree of ambivalence.[15] Clergymen of all stripes continued to mix socially and professionally: in educational endeavours and at visitation sermons, for example. Nevertheless, partisan lines were becoming clearer. One axis was doctrinal. Evangelicals proclaimed vociferously their adherence to the founding doctrines of the Anglican reformers as expressed in the Articles, Liturgy and Homilies, and their opponents' departure from

[10] Bateman, *Daniel Wilson*, I: 151.
[11] Daniel Wilson, *A Defence of the Church Missionary Society* (11th edn: London, 1818), 12–14.
[12] *Ibid.*, 16.
[13] *Ibid.*, 35.
[14] Wilson, *Defence*, 26–7.
[15] Lord Liverpool to anon., 19 Mar. 1821, Correspondence and Papers of 2nd Earl of Liverpool, BL Add. MS 38289, fo. 117.

them. '*We* then are the TRUE CHURCHMEN,' John Overton trumpeted, '... they are *Schismatics*.'[16] Anti-Evangelical polemicists responded that Original Sin, spiritual conversion and salvation by faith alone were alien doctrines that subverted ecclesiastical unity and political order, arguments that were advanced in several of Oxford's Bampton Lectures.[17] Yet the more significant source of friction, as Mark Smith has suggested, was the development of Evangelicalism organizationally.[18] Wilson's emphasis on the private nature of CMS membership was, after all, a concession: this was a society of churchmen, not a Church society. And if Evangelicals pointed the way towards innovations that others would eventually take up, in the process they also created institutions that, whether they liked it or not, marked them out as an increasingly distinct body. Nevertheless, this was not a pre-planned programme. There was little agreement as to how far churchmen ought to collaborate with dissenters, while among the Orthodox, too, there were deep divides between those who embraced organizational innovation and those who remained suspicious of it. This chapter uses debates surrounding the Bible Society, Prayer Book and Homily Society, SPCK and CMS to illuminate both where the battle-lines were and the issues that cut across those lines. It then turns once more to patronage, completing the narrative begun in Chapter 1 by showing how Evangelicals unlocked senior ecclesiastical appointments. In most respects this is a story of success. Yet success served also to restate some thorny questions. What did it mean to be both Anglican and Evangelical? How were the claims of the visible church to be balanced against those of the invisible communion of all believers? How far ought loyal churchmen to involve themselves in ecumenical concerns or projects of 'general benevolence', and on what basis? This was undoubtedly a formative period for Evangelicalism. But it also bequeathed internal tensions that would trouble the movement for decades to come.

---

[16] John Overton, *The True Churchmen Ascertained* (2nd edn: York, 1802), 397.

[17] Richard Laurence, *An Attempt to Illustrate those Articles of the Church of England, which the Calvinists Improperly Consider as Calvinistical* (Oxford, 1805); Thomas Le Mesurier, *The Nature and Guilt of Schism* (Oxford, 1807); Richard Mant, *An Appeal to the Gospel* (Oxford, 1812); John Hume Spry, *Christian Union Doctrinally and Historically Considered* (Oxford, 1816). For Hannah More's reaction to Spry's lectures, see More to Wilberforce, n.d. [March 1816], Rubinstein Library, Duke University, Wilberforce Papers, Box 3, Folder 2.

[18] Smith, 'Bath CMS'.

Evangelical Societies and Partisanship

The gospel clergy were understandably slow to embrace large-scale inter-denominational endeavour. Having largely steered clear of the LMS, they were also initially wary of the Religious Tract Society, founded in 1799 and, like the older body, dominated in its early days by nonconformist ministers and metropolitan laymen who had little time for clerical scruples.[19] They thus played no part in the RTS meetings between 1802 and 1804 where the idea of a Bible Society was mooted and developed. It was symbolically significant that many of these gatherings took place on business premises: at Joseph Hardcastle's 'counting house' at 9 Old Swan Stairs, near London Bridge. Hardcastle and his business partner Joseph Reyner (1754/5–1837) were cotton importers and shippers and they, along with a third Independent, the banker William Alers Hankey (d. 1859) and another layman, the Anglican leather merchant Samuel Mills (c. 1769–1847), propelled the new project forward.[20] They were determined from the outset to set the Bible Society on an efficient, professional footing. Its committee was thus to be composed entirely of laymen, potential accusations of imbalance being circumvented through strict quotas: fifteen churchmen, fifteen dissenters and six foreigners resident in London. The sole object of the new endeavour was, as its first law put it, 'to encourage a wider circulation of the Scriptures'. 'The only copies in the languages of the United Kingdom to be circulated by the Society, shall be the authorized version, without note or comment.'[21] This famous principle was not merely a statement of interdenominational intent. It served to underline the deliberately dispassionate basis of the Bible Society's operations. 'It is a society for furnishing the means of religion,' explained the Quaker minister and scientist Luke Howard (1772–1864), 'but not a religious society.'[22] Anyone might participate: there was no doctrinal test, nor were there prayers at meetings. The society thus not only sidestepped the Conventicle Act but signalled its openness to support from any quarter.

The British and Foreign Bible Society was inaugurated on 7 March 1804 at a suitably secular venue: the London Tavern on Bishopsgate

---

[19] Roger H. Martin, *Evangelicals United: Ecumenical Stirrings in Pre-Victorian Britain, 1795–1830* (Metuchen, NJ, and London, 1983), 148–56.

[20] The best recent account is Leslie Howsam, *Cheap Bibles: Nineteenth-Century Publishing and the British and Foreign Bible Society* (Cambridge, 1991), 1–34.

[21] *Reports of the British and Foreign Bible Society ... Volume the First, for the Years 1805, to 1810, inclusive* (London [1810?]), 3.

[22] William Canton, *A History of the British and Foreign Bible Society*, 5 vols (London, 1904–10), I: 359.

Street. Thanks to the circulation of a printed prospectus and adverts in metropolitan and provincial newspapers, it had already attracted subscriptions. Intensive lobbying by Wilberforce and his connections secured as vice-presidents Bishops Porteus, Barrington and Burgess, as well as John Fisher (1748–1825) of Exeter, Sir William Pepperell and Vice-Admiral James Gambier. They were supplemented by Wilberforce and the East India Director Charles Grant, both MPs, while their Clapham intimate, Henry Thornton, was Treasurer and John Shore, Lord Teignmouth, President. Yet Evangelical clergymen were reticent about taking part, so ingrained was their disapproval of irregularity. One representative example is John Owen (1766–1802), curate of Fulham and chaplain to Porteus, who thought the combination of dissenters and Anglicans 'utterly chimerical', and so took 'little pains either to understand or to recommend it'.[23] Attending the London Tavern nevertheless, his mind was completely changed by what he heard and saw: 'it appeared to indicate the dawn of a new era in Christendom; and to portend something like the return of those auspicious days, when "the multitude of them that believed were of one heart and of one soul;" and when, as a consequence of that union, ... "the Word of God mightily grew and prevailed".'[24] A few weeks later he consented to be the society's Anglican secretary, alongside the Baptist minister Joseph Hughes, representing dissent, and the Reverend Karl Friedrich Adolf Steinkopf of the Savoy Lutheran Chapel for the 'Foreign Department'.[25] Not everyone was so easily convinced. In Cambridge, Charles Simeon was reluctant to spend carefully husbanded credit on the BFBS.[26] Richard Lloyd (1764/5–1834), the outspoken Vicar of St Dunstan-in-the-West – a Thornton Trust living controlled by Evangelical patrons – opposed it as unchurchmanlike.[27] As time went on, though, the bulging coffers of the BFBS and its eminent patrons became unanswerable arguments in its favour.

This euphoria was not, though, shared by the 'Hackney Phalanx', an influential group of churchmen that coalesced at the turn of the century around the wine merchant Joshua Watson and his brother-in-law Henry Handley Norris. The Phalanx was to Orthodox or High churchmanship what the Clapham Sect was to Evangelicalism: an extensive set of

[23]   John Owen, *The History of the Origin and First Ten Years of the British and Foreign Bible Society*, 2 vols (London, 1816), I: 37.

[24]   *Ibid.*, 44.

[25]   For Steinkopf, see Nicholas Railton, *No North Sea: the Anglo-German Evangelical Network in the Middle of the Nineteenth Century* (Leiden, 1999), 71–8.

[26]   Charles Simeon to Joseph Tarn, 14 Aug. 1804, cited in Martin, *Evangelicals United*, 85.

[27]   Richard Lloyd, *Two Letters, Addressed to a Young Clergyman ...* (London, 1818).

friendship and kinship connections from mercantile and banking families which combined lay business acumen with access to patronage and political influence.[28] They, too, were keenly aware of the importance of publicity: Watson purchased the *British Critic* in late 1811 and later co-founded the *Christian Remembrancer*, both of which championed the Tory politics and churchmanship of the majority of the Anglican clergy. The Phalanx and its associates were not, then, opposed to innovation; but they were uneasy about bodies such as the BFBS that seemed to subvert the hierarchical and territorial discipline of the Church of England. Thomas Sikes of Guilsborough (1766–1834) – 'A Country Clergyman' – lashed Porteus and Teignmouth regarding the 'promiscuity' of a body that placed schismatics on a level with loyal churchmen. Anglicans, he warned, would be outvoted by 'coal-heaving ministers, bird-catching ministers, Baptist ministers of all trades, those of the Roman Catholic communion, together with the green-aproned female ministers of the friends.'[29] Such proceedings were not only dangerously democratic; they undermined the very principle of religious truth. 'A Bible given away by a Papist, will be productive of popery. The Socinian will make his Bible speak, and spread Socinianism: while the Calvinist, the Baptist, and the Quaker, will teach the opinions peculiar to their sects,' Sikes asserted. 'Supply these men with Bibles, (I speak as a true Churchman) and you supply them with arms against yourself.'[30]

Defenders of the Bible Society, both Evangelical and Orthodox, took their stand on simple grounds: that the benefits of distributing the Word of God vastly outweighed its disadvantages. They took cover behind the Society's careful demarcation between business and religion, a case put eloquently by the Staffordshire clergyman Edward Cooper (1770–1835):

> On going to the committee room, or to the hall, I make no compromise of principle, even in appearance, in any way. I offend not, either in letter or spirit, against any one article of the Church. I break no law, or canon which I have subscribed. I violate no duty which I owe to my ecclesiastical rulers. I am countenanced by many of my superiors, by some of the highest authority in my Church. When I have transacted the business on which I have attended I leave the assembly, I trust,

---

[28]   See A.B. Webster, *Joshua Watson: the Story of a Layman, 1771–1855* (London, 1954); Clive Dewey, *The Passing of Barchester* (London, 1991); Robert M. Andrews, *Lay Activism and the High Church Movement of the Late Eighteenth Century* (Leiden, 2015).

[29]   'A Country Clergyman' [Thomas Sikes], *An Humble Remonstrance to the Lord Bishop of London* (London, 1806), 50.

[30]   'A Country Clergyman' [Thomas Sikes], *An Address to Lord Teignmouth...* (London, 1805), 13

uncontaminated by the work in which I have been engaged, or by the persons with whom I have associated.[31]

Yet this cut little ice with polemicists concerned about the crumbling social and political purchase of the Church of England: concerns that were exacerbated in 1811 by the abortive attempt of the Home Secretary, Lord Sidmouth (1757–1844), to tighten the terms on which dissenters were licensed, and in 1813 by the Unitarian Toleration Act.[32] For them the activities of the Bible Society were part of the problem rather than the solution. The Almighty was a God of order who spoke through his Church.

If these years witnessed the politicization of evangelical dissent, as Michael Rütz has argued, they also, then, marked a hardening in attitudes among the clergy towards cross-denominational activism in general. The Royal Lancasterian Institution for the Education of the Poor of Every Religious Persuasion, instituted formally in 1810, attracted vicious abuse. Sarah Trimmer (1741–1810) declared its founder, the Quaker educationalist Joseph Lancaster (1778–1838), to be the 'Goliath of Schismatics', while the acerbic Archdeacon of Salisbury, Charles Daubeny (bap. 1745, d. 1827), who had assailed Hannah More's Mendip Sunday Schools on similar grounds in the 1790s, went one better in dubbing Lancaster a new Julian the Apostate and an emissary of Satan.[33] The British and Foreign School Society, as it later became, mirrored the Bible Society both in its patriotic title and in its reasonable defence of its activities: it made much of George III's oft-quoted wish 'that every child in his dominions might be able to read the Bible, and have a Bible to read'.[34] It also mobilized prominent lay support, attracting the patronage of the Duke of Kent and of Whig educational enthusiasts such as James Mill (1773–1836), Henry Brougham (1778–1868) and Samuel Whitbread, as well as nonconformists and some Evangelicals.[35] Clerics already tetchy about lay-controlled endeavours condemned this as a toxic alliance that married theological heterodoxy to secular-minded radicalism. For them religious neutrality meant religious indifference or worse. 'Our

[31] Edward Cooper, *Conduct of the Clergy in Supporting the Bible Society Vindicated* (London, 1818), 23–4.

[32] Michael A. Rütz, 'The Politicizing of Evangelical Dissent, 1811–1813', *Parliamentary History*, 20 (2001), 187–207.

[33] Robert, Caroline and Charles Robert Southey (eds), *The Life of the Rev. Andrew Bell*, 3 vols (London, 1844), II: 132. For the broader debate, see R.A. Soloway, *Prelates and People: Ecclesiastical Social Thought in England, 1783–1852* (London, 1969), 370–9.

[34] H.B. Binns, *A Century of Education: Being the Centenary History of the British & Foreign School Society 1808–1908* (London, 1908), 14.

[35] *Ibid.*, 51–2, 73–2.

utility will cease,' warned Herbert Marsh in an apocalyptic 1811 charity schools sermon in St Paul's Cathedral. 'We shall lose the *power* of doing good. No residence, no preaching, no catechising will further avail. Our flocks will have deserted us; they will have grown wiser than their guides; and the *national* Creed will have become too narrow for minds accustomed to the liberal basis.'[36] One result was the formation of the National Society for Promoting the Education of the Poor in the Principles of the Established Church in autumn 1811. It was supported by a wide spectrum of churchmen, including numerous Evangelical Anglicans, many of whom had remained aloof from the Lancasterian body.[37]

Hence, the BFBS remained a divisive subject. By 1811 it could claim the countenance of several episcopal vice-presidents: although Porteus had died, Barrington, Burgess and Fisher had now been joined by Bathurst of Norwich, William Lort Mansel (1753–1820) of Bristol and three Irish prelates: John Porter (d. 1819) of Clogher, William Bennet (1746–1820) of Cloyne and Archbishop Charles Brodrick (1761–1822) of Cashel. Several more were members.[38] But the rapid growth of the society after local auxiliaries began to spring up in 1809 turned a relative truce regarding its activities into open warfare. At Colchester in 1810[39] and Gloucester in 1812,[40] controversy erupted around the refusal of diocesans to give public countenance to the BFBS, while at Hackney in 1814[41] local clergy opposed the formation of auxiliaries, with pamphleteers on both sides connecting all these disputes

---

[36]   Herbert Marsh, *The National Religion the Foundation of National Education* (5th edn: London, 1811), 29.

[37]   H.J. Burgess, *Enterprise in Education: The Story of the Work of the Established Church in the Education of the People prior to 1870* (London, 1958), 21–2. Geoffrey Best is mistaken in reckoning that evangelicals as a body supported Lancaster: see G.F.A. Best, 'The Evangelicals and the established Church in the early nineteenth century', *Journal of Theological Studies*, n.s., 10 (1959), 72–3. 'Dr Bell's system' was favoured in Sierra Leone: *Second Report of the African Institution* (London, 1808), 12.

[38]   See William Otter, *A Vindication of Churchmen who Become Members of the British and Foreign Bible Society ...* (Cambridge, 1812).

[39]   See Christopher Wordsworth, *Reasons for Declining to become a Subscriber to the British and Foreign Bible Society ...* (London, 1810). There were published replies from Teignmouth, William Ward of Myland (c. 1762–1838), and William Dealtry.

[40]   'Clericus', *A Letter to the Right Reverend the Bishop of Gloucester ...* (Canterbury, 1813); Thomas Gisborne, *A Letter to the Right Reverend the Lord Bishop of Gloucester ...* (London, 1815).

[41]   Henry Handley Norris, *A Practical Exposition of the Tendency and Proceedings of the British and Foreign Bible Society* (London, 1813). There were replies from Dealtry and from the Unitarian Robert Aspland (1782–1845).

into a struggle for the soul of the nation.[42] Yet that struggle did not divide churchmen straightforwardly along party lines. When Herbert Marsh and Edward Maltby (1770–1859) took on the Cambridge Bible Society Auxiliary in one of the most prominent such conflicts, they were inundated with tracts not just from Evangelicals – William Dealtry (1775–1847), Isaac Milner, J.W. Cunningham (1780–1861), Charles Simeon and the MP Nicholas Vansittart – but also from Orthodox moderates such as William Otter, later Bishop of Chichester.[43] Especial obloquy was reserved for Owen. 'Jack [John Owen] was a Jacobin once, and Jack is a Jacobin still,' Sikes told Norris in 1812. 'He has only changed colour, as the complexion of times and places require.'[44] When Bishop Randolph of London's requirement that Owen reside in his Essex parish forced him to resign his Fulham curacy in 1813, it was widely interpreted as punishment. 'YOU ARE THE PROTOMARTYR OF THE BIBLE SOCIETY,' his Baptist colleague Hughes told him.[45] The threat of such treatment seems to have led to several defections from the BFBS in the late 1810s, meaning that in some localities it was impossible to maintain the prescribed balance between Church and dissent.[46]

The most telling argument against clerical involvement in the BFBS was that it diverted support and funds away from the SPCK. 'The Church already has its Bible Society,' protested Sikes.[47] By the mid 1810s, as Mark Smith points out, commentary on the relationship between the two societies 'had become a common feature in episcopal charges.'[48] For Samuel Goodenough (1743–1827) of Carlisle and G.H. Law (1761–1845) of Chester this was a zero-sum game: monies donated to the non-denominational BFBS would be better spent by the SPCK. Others differed.[49] Ryder pointed out wryly in his 1816 Charge that there was no essential conflict: ministers might 'by a little further stretch of self-denial' dip deeper into their pockets

[42] 'A Presbyter of the Church of England', *Papers Occasioned by Attempts to Form Auxiliary Bible Societies in Various Parts of the Kingdom* (London, 1812).

[43] The best account is in Ford K. Brown, *Fathers of the Victorians: the Age of Wilberforce* (Cambridge, 1961), 285–316.

[44] Thomas Sikes to Henry Handley Norris, 22 Dec. 1812, Bodleian Library, MS Eng. Lett. c. 789, fos. 38–9.

[45] John Leifchild, *Memoir of the Late Rev. Joseph Hughes* (London, 1835), 252-3.

[46] Martin, *Evangelicals United*, 109–10.

[47] 'A Country Clergyman' [Thomas Sikes], *A Second Letter to Lord Teignmouth* (London, 1810), 50.

[48] Henry Ryder, 'A Charge Delivered to the Clergy of the Diocese of Gloucester in the Year 1816', ed. Mark A. Smith, in *idem* and Stephen Taylor (eds), *Evangelicalism in the Church of England c. 1790–c. 1890* (Woodbridge, 2004), 81.

[49] E.g. Thomas Burgess, *A Charge Delivered to the Clergy of the Diocese of St David's in September 1813* (2nd edn: Durham, 1813), 19–32.

and support both.[50] Speaking at the inception of the Staffordshire Auxiliary in 1812, Thomas Gisborne told assembled county notables that he
had been a member of both the SPCK and SPG 'for about six and twenty
years', but thought support for the new organization justified on the basis
that it met spiralling demand which they were unable to fulfil.[51] As for
the 'treachery' of associating with nonconformists, Gisborne drew the
attention of his listeners to the Naval and Military Bible Society (NMBS),
established in 1780 and 'equally open in all its office, open without any
limitation whatsoever as to proportionate numbers, to members of the
Established Church and to Dissenters'. Like the BFBS, the NMBS distributed the Authorized Version without accompanying notes. It was also
dominated by Evangelicals, a fact that Gisborne understandably chose not
to mention. But unlike its younger sister, the NMBS enjoyed the imprima-
tur of establishment support, with the Duke of York (1763–1827) as Patron,
the Duke of Gloucester (1776–1834) as Vice-Patron and the Archbishop of
Canterbury as President.[52] Support for the Bible Society was thus neither
unpatriotic nor unsanctioned by past precedents.

Events within the SPCK, however, served to exacerbate divisions. In
1811 Watson, Norris, Christopher Wordsworth (1774–1846) and John
Bowles (1751–1819) took a leaf out of the Evangelical book, overriding the
protestations of traditionalists on the committee to sponsor the foundation of a Colchester District Meeting in deliberate competition with
its Bible Society counterpart. While the subsequent spread of regional
branches trebled the annual income of the SPCK, it also helped to cement
its reputation as a bastion of well-starched churchmanship.[53] Evangelical
subscribers had never taken a leading part in SPCK affairs on a national
level. But despite their growing influence and numbers they still found
themselves frozen out of decision-making.[54] There were also widespread
fears that gospel clergymen might find themselves blackballed: this seems
to have happened to Simeon more than once.[55] 'A great proportion of the

[50] Ryder, 'Charge', ed. Smith, 105.
[51] Thomas Gisborne, *The Substance of the Speech of the Rev. Thomas Gisborne ... in the County Hall at Stafford ...* (London, 1812), 13.
[52] *Ibid.*, 23–6.
[53] E.A. Varley, *The Last of the Prince Bishops: William Van Mildert and the High Church Movement of the Early Nineteenth Century* (Cambridge, 1992), 68–9.
[54] Josiah Pratt to J.A. Woodhouse, 3 Jan. 1814, cited in Charles Hole, *The Early History of the Church Missionary Society for Africa and the East* (London, 1896), 406–7.
[55] 'Religious Intelligence. Prayer-Book and Homily Society' *Christian Observer*, 11 (1812), 394; Alfred Blomfield, *A Life of Charles James Blomfield*, 2 vols (London, 1863), I: 75.

most active clergy are shut out from the advantages of getting prayerbooks from the Society ... through fear of the ballot,' lamented the chaplain of Bridewell Hospital, Henry Budd (1774–1853). Yet nor, he added, did such men want to support a society 'which distributes heterodox tracts'.[56] He probably had in mind Richard Mant (1776–1848), whose 1812 Bampton Lectures, *An Appeal to the Gospel*, were a deliberately anti-Evangelical manifesto. Mant insisted that Christian works were 'a necessary condition of salvation', drawing on the Prayer Book, the Bible and the Fathers to argue that regeneration was the product of baptism, 'rightly administered'. 'The language cannot be plainer', he declared.[57] Although Evangelical opinions on the subject were far from monolithic, Mant's views cut against their touchstone doctrines: salvation by faith alone and conversion through the 'New Birth'. Insult was added to injury in 1815 when the SPCK excerpted Mant's chapters on baptismal regeneration and against 'special and instantaneous conversion' as a tract and circulated them with its annual report.[58]

Dismayed by this, and stung by accusations that the distribution of the Bible without the Prayer Book was unchurchmanlike, during the spring and summer of 1812 Budd masterminded the establishment of a new organization, the Prayer Book and Homily Society (PBHS).[59] It boasted prominent backers, including six peers (Earl Ferrers [1765–1827], Viscount Valentia [1744–1816] and Lords Calthorpe, Headley [1784–1840], Gambier and Teignmouth), and five MPs (Sir Thomas Baring, Thomas Babington, Charles Grant, William Wilberforce and Henry Thornton). Its proclaimed aim was simple: to promote the circulation of the formularies of the Church of England, i.e. the Book of Common Prayer and the Book of Homilies, 'without note or comment'. Evangelicals were by no means alone among late-Hanoverian churchmen in advocating a heartfelt devotional spirituality based on the Liturgy.[60] The membership of the PBHS in its early years was, however, almost exclusively Evangelical, and it was clearly designed to complement the BFBS and to circumvent criticism of the involvement of churchmen in it. In fact, Budd's introductory pamphlet reasoned, the distribution of Bibles ought to have created an expanded readership for

[56]   Henry Budd to C.J. Bird, 22 May 1812, cited in Henry Budd, *A Memoir of the Rev. Henry Budd* (London, 1855), 150.

[57]   Mant, *Appeal to the Gospel*, 334–6.

[58]   Richard Mant, *Two Tracts* (London, 1815).

[59]   For its manifesto, see 'Religious Intelligence. Prayer-Book and Homily Society', *Christian Observer*, 11 (1812), 247–9.

[60]   Ryder, 'Charge', ed. Smith, 71.

other religious literature.[61] Advance proposals for the PBHS thus billed it alongside the SPCK, NMBS and National Society as dedicated to Church interests: it was instituted 'by members of the Established Church'. Yet there was a widespread sense among its friends and enemies alike that the new society sought not just to supplement the SPCK but to supplant it. Clerical members – many of them unable to take advantage of SPCK discounts – were assured that the PBHS would keep prices low, and that those remitting congregational collections would receive three-quarters of the total in books at cost price.[62] Its ordained membership grew particularly quickly, reaching 298 by 1816: between a quarter and a third of the gospel clergy at large. The involvement of several military men, including Admiral Gambier, signalled that, like the SPCK, the PBHS promised to pay especial attention to the armed forces: a canny move given the power of patriotic discourse in wartime Britain. Translations of the Prayer Book or selected portions of it into 'Hindoostanee' (1816), Bullom (1817) and Chinese (1819) meant that the PBHS could also claim to be spreading Church of England principles abroad: in this respect, too, it stole a march over the SPCK.[63]

Most importantly, the PBHS embodied the conviction of Evangelicals that they were the true bearers of the Anglican flame. 'The grand distinction between Protestant *Churchmen* and Protestant *Dissenters*', Marsh had urged against the Bible Society, 'lies in the adoption or rejection of the Liturgy.'[64] To overthrow it was, as the Commonwealth showed, to overthrow Church and King too. Against such slurs, Evangelicals had long retorted that the Prayer Book was not the only source of authentic churchmanship: that the more avowedly reformed Homilies and Articles were being deliberately detached from the Liturgy that they were intended to explain and safeguard. This complaint was given piquancy by Mant's assertions regarding the baptismal service. Budd's reading of sixteenth- and seventeenth-century divinity convinced him, like many others, that 'real Christianity' was embedded in the warp and woof of the national establishment, if only one looked hard enough. He deplored the dishonesty of anti-Calvinists who dismissed the reformed theology of the Homilies or crypto-Socinians who explained away Trinitarian Articles to which they

---

[61]   'Religious Intelligence. Prayer-Book and Homily Society', *Christian Observer*, 11 (1812), 248.

[62]   J.W. Cunningham, *A Sermon Preached ... Before the Prayer Book and Homily Society* (London, 1813), vii.

[63]   D.N. Griffiths, 'Prayer-Book Translations in the Nineteenth Century', *The Library*, 6 (1984), 3.

[64]   Herbert Marsh, *An Inquiry into the Consequences of Neglecting to Give the Prayer Book with the Bible* (4th edn: Cambridge, 1812), 30n.

had supposedly subscribed *ex animo*. The eighty-seven questions which Marsh, as Bishop of Peterborough, put to ordination candidates ('cobwebs to catch Calvinists') Budd branded 'the complete subversion of the thirty-nine Articles'. 'Let the Bishops generally act on this principle, and farewell to the Church of England.'[65] Bearing in mind that Prayer Books were often distributed without the Articles attached, and that no new edition of the Homilies had appeared for years, one of the chief aims of the PBHS was, then, to make latitude more difficult to sustain.[66] It also offered a powerful explanation of the growth of dissent, exonerating voluntary endeavour and placing blame at the door of the Anglican establishment instead. Was it not a disgrace, asked the *Christian Observer*, that 'while the writings of the Puritan divines are to be found in almost every village and hamlet in the kingdom the writings of our own Reformers, the founders and fathers of our church, expressly designed for the instruction of the poor and ignorant, should be altogether unknown to the great mass of our population?'[67] Small wonder that flocks had wandered away from their appointed shepherds. 'Know thou the God of thy father' was the text of the first anniversary sermon in 1813, and it was a theme that preachers returned to with relish.[68]

Such arguments were part of a broader assumption, embedded in the founding myths of a number of Evangelical endeavours, that the existing Anglican bodies were at best inadequate to their task and at worst slothful in tackling self-evident shortages of religious literature. Undoubtedly the most cherished of these was and remains the tale of Mary Jones (1784–1864) and her initially fruitless search for a Welsh Bible. It was her plight, the story goes, that induced Thomas Charles (1755–1814) of Bala to take a leading part in the formation of the BFBS. How far Mary Jones's case indicates a genuine shortage of (SPCK-printed) Welsh Bibles is a moot point: it became a *cause celebre* only in the late nineteenth century.[69] Either way, it was rhetorically necessary for the new Evangelical societies to present the SPCK and SPG as moribund, and to see themselves as fulfilling unmet needs. Hence the passions on both sides, for while defenders of the new initiatives declared ever more strenuously that they were supplementing

---

[65] Budd, *Memoir*, 349–50.
[66] 'Publications of the Prayer-Book and Homily Society', *Christian Observer*, 37 (1838), 322–34.
[67] 'Review of *Select Homilies of the Church of England*', *Christian Observer*, 10 (1811), 633.
[68] Cunningham, *Sermon*, 1.
[69] It was first set out in R.O. Rees, *Mary Jones, y Gymraes fechan heb yr un Beibl : a sefydliad y Feibl-Gymdeithas* [Mary Jones, the Welsh Girl without a Bible: the Organisation of the Bible Society] (Wrexham, 1879).

patchy provision, their opponents replied equally vehemently that the means already existed to address them, if only people would support the older societies.

Naturally, then, the SPCK remained a cockpit for combative partisans. In February 1816 Daniel Wilson and a group of eminent Evangelicals scandalized the society's meeting when they called for Mant's *Two Tracts* to be struck off the publications list.[70] 'We separated, half dead with heat and fatigue, but cheered by a success greater than we had dared to expect,' Wilson crowed.

> The consternation of the members was laughable. Dr. Mant ballotted [*sic*] on his own tract. The next meeting will be crowded. Every body is speaking of it. May God's spirit guide and direct us. I cannot describe to you the exact state of things. They began by attempting to trample us under their feet. They were driven off ... The ballot itself showed our power ... We hoped everything, and the truth sustained us. All our friends must be in town on the 5th March.[71]

When the society reassembled later in the month it was with ecclesiastical heavyweights present to maintain order: Archbishop Manners-Sutton (1755–1828) in the chair, flanked by Bishop Howley (1766–1848) of London.[72] Although Dealtry, the Evangelical spokesman, was excluded from the committee appointed to examine Mant's work, Wilson considered the result – a corrected edition – to be a triumph.[73] This did nothing to bridge deepening divisions over baptismal regeneration.[74] Bartlett's Buildings was to remain a key skirmishing ground, partly because of its publishing reach but also because of its symbolic importance. Evangelicals, the Orthodox and later Tractarians all sought to use it as a platform. In the 1810s partisan divisions were not yet so deep: there remained plenty who saw no need to rock the boat. Pugilists like Wilson, however, could afford to be assertive because they had strongholds to fall back upon, not least Evangelical societies with ever-lengthening subscription lists. Ranged against them, though, were well-entrenched opponents. When Wilson preached before Oxford

---

[70]   Bateman, *Daniel Wilson*, I: 140–4. See also Daniel Wilson, *A Respectful Address to ... the Society for Promoting Christian Knowledge, on Certain Inconsistencies and Contradictions ...* (London, 1816).

[71]   Bateman, *Daniel Wilson*, I: 142–3.

[72]   See CUL, SPCK.MS A1/37, Committee Minute Book 1815–16, fos. 425–6; 433–6.

[73]   See Grayson Carter, *Anglican Evangelicals*, 132–4.

[74]   See e.g. James Pereiro, *'Ethos' and the Oxford Movement: at the Heart of Tractarianism* (Oxford, 2008), 17–25.

University in 1817, again on the necessity of 'New Birth', he infuriated the authorities. 'It is a doctrine which I am more bound to maintain, because of the part I have taken in London, both in the "Address" I have printed, and the opinions I have expressed at the Christian Knowledge Society,' he decided.[75] But on asking to have the sermon printed at the University press, Wilson received the bluntest of responses from the Vice-Chancellor, Thomas Lee (1761–1824). 'It savours of St Edmund's Hall,' he uttered, 'the press is engaged.'[76]

The 'Pious Clause' and the Anglican Missionary Spirit

Nevertheless, there were areas of activity where partisanship was muted. Overseas missions was one of them. The EIC's parliamentary charter was due to be renewed in 1813, and the moral and religious state of its possessions was to be a central issue. Tempers had been running high since 1806, when the Vellore Mutiny sparked a heated dispute between champions of proselytization and mercantile interests who blamed the affair on missionary interference.[77] Contradictory religious imperatives exacerbated matters. Evangelicals already had a stake in the Company thanks to pious directors such as Charles Grant and Edward Parry. While they sympathized with LMS and Baptist missionaries, who found their activities circumscribed by wary officials, Evangelical churchmen also thought nonconformists hot-headed and potentially disruptive. Mainstream churchmen, for their part, were as suspicious of dissent and the unfettered distribution of Bibles abroad as they were at home. The patrician disdain of the Whig churchman and wit Sydney Smith for 'little detachments of maniacs' drawn from the 'lowest of the people' was widely echoed.[78] Yet Smith's dismissal of providential arguments, his pragmatic pluralism and his respect for Indian civilization were beginning to look old-fashioned at a time when the idea of an ecclesiastical establishment for India was gaining currency. Evangelical strategists played no small part in this development, but they were keen to include others in the same cause. This imperative owed much to the experiences of Grant and Wilberforce during the previous renewal of the Company's charter in 1793. There, too, their instinct had been to seek allies.

[75] Bateman, *Daniel Wilson*, I: 145.
[76] *Ibid.*, 147. It was published by Hatchard: Daniel Wilson, *The Doctrine of Regeneration Practically Considered* (London, 1817).
[77] Jörg Fisch, 'A Pamphlet War on Christian Missions in India 1807–1809', *Journal of Asian History*, 19 (1985), 22–70.
[78] [Sydney Smith], 'Indian Missions', *Edinburgh Review*, 12, 23 (1808), 179.

On Grant's return from India in 1790, for instance, he joined the SPCK East India Mission Committee. His *Observations on the State of Society among the Asiatic Subjects of Great Britain, Particularly with Respect to Morals* (1792) was couched in terms that were humanitarian and civilizational as much as religious.[79] Yet the attempt to introduce a 'Pious Clause' declaring Britain's duty to promote Christianity in India foundered, partly because they put the wind up leading Company men, but also because they failed to enthuse the bench of bishops. 'They never like to give the reins into the hands of men of warm imaginations,' warned a friend, an accurate prediction at a time when scaremongers saw 'Methodism' and Jacobinism as practically synonymous.[80]

It is important not to conclude from this that the Orthodox majority were uninterested, as Evangelical writers then and since have often assumed. The set-piece annual sermons preached by bishops for the SPG and SPCK could be as dismissive of Indian culture and as fiery about British failure to proselytize as anything that issued from an Evangelical pulpit.[81] Yet recent scholarship on Anglican imperial rhetoric has sometimes seemed to mistake words for actions. By the turn of the century, Evangelicals were frustrated enough to take matters into their own hands. One aspect of this was the foundation of the CMS. Another was the exploitation of Company connections to secure appointments to a string of official chaplaincies. These were staffed by Cambridge men painstakingly selected by Simeon in conjunction with Grant.[82] They were fêted by missionary hagiographers, none more so than Henry Martyn, who came to be regarded as the prototypical modern Anglican martyr-saint after his death in Persia in 1812.[83] More significant practically, though, was Claudius Buchanan, whose commitment to working with the establishment grain and shrewd appreciation of the importance of publicity allowed Evangelicals to shape the religious agenda regarding India.

Buchanan came to prominence in 1800, when he preached a sermon on the recent British victory in Mysore that impressed the Governor-General,

---

[79] Allan K. Davidson, *Evangelicals and Attitudes to India, 1786–1813* (Sutton Courtenay, 1990), 46–56.

[80] Thomas Raikes to Charles Grant, 5 Apr. 1788, cited in Henry Morris, *The Life of Charles Grant* (London, 1904), 115.

[81] Rowan Strong, *Anglicanism and the British Empire, c. 1700–1850* (Oxford, 2007), 118–97.

[82] See this book, 219–20.

[83] Brian Stanley, '"An Ardour of Devotion": the Spiritual Legacy of Henry Martyn', in Richard Fox Young (ed.), *India and the Indianness of Christianity* (Grand Rapids, 2009), 108–26.

Marquess Wellesley (1760–1842).[84] Wellesley made Buchanan Vice-Provost of Fort William College, Calcutta, a newly founded institution intended to train civil servants in Indian languages, culture and history. While the College was attacked by the Company's directors as an unwarranted extravagance, for Buchanan it became his platform, as is discussed in a later chapter. The generous essay and poetry prizes he offered out of his own pocket to British universities and leading public schools in 1803 and again in 1805 elicited numerous entries on the designs of providence in subordinating India to British rule, several of which were published. In Britain, Buchanan's *Memoir of the Expediency of an Ecclesiastical Establishment for British India* (1805), meanwhile, imbued its subject with a new urgency. Written at the suggestion of Porteus and dedicated to the Archbishop of Canterbury, it combined a lurid portrayal of Indian religion and civilization with sweeping prescriptions designed to appeal to a broad spectrum of churchmen: bishops to preserve religion among the British in India, scores of chaplains and missionaries to bring the 'natives' into the fold.[85] Buchanan was lionized on his return to Britain in 1808, embarking on a preaching tour of England and Scotland and dining with favourably disposed bishops. His *Star in the East*, a sermon preached in Bristol for Biddulph, became a bestseller, proclaiming that 'the time for diffusing our religion in the East is COME.'[86] As yet, however, it was unclear how this might come about. When Buchanan visited Auckland Castle he was impressed by Bishop Barrington's boycott of the *Edinburgh Review*, whose recent anti-missionary articles, from the scurrilous pen of Sydney Smith, had 'grossly insulted religion'. But when Barrington enquired after Buchanan's impression of the country after twelve years abroad, his guest lambasted the bishops' inability to reach out beyond the bench, the clergy or indeed the Church of England to 'men of piety and learning'. 'They were like twenty-four insulated kings or barons in their castles, while the enemy was scouring the plains.'[87] Buchanan clearly had trenchant views: too trenchant, in Simeon's opinion. But his comments capture something of Evangelical impatience with what they saw as ecclesiastical rigidity.

Thus it was that in 1812 the Society for Missions to Africa and the East received a facelift. One change was in its name: the geographical

---

84   Claudius Buchanan, *A Sermon, Preached at the New Church of Calcutta* ... (Calcutta, 1800).

85   Claudius Buchanan, *Memoir of the Expediency of an Ecclesiastical Establishment for British India* (London, 1805).

86   Claudius Buchanan, *The Star in the East* (2nd edn: London, 1809), 34.

87   Hugh Pearson, *Memoirs of the Life and Writings of the Rev. Claudius Buchanan*, 2 vols (Oxford, 1817), II: 192.

qualifications designed to placate the existing Anglican societies were now relegated to the small print, in favour of the simpler and more assertive Church Missionary Society. Another alteration was in its hierarchy: for the first time since its foundation, the CMS was to have a President – Lord Gambier – while the eight governors of the society were rechristened as vice-presidents, and four more influential public figures added to give extra lobbying firepower: Earl Ferrers, Lord Teignmouth, Nicholas Vansittart and another MP, Charles Noel Noel (1781–1866). Also important symbolically was a change of venue: having met hitherto in William Goode's study in Blackfriars Rectory, the committee now moved to business premises, engaging the publisher L.B. Seeley for the permanent use of an office in his house at 169 Fleet Street, on the corner of Red Lion Court, and paying £30 a year for fire, candles and the care of the society's library.[88] Having spent more than a decade in the doldrums, the CMS was to become the spearhead for an ecumenical cause: the Christianization of India. This was not as fanciful as it sounds. The foundation of the National Society had recently underlined the common churchmanship of Evangelicals and the Orthodox and, in March 1812, Wilberforce approached J. H. Pott (1758–1847), the outgoing SPCK Treasurer and an associate of the Hackney Phalanx, regarding further co-operation.[89] Despite the opposition of the splenetic Randolph, a 'very full' SPCK meeting on 'East India Christianising' gathered at Bartlett's Buildings on 5 May, with Archbishop Manners-Sutton in the chair and Wilberforce, Babington, Zachary Macaulay and the Methodist MP Thomas Thompson present 'by special summons'.[90] Guided by Wilberforce, the committee adopted a version of Buchanan's *Memoir*, and suggested that Wilberforce should present a petition in parliament on behalf of the society. The SPCK's resolutions were then sent to the Prime Minister, the Chancellor of the Exchequer, the President of the Indian Board of Control and the Directors of the EIC, 500 further copies being printed for the use of MPs. Wilberforce then moved to mobilize his natural constituency. The next day he spoke at an 'immense meeting' of the BFBS, while for the May number of the *Christian Observer* he wrote a lengthy anonymous letter under the ecumenical moniker 'A CHRISTIAN', drawing on Buchanan's shocking accounts of widows' *sati* and infanticide to urge all believers to devote themselves to the cause of India.[91] His call to arms was shot through

---

[88]   Hole, *Church Missionary Society*, 208–9.
[89]   The best account is in Penelope Carson, *The East India Company and Religion, 1698–1858* (Woodbridge, 2012), 124–5.
[90]   Wilberforce, *Life*, IV: 22–3; Varley, *Last of the Prince Bishops*, 75–6.
[91]   Wilberforce, *Life*, IV: 22; 'A Christian' [William Wilberforce], 'Letter to a friend ON THE DUTY OF GREAT BRITAIN TO DISSEMINATE CHRISTIANITY IN INDIA',

with the languages of paternalism, patriotism and impending national judgment that had proven so successful in pushing through slave trade abolition only a few years earlier.[92] He and Buchanan also lobbied the General Assembly of the Church of Scotland to take up the cause, while the latter urged Cambridge to petition parliament.[93]

To interest evangelical dissenters, Wilberforce and his coadjutors faced a complex balancing act. On one hand, they needed to convince spokesmen like the Baptists Andrew Fuller (1754–1815) and John Ryland (1753–1825), the Wesleyan Joseph Butterworth and the Independent George Burder (1752–1832) that Buchanan's plan for an ecclesiastical establishment would unlock India to nonconformists as well. There was 'room enough in the East for all Denominations of xtians', Wilberforce told Ryland, 'and it [will] be my earnest endeavour to have free scope for the execution of all'.[94] On the other hand, they needed to reassure churchmen who might take fright at 'meetings petitions &c. among the religious world'.[95] The Committee of the Three Denominations, the Wesleyan Committee of Privileges and the Protestant Society for the Protection of Religious Liberty (PSPRL), founded in 1811 to fight Sidmouth's proposed bill, were encouraged to keep a low profile while Wilberforce spoke to the SPCK. It was agreed that different denominations and missionary societies should lobby government ministers and the Company separately, albeit with a high degree of co-ordination behind the scenes.[96] That this arrangement functioned at all suggests that nonconformist leaders knew that success depended on connections within the establishment. It should therefore come as no surprise that the CMS deputation was especially influential, securing promises regarding an episcopal establishment, training seminaries for native ministers and the licensing of missionaries from the new Prime Minister, Lord Liverpool, when Wilberforce, Grant and Babington visited him in July 1812.[97]

Nevertheless, by early 1813, with the Company seeking to retain control of who should enter its territories, dissenting bodies were anxious that they might be sold short. Wilberforce agonized over how to proceed. 'We may

Christian Observer, 11 (1812), 261–72.

[92]   See Boyd Hilton, '1807 and All That: Why Britain Outlawed her Slave Trade', in Derek R. Peterson, *Abolitionism and Imperialism in Britain, Africa, and the Atlantic* (Athens, OH, 2010), 63–83.

[93]   Carson, *East India Company*, 125–6; Pearson, *Claudius Buchanan*, II: 279–80.

[94]   Wilberforce to Ryland, 3 Jun. 1812, cited in Carson, *East India Company*, 124.

[95]   Henry Thornton to Hannah More, 25 Apr. 1812, 'Family Letterbook and Recollections', CUL, MS Add.7674/1/N, fo. 343.

[96]   Wilberforce, *Life*, IV: 1, 10, 12.

[97]   Hole, *Church Missionary Society*, 229.

lose all by striving for too much,' he warned Burder.[98] While some pious commentators talked iconoclastically about dismantling the Company's monopoly, Grant and Parry were wary of such language: they wanted to advance missions but also spoke for a Company wary of interference and expense.[99] The declaration of Lord Castlereagh (1769–1822) on 22 March 1813 that the government intended to provide a bishop and an archdeacon for India, however, was almost as unsatisfactory to Evangelical churchmen as it was to dissenters. It did not guarantee missionary access, and it fell short of being a full-blooded commitment to broadcast Christianity among the millions placed under Britain's care. It was at this point that the religious public were called into play. A London-based committee under the chairmanship of Macaulay sent out some 100,000 circulars to ministers throughout the kingdom, enlisting them as local intermediaries.[100] English denominational bodies and missionary societies were joined by the Scottish SPCK, Church of Scotland and Scottish dissenters in an enormous campaign that deluged the Houses of Parliament with 908 petitions during April and May. The measure was passed in July.

Although in public Evangelicals trumpeted Section 33 of the new charter – the 'Pious Clause' – as a success, in private many were disappointed at its ambiguity. The established churches received what they wished for: there would be a Church of England bishop and three archdeacons, while the Company also agreed to provide three Church of Scotland chaplains. Official recognition of Britain's duty 'to promote the interests and happiness of the native inhabitants' through 'religious and moral improvement', moreover, was undoubtedly significant symbolically, especially so given the opposition missionaries faced from colonial authorities in the West Indies, South Africa and Ceylon.[101] As in other spheres, public statements regarding Britain's providential obligations were welcomed almost as warmly as hard policies. Immediate difficulties in securing licences for BMS and CMS missionaries, though, confirmed an impression that the campaign had stopped short, an impression intensely felt among dissenters especially.[102] For them this underlined the need for complete religious freedom at home and abroad, a stance that put them at odds with churchmen and contributed

---

[98]   Wilberforce to Burder, 10 May 1813, cited in Carson, *East India Company*, 135.

[99]   See e.g. *Ibid.*, 125.

[100]   Viscountess Knutsford, *Life and Letters of Zachary Macaulay* (London, 1900), 297–8.

[101]   See Andrew Porter, *Religion versus Empire? British Protestant Missionaries and Overseas Expansion, 1700–1914* (Manchester, 2004), 64–90.

[102]   Carson, *East India Company*, 151–82.

to the unravelling of pan-evangelical endeavours in the 1820s and 30s.[103] Yet neither was the new bishop everything Evangelicals could have wished for. In January 1814 the post was first offered to Christopher Wordsworth, who declined, before being accepted by the Archdeacon of Huntingdon, Thomas Fanshaw Middleton (1769–1822), another energetic churchman with Hackney connections.[104] Wilberforce did his best to paper over the cracks, inviting Middleton to dinner, along with Teignmouth and Grant: 'he seems very earnest and pondering to do good – hopes for churches in different parts of India – favourable to schools and a public library – a college with discipline – his powers greater than we conceived.'[105] But when Middleton proposed co-operation with the Calcutta branch of the BFBS, he horrified his High Church connections. 'What will he do thereby for Education – what for Truth – what for the Liturgy – what for Missions'? Wordsworth fulminated to Norris in February. Would not a better solution be 'a grand Oriental Auxiliary Society for Promoting Christian Knowledge' that would promote the 'Madras System' – the firmly Anglican rival of Lancaster's monitorial scheme – and which 'all respectable persons' going out to India could be quietly encouraged to favour?[106]

These tensions resurfaced once Middleton arrived in India. As will be seen in Chapter 6, the ecclesiastical scene in Calcutta had for many years been strongly tinged with Evangelicalism. There, as in Britain, Evangelicals were in general readier to exploit the proselytizing and philanthropic opportunities afforded by an expanding public sphere. They were also open to ecumenical initiatives and friendship. Given the inaction or refusal of the 'National Church' to act institutionally, Grant explained in a pained letter to Middleton, he 'could not but' wish success to Protestant dissenters.[107] Middleton, for his part, had been instructed by Manners-Sutton 'to put down enthusiasm and to preach the Gospel', and the tussles hinted at by his biographer over vestries, schools and societies show how disagreements with Evangelicals about episcopal authority and lay leadership were replicated overseas.[108] 'No man can well be more unpopular than the bishop is,' reported Daniel Corrie.[109] A lack of clarity

[103] Susan Thorne, *Missions and the Making of an Imperial Culture in Nineteenth-Century England* (Stanford, CA, 1999), 53–88.
[104] Varley, *Last of the Prince Bishops*, 76–7.
[105] Wilberforce, *Life*, IV: 200.
[106] Wordsworth to Norris, 3 Feb. 1814, cited in Varley, *Last of the Prince Bishops*, 77.
[107] Grant to Middleton, August 1817, cited in Morris, *Charles Grant*, 337–8.
[108] Webster, *Joshua Watson*, 123.
[109] Corrie to Josiah Pratt, 4 Feb. 1819, CRL, Church Missionary Society Archive, North India Mission, XCMS/B/OMS/I/C I1 E2/45.

regarding his authority over Company chaplains further compounded matters. In 1816 Simeon complained to Wilberforce about Middleton's high-handed 'usurpations', hoping that the return of Grant to the chairmanship of the EIC would put paid to this. 'The Bishop's remedy for all, is ... fine Churches, two more bishops three better paid chaplains. Mine would be pious ministers, good schools, and a *more spiritual* bishop, with the divine blessing.'[110]

Yet Evangelicals, too, could be wary about ecumenism. The new mania for missions took time to catch on among gospel clergymen accustomed to teetering on the tightrope of ecclesiastical regularity. The adoption of local CMS associations from 1813 onwards certainly filled the society's coffers, but some thought that this smacked of LMS or BFBS irregularities.[111] Similarly, fundraising tours initially evoked comparisons with Methodist itinerancy. Opening his pulpit on a weekday, insisted John Scott (1777–1834) of Hull, 'would be very distasteful to church folk and give the whole affair an irregular and unchurchlike appearance.'[112] Basil Woodd of Bentinck Chapel, Marylebone, echoed him. 'I do not see the expediency of sending ministers from London to Yorkshire,' he declared. 'It has an aspect of publicity which I do not like. I am willing to succour the cause in my own little sphere, but do not ask me to take long journeys.'[113] Eventually Woodd relented and, on 21 July 1813, set out with his wife for the North by postchaise, resolved to preach twice a day if pulpits could be found for him.[114] The trip's financial success made missionary tours a central plank of CMS policy. One of the main perpetrators was Pratt. 'Remember that I am not only the *Sedentary Secretary* of the Society, but the *Travelling Preacher*, and everywhere I find the hearts of our English Christians open towards India,' he informed a friend with glee.[115] 'I am just returned from a most successful Missionary tour,' he remarked elsewhere, 'Bristol (as you know), £800; Manchester, £700; Staffordshire, £250; Derbyshire, not yet known.'[116] Booming receipts encouraged Pratt and his colleagues to paint on broader and broader canvases. 'It is a peculiar glory of institutions like ours, that they connect every one of their members with the whole race of their

---

[110] Simeon to Wilberforce, 18 Nov. 1816, Bodl., MSS Wilberforce, c.3, fo. 154.
[111] For an exhaustive account, see Hole, *Church Missionary Society*, 251–64, 274–96, 306–60.
[112] Eugene Stock, *The History of the Church Missionary Society*, 4 vols (London, 1899–1916), I: 134.
[113] *Ibid.*, 132.
[114] Hole, *Church Missionary Society*, 294.
[115] Pratt, *Josiah Pratt*, 79–80.
[116] *Ibid.*, 128.

fellow-men,' Pratt enthused. 'They are drawn out, by these contributions, beyond the little circle of their own interests and concerns; and begin to understand and to appreciate the high honour of being allowed to take a share in the chief work of mercy – the SALVATION OF THE WORLD.'[117] Only now, argued Daniel Wilson, was Britain awakening to her destiny: to fulfil the Great Commission by spreading the Gospel to all nations.[118] This was certainly true of the Evangelical clergy.

There were still efforts among churchmen to maintain the united front that had secured the passage of the 'Pious Clause'. In the face of the lurid pictures painted in missionary periodicals of the rituals of *sati*, the notorious *thuggees* and the suicidal devotees at Juggernaut, perhaps even the most unbending High Churchman and the most one-eyed gospel clergyman might agree that theirs was a common aim. Little came, however, of a scheme for union between the CMS and SPG drawn up by Reginald Heber, a member of both societies who later succeeded Middleton as Bishop of Calcutta.[119] It took Archdeacon Thomas's overinflated claims on behalf of the SPG at Bath in late 1817 to prompt efforts to rejuvenate it. Significantly, though, these came from all sides. Joshua Watson helped to secure a King's Letter requiring all clergymen to preach in its favour in 1819.[120] The SPG was also puffed by Josiah Pratt, Secretary of the CMS between 1802 and 1824, and a powerful and ubiquitous figure in metropolitan committee rooms. Through his *Missionary Register*, begun in January 1813, Pratt had taken upon himself the task of assembling bulletins from all missionary concerns, including the SPCK, into one periodical. Now he sought to apply Evangelical-style publicity to the SPG, detailing its history and activities in a book published anonymously so as not to scare people off.[121] 'True, numbers will make this a reason for not aiding [the CMS];' he reflected, 'but they will be made to aid that Cause which is dearer, we trust to all our hearts, than any consideration respecting ourselves.'[122] The organization of SPG parochial and district committees in the 1820s resulted in a marked rise in its voluntary income.[123] Also in 1819, the Colonial Service Act was passed, allowing candidates to be ordained direct to the mission

[117] *Ibid.*, 138.

[118] Wilson, *Defence*, 3–10.

[119] Heber, *Reginald Heber*, I: 492–8.

[120] Edward Churton, *Memoir of Joshua Watson* (2nd edn: London, 1863), 96–106. See also the sources cited in Bob Tennant, *Corporate Holiness: Pulpit Preaching and the Church of England Missionary Societies, 1760–1870* (Oxford, 2013), 169–72.

[121] [Josiah Pratt], *Propaganda: Being an Abstract of the Designs and Proceedings of the Incorporated Society for Propagating the Gospel in Foreign Parts* (London, 1819).

[122] Josiah and John Henry Pratt, *Memoir of the Rev. Josiah Pratt* (London, 1849), 154.

[123] Tennant, *Corporate Holiness*, 123–4.

field. Matching grants of £5,000 apiece from the SPCK, SPG, CMS and BFBS were advanced for what became Bishop's College, Calcutta. Appropriately enough, Ryder was asked to preach the 1819 SPG anniversary sermon. This pooling of resources galvanized other projects, too. When the wealthy clergyman Lewis Way (1772–1840) effectively bought dissenters out of the London Society for Promoting Christianity Amongst the Jews in 1815, for instance, it was done with an eye to attracting support from reticent churchmen; likewise the formal division of the RTS between the Church and dissent along BFBS lines.[124] The Church Building Society, founded in 1818, was the outcome of many years of planning on the part of the Earl of Harrowby (1762–1847) and Nicholas Vansittart, in coalition with Christopher Wordsworth and Joshua Watson, and it pulled in a range of friends of the Church, including Wilberforce.[125]

The late 1810s thus represents an important if confused period in the development of parties within the Church of England. On many issues there was little difference between Evangelicals and the Orthodox. Patriotic-providential rhetoric was not the preserve of any group. If Evangelicals were quicker to project a global vision that transcended national boundaries, and bought more readily into voluntary activity and fundraising, the older societies, too, were coming to appreciate the importance of cultivating an engaged missionary public. Yet it was only later, with the establishment of the Colonial Bishoprics' Fund in 1841, that they came to conjoin this decisively with their cherished aim of expanding the Church of England overseas. For the time being, most churchmen sought government support for church establishments in the settler colonies: a slow-moving process, but one that accorded with Anglican missionary ideas as they had developed over many years, and which only began to crumble with the withdrawal of the government's annual grant to the SPG in 1832.[126] Co-operation did not, then, entirely subsume methodological differences. Indeed, in trying to shame the SPG and SPCK into moving more quickly, Evangelicals probably perpetuated the partisanship they purported to deplore. 'What shall we *think* of a body of men', asked Richard Warner of Bath (1763–1857), 'who, though inhabitants of the building themselves,

---

[124] Martin, *Evangelicals United*, 187–8, 153.

[125] M.H. Port, *Six Hundred New Churches* (London, 1961), 6–19; Wilberforce, *Life*, IV: 368. Others involved included R.H. Inglis and Sir Thomas Dyke Acland, both associates of the Saints. Acland married Lydia, daughter of the pious banker Henry Hoare.

[126] See Brian Stanley, 'Anglican Missionary Societies and Agencies in the Nineteenth Century', in Rowan Strong (ed.), *The Oxford History of Anglicanism, Volume III: Partisan Anglicanism and its Global Expansion, 1829–c. 1914* (Oxford, 2017), 116–40; Tennant, *Corporate Holiness*, 211–12.

are loudly and perpetually crying out on the irregularity of some, and the inutility of other, of its departments?'[127]

Friends in High Places?

The foundation of the Isle of Thanet Auxiliary Bible Society in October 1821 symbolized everything that critics of the BFBS loathed. The Cobb family who played a leading part in it were prominent Margate bankers and merchants who mixed anti-slavery agitation with pan-denominational activism, attending the Baptists, the Countess of Huntingdon's Connexion or Holy Trinity, the 'new Church' which they had helped to found, as they chose.[128] Imagine then the consternation of Henry Handley Norris when he read, first in the *Morning Herald* and then placarded around Borough, a speech given in Margate by the Prime Minister, the Earl of Liverpool, explaining why he had agreed to become President of the Thanet Auxiliary.[129] The Bible Society, explained the noble Lord, was 'in perfect accordance with my principles'. While he was a member of the SPCK and a sincere churchman, he also supported the spread of Protestant Christianity more generally, both at home and in Catholic Ireland: 'shall we withhold the Scriptures because *all* will not receive the Prayer Book with them?' Britons owed a duty to God arising out of their overseas possessions, and for this reason too, he pointed out, the BFBS ought to be supported by all genuine patriots. Norris's fury was understandable: he thought Liverpool's words were being used to justify aggression against the SPCK, and his *Respectful Letter to the Earl of Liverpool* sparked a lively spat.[130] In truth, there was nothing surprising about it: Liverpool had been President of the Cinque Ports Auxiliary since 1812 and a national vice-president since 1815–16, and had expressed himself before in similar terms.[131] Partisan distinctions often

---

[127] Richard Warner, *A Letter to the Hon. and Rt. Rev. Henry Ryder ... on the Admission to Holy Orders of Young Men Holding (What are Commonly Called) Evangelical Principles* (Bath, 1818), 6.

[128] Toby Ovenden, 'The Cobbs of Margate: Evangelicalism and Anti-Slavery in the Isle of Thanet, 1787–1834', *Archaeologia Cantiana*, 133 (2013), 15–19.

[129] Reproduced in *A Respectful Letter to the Earl of Liverpool, Occasioned by the Speech Imputed to his Lordship at the Isle of Thanet Bible Society Meeting* (2nd edn: London, 1823), xxxii.

[130] See 'Warwickshire Bible Society Meeting', *Christian Remembrancer*, 3 (1821), 743–53.

[131] 'Cinque Ports Auxiliary Bible Society', *Christian Observer*, 11 (1812), 746; *Ibid.*, 14 (1815), 840. Liverpool succeeded Pitt as Lord Warden of the Cinque Ports, serving from 1806 until 1827.

made more sense to the clergy than they did to the laity. Instead of seeing Liverpool as 'at heart ... a liberal evangelical', as Norman Gash did, we can place him among the many friends to established order who willingly invested in Evangelical societies, seeing in their flexibility a pragmatic solution to pressing ills.[132] Yet this episode also serves to highlight a problem that confronted Evangelicals with growing urgency. How was their success in attracting prominent lay supporters into their societies to be translated into ecclesiastical capital? In particular, how were they to access higher positions within the Church?

As we have seen, the informal networks of earlier years had evolved into a set of powerful metropolitan pressure-group organizations that raised and spent tens of thousands of pounds a year. Their interlocking bureaucracies, connected with local associations in the provinces and, increasingly, the colonies, gave the movement a reassuringly solid institutional and cultural framework. But without episcopal representation, the gospel clergy believed that they were still being treated as interlopers. And with some reason: their pursuit of lectureships and presentations to parish livings elicited fulminating allegations of simony and conspiracy against Church and constitution.[133] In the mid 1810s, the Evangelical leadership could only stand by as the Indian ecclesiastical establishment they had fought for was parcelled out among High Churchmen. Now, in the early 1820s, they faced crisis in Ireland, the growing prominence of 'Sectaries and Seceders' in the Hibernian Bible Society having prompted the public withdrawal of the Primate, Archbishop William Stuart (1755–1822) of Armagh, and the Archbishop of Dublin, Lord John Beresford (1773–1862), and a slew of denunciatory charges and circulars.[134] No wonder, Norris chortled, that they needed to buttress their 'shaken fabric' with a half-imagined Prime Ministerial endorsement.[135] Liverpool's cordial attachment to the established Church as Norris understood it, he pointed out, was demonstrated 'by the persons preferred, through your Lordship's intervention with his Majesty, to many of its most responsible offices'.[136] Liverpool, in short, preferred highish mainstream churchmen. As a key player in this process – dubbed by some 'the Bishop-maker' – Norris's smugness was palpable.[137]

---

[132] Norman Gash, *Lord Liverpool* (London, 1984), 201.

[133] See e.g. William Downes Willis, *Simony. A Sermon* (London, 1842).

[134] Norris, *Respectful Letter*, 4–7.

[135] *Ibid.*, 7.

[136] *Ibid.*, 9.

[137] Thomas Mozley, *Reminiscences: Chiefly of Oriel College and the Oxford Movement*, 2 vols (2nd edn: London, 1882), I: 338. Although William Gibson, 'The Tories and Church Patronage, 1812–1830' *Journal of Ecclesiastical History*, 41 (1990), 266–74,

Evangelical frustration with this state of affairs went back many years. During the 1780s and 90s Wilberforce's friendship with William Pitt seemed to offer a promising route towards prebends, deaneries and bishoprics. In 1788, for example, he asked unsuccessfully for the Mastership of Trinity College, Cambridge for his friend Isaac Milner, but in 1791 secured him the Deanery of Carlisle through Pitt's ecclesiastical patronage-broker, Bishop George Pretyman of Lincoln.[138] There, however, Milner stalled, notwithstanding repeated attempts by Wilberforce to have the Deanery of York set aside in anticipation of the death of its venerable incumbent, John Fountayne (1715–1802).[139] Even here, calculation played a part: 'Was Milner likely to live very long?' Wilberforce asked his physician, William Hey, in 1799. 'The Injury might be great to the Interest of Religion … from putting in a man whose Life in the Businesslike phrase, was worth only a few years purchase.'[140] As the 1790s progressed, Wilberforce's ever more public Evangelicalism clashed with a growing antipathy on the part of the Prime Minister. 'We spent some hours together at a tête-a-tête supper,' he wrote in 1800,

> and I confess I never till then knew how deep a prejudice his mind had conceived against the class of clergy to whom he knew me to be attached. It was in vain that I mentioned to him Mr. Robinson of Leicester, Mr. Richardson of York, Mr. Milner of Hull, Mr. Atkinson of Leeds, and others of similar principles; his language was such as to imply that he thought ill of their moral character, & it clearly appeared that the prejudice arose out of the confidence he reposed in the Bishop of Lincoln.[141]

There were some signal triumphs, not least when Wilberforce succeeded in having the learned Henry William Coulthurst appointed to St John the Baptist, Halifax in 1790, placing an enormous parish with fourteen sub-chapelries in Evangelical hands.[142] Yet Wilberforce's success there and

---

argues that William Howley and Charles James Blomfield (1786–1857) were Liverpool's primary advisors.

[138] Reider Payne, *Ecclesiastical Patronage in England, 1770–1801: a Study of Four Family and Political Networks* (Lewiston, ME, Queenston, ON, and Lampeter, 2010), 249–51, 255.

[139] Henry Addington to William Wilberforce, 24 Sep. 1801, Bodl., MSS Wilberforce, d.13, fo. 9.

[140] Wilberforce to William Hey, 27 July 1799, Bodl., MSS Wilberforce d. 15/2, fo. 168.

[141] Wilberforce, *Life*, II: 364.

[142] William Pitt to William Wilberforce, 26 Aug. [1790], Rubinstein Library, Duke University, Wilberforce Papers, Box 1, Folder 3.

in York probably represents the patronage due to a county MP rather than any unusual influence. He continued to badger Pitt about senior appointments. 'My dear P, let me intreat you, as I see another Bishop is dead, to consider well whom you appoint,' Wilberforce urged in 1797 regarding the vacant see of Chichester. 'I am persuaded that if the clergy can be brought to know and to do their duty, both the religious and civil state of this country would receive a principle of new life.'[143] Being unable to convince Pitt, however, he was reduced to private grumbling. The appointment of William Lort Mansel as Master of Trinity in 1798, he commented acidly to a friend, was, 'I must say, by no means such as I could approve.'[144]

Evangelical hopes reawakened in the early 1810s, coalescing around the Honourable Henry Ryder. Ryder was worlds away from the popular caricature of a gospel minister; indeed, when he was appointed to the livings of Lutterworth and Claybrook in Leicestershire in 1801, Ryder had held decidedly anti-Evangelical opinions. In the late 1800s growing respect for and then friendship with Thomas Robinson of Leicester encouraged a gradual change in his views. By 1811 Ryder had come out as an Evangelical, even being prepared to take the chair of the Leicester Auxiliary Bible Society. This notwithstanding, Ryder was well placed for promotion: his brother Dudley Ryder, Earl of Harrowby (1762–1847), was a school friend of the Prime Minister, Spencer Perceval, and sat in his cabinet, while another brother, Richard Ryder (1766–1832), was Home Secretary. Perceval seems to have favoured Ryder, although not necessarily for the reasons one might assume. For although he was personally and in some respects fiercely devout, Perceval was reluctant to align himself with any ecclesiastical faction, patronizing among others the High Churchman William Van Mildert (1765–1836).[145] The occasionally fractious independence of the Saints clearly frustrated him, and he was not close to the Wilberforce circle socially, despite living in Clapham.[146] Indeed, the notion that he was an Evangelical has been questioned.[147] The health of the Church of England was uppermost in his mind: on the question of dissenting missionary access to India he dragged his feet, while his ministry was characterized

---

[143] William Wilberforce to William Pitt, 1 Aug. 1797, National Archives, William Pitt, first Earl of Chatham, PRO 30/8/189, fo. 175.

[144] William Wilberforce to Dr Frewen, 16 May 1798, Bodl., MSS Wilberforce, d.15/2, fo. 220.

[145] See Varley, *Last of the Prince Bishops*, 49–51.

[146] Dennis Gray, *Spencer Perceval: the Evangelical Prime Minister 1762–1812* (Manchester, 1963), 25–7, 202–6, 260–1.

[147] Edward Hicks, '"Christianity Personified": Perceval and Pittism' (unpublished D. Phil. thesis, University of Oxford, 2018).

by reforms to bolster the Church, including measures to reduce non-residence, to improve clerical stipends and to build new churches where they were needed.[148] This broad-based programme was set forth by a cabinet that contained devout Anglicans of a range of stripes – Liverpool, Vansittart, Sidmouth, the Ryders – and it emphasizes how the priorities of different brands of late-Hanoverian churchmanship often coincided. It was a vision with which Ryder's conscientious parochial ministry accorded well. He was made Dean of Wells in 1812. In 1814, however, he became the first dignitary to preach the annual CMS sermon, also preaching at the LSPCJ anniversary the same year: actions that pleased Evangelicals but attracted unfavourable commentary elsewhere.[149] Nevertheless, Perceval's assassination in May 1812 was seen as a blow to his prospects. 'Alas, I fear that Mr. Henry Ryder's being a Bishop, as humanly speaking he soon would have been, will be prevented,' lamented Wilberforce.[150] Chester went to Law in August, and London to Howley in 1813. Vital religionists watched with bated breath. 'God grant that the Dean of Wells may be the new bishop,' fretted Budd, 'though it is said there is great opposition made to his appointment.'[151] 'The Dean of Wells (very probably near the bench) preaches our next Anniversary Sermon. Only give us time,' Pratt wrote tersely.[152]

Prominent among the obstacles to Ryder's elevation was the question of his 'Calvinism', a derogatory term fired at Evangelicals as a matter of course. One admittedly sympathetic reviewer noted in 1812 that 'Calvinist' had replaced 'Methodist' as the term of general abuse for 'any clergyman, nay any layman, who appears more anxious than his neighbour on the subject of religion'.[153] Those who unchurched Calvinists, he added, were descending to the level of their supposedly sectarian targets.[154] Yet if 'Calvinist' was an inaccurate label, it was effective as a boo-word. It conjured up unpleasant memories of the Commonwealth and regicide republicanism, and of foreign influences that loyal churchmen had long stigmatized. It was also a satisfyingly abusive shorthand for doctrines that Evangelicals undoubtedly *did* hold: justification by faith alone, a strong awareness of Original Sin and the New Birth. For Evangelicals these doctrines were validated both by their

---

[148] Stewart J. Brown, *The National Churches of England, Ireland, and Scotland, 1801–1846* (Oxford, 2001), 64–7.

[149] Ryder, 'Charge', ed. Smith, 57–8.

[150] Diary, 16 May 1812, cited in Wilberforce, *Life*, IV: 27. The date of this entry is, however, suspect: see Ryder, 'Charge', ed. Smith, 58.

[151] Henry Budd to C.J. Bird, 26 Jun. 1815, cited in Budd, *Memoir*, 8–9.

[152] Pratts, *Josiah Pratt*, 85.

[153] 'Bishop of Lincoln on Calvinism', *British Review*, 3 (1812), 244.

[154] *Ibid.*, 235.

own experiences and the formularies. For their opponents such notions were 'enthusiastic', producing divisions within congregations between the elect and the unregenerate that destroyed social harmony. Herein lay the grounds of Pitt's aversion to the gospel clergy, and the probable reason behind Milner's failure to advance further than Carlisle.[155] Thus, although Ryder was a convinced Arminian, he still felt the need to rebut the charge, turning the notes that accompanied his published commemorative sermon on Robinson into a commentary on the soteriological differences between him and his friend.[156] 'I never did preach the Calvinistic doctrines,' he reassured his brother, pointing to the many impeccable authorities who saw the Articles as accommodating both traditions.[157] Harrowby seems at this point to have been instrumental in pushing his younger brother's appointment: 'if Dr. Ryder is not fit to be a bishop,' he threatened the House of Lords, 'Lord Harrowby is not fit to be Lord President of the Council.'[158] Despite carping from several members of the bench, including the Archbishop of Canterbury, Liverpool made Ryder Bishop of Gloucester in August 1815.[159]

By the early 1820s, when Norris broadcast his opinions on the matter, Evangelical spokesmen were beginning to argue that their numerical strength warranted further representation. Indeed, the impression that they were being frozen out became for some an obsession. The ambitious Vicar of Harrow, J.W. Cunningham, repeatedly pestered Harrowby to inform the Prime Minister that he was an Arminian, refusing the Secretaryship of the BFBS for fear of being considered a '*party man*' and 'incurring the displeasure of Lord Liverpool.'[160] Yet the stigma of Calvinism proved difficult to shift, notwithstanding withering attacks by the *Christian Observer* and its allies on high predestinarians.[161] The subject certainly weighed

---

[155] Milner defended the doctrine of justification by faith alone for his B.D. degree in 1786. See Mary Milner, *The Life of Isaac Milner* (London, 1842), 31–2.

[156] Henry Ryder, *A Sermon Preached for the Benefit of St Mary's School, in Leicester* (Lutterworth, 1813).

[157] Henry Ryder to Earl Harrowby, n.d., 1815; n.d., 1815, Harrowby MSS, v, fos. 124–6, 127–9.

[158] G.C.B. Davies, *First Evangelical Bishop: Some Aspects of the Life of Henry Ryder* (London, 1958), 8.

[159] For a detailed account of the issues surrounding Ryder's appointment, see Ryder, 'Charge', ed. Smith, 57–62.

[160] J.W. Cunningham to Earl Harrowby, 16 Jul. 1822, Harrowby MSS, 2nd ser., vol. 40, Supplementary Volume, xl, fos. 14–16; J.W. Cunningham to Earl Harrowby, 14 Dec. 1822, Harrowby MSS, 1st ser., vol. 40, General Correspondence, xiv, fos. 213–16.

[161] See e.g. 'Review of Scott's Articles of the Synod of Dort', *Christian Observer*, 18 (1819), 797; 'Review of Chalmers's Civic Economy – Nos. V and VI', *Ibid.*, 20 (1821), 711; 'Review of the Life of the Rev. Thomas Scott', *Ibid.*, 21 (1822), 655; 'Review of

heavily with Wilberforce, who bombarded the long-suffering Liverpool with letters about it. Although the Premier supported the BFBS, Wilberforce complained, 'all your preferment has been given to its Enemies, nay to those who have been its most notorious and bitter opponents'.[162] Liverpool's response was revealing. 'I own to you I have a great horror of the doctrines of Calvinism,' he wrote, adding that while he recognized the 'amiable and virtuous' qualities of predestinarians past and present, he considered this to be unrelated to their pernicious beliefs. 'If I have not been instrumental in promoting one particular class of clergy,' Liverpool declared, 'it has been from a sincere opinion that their opinions are erroneous.'[163] In reply Wilberforce sought to clarify what Calvinism really was: 'I myself am no Calvinist, because my religion opinions have long been before the World, and they certainly are much less Calvinistic than the Articles of the Church of England, as explained by Bishop Burnet, who I dare say you know was no Calvinist either.'[164] Some of the greatest Anglican divines, men such as James Ussher (1581–1656), Richard Hooker (1554–1600) and Robert Leighton (bap. 1612, d. 1684), had held reformed convictions. Gospel clergymen, he went on, stood in the same tradition, but upheld it 'in a far more relaxed and even doubtful way, than their predecessors of a former Generation'. Several, including Ryder ('a strong anti-Calvinist'), in fact opposed predestinarianism. In London, 'moderate Calvinists' such as Gerard Noel (1782–1851) at Percy Chapel, 'Dr Jenyns', i.e. Philip Jennings (c. 1783–1849) of Welbeck, Daniel Wilson of St John's, Bedford Row and Basil Woodd of Bentinck were men whose exemplary lives, he maintained, were well known.[165] In many respects Wilberforce was arguing past the Prime Minister, whose definition of 'Calvinists' revolved more around the potential effects of their perceived separatism than their soteriology. Why favour self-proclaimed 'Evangelicals', Liverpool wearily asked a friend, as though

---

Cottle's Strictures on Antinomianism', *Ibid.*, 22 (1823), 709–28; 'Review of the Life and Times of Arminius and Bishop Hall', *Ibid.*, 26 (1827), 628, 695.

[162] William Wilberforce to 2nd Earl of Liverpool, 16 Sep. 1820, Liverpool Papers, BL Add. MS 38191, fo. 274.

[163] Lord Liverpool to anon., 26 Sep. 1820, Liverpool Papers, BL Add. MS 38287, fos. 272–8. Best considers this to have been addressed to Wilberforce. Best, 'Evangelicals and the Established Church', 74–5.

[164] William Wilberforce to 2nd Earl of Liverpool, 30 Sep. 1820, Liverpool Papers, BL Add. MS 38191, fo. 280. Gilbert Burnet (1643–1715) had argued influentially in his *Exposition of the Thirty Nine Articles* (1699) that they could be held in a non-predestinarian sense.

[165] William Wilberforce to 2nd Earl of Liverpool, 30 Sep. 1820, Liverpool Papers, BL Add. MS 38191, fo. 280.

they deserved different treatment from those who performed their clerical duty without ostentation?[166]

Turbulence in the Evangelical world in the early 1820s did little to reassure their Anglican critics. Debates about the Apocrypha wracked the BFBS, while the rise of angry firebrands such as the Scottish Presbyterian Edward Irving (1792–1834) and the Baptist Robert Haldane (1764–1842), proclaiming hard-edged Calvinism, high doctrines of scriptural inspiration, a disdain for human 'means' and the imminent end of the world, marked a sharp challenge to the pragmatism of the older generation. Cracks in pan-evangelical unity, however, also opened up fresh prospects of cross-partisan rapprochement. 'A moderate spirit is growing up, both in High Churchmen, and the better kind of evangelicals,' rejoiced Bishop Jebb (1775–1833) of Limerick in 1826. 'There is a wish that there should be a coalition, between the sane and safe part of the Bible Society, and that for promoting Christian Knowledge.'[167] Suspicion of nonconformist and Catholic campaigns for emancipation represented further shared ground. Yet even cultured and urbane moderates could still be regarded with suspicion. The King would only accept Ryder's translation to Lichfield and Coventry in 1824 with the proviso that this preferment should be his last, worrying that if his opinions infected his brother bishops this might be 'attended with great inconvenience to the State.'[168] It was thus significant that the next two Evangelical bishops, the brothers John Bird and Charles Richard Sumner, only identified themselves as such in the years after they were consecrated. Distant cousins of William Wilberforce, both attended Eton and Cambridge, John (1780–1862) going to King's College, where he became a fellow, before returning to Eton as a master, and Charles (1790–1874) to Trinity. There is no firm evidence that either of them at this stage held Evangelical views: his biographer's assumption that John came under the influence of Simeon at Cambridge is no more than guesswork,[169] while the book that made his name, *Apostolical Preaching Considered* (1815), was markedly anti-Calvinistic, being sufficiently unevangelical on the question

---

[166] Lord Liverpool to anon., 19 Mar. 1821, Liverpool Papers, BL Add. MS 38289, fo. 117. Gibson reckons this letter to have been addressed to the Bishop of Bristol, John Kaye (1783–1853), whereas Payne argues for Howley. William Gibson, 'The Tories and Church Patronage', 269; Payne, *Ecclesiastical Patronage*, 265n.

[167] Charles Forster (ed.), *Thirty Years' Correspondence Between John Jebb ... and Alexander Knox*, 2 vols (2nd edn: London, 1836), 546.

[168] A. Aspinall (ed.), *The Diary of Henry Hobhouse* (London, 1947), 32–3.

[169] The references given in Nigel Scotland, *John Bird Sumner: Evangelical Archbishop* (Leominster, 1995), 5–8, do not bear out the assertion that he left university 'a convinced Simeonite'.

of baptism that it helped to move John Henry Newman (1801–1890) away from his youthful creed.[170] In temperament, too, the mild-mannered Sumner was not a party man; and it seems likely that it was this, combined with his writings and his dedicated pastoral ministry around Windsor and later in his parish at Mapledurham, that recommended him to Barrington, who made him a prebendary of Durham in 1820.[171]

Charles's career, on the other hand, exemplifies Cowper's observation: 'Church ladders are not always mounted best / By learned clerks and Latinists professed … The Parson knows enough who knows a Duke.'[172] His first steps up that ladder were taken when he accompanied two sons of the Marquess Conyngham (1766–1832) on a tour of the Continent. It was through the Conyngham interest that Sumner became curate of Highclere, Hampshire; and it was through them, too, that he was introduced to George IV at Brighton in 1820: Elizabeth, Marchioness Conyngham (1769–1861), was in the process of becoming the King's latest and last mistress. Having made a favourable impression on the King, Sumner's rise thereafter was nothing short of meteoric. In 1821 he was made historiographer to the crown, chaplain to the household at Carlton House and librarian to the king, as well as private chaplain at Windsor, with £300 a year 'and a capital house … opposite the park gate', becoming chaplain-in-ordinary in January 1823 and deputy clerk of the closet in March 1824.[173] In September 1821 he became Vicar of St Helen's, Abingdon, then in March the next year Canon of Worcester and in 1825 Canon of Canterbury. In January 1824 he was offered the newly created bishopric of Jamaica, but the King refused to sanction his leaving England. In July 1825 Sumner received a Cambridge doctorate in divinity by royal command. 'Mr. Sumner by this time must have been accustomed to receive letters and dispatches on the subject of preferment', remarks his biographer drily.[174] By 1826 he was Bishop of Llandaff and only eighteenth months later he was moved to richer pickings at Winchester, also becoming Prelate of the Order of the Garter. He was still only thirty-seven. Hints about his churchmanship at this stage are difficult to glean. Liverpool successfully opposed his appointment as Canon of Windsor in 1821, but it seems probable that this was on the grounds of Sumner's inexperience or the discredit that might

---

[170]   See Gareth Atkins, 'Evangelicals', in Frederick D. Aquino and Benjamin J. King (eds), *The Oxford Handbook of John Henry Newman* (Oxford, 2018), 182–4.

[171]   Scotland, *Sumner*, 31.

[172]   The quotation is from 'Tirocinium: or, a Review of Schools' (1784). Robert Southey (ed.), *The Works of William Cowper*, 8 vols (London, 1854), VI: 174.

[173]   G.H. Sumner, *Life of Charles Richard Sumner* (London, 1876), 62.

[174]   *Ibid.*, 85–6.

accrue to the Church from his connection with Lady Conyngham. The Bishop of Oxford, Charles Lloyd (1784–1829), was certainly unimpressed, damning his new colleague as 'neither with or without learning, neither with or without ability'. 'He is unexceptionable as a moral man', he wrote, 'and a bit of a Methodist, and will, consequently, have the support of all the Evangelical party in England.'[175] It was an accurate prediction: Ryder wrote immediately to congratulate him, while in 1828 Sumner preached the CMS annual sermon, thus allying himself with the Evangelical wing of the Church.[176] His brother was hailed by the King only slightly less enthusiastically as 'that excellent man Dr Sumner': he declined Sodor and Man in 1827 but was elevated to Chester in 1828.[177]

More work is needed on the ecclesiastical landscape of the 1820s and 30s and on the place of middle-men like the Sumners in it. Partisan positions took time to develop, and they were cut across by personal relationships, patronage and educational ties. In most respects the gap between church and dissent remained wider than gaps between ecclesiastical parties, although, as Frances Knight points out, conflicts that would have been unimaginable in earlier decades signalled that faultlines were becoming more firmly drawn.[178] Yet party positioning did not determine behaviour. The Sumners were unusual among English bishops in becoming vice-presidents of the Bible Society, but they were not unique. While Bishop Van Mildert of Durham could regard even the mild John Bird Sumner as an accessory in a 'smooth and plausible and undermining confederacy' to undermine the Church, plenty of others then and since would place the Sumners alongside reforming contemporaries like Howley and Kaye in their concern for church extension and education.[179]

What is beyond doubt is that episcopal representation opened avenues for preferment.[180] At Gloucester, Ryder appointed John Kempthorne (1775–1838) to be his Examining Chaplain, as well as collating gospel clergymen to

[175] Charles Lloyd to Robert Peel, 28 Dec. 1827, Peel Papers, BL Add. MS 40343, fo. 96.

[176] Sumner, *Charles Richard Sumner*, 102–3, 141.

[177] George IV to George Canning, 6 May 1827, cited in A. Aspinall and E. Anthony Smith (eds), *English Historical Documents, Volume VIII: 1783–1832* (London, 1959), 182.

[178] Frances Knight, *The Nineteenth-Century Church and English Society* (Cambridge, 1995), 174–7.

[179] Van Mildert to Archdeacon Charles Thorp, 25 Jul. 1831, cited in Varley, *Last of the Prince Bishops*, 157. See Arthur Burns, *Diocesan Revival in the Church of England, c. 1800–1870* (Oxford, 1998).

[180] The episcopal bench nominated to some 12 per cent of parochial livings. See Peter Virgin, *The Church in an Age of Negligence: Ecclesiastical Structure and Problems of Church Reform, 1700–1840* (Cambridge, 1989), 173.

livings under his control and ordaining candidates for overseas missions.[181] On Ryder's translation to Lichfield in 1824, he appointed three serious clergyman to be the archdeacons of his rapidly urbanizing diocese: in 1827 Wilberforce's brother-in-law William Spooner (1778–1857) for Coventry, in 1828 Edward Bather (1779–1847) for Shropshire and in 1829 the former Magdalene fellow George Hodson (1788–1855) for Stafford.[182] Kempthorne became a Prebendary in 1825. When John Bird Sumner arrived at Chester in 1828, he summoned his Eton contemporary Henry Raikes (1782–1854) to become Examining Chaplain, making him Chancellor of the diocese in 1830. 'His society, as you will suppose, is a great comfort to me here, and a great advantage to the place,' Sumner told a friend.[183] The appointment to the deanery of the soporific but serious George Davys (1780–1864), tutor to the future Queen Victoria and later Bishop of Peterborough, took place in 1831. Sumner was also a hearty supporter of the Church Pastoral Aid Society (CPAS), which during his tenure supplied grants for thirty extra curates to serve in urban parishes.[184] At Winchester, Charles Sumner, too, packed the cathedral establishment with Evangelical talent. A.R.C. Dallas (1791–1869) and Philip Jacob (1803–1886) joined him initially as domestic chaplains; Charles James Hoare (1781–1865) became Archdeacon of Winchester in 1829 and Rural Dean of South-East Ewell in 1829, adding a canonry in 1831; Dealtry was appointed Chancellor in 1830; William Wilson (1783–1873) arrived as a canon in 1831; Gerard Thomas Noel was given a prebend in 1834.[185] Others reached higher preferment through different routes: Hugh Nicholas Pearson (1776–1856), another cultivated Cambridge man noticed by George IV, became first a royal domestic chaplain and then in 1823 Dean of Salisbury. Such appointments further cemented the Evangelical position, but they also set the seal on longer-term processes of party formation. As elder statesmen in the 1840s and 50s, these men clove to the establishment because they were convinced that its doctrines were sound. Yet they were now also becoming a distinct group within it: one whose

[181] Kempthorne to Simeon, 10 May 1813, Ridley Hall, Cambridge, Charles Simeon Papers.

[182] Davies, *First Evangelical Bishop*, 14.

[183] John Bird Sumner to Edward Hawke Locker, 27 Dec. 1832, Huntington Library, Edward Hawke Locker Papers, mssLR, fos 61–4.

[184] Scotland, Sumner, 52. See also 'Currer Bell' [Charlotte Brontë], *Shirley*, 3 vols (London, 1849), I: 1: 'of late years, an abundant shower of curates has fallen upon the north of England.'

[185] Desmond Bowen, 'A.R.C. Dallas: the Warrior Saint', in T. Phillips (ed.), *The View from the Pulpit* (Toronto, 1978), 17-44. Jacob married Sophia Noel, daughter of his colleague Gerald Thomas Noel.

conventions, emphases and career structure were beginning to mark it out as an establishment in its own right.

An Embarrassment of Riches?

Evangelicals in the 1820s knew well that the position they enjoyed was beyond the fondest imaginings of their forebears. By the end of the decade they could boast three English bishops and an Irish archbishop, Power Le Poer Trench of Tuam (1770–1839),[186] as well as a raft of cathedral appointees and senior clergymen. Through proprietary chapels and city lectureships they wielded weight in London, quite aside from the prosperous national societies also based there. Serious ministers appeared to be leavening the Anglican lump. 'We hear, for instance, in very few sermons, such notoriously unscriptural statements respecting the justification of a sinner before God, as were quite current fifty years ago,' noted the *Christian Observer* in 1829.[187] Yet acceptance did not always sit easily with those used to swimming against the tide. 'Evening lectures have now become common, and can no longer be accounted what they once were, a kind of discriminating test, both of principle and of ardour in religion,' mused Edward Vaughan (1772–1829).[188] For Charles Jerram, regret mixed with satisfaction in the observation that 'to be a member of the Church Missionary Society was long considered as a test of character'.[189]

Success undoubtedly pointed up tensions that had long been inherent in the Evangelical mindset. 'I am sorry to say, that worldly prudence, and the desire of making provision for families, not only for necessary things, but for gentility and affluence is, in my opinion, eating out the life of spirituality, and simple trust in the Lord, even among those who preach scriptural doctrine,' lamented Thomas Scott. 'The spirit of the commercial world, having long corroded the professors of the gospel, is now making havoc among ministers.'[190] Evangelicals were already beginning to show the yearning for an earlier, earthier generation that would become so noticeable in the later nineteenth century; that sense that while much had been gained, something

---

[186] J. D'A. Sirr, *Memoir of the Honourable and Most Reverend Power Le Poer Trench, Last Archbishop of Tuam* (Dublin, 1845).

[187] 'Review of Visitation Sermons', *Christian Observer*, 28 (1829), 774.

[188] Edward T. Vaughan, *Some Account of the Life, Ministry, Character, and Writings of the Late Rev. T. Robinson* (London, 1815), 101.

[189] James Jerram, *The Memoirs and a Selection from the Letters of the Late Reverend Charles Jerram* (London, 1855), 295.

[190] John Scott, *The Life of the Rev. Thomas Scott* (4th edn: London, 1822), 403.

had been lost in the process. Perversely, they admired those of their ancestors who had scorned place and position. 'I am endeavouring, my Lord, to gain preferment in another world, where no one fails who attempts it,' was how William Bromley Cadogan refused a would-be benefactor.[191] The newly graduated Henry Venn Elliott (1792–1865), by contrast, could resolve 'to read at Cambridge for his Fellowship; to take pupils; to spend his long vacations in choice country spots; and, besides enjoying the intimacy of his own family, to cultivate the society of such friends as Hannah More, the Wilberforces, the Hoares, and the Trevelyans.'[192] It was a far cry from the white heat of earlier years. And for younger, more radical figures it might have raised an unsettling thought: that those who had set out to ginger up the establishment were now indistinguishable from it.

---

[191] Richard Cecil, *Discourses of the Honourable and Reverend William Bromley Cadogan* (London, 1798), lxi.
[192] Josiah Bateman, *The Life of the Rev. Henry Venn Elliott* (London, 1868), 42.

Chapter Four

Forging an Evangelical Empire:
Sierra Leone and the Wider British World

In 1815 William Wilberforce exchanged letters with the Secretary of State for War and the Colonies, Earl Bathurst (1762–1834), on the subject of Ceylon. He was concerned that the Governor, Sir Robert Brownrigg (1759–1833), seemed to be obstructing Methodist missionaries. Had Brownrigg perhaps taken advice from 'some person who is indisposed to Xtianity'? Bathurst was anxious to placate his correspondent, forwarding a letter from Brownrigg which spoke highly of the missionaries in Ceylon and the Church of England chaplain there. Even so, Wilberforce came close to taking matters into his own hands. 'If Genl Brownrigg were not a man of very high connections,' he told the Wesleyan MP Joseph Butterworth, 'I should be tempted to endeavour to get him removed.'[1] Such episodes were fairly frequent in the post-war years, as governors obliged by treaty to protect the religious rights of new subjects in Malta, the Ionian Islands and Ceylon found themselves squeezed between proselytizing Evangelicals, local sensitivities and a Westminster government bent on retrenchment.[2] Bathurst was himself a staunch churchman and a convinced opponent of slavery, but was constantly pestered by Evangelicals who thought that he was not doing enough to help them. The most prominent was Wilberforce, who spoke for a number of campaigning groups. His position at the head of the increasingly powerful religious public described in the previous chapter meant that his word carried weight, most obviously in 1814–15, when a deluge of petitions forced the government to prioritize international abolition in the peace negotiations. Defying the Saints, Liverpool told Castlereagh and Wellington, would cause a storm 'very difficult to weather.'[3]

---

[1] Wilberforce to Butterworth, 28 Sep., 22 Nov. 1815; 20 Dec. 1816, Bodl., MSS Wilberforce, d.56, fos. 63, 64, 65.

[2] Thomas W. Gallant, *Experiencing Dominion: Culture, Identity, and Power in the British Mediterranean* (Notre Dame, IN, 2002), 175–209.

[3] Liverpool to Castlereagh; Liverpool to Wellington, 23 Sep. 1814, cited in Paul Michael Kielstra, *The Politics of Slave Trade Suppression in Britain and France, 1814–48*

Yet to view Evangelicals as amateurs or outsiders is misleading. Between the late 1780s and the 1820s imperial expansion in West Africa, New South Wales, New Zealand, Cape Colony and India allowed them to expand their reach abroad, giving them influence over not just appointments but policy too. That Wilberforce could consider cold-bloodedly wrecking Brownrigg's career underlines the strength of their position. 'It is the fashion to speak of Wilberforce as a gentle, yielding character,' grumbled one Colonial Office official years later, 'but I can only say that he is the most obstinate, impracticable fellow with whom I ever had to do.'[4] None of this should come as any surprise. As C.A. Bayly observed, 'Britain's new imperial age' – the generation or so following the loss of America – was infused with 'Anglican providentialism', professionalism and moral seriousness.[5] Evangelicals were not the only purveyors of such ideas, but they shaped them powerfully, especially in the golden years following slave trade abolition in 1807. They were also instrumental in establishing the institutions that promulgated them, such as Haileybury College and Fort William College, Calcutta, where 'British values' were drummed into generations of EIC servants.[6] Historians have given little sustained attention, however, to their penetration of imperial officialdom and the military. The Royal Navy will be the focus of Chapter 5, while the EIC will be dealt with in Chapter 6. This chapter will concentrate initially on Sierra Leone. For it was Sierra Leone that granted Wilberforce and his circle access to power, first as co-projectors of the 'Province of Freedom' founded in 1787; then as leading lights in the Sierra Leone Company, which emerged in 1790–1 from the wreckage of the earlier venture; and, finally, via the African Institution, which continued to shape policy and appointments even after Sierra Leone became a crown colony in 1808. It then broadens to consider colonial affairs more generally, suggesting that Evangelical strength in metropolitan institutions rested, to some extent, on their connections overseas. The stakes were therefore very high indeed.

Central to this story is the loss of America. The need to place convicts, loyalist refugees and to source naval supplies all prompted fresh initiatives, both from within government and from extra-governmental interest groups. The 'new' empire provided Evangelicals with some of their most

(London, 2000), 47.

4   Wilberforce, *Life*, V: 243.

5   C.A. Bayly, *Imperial Meridian: the British Empire and the World, 1780–1830* (London, 1989), 133–63.

6   See this book, 224–6, 235–6.

promising openings.[7] This matters because although recent scholarship has rightly emphasized the growing centrality of missions and anti-slavery to middle-class identities in this period, such research has often downplayed the imbrication of voluntaristic activism with state action.[8] It has also been fashionable to downplay or dislike the role of Wilberforce and the Clapham Sect.[9] Yet it is impossible to consider either side of the equation without the other. Mass mobilization gave Evangelical parliamentarians one of their most powerful tools, while philanthropic organizations in turn leaned on friends in high places. Connections in naval administration, for instance, made for close co-operation between government and the London-based societies: from the late 1790s onwards, missionaries frequently travelled as non-paying passengers in His Majesty's ships.[10] This did not make them agents of the imperial state, as such.[11] But although nonconformists in particular often distanced themselves from political establishments, churchmen tended to take advantage of the openings provided by state employment. Military officers and chaplains, missionaries and merchants formed a flourishing web that gathered intelligence on a wide variety of subjects. Knowledge was power, and it was circulated between pious politicians, clergymen and missionary strategists, to be deployed as currency in dealings with government or other establishment figures. In a world in which interest groups and institutions vied for ministerial attention,

[7]   Emma Christopher, 'The Slave Trade is Merciful Compared to [This]', in Christopher, Cassandra Pybus and Marcus Rediker (eds), *Many Middle Passages: Forced Migration and the Making of the Modern World* (Oakland, CA, 2007), 109–28.

[8]   See, for example, David Brion Davis, *The Problem of Slavery in the Age of Revolution, 1770–1823* (Ithaca, NY, 1975); James Walvin, *The Abolition of the Atlantic Slave Trade: Origins and Effects in Europe, Africa and the Americas* (Madison, WI, 1981); David Turley, *The Culture of English Antislavery, 1780–1860* (London, 1991); J.R. Oldfield, *Popular Politics and British Anti-Slavery: the Mobilisation of Public Opinion Against the Slave Trade, 1787–1807* (Manchester, 1995); Judith Jennings, *The Business of Abolishing the British Slave Trade, 1783–1807* (London, 1997); Catherine Hall, *Civilising Subjects: Metropole and Colony in the English Imagination, 1830–1867* (Chicago, IL, 2002).

[9]   Christopher Leslie Brown, *Moral Capital: Foundations of British Abolitionism* (Chapel Hill, NC, 2006), 379–80.

[10] See this book, 190-1, 205.

[11] Revisionists have tended to argue that they had their own agenda that often cut against those of imperial authorities. See Brian Stanley, *The Bible and the Flag: Protestant Missions and British Imperialism* (Leicester, 1990); Andrew Porter, *Religion versus Empire? British Protestant Missionaries and Overseas Expansion, 1700–1914* (Manchester, 2004); Norman Etherington (ed.), *Missions and Empire* (Oxford, 2005).

influence and commercial contracts, Evangelical networking and expertise helped to ensure that they would be heeded by those who mattered.[12]

All this has important consequences for how we see Sierra Leone. The endeavours of the Clapham Evangelicals to use it as a proving ground for the superiority of free labour over slave production have attracted considerable attention.[13] So too, more lately, have the serious shortcomings of their management of it, ranging from racial condescension to political repression and profiteering.[14] This chapter does not dismiss these judgements, but it echoes Richard Huzzey's call to decouple our idea of anti-slavery 'from anachronistic expectations of antiracism, anticolonialism, or humanitarianism'.[15] It suggests, in short, that Evangelicals had both their own vision and the leverage to pursue it. Sierra Leone was intended to be a blueprint for the more intensely Christian empire they wanted to build: a symbiosis of moral government, mission, civilization and commerce. Hence the energy they expended on it; the changes of direction as they cast about for a workable formula; and the ruthlessness with which they stifled unrest in the colony and opposition at home. Whether or not we approve of their actions is beyond the remit of this chapter: the aim is to explain what they were trying to do. As we shall see, success was to be evaluated not in terms of enlightened government, economic success nor even in the price Britain was prepared to pay in men, ships and money to rescue 'recaptives' from the clutches of slave traders, important subsidiary aims though these were. It was to be measured in the forging of an Evangelical empire: in influence

[12] For this insight I am indebted to Zoe Laidlaw, *Colonial Connections, 1815–45: Patronage, the Information Revolution and Colonial Government* (Manchester, 2005).

[13] Seymour Drescher, *The Mighty Experiment: Free Labour versus Slavery in British Emancipation* (New York, 2002), 88–105; Suzanne Schwarz, 'Commerce, Civilization and Christianity: the Development of the Sierra Leone Company', in David Richardson, Suzanne Schwarz and Anthony Tibbles (eds), *Liverpool and Transatlantic Slavery* (Liverpool, 2007), 252–76; Paul E. Lovejoy and Suzanne Schwarz (eds), *Slavery, Abolition, and the Transition to Colonialism in Sierra Leone* (Trenton, NJ, 2015).

[14] Michael J. Turner, 'The Limits of Abolition: Government, Saints, and the "African Question", c. 1780–1820', *English Historical Review*, 112 (1997), 319–57; Simon Schama, *Rough Crossings: Britain, the Slaves and the American Revolution* (London, 2005), 255–383; Cassandra Pybus, *Epic Journeys of Freedom: Runaway Slaves of the American Revolution and their Global Quest for Liberty* (Boston, MA, 2006), 139–56, 169–202; Maeve Ryan, '"A Moral Millstone"?: British Humanitarian Governance and the Policy of Liberated African Apprenticeship, 1808–1848', Slavery and Abolition, 37 (2016), 399–422; Padraic Scanlan, *Freedom's Debtors: British Antislavery in Sierra Leone in the Age of Revolution* (New Haven, CT, 2017).

[15] Richard Huzzey, *Freedom Burning: Anti-Slavery and Empire in Victorian Britain* (Ithaca, NY, 2012), 19; see also Brown, *Moral Capital*, 355.

over appointments and policy at home and in infusing imperial discourse with a new moral energy. That the Saints succeeded can be seen in the support of Victorian governments for humanitarian and missionary endeavours, and perhaps above all in the purchase of anti-slavery as a 'hegemonic ideology': one whose hard-edged certainties undergirded the myth of Britain's moral superiority and drove the expansion of her dominion.[16]

Foundation and Early Years, 1787–92

The foundation of Sierra Leone took place almost by accident. It represented the confluence of several streams emerging from the moral crisis that attended defeat in America in 1783: intensifying antipathy towards slavery among Quakers and other radical and pacifist sects; the identification by Anglican Evangelicals of the slave trade as the great ill at the heart of empire; above all, perhaps, the visible plight of London's 'black poor', including freed loyalist slaves, many of whom had served in the British armed forces. One response was the formation of a Committee to Relieve the African Poor in 1786, led by the veteran philanthropist Jonas Hanway (1712–1786), a figure who well exemplifies how nascent Evangelical networks intersected with existing philanthropic circles in the reforming 1780s.[17] His fellow Russia merchants J.J. Angerstein and the Evangelical John Thornton both took up the cause.[18] Thornton seems to have drawn in Hannah More and her friends Sir Charles and Lady Margaret Middleton (d. 1792), hosts of the Evangelical circle that met at Barham Court in Teston, Kent, along with Henry Thornton and the angular anti-slavery campaigner Granville Sharp (1735–1813).[19] Soup kitchens and outdoor relief were not, however, a lasting solution, and the free blacks were not prepared to be passive objects of charity. In North America and London they lobbied hard

[16] See Huzzey, *Freedom Burning*.

[17] James Stephen Taylor, *Jonas Hanway, Founder of the Marine Society: Charity and Policy in Eighteenth-Century Britain* (London, 1985); Donna T. Andrew, *Philanthropy and Police: London Charity in the Eighteenth Century* (Princeton, NJ, 1989), 74–134. For a detailed recent analysis of overlapping philanthropic circles, see Roshan Allpress, 'Making Philanthropists: Entrepreneurs, Evangelicals, and the Growth of Philanthropy in the British World, 1756–1840' (unpublished D.Phil. thesis, University of Oxford, 2015), 162–71.

[18] Stephen J. Braidwood, *Black Poor and White Philanthropists: London's Blacks and the Foundation of the Sierra Leone Settlement, 1786–1791* (Liverpool, 1994), 64–5.

[19] For detail, some of it unreliable, see Prince Hoare, *Memoirs of Granville Sharp* (London, 1820), 257–379. For the Teston circle, see Brown, *Moral Capital*, 341–89.

to be recognized as British subjects.[20] Other black figures, such as the abolitionist writers Ottobah Cugoano (c. 1757–c. 1791) and Olaudah Equiano (c. 1745–1797), the latter an associate of the Teston Evangelicals, championed their cause.[21] This humanitarian upsurge helped to float the long-cherished scheme of the naturalist and adventurer Henry Smeathman (1742–1786) for a free labour settlement on the coast of West Africa, and it was taken up by Treasury officials.[22] The plan was eagerly supported by Sharp, whose reverence for Anglo-Saxon primitive democracy and the common-law tradition meant that he was less interested in profit than in designing public institutions from scratch along archaic lines. On the sudden death of Smeathman in spring 1786, however, Sharp shouldered sole administrative responsibility, and in April 1787 several hundred settlers were despatched under naval escort, bound for what he optimistically dubbed the 'Province of Freedom.'[23]

At this stage Wilberforce, Henry Thornton and the Testonites remained in the background, although their connections were useful. As Comptroller of the Navy, Middleton was instrumental in assembling the expedition, placing his Kentish neighbour Thomas Boulden Thompson (1766–1828) in command of its escort, HMS *Nautilus*, and almost certainly recommending Equiano as Commissary of Provisions and Stores.[24] An early high-water mark in Evangelical influence came in 1787, in that they also shaped the composition of the First Fleet to Botany Bay, which sailed only five weeks later. Its chaplain, Richard Johnson (1755–1827), was chosen by Wilberforce and John Newton, while Middleton's erstwhile shipboard surgeon and confidential secretary James Ramsay (1733–1789) appears to have selected the colony's medical establishment.[25] News from the 'Province of Freedom,'

---

[20] *Ibid.*, 259–330.

[21] Braidwood, *Black Poor*, 79.

[22] Brown, *Moral Capital*, 314–20.

[23] Granville Sharp, *A Short Sketch of Temporary Regulations (Until Better Shall be Proposed) for the Intended Settlement on the Grain Coast of Africa near Sierra Leone* (3rd edn: London, 1788).

[24] Olaudah Equiano, *The Interesting Narrative of the Life of Olaudah Equiano, or Gustavus Vassa, the African*, ed. Werner Sollors (New York and London, 2001), 171–5. Thompson's religion has never attracted much notice, but it may be significant that he was Middleton's neighbour in Kent, supported missions and married a daughter of the Sunday School pioneer Robert Raikes.

[25] John Newton to Middleton, 7 Dec. 1786, Bodl., MSS Wilberforce c.49, fo. 126; J. Watt, 'James Ramsay, 1733–89: Naval Surgeon, Naval Chaplain and Morning Star of the Anti-Slavery Movement', *Mariner's Mirror*, 81 (1995), 166. A key intermediary may have been the prominent Pittite civil servant and spymaster Evan Nepean, the

however, was almost unremittingly bad: illness, poor soil and the coun-ter-attractions of the slave trade crippled it even before the local Temne destroyed the main settlement in 1789. It was at this point that the Middle-ton–Wilberforce–Thornton axis stepped in to bail out the failing colony. Their intervention marked a change of emphasis. Being keen from the outset to interest respectable opinion in their cause, they shelved Sharp's eccentric vision in favour of a trading concern controlled from Britain. Pitt and the incoming Home Secretary, Henry Dundas (1742–1811), sup-ported the plan, and a bill incorporating a joint-stock company was pushed through parliament in the face of West Indian opposition, passing in June 1791.[26] The timing could not have been more opportune. During the late 1780s it was popular petitioning that had impressed politicians with the extent of public anti-slavery feeling. But in April 1791, against a backdrop of unrest in France and slave rebellion in Haiti, Wilberforce's first anti-slavery motion had been badly defeated. Sierra Leone offered the chance to dis-tance the cause from sentimental effusions and madcap radicalism. 'Our credit and Judgment is at stake,' counselled Middleton.[27]

Already this was, then, much more than the mere addition to the Claphamites' philanthropic portfolio that some accounts suggest.[28] Frenetic planning and negotiation occupied most of the energies of what remained a small group. Cryptic references to 'City – Sierra Leone' abound in Wilber-force's papers. 'I find that I can hardly keep an account of time,' he wearily remarked in December 1791. 'H. Thornton has been at it the whole day for some months.'[29] By October 1791 matters had advanced far enough to hold a public meeting at the King's Head Tavern in the Poultry, London.[30] Thornton was to be chairman, and twelve other directors were elected. Four were Evangelical abolitionists: Wilberforce, Middleton and the cam-paigner Thomas Clarkson (1760–1846), along with Sharp, now sidelined

---

colony's co-planner. He participated in many Evangelical projects, supporting mis-sionaries while Governor of Bombay in 1812–19.

26 Danby Pickering (ed.), *The Statutes at Large, from Magna Charta to the End of the Eleventh Parliament of Great Britain, Anno 1761 Continued*, 37 (1791), 367–8.

27 Middleton to Wilberforce, n.d., [1791], Duke University, Wilberforce Papers, Box 1, Folder 3.

28 E.g. E.M. Howse, *Saints in Politics: the 'Clapham Sect' and the Growth of Freedom* (London, 1953), 45–51; John Pollock, *Wilberforce: God's Statesman* (London, 2001), 109–16.

29 Diary, 15, 16 Dec. 1791, 10, 12 Jan. 1792, cited in Wilberforce, *Life*, I: 314–16, 322, 325–6, 334–6; II: 23.

30 *Substance of the Report of the Court of Directors of the Sierra Leone Company to the General Court held at London on Wednesday the 19th of October, 1791* (London, 1792), n.p.

given the gap between what his biographer delicately called his 'highly visionary' aims and the commercialism of the Company.[31] Six directors were London businessmen prominent in Evangelical philanthropy: Philip Sansom (d. 1815), Joseph Hardcastle, John Kingston (1736–1820), Samuel Parker (fl. 1780s–90s), William San(d)ford (?d. 1809) and John Vickris Taylor (probably 1748–1828). Bearing in mind the importance of the Quaker-dominated London Abolition Committee in anti-slavery campaigning, it is striking that only Taylor was a member of the Society of Friends: social and political respectability were evidently essential. The other two directors were the naval officer, colonial projector and abolitionist Admiral Sir George Young (1732–1810) and the Danish Consul-General George Wolff, a participant in many Evangelical endeavours.[32] Although the resemblance was superficial, it is significant that the procedures and language employed by the SLC – a 'Court of Directors' elected annually by the 'Court of Proprietors', among whom votes were apportioned according to stock holdings – resembled those of the EIC. Later the pomp and pageantry of the SLC's meetings would be derided. In 1791, however, its ambition seemed justified. Even before trade receipts, an agreed quit-rent of 2s. on each of the colony's 250,000 acres would guarantee an annual return of £12,500, while the directors confidently projected high profits from a market 'to the demands and extent of which it is difficult to assign a limit'.[33] The ninety-five original proprietors named in Thornton's act were joined by a plentiful stream of subscribers and the Company's proposed capital was rapidly augmented from £100,000 to £150,000. By the time subscriptions closed in June 1792, £235,280 had been raised.[34]

Anti-slavery colonization was an idea whose time seemed to have come. Entrepreneurs had long fantasized about a permanent settlement on the African coast, and SLC publications presented a beguiling picture in which profit and philanthropy went hand-in-hand.[35] There was no need to combat the slave trade: it would wither on the vine. Yet if the directors'

[31]   Prince Hoare, *Granville Sharp*, 364.
[32]   See Alan Frost, *Dreams of a Pacific Empire: Sir George Young's Proposal for a Colonization of New South Wales, 1784–5* (Sydney, 1980); Peder Borgen, 'George Wolff (1736–1828): Norwegian-born Merchant, Consul, Benevolent Methodist Layman, Close Friend of John Wesley', *Methodist History*, 40 (2001), 17–28.
[33]   *Postscript to the Report of the Court of Directors ... on Wednesday the 19th of October, 1791* (London, 1792), 4–5.
[34]   *Substance of the Report Delivered by the Court of Directors ... on Thursday 27th March 1794* (London, 1794), 30.
[35]   P.D. Curtin, *The Image of Africa: British Ideas and Action, 1780–1850*, 2 vols (Madison, WI, 1964), I: 121–286.

economic self-assurance was founded on Adam Smith's comments in *The Wealth of Nations* (1776) regarding the inefficiency of slave labour, they also insisted that involvement in the project was an ethical investment.[36] Granville Sharp's *Law of Retribution* (1776) made the parallel between Britain and Israel as godly nations, warning that failure to provide restitution for the wrongs suffered by the slaves would incur 'a severe *National Retribution*'.[37] Here was an opportunity both for individuals who felt for the wrongs of Africa to bind up her wounds and for Britain to atone for inflicting them. Such were the directors' convictions. But what of the proprietors? The two-stage system whereby putative subscribers were recommended by existing proprietors and then balloted was undoubtedly designed to prevent infiltration by West Indian sympathizers. The requirement that proprietors be 'well-affected to the objects of the Company' was, however, open to interpretation.[38] The anti-slavery movement brought Evangelicals together with some strange bedfellows – deists, radical democrats, Whig humanitarians – and it was inevitable that this should be reflected in the Company's composition. Periodically this posed problems, such as when 'one Man in the Garb of a Democrat' raged in an 1800 meeting against a proposed new Charter of Justice: '"He never could be accessory to the introduction of the complicated evils of English Law into a Colony founded with the express view of opposing truth and utility to every established institution."'[39]

Curiously, although a full subscription list for the SLC survives, historians have never made more than piecemeal use of it.[40] It serves to underline that here, as in so many other endeavours, Evangelicals co-ordinated a much wider set of interests. Its geographical reach is striking: the list includes prominent anti-slavery campaigners from across England and Scotland, including William Rathbone IV (1757–1809) and John Yates (1755–1826) in Liverpool, Thomas Walker (1749–1817) in Manchester and the Elfords in Plymouth. Luminaries who had co-ordinated the provincial petitioning of 1787–8 clearly also took up shares in 1791–2 in places such as York, Manchester, Northampton, Norwich, Chester, Derby, Shrewsbury, Reading

[36]   Roger Anstey, *The Atlantic Slave Trade and British Abolition, 1760–1810* (London, 1975), 117–18; Drescher, *Mighty Experiment*, 19–33.

[37]   Granville Sharp, *The Law of Retribution; or, a Serious Warning to Great Britain and her Colonies* (London, 1776), 3.

[38]   *Substance of the Report ... 1791*, 58–9.

[39]   Zachary Macaulay to Thomas Babington, 1 April 1800, Trinity College, Cambridge, Papers of the Babington Family of Rothley Temple, Trinity/BABINGTON, Box 26/26.

[40]   See C.B. Wadström, *An Essay on Colonization*, 2 vols (London, 1794–5), II: 341–53.

and Leeds, where Evangelical and abolitionist networks were strong.[41] The list also contains twenty-nine MPs. Some of these were known for their piety, but for the most part they were personal acquaintances or relations of the directors: Sir William Dolben (1727–1814), Henry Duncombe, William Smith and Samuel Whitbread were friends and fellow abolitionists; Gerard Noel Edwards, Edward Eliot, William Morton Pitt (1764–1836) and Dudley Ryder were members of the Pitt–Wilberforce circle; Robert and Samuel Smith and the Thorntons were all cousins. Close links can also be discerned between the four peers who volunteered support and the Company's leaders: Earl Spencer (1758–1834) and Viscount Garlies (1768–1834) were naval colleagues of Middleton; the Earl of Gainsborough (1743–1798) was Edwards's uncle; Lord Balgonie (1749–1820) was Thornton's brother-in-law.[42] The enlistment of family connections and political acquaintances, many of whom took up only one or two symbolic shares, was an important way of gaining cheap gravitas.

It should not be forgotten, though, that the Company was a genuine trading venture. Both in terms of numbers and financial commitment, the most significant investors were merchants and bankers. Shares were floated at £50, well within the means of the upper middle classes. Out of the 1,844 proprietors some 1,192 (65 per cent) gave a London address, significant numbers being based in the financial district around Lombard Street and the Bank of England, and at the General Post Office, EIC and Navy Office, all institutions where there was a strong Evangelical presence. Other addresses lay further east, and although occupational information is only available for a few, many were small-scale businessmen: merchants, coal factors, sugar refiners and the like. As befitted the chairman, Henry Thornton held the most shares (fifty-eight), but eighty-six others held ten or more, representing a sizeable outlay of £500 in each case. While some might have been attracted by hype about untapped African markets, the presence among this number of the directors Middleton, Hardcastle, Parker, Wilberforce and Wolff, as well as their serious acquaintances Samuel Hoare junior, William Hey and Joseph Reyner, Quakers such as Gamaliel Lloyd (1744–1817) and the abolitionists Josiah

---

[41]   See F.E. Sanderson, 'The Liverpool abolitionists', in Roger Anstey and P.E.H. Hair (eds), *Liverpool, the African Slave Trade and Abolition* (enlarged edn: Liverpool, 1989), 198–203, 206, 214, 216; Jennings, *Business*, 70, 82; Drescher, *Mighty experiment*, 93. For an overview of the petitioning campaign, see Oldfield, *Popular politics*, 96–154.

[42]   Henry Noel, 6th Earl of Gainsborough to Gerard Noel Edwards, 31 Jan. 1792, Record Office for Leicestershire, Leicester and Rutland, Records of the Noel Family, DE3214/45/4.

Wedgwood (1730–1795) and Samuel Whitbread, suggests that abolition-ist sentiment, often coupled with religious dissent and political radical-ism, was a deciding factor. Many smaller-scale proprietors were drawn from the pious metropolitan milieux explored in the previous chapter, including William Cardale, Henry Hoare, Ambrose Martin, the china manufacturer James Neale (c. 1740–1814), the insurance broker William Terrington (d. 1821) and the tea-broker Edward Venn (1752–1830).[43] In the industrializing areas of Lancashire and Yorkshire, too, the Company found a ready audience. While some, like the famed Preston-born inven-tor and cotton magnate Sir Richard Arkwright (1732–1792), may have speculated on the promise of cheap raw materials, we should be cautious about distinguishing between 'business' and 'philanthropy': Arkwright's partners were both members of the Manchester abolition committee and contributors to the LMS.[44] On the east coast, meanwhile, the Wilber-force–Thornton–Sykes conglomerate seems to have spread word about the Company. Thirty-nine Hull residents invested in it, chiefly Baltic traders, bankers and merchants, most of whom were also prominent in Wesleyan or Evangelical congregations.[45]

Clergymen took little part in the day-to-day running of the SLC, but they comprise one of the largest identifiable occupational groups on the subscription list, with 121 names. In most cases their investment was min-imal, but many compensated for this by their zeal. 'I contrived (by a sort of lyrical transition in my sermon)', boasted William Mason (1724–1797), Canon and Precentor of York Minster, 'not only to applaud the plan of the new colony of Sierra Leone, but also to exhort my audience to renew their petitions for the Abolition.'[46] Pro-Sierra Leone sentiment clearly stemmed from a variety of theological bases, and had as much to do with personal links as churchmanship. John Newton and Charles Simeon rubbed shoul-ders not only with the sympathetic mainstream churchmen Shute Barring-ton, Thomas Burgess and Beilby Porteus, but also with others who stood outside the bounds of orthodox belief, such as the Unitarians William Frend and William Smith. Wilberforce eagerly enlisted his Yorkshire friend and electoral agent Christopher Wyvill (1740–1822), a cleric of decidedly

---

[43] Charles Hole, *The Early History of the Church Missionary Society for Africa and the East* (London, 1896), 642–3.

[44] R.S. Fitton, *The Arkwrights: Spinners of Fortune* (Manchester, 1989), 215–6, 272–3.

[45] J.A.S.L. Leighton-Boyce, *Smiths the Bankers 1658–1958* (London, 1958), 213, 219–20; Gordon Jackson, *Hull in the Eighteenth Century: a Study in Economic and Social History* (London, 1972), 288–99.

[46] Mason to Thomas Gisborne, 29 Dec. 1791, Bodl., MSS Wilberforce, d.17, fo. 20.

latitudinarian views, to bang the drum in North Yorkshire, while his connections in the City of York also bore fruit.[47] Wilberforce's Cambridge tutor, William Cookson (1754–1820), took one share, while Archdeacon Joseph Plymley (1759–1838) of Shropshire, a close friend of Clarkson and another liberal-leaning clerical abolitionist, also invested.[48] Another supporter was the Master of Magdalene College, Cambridge, Peter Peckard, an 'earnest but rational' champion of universal benevolence. Although suspected of anti-Trinitarian views, Peckard was nevertheless closely linked to abolitionist circles, through the Evangelicals of his college and through his friendship with Equiano. Peckard preached some of the earliest Anglican sermons against slavery, probably coining the phrase 'Am I not a man and a brother?' in a 1788 pamphlet addressed to parliament, and set the prize essay that prompted Thomas Clarkson to take up the cause.[49] 'Through him', Peckard wrote, 'I took upon myself as in some degree a Promoter of the glorious attempt to set the slave at liberty.'[50]

From Company to Colony, 1792–1808

The early SLC was not, then, a narrow-minded concern. Civilization, commerce and Christianity provided a banner that most anti-slavery supporters could march under. Naturalists and geostrategic thinkers, too, took a keen interest: the Swedish botanist Adam Afzelius (1750–1837) travelled to Sierra Leone on the recommendation of Sir Joseph Banks (1743–1820).[51] Most importantly, the scheme could also claim the backing of the government, for which it was a solution to several nagging problems. Ministers expedited the Company's despatch of Lieutenant John Clarkson (1764–1828) of the Royal Navy to recruit settlers from among the black American

[47] Wilberforce to Wyvill, 8 Aug, 24 Aug, 3 Dec., 19 Dec. 1791; 18 Jan. 1792; Wyvill to Wilberforce, 18 Jan. 1792, North Yorkshire CRO, Northallerton, Wyvill of Constable Burton Papers, ZFW 7/74/12–17; Ellen Gibson Wilson, *Thomas Clarkson: a Biography* (London, 1989), 68.

[48] Douglas Grounds, *Son and Servant of Shropshire: the Life of Archdeacon Joseph (Plymley) Corbett* (Logaston, 2009), 45–6; Wilson, *Thomas Clarkson*, 41, 66–78.

[49] John Walsh and Ronald Hyam, 'Peter Peckard: Liberal Churchman and Anti-Slave Trade Campaigner', *Magdalene College Occasional Papers*, 16 (1998).

[50] Peter Peckard, *Justice and Mercy Recommended* (London, 1788), ix.

[51] Alexander Peter Kup, *Adam Afzelius: Sierra Leone Journal, 1795–1796* (Uppsala, 1967).

loyalists at Nova Scotia.[52] 'The Eyes of England are upon you and this Infant Colony,' enthused his brother, Thomas.

> No Establishment has made such a Noise as this in the Papers or been so generally admired ... To your lot it falls to be Governor of the Noblest Institution ever set on foot, an Institution which embraces no less than an Attempt to civilize and Christianize a great Continent, to bring it out of Darkness, and to abolish the Trade in Men.[53]

There seemed few limits to what the Company might achieve. It was only a matter of time, the directors believed, before the African Company, its Gold Coast forts and its £13,000 annual subsidy would be turned over into their hands. Proposals were already being advanced for a second settlement at Cape Mesurado (now in Liberia), while the expedition of Daniel Houghton (1740–1791) up the Gambia River to Timbuktu hinted at the possibility of trade with the interior. The anticipated profits might allow the directors to buy out the local slavers at nearby Bance Island, or even to purchase Gambia Island in order to block the French as well as the British traffic. Although these plans soon seemed laughably overambitious, they serve to underline the providential optimism that for the time being welded together an otherwise disparate anti-slavery movement.

The Company's momentum did not go unchecked, however. Pro-slavery interests at Westminster and in the City found government support for it hard to stomach, and they mounted a sustained campaign to blacken its reputation, insinuating that its humanitarian rhetoric masked commercial aims, playing up the religious extremism of its members and, most damagingly of all, suggesting that they might be unwitting patsies for a levelling Jacobin conspiracy. It was a tactic designed to lever open cracks in the broader abolition movement, as Evangelicals mostly moved to the right and others continued to champion political change amid growing anxiety about the spread of revolutionary principles from France.[54] Thomas Clarkson's appearance at a 1791 anniversary dinner commemorating the storming of the Bastille prompted an incredulous letter from Dundas to Wilberforce. 'It is absolutely necessary to keep clear from the subject of

[52] Henry Thornton to Dundas, 3, 4, 17, 30 Aug. 1791, National Archives, Colonial Office Papers, CO 267/9; Dundas to Wilberforce, 11 Aug. 1792, cited in Wilberforce, *Life*, I: 364.

[53] Thomas to John Clarkson, n.d., [1792], Clarkson Papers, BL Add. MS 41262A.

[54] Seymour Drescher, 'Public Opinion and Parliament in the Abolition of the British Slave Trade', *Parliamentary History*, 26 (2007), 55–7.

the French Revolution,' Wilberforce instructed Clarkson.[55] Almost half a century later, Wilberforce's sons revealed that Samuel Smith might have given more than £50 to the SLC had it not been for Clarkson's indiscretions, while Sir James Stephen, too, was still fuming.[56] 'By alarming George the 3d, Mr Pitt and the whole race of Anti-Jacobins, I believe that Clarkson did as much to frustrate and delay the abolition, as he ever did to promote it.'[57] Another proprietor, the Swedenborgian and international abolitionist Carl Bernhard Wadström (1746–1799), subscribed to a utopian proposal for a radical Christian settlement 'intirely independent' of existing European laws in which property (including wives) would be held in common. He was made an honorary citizen when he moved to France in 1795.[58] Small wonder that in the late 1790s Wilberforce broke off correspondence on the subject of politics with his onetime radical friend Wyvill.[59] This context has often been lost in the many recent retellings of the 'unknown story' of the black settlers. It is hardly surprising that 'none of the directors ... had concern for the aspirations for dignity and self-determination among these runaway slaves.'[60] Like many of their contemporaries, they saw 'self-determination' as a synonym for anarchy. Gradual abolition was their frequently repeated aim. 'Whether you will have strength to maintain the principle of universal Freedom or whether you must awhile connive and temporize, I think depends on circumstances at the place,' Thornton advised Clarkson.[61]

The refusal of the Nova Scotians to accept Company edicts thus presented problems at home as well as abroad. Independent-minded nonconformist evangelicalism was central to their identity, and they likened their voyage to the Israelites' journey out of Egypt. Once in the Promised Land, however, they resented the burdensome quit-rent and the heavy-handed tone of the authorities, and relations between the Company and those it regarded as its subjects – or debtors – deteriorated. Initially the SLC establishment was impressed with the settlers' religiosity. The 1794 Report

55   Wilberforce, *Life*, I: 343–4.
56   Wilberforce, *Life*, II: 54.
57   James Stephen to Robert Isaac Wilberforce, 25 Sep. 1833, Bodleian Library, Wrangham Papers, Box O. For further details of the spat, see J.R. Oldfield, '*Chords of Freedom': Commemoration, Ritual and British Transatlantic Slavery* (Manchester, 2007), 33–55.
58   Deirdre Coleman, *Romantic Colonization and British Anti-Slavery* (Cambridge, 2005), 63–105.
59   Wilberforce to Wyvill, n.d., 10 Mar. 1796, 24. Jan. 1797, North Yorkshire CRO, Northallerton, Wyvill of Constable Burton Papers, ZFW 7/106/20-2.
60   Pybus, *Epic Journeys*, 109.
61   Henry Thornton to John Clarkson, 30 Dec. 1791, Clarkson Papers, BL Add. MSS 41262B, fos. 33–44.

remarked on their discipline, sobriety, moral probity and sabbath-keeping, while one visitor remembered that she never woke at night 'without hearing preachings from some quarter or another'.[62] The first chaplains to the colony, the cousins Nathaniel Gilbert (1761–1807) and Melville Horne, were onetime Wesleyan Methodists, and their eirenic approach encouraged the black congregations to attend Anglican services too. Relations gradually soured, however. The charismatic 'revelations' and 'visions' recounted in the 1798 Report were anathema to Anglicans who valorized self-control, and for whom emotional assurance of salvation appeared unbiblical and presumptuous.[63] Wesleyan and Baptist missionaries sent out to the colony also proved hard to govern.[64] Attempts to enforce confessional orthodoxy with morning and evening prayer and marriage along Church of England lines served only to reinforce the authority of the Wesleyan, Baptist and Countess of Huntingdon's Connexion preachers who had led the Nova Scotians from North America.[65] When a new Church of Scotland chaplain, John Clarke (fl. 1790s), took them to task for their religious ignorance and the indiscipline of their worship, he was curtly rebuffed. 'We don't want you,' they informed him. 'We are in Christ already and have been for these last twenty-two years.'[66] This was a clash between two very different outworkings of religious revival.

As with most late-Hanoverian colonial ventures, slow communications and a lack of reliable information about climate, crops and indigenous politics gave men on the spot disproportionate power to shape policy. 'Admirable in themselves ... but ... not calculated for us in our present state,' was Clarkson's verdict on the directions he received from London.[67] His difficulties were compounded by problems with the Company's personnel, who squabbled, drank, took mistresses, absented themselves from church and – in one or two notorious cases – absconded to become slave traders.[68] Understandably, Clarkson's reports were received in London with concern.

---

[62] *Substance of the Report ... 1794*, 58–9; Anna Maria Falconbridge, *Narrative of Two Voyages to the River Sierra Leone during the years 1791 – 1792 – 1793*, ed. Christopher Fyfe (Liverpool, 2000), 98.

[63] *Substance of the Report ... Thursday the 29th March, 1798* (London, 1798), 47.

[64] Andrew F. Walls, 'A Christian Experiment: the Early Sierra Leone Colony', *Studies in Church History*, 7 (1970), 107–29.

[65] Viscountess Knutsford, *Life and Letters of Zachary Macaulay* (London, 1900), 143–7.

[66] Zachary Macaulay's Journal, 23 Apr., 17 Jun. 1796, cited in Pybus, *Epic Journeys*, 186–7.

[67] John to Thomas Clarkson, 28 Mar. 1792, Clarkson Papers, BL Add. MS 41262A.

[68] Falconbridge, *Narrative*, 74.

'You have been cheated in every department, ships, stores and cargo,' he brutally told the directors in April 1792.[69] Initially they welcomed his forthrightness, but before long hints began to appear in correspondence that the character of 'your Nova Scotians' was at fault.[70] The pronoun was significant. The settlers saw Clarkson as the Moses who had led them to freedom, and he reciprocated by championing their interests. 'Your government', he berated his brother, 'is of the most absurd kind and calculated to make miserable those valuable people I brought with me from America.'[71] It did not help that he did not always see eye to eye with the directors on religious matters. He had not been their first choice as governor: the directors had canvassed several others, including the Royal Marine officer and Evangelical Andrew Burn.[72] While vital religion does not seem to have been a requisite in those appointed, Evangelical connections figured heavily in the SLC's recruitment and crop up throughout correspondence. The pious surgeon John Pearson gave advice on medical appointments, for instance, while Hannah More informed a correspondent in 1794 that 'our friends the directors are writing to me to get them clergymen, missionaries, and schoolmasters'.[73] One of the few potential employees Clarkson considered competent, the naval officer Samuel Wickham (1758–1816), was passed over because one (unnamed) member of the committee heard him swear, and so could not 'in conscience take him by the Hand'. 'I will now sware [*sic*] for the first time for I never was given to it in my Life and I will say curse illiberality and all such ignorant childish, Methodistical notions,' raged Clarkson.[74] By this time, however, he had already been dismissed and members of his 'party' purged from the Company.[75] 'Religion which ought to have been the sheet anchor of the Colony', he sighed, 'will be its Ruin.'[76]

Unsurprisingly, the Evangelical credentials of Clarkson's successors were impeccable, and they illustrate the growing reach of the Clapham circle across the imperial world. William Dawes (1762–1836), Governor

---

[69] John Clarkson to Henry Thornton, 18 Apr. 1792, Clarkson Papers, BL Add. MS 41262A, fos. 76–81.

[70] Thornton to Clarkson, n.d., cited in Wilson, *John Clarkson*, 121.

[71] John to Thomas Clarkson, 28 Mar. 1792, cited in Wilson, *John Clarkson*, 90.

[72] John Allen (ed.), *Memoirs of the Late Major-General Andrew Burn, of the Royal Marines*, 2 vols (London, 1815), I: 112.

[73] Knutsford, *Zachary Macaulay*, 132; Hannah More to Elizabeth Bouverie, 31 Jan. [1794], cited in Lady Georgiana Chatterton (ed.), *Memorials, Personal and Historical, of Admiral Lord Gambier*, 2 vols (London, 1861), I: 239.

[74] John Clarkson to Lawrence Hartshorne, 4 Aug., [23] Sept. 1793, Clarkson Papers, BL Add. MS 41263.

[75] It may be significant that Thomas Clarkson sold his ten shares in August.

[76] John Clarkson to Isaac Dubois, 1 Jul. 1793, Clarkson Papers, BL Add. MS 41263.

from 1792–4, 1795–6 and 1801–3, was a half-pay Royal Marine officer and engineer who left Botany Bay under a cloud, having refused to participate in a punitive expedition against the aborigines. But although he impressed Wilberforce as 'an avowed friend of religion and order', his overbearing manner led the Nova Scotians to dub him 'Pharaoh'.[77] Zachary Macaulay (Governor 1794–5, 1796–9) was a globetrotting Scot who had been assistant overseer on a Jamaica sugar plantation, before returning to Britain, where he was introduced to the Clapham circle by his sister's husband, the banker Thomas Babington of Rothley Temple in Leicestershire. Macaulay, likewise, was not popular. These problems were, however, dwarfed by the disaster of 1795, when the pillage of Freetown in a French raid almost ended the Sierra Leone experiment overnight. Cutbacks ensued: the home establishment was slashed and expenditure in the colony reduced 'within narrow limits'.[78] Financial pressures intensified the disenchantment of the SLC establishment regarding the Nova Scotians, whom they damned as ungrateful incorrigibles. The establishment of schools in the colony and the new 'African Academy' at Clapham marked a concerted attempt to indoctrinate a new generation.[79] 'In the children ... of the Nova Scotian blacks', the 1798 Report maintained, 'the Proprietors may reasonably hope for a body of colonists of a different description from their parents.'[80] Year after year annual reports promised shareholders jam tomorrow, blaming privateers, colonists, insects, bad weather, bad fortune. But the colony's inability even to feed itself gave a hollow ring to repeated assurances about cultivating and civilizing a continent. By 1801 the Company's capital had more than halved to £95,567. 7s. 11d., its shares were trading at a 95 per cent discount and the Nova Scotians were in open revolt.[81]

The most significant consequence was a growing closeness to government. Far-flung colonies were strategically important in the global struggle against France, but the arrival of Jamaican Maroons exiled after a recent rebellion, in return for a supplementary £4,000 annually, bound Sierra Leone irrevocably into the imperial system. Not only did this answer the Company's need for financial support and for manpower that it could use to suppress unrest; it gave it a bargaining chip. The directors had long

---

[77] Phyllis Mander-Jones, 'Dawes, William (1762–1836)', in *Australian Dictionary of Biography*, online. http://adb.anu.edu.au/biography/dawes-william-1968, last accessed 26 Sep. 2017.

[78] *Substance of the Report ... 30th March 1796* (London, 1796), 5.

[79] Bruce L. Mouser, 'African academy – Clapham 1799–1806', *History of Education*, 33 (2004), 87–103.

[80] *Substance of the Report ... 1798*, 50.

[81] *Substance of the Report ... 1801*, 10–17.

lobbied pious acquaintances at the Admiralty for naval protection, and now they also secured large sums to improve the colony's fortifications.[82] "'Marianne, do you not wish me joy?'" Henry Thornton reportedly asked his wife. "'I have seven thousand a year given to me.'"[83] Between 1801 and 1805 the SLC received £67,000, which brought it into line with the other African forts supported by government grants. Later on, the colony became an important recruiting ground for the West India regiments.[84] In 1800 the Company was granted a Charter of Justice, making Sierra Leone 'a colony, governed indisputably from London, the directors exercising the powers normally exercised in other Colonies by the Secretary of State'.[85] Quietly inverting their original arguments, supporters of the SLC began to claim that the colony had been stifled by the slave trade, rather than out-competing it, as they had hoped.[86] West Indian MPs continued to seethe about the SLC's privileged position and were furious that 'a speculation which ha[s] failed' should be bailed out at public expense.[87] 'The Company could scarce be said to exist,' protested one MP in 1800, warning that 'nobody knew how they applied the money which they received'.[88] His complaint reflects the change of direction that the project was again undergoing. Instead of selling African commodities for profit, the SLC was now effectively a government contractor.

These arguments were reprised in 1807, when in the aftermath of the Slave Trade Abolition Act, passed in March, the Sierra Leone Transfer Bill came before parliament. The Saints came out in force to support it, and the speeches of Wilberforce and Thornton were larded with the language of atonement for past sins that had so palpably infused parliamentary debates earlier in the year.[89] Since 1792, they contended, the SLC had paid the price for others' sins. Against the contention that it be held liable for funds it had swallowed, they insisted that British debts to Africa had only partially been

---

[82]   See e.g. Henry Thornton to Zachary Macaulay, 23 Sep. 1794, CUL, MS Add.7674/1/M, fo. 3; Wilberforce, *Life*, II: 344; Evan Nepean to William Wilberforce, 10 Jan. 1800, Bodl., MSS Wilberforce, d.17, fo. 99.

[83]   Zachary Macaulay to Selina Mills, 20 June 1799, cited in Knutsford, *Zachary Macaulay*, 226.

[84]   Scanlan, *Freedom's Debtors*, 130–66.

[85]   Christopher Fyfe, *History of Sierra Leone* (London, 1962), 86.

[86]   See Wilberforce's speech, *Parliamentary Debates from the Year 1803 to the Present Time*, 9 (5 Mar.–14 Aug. 1807), col. 1002.

[87]   *Ibid.*, 2 (5 Apr.- 31 Jul. 1804), cols. 966–7.

[88]   *The Times*, 21 Jul. 1800, 2.

[89]   Boyd Hilton, '1807 and All That: Why Britain Outlawed her Slave Trade', in Derek R. Peterson (ed.), *Abolition and Imperialism in Britain, Africa, and the Atlantic* (Athens, OH, 2010), 63–83.

discharged. The colony had failed, Thornton observed, because it lacked the advantages of other African settlements, 'to which parliament had been used to grant from £20,000 to £30,000 per annum'.[90] Instead of being abandoned it should be developed and supported. Although their arguments were strongly opposed by West Indian interests, they were broadly well received and the bill passed in August 1807. Henceforward the Company would disavow all claims to governance: 'it would be for the parliament and the government to act hereafter as might ... appear expedient'.[91] Such comments were, however, slightly disingenuous. 'I have no doubt that Government will be disposed to adopt almost any plan which we may propose to them with respect to Africa provided we will but save them the trouble of thinking,' boasted Macaulay in a letter to Thomas Ludlam (1775–1810), Governor from 1799–1800, 1803–5 and 1806–8.[92] It was a revealing comment that would be damaging when it was made public later on. For the time being, though, the Saints were riding high.

The African Institution and the Colonial Office

The African Institution was founded in April 1807 amid a mood of benevolence towards wounded Africa.[93] Billed as an opportunity to promote 'civilization and happiness', it drew support from across the political spectrum, including the leading Whigs Charles, later Earl Grey (1764–1845), Lord Henry Petty (1780–1863) and Henry Erskine (1746–1817); the Pittites George Canning, William Huskisson, Spencer Perceval, Nicholas Vansittart and J.C. Villiers (1757–1838), as well as the leading parliamentary Saints.[94] This was not an organization that could be accused of fanaticism or radicalism: it was unashamedly elitist. 'Where delicate negociations [*sic*] are to be managed by the backstairs ... [t]he intermeddling of popular committees and popular meetings spoils everything,' one member later commented.[95] The *Christian Observer* revelled in its 'distinguished patronage', seeing this as unmistakable evidence of the 'march of wisdom, justice,

---

[90] *Parliamentary Debates*, 9 (5 Mar.–14 Aug. 1807), col. 1005.
[91] *Ibid.*
[92] Macaulay to Ludlam, 4 Nov. 1807, University of Hull, Brynmor Jones Library, Papers of Thomas Perronet Thompson relating to Sierra Leone, DTH 1/2/4.
[93] Wayne Ackerson, *The African Institution (1807–1827) and the Antislavery Movement in Great Britain* (New York, Queenston, ON, and Lampeter, 2005).
[94] *Report of the Committee of the African Institution* (London, 1807), vii–viii.
[95] George Stephen, *Anti-Slavery Recollections* (London, 1854), 57.

benevolence, and mercy'.[96] Indeed, the African Institution is perhaps the most important site for what Abraham Kriegel called 'a convergence of ethics' between Whig humanitarianism and Evangelical philanthropy: the late Prime Minister Lord Grenville and the up-and-coming barrister Henry Brougham were key participants and, although Sydney Smith had sharp words for the spread of 'fanaticism' in public life, the *Edinburgh Review* was among the Institution's fiercest champions.[97] Lessons had been learned from the muddled quasi-commercialism of the SLC: here was a solely philanthropic enterprise in which social eminence was to be given due weight, with subscriptions graded from one guinea (annual membership) to a hefty sixty guineas (hereditary governorship).[98] Its President was the Duke of Gloucester, and the first General Meeting was set for 15 July. 'A magnificent day,' reported a jubilant Wilberforce, 'between five and six hundred people, ten or twelve noblemen, and forty or more MPs.'[99] The first report stressed that the Institution was no 'rash and visionary project': it ostentatiously disavowed religious and commercial motives, emphasizing that the new body was not a continuation of the SLC.[100]

Yet whatever they pretended, this was a triumph for the Saints. The African Institution was an elite vehicle for enforcing an Act they had helped to draw up. It oversaw the governmental takeover of Sierra Leone and in 1821 presided over the suppression of the African Company and the transfer of the Gold Coast forts to the crown. It helped that the unsettled politics of the 1800s and early 1810s magnified their parliamentary influence. They had managed, 'when parties have been nearly equal ... to hold the balance of power ... and have thus acquired an importance which neither their numbers nor their talents would otherwise have entitled them', fulminated one pro-slavery pamphleteer.[101] Other critics were quick to point out that no fewer than eight out of the fourteen directors of the SLC for 1807–8 were also on the committee of the new body.[102] Most blatantly of all, Macaulay moved from being Secretary of the Company to the same post in the Institution. Nevertheless, anti-slavery sentiment was running high and the Institution channelled this towards ministers who in any case were already

---

[96]   'Religious Intelligence. African Institution', *Christian Observer*, 6 (1807), 270–3.
[97]   Abraham D. Kriegel, 'A Convergence of Ethics: Saints and Whigs in British Antislavery', *Journal of British Studies*, 26 (1987), 423–58.
[98]   *African Institution Report* (1807), 72–3.
[99]   Wilberforce, *Life*, III: 361.
[100] *African Institution Report* (1807), 10.
[101] Joseph Marryat, *Thoughts on the Abolition of the Slave Trade, and Civilization of Africa; with Remarks on the African Institution* (London, 1816), 230.
[102] Babington, Clarkson, Grant, Hardcastle, Sharp, Teignmouth, Thornton, Wilberforce.

sympathetic. For perhaps a decade after its foundation the Institution was 'almost a de facto slave-trade department of the Foreign Office'.[103] Among its key members was James Stephen, the MP and lawyer whose expertise in maritime law lay behind the Slave Trade Act, and whom Spencer Perceval made Master in Chancery in early 1811. 'I am never refused any thing at the Colonial Office,' he boasted, the appointment of his son, also James, as legal adviser being a case in point.[104] Official and unofficial intelligence-gathering networks overlapped: Institution officers were granted access to Customs House records; tip-offs from informants in Brazil, Sierra Leone and the Canaries prompted searches of homecoming ships; and government agents such as the British Consul-General at Rio de Janeiro, James Gambier (1772–1844) – cousin of the Evangelical Admiral – were instructed to keep tabs on British slavers calling there.[105]

Gallingly for those who had rejoiced at the struggles of the SLC, the Saints also preserved their hegemony over Sierra Leone. Yet this was a mixed blessing. The first Crown Governor, Thomas Perronet Thompson (1783–1869), was one of their protégés.[106] Son of the Hull banker, Methodist and MP Thomas Thompson, Thompson junior had been immersed in Evangelical influences from an early age, attending Hull Grammar School under Joseph Milner and then Queens' College, Cambridge, under Isaac Milner, where he was briefly a fellow, before going to sea in 1803 under Gambier on HMS *Isis*.[107] Thompson's energy made him a natural choice for the stagnating colony, or so Wilberforce thought.[108] Yet privately he was impatient with the pious respectability of his sponsors. 'I am already blasted with good names; grave, steady, hopeful, promising, and all the other titles which being interpreted mean fool,' he told his fiancée. 'I should not wonder at waking up some morning an established character on Clapham common with a seat in the Church, the House of Commons and the East

---

[103] David Eltis, *Economic Growth and the Ending of the Transatlantic Slave Trade* (New York, 1987), 105.

[104] Stephen to Wilberforce, n.d., [1811], cited in Wilberforce, *Life*, IV: 240.

[105] Ackerson, *African Institution*, 77–104

[106] Correspondence was already going to and fro over potential governors in 1807. See Spencer Perceval to Wilberforce, n.d., [1807], Rubinstein Library, Duke University, Wilberforce Papers, Box 2, Folder 2. For Thompson, see Leonard George Johnson, *General T. Perronet Thompson, 1783–1869* (London, 1957).

[107] T.P. Thompson to Wilberforce, 3 Mar. 1806, Bodl., MSS Wilberforce, d.14, fo. 288.

[108] William Wilberforce to Lord Castlereagh, 19 Jan. 1809, Colonial Office: Sierra Leone Original Correspondence, CO 267/25. See also Isaac Milner to Charles Ignatius La Trobe, 26 Feb. 1808, cited in Mary Milner, *The Life of Isaac Milner* (London, 1842), 356.

India directory.'[109] He found Ludlam and Macaulay, his only sources of first-hand information, opaque, but worse was to come *en route* to Africa, when Dawes informed him that he had 'always thought slavery necessary in the colony'. While this comment seems improbable, Thompson certainly differed from Dawes in his attitude to 'apprenticeship', whereby freed slaves ('recaptives') were indentured as labourers or to military service. The African Institution justified this a necessary step towards freedom; Thompson saw it as slavery by another name.[110] His unease was heightened when he arrived in a colony whose agriculture, economy and military bore little resemblance to the picture painted by its advocates. Convinced that they had been 'most egregiously deceived', Thompson despatched a blizzard of graphic memoranda to Macaulay, Wilberforce and the Secretary of State for War and the Colonies, Lord Castlereagh.[111] While the Saints initially tried to reason with Thompson, they rapidly came to realize that he was a loose cannon who was turning his fire against them.[112] 'The accounts from S. Leone have shocked me a great deal', shuddered Macaulay. 'Thompson I think must be mad.'[113]

What happened next demonstrates the reach of the Saints. Thompson was recalled in early 1809. Most of his attempts to arrange meetings with ministers were frostily ignored.[114] His calls for a parliamentary enquiry were blocked in the House of Commons by anti-slavery members, his father included.[115] Thompson was enraged by what he saw as the dishonesty of his erstwhile patrons:

> At the African Institution they impudently declare that they have
> no concern either with commerce or with missions; they step into

---

[109] Thompson to Nancy Barker, 27 May 1808, cited in Johnson, *Perronet Thompson*, 32.

[110] Thompson to Nancy Barker, 23 Jul. 1808, Draft Biography, Papers of Thomas Perronet Thompson, DTH 4/1, 455–61.

[111] Thompson to African Institution (draft), 2 Nov. 1808, Papers of Thomas Perronet Thompson, DTH 1/27.

[112] Wilberforce to Thompson, 19 Oct. 1808, Papers of Thomas Perronet Thompson, DTH 1/61/8. For a fuller account of the cover-up, see Turner, 'Limits of Abolition', 347–51.

[113] Macaulay to Babington, May 17 1809, Trinity/BABINGTON, Box 26/114.

[114] Draft letters, Thompson to Lord Liverpool, 13 Dec. 1810–4 Jan. 1811, Papers of Thomas Perronet Thompson, DTH 1/97/4.

[115] *Parliamentary Debates*, 19 (22 Feb.–10 May 1811), cols. 461–2, 570. Wilberforce to Thomas Thompson, 28 Aug. 1810, Papers of Thomas Perronet Thompson, DTH 4/2, 1224–7; Arthur R.B. Robinson, *The counting house: Thomas Thompson of Hull 1754–1828 and his family* (York, 1992), 34, 61. Thompson to Nancy Barker, 27 Oct. 1810, cited in Johnson, *Perronet Thompson*, 66–7.

their coaches and presto – they are the Sierra Leone Company – hey pass and they are the Society for Missions to Africa and to the East; another transformation makes them the Society for the Suppression of Vice, a fourth carries them to the East India House, and a fifth lands them in the House of Commons. This marvellous property of being everywhere is not one of their least dangerous qualifications.[116]

While Thompson was unable to make his allegations stick, they provided potent ammunition for his friend Robert Thorpe (c. 1764–1836), Chief Justice to Sierra Leone, who sought on his return in 1813 to expose how the colony and its affairs had been mispresented. On the whole the Saints were not, he thought, wilfully deceptive or corrupt. But a combination of bad character judgement, broken promises, mis-spent money, cover-ups and misapplied influence out of the public eye meant that 'Upas like, they poison every thing [*sic*] salutary within their influence.'[117]

His main target was Zachary Macaulay, whose firm, Macaulay and Babington, perpetuated the effective monopoly of the SLC over trade, shipping supplies, proving wills and even the minting of coins. Particularly repulsive to Thorpe was the stranglehold of the Macaulay empire on the Vice-Admiralty Court that decided what government would pay for captured slaving vessels and their human cargoes. Prize money had always been an incentive for naval commanders and their crews to disrupt enemy trade, and it seems to have been James Stephen's inspiration to use this to cut off the supply of slaves to the British West Indies.[118] The African Institution did everything in its power to encourage this, pestering policymakers to put in place a 'West Africa Squadron' and publicizing the financial benefits of what Padraic Scanlan calls 'anti-slavery entrepreneurship' among naval officers.[119] In Sierra Leone, however, Macaulay and Babington's agents, including Kenneth Macaulay (1792–1829), Zachary's cousin, took a cut of the proceeds at every stage, providing officers for the Court, acting as

---

[116] Thompson to captain of a vessel [unknown], 3 Aug. 1809, Papers of Thomas Perronet Thompson, DTH 1/41.

[117] The Bohun Upas ('Poison Tree') of Java was thought to kill all that came near it. Robert Thorpe, *A Reply 'Point by Point' to the Special Report of the Directors of the African Institution* (London, 1815), 72.

[118] Roger Anstey, *The Atlantic Slave Trade and British Abolition, 1760–1810* (London, 1975), 350–6.

[119] Tara Helfman, 'The Court of Vice Admiralty at Sierra Leone and the Abolition of the West African Slave Trade', *Yale Law Journal*, 115 (2006), 1122–56; Padraic X. Scanlan, 'The Rewards of their Exertions: Prize Money and British Abolitionism in Sierra Leone, 1807–1823', *Past and Present*, 225 (2014), 187.

prize agents for naval officers and superintending 'captured negroes'. They thus also perpetuated the system of 'vassalage' that Thorpe, like Thompson, thought tantamount to slavery. Given the unpalatability of pricing freed slaves to modern sensibilities, recent research has tended to see Evangelical moralizing as insulating British people from their complicity in systems of racial and economic exploitation.[120] Nevertheless, contemporary pious publicists regarded the price paid to 'redeem' recaptives from servitude as a triumph, and celebrated the enormous sum devoted to compensation payments under the terms of the 1833 Emancipation Act. It was more difficult, though, for them to justify conflicts of influence in the colony. Macaulay's protest that he had 'never made the smallest effort to interest a single individual in this country, whether connected or not with the Sierra Leone Company, or with the African Institution, or with the Government, in the promotion of my commercial views' rang very thin indeed.[121] Incriminating extracts from his correspondence were reprinted at every opportunity by pro-slavery pamphleteers.[122] The Glasgow journalist and slave agent James MacQueen (1778–1870) calculated Macaulay's commission at '£13,000 per annum ... the very *"cheese parings and candle ends"* of which are annually worth more than the salary of the Prime Minister of Great Britain!'[123] Tory rags such as *John Bull* and the *Anti-Jacobin Review* raved about a conspiracy against Church and order underwritten by philanthropic profits, warning that the 'African faction' was purchasing church livings and parliamentary seats on a grand scale.[124]

Yet such attacks could not hold back the tide of anti-slavery opinion. In 1814–15 the African Institution co-ordinated an avalanche of petitions and addresses decrying the failure of British negotiators to enforce European abolition, containing perhaps 1,375,000 signatures.[125] Evangelical networks were crucial: Josiah Pratt, for instance, wrote to some 1,200 clergymen associated with the CMS in order to canvass their support.[126] 'They have

[120] Catherine Hall, Nicholas Draper, Keith McClelland, Katie Donington and Rachel Lang, *Legacies of British Slave-ownership: Colonial Slavery and the Formation of Victorian Britain* (Cambridge, 2016), 1–22.

[121] Zachary Macaulay, *A Letter to His Royal Highness the Duke of Gloucester* (2nd edn: London, 1815), 31.

[122] E.g. Robert Thorpe, *A Letter to William Wilberforce* (London, 1815), 39; *The Times*, 15 Feb. 1815, 3. For a fuller account, see Iain Whyte, *Zachary Macaulay, 1768–1838* (Liverpool 2011), 194–216.

[123] James MacQueen, *The Colonial Controversy* (Glasgow, 1825), 100.

[124] E.g. 'The African Institution and the Slave Trade', *Anti-Jacobin Review and True Churchman's Magazine*, 50 (1816), 645.

[125] Kielstra, *Slave Trade Suppression*, 30–1.

[126] *Ibid.*, 30.

literally so covered the floors of the Houses of Lords and Commons with petitions, as almost to awe the Legislature into … acquiescence', fumed Joseph Marryat (1757–1824).[127] As well as policing the British ban, the Institution also sought to force the pace on foreign abolition. 'To a meeting of the African Institution, previous to talking with different ministers about stopping Portuguese Slave Trade – Bissao', wrote Wilberforce in one typical diary entry. 'To Lord Castlereagh on getting Bissao from the Portuguese. To Lord Liverpool and Yorke, getting more naval force on the African coast.'[128] Even after the peace, they advocated the seizure of foreign slavers. 'With justice, honour and humanity on their side', proclaimed Stephen pugnaciously, '[Englishmen] have no reason to shrink from the attack of any power whatever.'[129] Rhetoric became reality with the bombardment of slave-holding Algiers by an Anglo-Dutch naval squadron in 1816. An ostentatious act of gunboat philanthropy intended at once to placate the Saints and to convince the Concert of Europe that Britain's abolitionism was not a covert attempt to ruin her rivals, it sent the Evangelical press into raptures.[130] Although recent scholarship has emphasized the coherence of pro-slavery thought and the strength of the West Indian lobby in the 1820s, it was increasingly difficult to compete with this potent combination of elite influence and public support.[131] By the 1830s the conjunction of patriotism with muscular anti-slavery was becoming a fixed point on the national moral compass.[132]

The Era of 'Proconsular Despotisms', c. 1800–40

If Evangelicals exercised significant clout in the Colonial Office, they also found ways to develop their influence in the dominions over which it presided. Networks were crucial. Information provided by chaplains in New South Wales, for instance, above all the long-serving Samuel Marsden, gave the Saints significant leverage in the colony for many years.[133] When in 1807

---

[127] Marryatt, *Thoughts*, 230–1.
[128] Wilberforce, *Life*, IV: 19.
[129] [James Stephen], *An Inquiry into the Right and Duty of Compelling Spain to Relinquish her Slave Trade in Northern Africa* (London, 1816), 71.
[130] 'Public Affairs – Algiers: Successful Attack', *Christian Observer*, 15 (1816), 616–18.
[131] Paula E. Dumas, *Proslavery Britain: Fighting for Slavery in an Era of Abolition* (New York, 2016); Michael Taylor, 'British Proslavery Arguments and the Bible, 1823–1833', *Slavery and Abolition*, 37 (2016), 139–58.
[132] Huzzey, *Freedom Burning*.
[133] Michael Gladwin, *Anglican Clergy in Australia, 1788–1850: Building a British World* (Woodbridge, 2015), 29–32.

Castlereagh directed the new governor William Bligh (1754–1817) to 'make the religious and moral state of the colony a prime regard' he was repeating a standard formula, but his instructions recommended Marsden's advice and gave Bligh permission to divert tax revenue to such causes as Marsden would recommend.[134] Evangelical networks also secured them the right to appoint to numerous minor posts. As the civil establishment of New South Wales expanded, Marsden and his metropolitan contacts recommended clergymen, masters and matrons for churches, orphanages and schools in the colony.[135] The pattern was replicated across the expanding Anglo-world. Just as significantly, the Saints also moulded the character of the ruling elite. The late-Hanoverian empire was, as Bayly observed, a chaotic federation of 'proconsular despotisms' in which ambitious autocrats, many of them military men, retained considerable freedom of local manoeuvre. Nevertheless, the Saints had Bathurst's ear and his long tenure (1812–27) gave them disproportionate influence over appointments.[136] Politically conservative Evangelicalism found natural affinities in the devout authoritarianism of men like Sir Ralph Darling (1772–1858), Governor of New South Wales from 1825–31, and Sir George Arthur (1784–1854), Governor of Van Diemen's Land from 1824–36. Both came to the notice of the African Institution when they took on local slaving interests, Arthur in British Honduras and Darling in Mauritius, and although neither owed their advancement to Evangelical connections, these evidently did no harm.[137] While both men were personally religious, they also warn against any anachronistic equation of humanitarianism with sentimental softness. The strict penal regime Arthur imposed on Van Diemen's Land was bitterly opposed among the press and local officials. But it was combined with the promotion of religion and education, alongside well-meaning attempts to dampen the unequal conflict between settlers and the aboriginal Tasmanians.[138] There, as in New South Wales, Evangelical networks supplied most of the early clergy.[139] Later on, the appointment of Charles Joseph La Trobe (1801–1875) to Port

---

[134] Andrew Sharp, *The World, the Flesh and the Devil: the Life and Opinions of Samuel Marsden in England and the Antipodes, 1765–1838* (Auckland, 2016), 180–1.

[135] *Ibid.*, 277; Stuart Piggin, *Evangelical Christianity in Australia: Spirit, Word and World* (Melbourne, 1996), 1–23.

[136] A scholarly study of Bathurst's appointments and influence is overdue. But see Neville Thompson, *Earl Bathurst and the British Empire* (Barnsley, 1999).

[137] A.G.L. Shaw, *Sir George Arthur, Bart, 1784–1854* (Melbourne, 1980), 61; B. H. Fletcher, *Ralph Darling: a governor maligned* (Melbourne, 1984), 183–205.

[138] For a nuanced recent interpretation of this, see Alan Lester and Fae Dussart, *Colonization and the Origins of Humanitarian Government: Protecting Aborigines across the Nineteenth-Century British Empire* (Cambridge, 2014), 37–76.

[139] Gladwin, *Anglican Clergy*, 30–1.

Philip in 1838 and eventually to be Lieutenant-Governor of Victoria, from 1851–4, bespeaks the continued importance of Evangelical patronage in Australian affairs.

Evangelicals thrived in the 'Regency Empire' because their aims and those of colonial authorities often coincided. The manpower and money they could mobilize made them attractive partners for cash-strapped governors keen to inculcate morality and to educate (and anglicize) their subjects. Stamford Raffles (1781–1826) in Java and Sumatra in the 1810s and 20s, for instance, was quick to forge connections with Wilberforce and the African Institution, sponsoring local Bible Society auxiliaries, missionary schools and scripture translation.[140] Likewise the Chief Justice and President of the Council at Ceylon, Sir Alexander Johnston (1775–1849), who took an active role in having 'Cyngalese' [Sinhalese] New Testaments printed at the BMS press in Serampore, as well as promoting the establishment of a Bible Society auxiliary along the lines of that at Calcutta: 'the Governor, and myself have agreed that nothing can be more advantageous for this Island.'[141] Societies cultivated such arrangements. To read the correspondence of Lord Teignmouth is to discern two obsessions: securing colonial positions for his protégés and promoting the BFBS, often in the same letter.[142] Lest we assume from this that officials saw religion and education merely as sedatives to deaden the desire for self-determination, it must be remembered that the connection between established religion and the maintenance of political authority was widely assumed. It is unhelpful to reduce the religious professions of a Raffles – which were fervent – to pragmatism pure and simple. Rather, we should see Evangelicals as being adept at negotiating a fluid colonial world whose frequently invoked values – British civilization and Protestant Christianity – were closely intermeshed, but meant different things to different people. Evangelical organizations readily inserted themselves into or worked around the patchy provision of military, garrison and company chaplains. They also took advantage of well-disposed local officials. One of the most influential citizens at the Cape, for instance, was William Wilberforce Bird (1758–1836) senior, a cousin of William Wilberforce who arrived in 1807 as slave prize agent, becoming Comptroller of Customs in 1810 and an adviser to Lord Charles Somerset (1767–1831), Governor from 1814–26.[143]

---

[140] Sophia Raffles, *Memoir of the Life and Public Services of Sir Thomas Stamford Raffles* (London, 1830), 411–12, 416–17, 585–93.
[141] Sir Alexander Johnston to Lord Teignmouth, 24 Feb. 1812, British and Foreign Bible Society Archive, BS/F3/Shore/93.
[142] See BS/F3/Shore.
[143] 'W.W. Bird, Esq', *Gentleman's Magazine*, 161 (1836), 433.

In few places was the notion of a Christian empire clearer than in Sierra Leone during the governorships of Charles Maxwell (1775–1848), from 1811–15, and Charles MacCarthy (1764–1824), from 1815–21. Their rule made moral improvement part of a grandiose religious-strategic vision. This served to justify aggressive campaigns against slaving vessels and even attacks on forts that lay outside the colony's jurisdiction, acts whose legality was questionable but which were trumpeted by the African Institution in Britain.[144] It also fuelled expansionism. Sierra Leone required an Anglican establishment, Maxwell told Bathurst, 'as the principal settlement of Great Britain throughout the whole extent of the western coast of Africa, and the point from which must issue every attempt to improve the religious and moral condition of the Natives of that vast Peninsula'.[145] Religious provision was, however, never a state preserve. Ever since the 1790s, the colony had been 'a sort of rusk on which infant missionary societies cut their teeth', with the Saints encouraging the CMS, LMS, Glasgow and Edinburgh societies, as well as Wesleyan Methodists, to use it as a base.[146] In the 1810s, the CMS and BFBS became quasi-government agencies. The villages in the mountain hinterland to which Liberated Africans were sent – Bathurst, Charlotte, Gloucester, Leopold, Waterloo, Wellington, Wilberforce – were supervised by CMS clergy and lay agents.[147] CMS salaries were augmented by government subsidies, while the state also paid for building materials for churches and stationery supplies for missionary schools.[148] As in other colonies, the education provided by institutions set up to train school-masters, catechists and clergymen was also a useful preparation for commerce and colonial administration: the CMS 'Christian Institution' of 1816 became Fourah Bay College in 1827.[149] Relations between Evangelicals and officialdom were not always straightforward. While many hailed MacCarthy's statistical reports, seeing in baptisms, weddings and school enrolments evidence of the advance of Christian civilization, his instrumental conception of baptism as an 'act of civilization' upset missionaries versed in the importance of heart religion.[150] When confronted, MacCarthy retorted that he would send people for Wesleyan baptism or else write for SPCK

---

[144] Scanlan, *Freedom's Debtors*, 153–66.
[145] Charles Maxwell to Earl Bathurst, 23 Dec. 1814, CO 267/38.
[146] Walls, 'Christian Experiment', 112–13.
[147] Scanlan, *Freedom's Debtors*, 167–209.
[148] Josiah Pratt to Earl Bathurst, 31 Aug. 1816, CO 267/44; Josiah Pratt to Henry Goulburn, 5 Nov. 1817, CO 267/46.
[149] Daniel J. Paracka, *The Athens of West Africa: A History of International Education at Fourah Bay College, Freetown, Sierra Leone* (New York, 2003), 21–33.
[150] *Fourteenth Report of the Directors of the African Institution* (London, 1820), 30.

missionaries to do it.[151] Nevertheless, Sierra Leone looked like the moral and civilizational success story that Evangelicals needed and by the early 1820s it was being cited as a place 'where the name of Briton [is] uttered with a blessing instead of a curse'.[152]

Elsewhere, Evangelicals used their connections to outflank their opponents. The Colonial Office fought constant battles with recalcitrant West Indian assemblies over the slave-trade ban in the 1810s and 20s.[153] It also crowbarred the Caribbean open for missionaries – William Dawes, onetime governor of Sierra Leone, ended his days supervising CMS schools for slaves in Antigua – although it could not help them to win favour with the rather hostile bishops installed in Barbados and Jamaica in 1824.[154] Occasionally the Saints overstepped the mark: Stephen senior had his knuckles rapped in 1813 for passing drafts of Jamaican colonial legislation to his abolitionist colleagues.[155] Yet even this episode serves to highlight their access to the corridors of power. Indeed, if anything their influence grew, thanks to the African Institution and, from 1823, the Anti-Slavery Society. Zoe Laidlaw has argued that the period from 1815–35 marks a distinct phase preceding the mass agitation of later years, one in which humanitarians pursued their aims through official bodies such as inquiries and parliamentary select committees. The Commission of Eastern Inquiry, for example, set up in 1822 to investigate colonial affairs in Ceylon, Mauritius and Cape Colony, became a vehicle for publicizing abuses of indigenous rights and ensuring that emancipation became official policy.[156] While the campaigns of the LMS missionary John Philip (1777–1851) against the government of Cape Colony regarding the civil disabilities of 'free persons of colour' and the human rights of the Khoi-Khoi people undoubtedly struck a chord among the religious public, this would have had little effect without the hearing secured for him by the MP Thomas Fowell Buxton, or without the tack away from political radicalism that Philip engineered

[151] William Jowett, *Memoir of the Rev. W.A.B. Johnson* (London, 1852), 94.

[152] *The Times*, 2 Nov. 1820, 3.

[153] Mary Reckord, 'The Colonial Office and the Abolition of Slavery', *Historical Journal*, 14 (1971), 723–34.

[154] Hans Cnattingius, *Bishops and Societies: a Study of Anglican Colonial and Missionary Expansion, 1698–1850* (London, 1952), 149–51.

[155] Henry Goulburn to James Stephen, 7 Apr. 1813, National Archive, Colonial Office, Jamaica Entry Books, CO 138/45.

[156] Zoe Laidlaw, 'Investigating Empire: Humanitarians, Reform and the Commission of Eastern Inquiry', *Journal of Imperial and Commonwealth History*, 40 (2012), 749–68.

within the LMS.[157] During the 1830s benevolent imperial trusteeship and the defence of indigenous land rights against white settlers became articles of faith at a Colonial Office led by Evangelicals and their allies.[158] Charles Grant, Lord Glenelg (Secretary of State 1835–9) and Sir James Stephen (Legal Adviser 1813–25, Permanent Legal Counsel 1825–34, Assistant Under-Secretary 1834–6, Permanent Under-Secretary, 1836–47) were second-generation Claphamites, while Sir George Grey (1799–1882), Under-Secretary in 1834 and from 1835–9, and the pious son of an equally pious naval officer and dockyard commissioner, was related to the Barings and married Anna Sophia (1805–1893), a daughter of Henry Ryder.[159] Although their Liberal attitude towards Church–state relationships was not always welcomed by more traditional-minded churchmen, they and their connections meant that the Colonial Office remained sympathetic to Evangelicals and pro-Christian lobbyists more broadly.

Their combination of institutional and associational strength also allowed Evangelicals to muscle in on the ecclesiastical affairs of settler colonies. Hilary Carey has talked of an empire of 'multiple establishments', as the British government and colonial authorities subsidized a mosaic of denominations and organizations.[160] This was fertile territory for well-connected Evangelical interest groups. The Newfoundland School Society, for instance, was founded in 1823 to provide elementary education in a largely Catholic colony. The rhetoric surrounding it was laced with patriotic providentialism and Protestant biblicism, and it attracted a glittering array of vice-presidents, including Liverpool, Bathurst, Ryder, Bexley and Wilberforce, later securing Queen Victoria as its patron. Yet it also rode roughshod over the SPG, which had hitherto monopolized schooling in Newfoundland, not to mention flouting episcopal authority in one of the few colonies that at this stage had an establishment. The financial support it secured from the Colonial Office was thus controversial.[161] Much more ambitious was the Colonial Church Society, which developed in 1838 out

---

[157] *Ibid.*, 758–62. Elizabeth Elbourne, *Blood Ground: Colonialism, Missions, and the Contest for Christianity in the Cape Colony and Britain, 1799–1853* (Montreal and Kingston, ON, 2002), 233–58.

[158] G.R. Mellor, *British Imperial Trusteeship, 1783–1850* (London, 1951).

[159] Ged Martin, 'Two Cheers for Lord Glenelg', *Journal of Imperial and Commonwealth History*, 7 (1979), 213–27; Paul Knaplund, *James Stephen and the British Colonial System 1813–1847* (Madison, WI, 1953); Mandell Creighton, *Memoir of Sir George Grey* (new edn: London, 1901), 1–30.

[160] Hilary M. Carey, *God's Empire: Religion and Colonialism in the British World, c. 1801–1908* (Cambridge, 2011), 52.

[161] *Ibid.*, 154–8.

of the Western Australia Missionary Society. From its office in Exeter Hall it sought 'to embrace all the Colonies of Great Britain' in sending missionaries and clergymen to minister to British settlers and to inoculate them against resurgent Roman Catholicism.[162] It boasted impressive support from a string of colonial governors and military officers, including the Governor of Western Australia, John Hutt (1795–1880); Sir Ralph Darling; Sir Peregrine Maitland (1777–1854) and the Arctic-exploring naval officers Sir William Edward Parry (1790–1855) and Sir John Franklin (1786–1847), again emphasizing the strength of Evangelically tinged piety in such circles.[163] The strategies the CCS adopted evince a sound knowledge of the colonial administrative mind: letters sent to the lieutenant-governors of New Brunswick, Nova Scotia and Newfoundland offered them salaried clergymen, so long as an extra £50 could be found locally to top up their income. It also made the most of connections in government, with Grey approaching the Foreign Office for matched funding on a similar basis. The CCS gained a foothold at the Cape, whose position en route to and from India was conducive to the development of a strong 'evangelical Anglo-Indian culture' that sat decidedly loosely to ecclesiastical niceties, with lay evangelists preaching in nonconformist and Wesleyan pulpits and even reportedly administering communion in prayer meetings.[164]

By the 1830s, however, the *modus operandi* that had served so well in the preceding decades was beginning to unravel. It was to be expected that the CCS would meet with opposition in an Atlantic world which had for many years been the province of the SPG and SPCK.[165] Bishop John Inglis (1777–1850) of Nova Scotia had championed SPCK local committees to counter the BFBS and BFSS, and when the CCS wrote to him he objected in strong terms.[166] More surprisingly, perhaps, the CCS was also given a frosty reception by the bishops of Calcutta, Bombay and Madras, two of whom were Evangelicals. This rebuff serves to underline the growing institutionalization of imperial Anglicanism. To some extent this was driven from abroad, by episcopal autocrats such George Augustus Selwyn (1809–1878) in New Zealand and the Evangelical Daniel Wilson in Calcutta, who sought

---

[162] *Ibid.*, 158–62.

[163] Janice Cavell, *Tracing the Connected Narrative: Arctic Exploration in British Print Culture, 1818–1860* (Toronto, 2008), 101–16.

[164] Joseph Hardwick, *An Anglican British World: the Church of England and the Expansion of the Settler Empire, c. 1790–1860* (Manchester, 2014), 171–4.

[165] Richard W. Vaudry, *Anglicans and the Atlantic World: High Churchmen, Evangelicals, and the Quebec Connection* (Ithaca, NY, 2003), 34–8, 97–167.

[166] Judith Fingard, 'Inglis, John', *Dictionary of Canadian Biography*, online. http://www.biographi.ca/en/bio/inglis_john_7E.html, last accessed 27 Sep. 2017.

to impose their authority on a patchwork of chaplains, missionaries and other clergy.[167] But it was also taking place in Britain, where from 1824 an Ecclesiastical Board took responsibility for providing the colonies with clergymen. Although formally a branch of the Colonial Office, it placed the process more decisively under the authority of the Bishop of London and the archbishops.[168] This coincided with a growing ambivalence towards the principle of establishment among devout but tolerant colonial governors such as Richard Bourke (1777–1855) in New South Wales and Lord William Bentinck (1774–1839) in India.[169] Glenelg at the Colonial Office – a Canningite and a Liberal as well as an Evangelical – concurred: in places 'comprising great numbers of Presbyterians and Roman-catholics, as well as members of the Church of England, it is evident that the attempt to select any one Church as the exclusive object of public endowment … would not long be tolerated'.[170] Despite misgivings, many churchmen embraced this shift, seeing it as an opportunity to wean the Church off its unhealthy dependence on an increasingly ambivalent state. Probably the most important expression of this was the Colonial Bishoprics' Fund, founded in 1841, which raised money to endow bishoprics across the globe.[171] Although the CBF had close links with the Orthodox- and Tractarian-dominated SPG, Evangelicals participated in it enthusiastically. But having existed hitherto in a world where the writ of government mattered more than that of distant bishops at home, they would now have to learn to live within a more solidly ecclesiastical framework: one increasingly coloured, moreover, by advanced High churchmanship.[172]

[167] Robert William Keith Wilson, *George Augustus Selwyn* (Farnham, 2014), 69–110; T.E. Yates, *Venn and Victorian Bishops Abroad: the Missionary Policies of Henry Venn and their Repercussions upon the Anglican Episcopate of the Colonial Period 1841–1872* (Uppsala, 1978), 30–42.

[168] Hardwick, *Anglican British World*, 30.

[169] Penelope Carson, *The East India Company and Religion, 1698–1858* (Woodbridge, 2012), 183–205; David Stoneman, 'Richard Bourke: for the Honour of God and the Good of Man', *Journal of Religious History*, 38 (2014), 341–55.

[170] Glenelg to Bourke, [30 Nov. 1835], cited in 'Religion and Education in New South Wales', *Asiatic Journal and Monthly Miscellany*, 31 (1840), 218.

[171] Rowan Strong, *Anglicanism and the British Empire, c. 1700–1850* (Oxford, 2007), 198–282.

[172] G.A. Bremner, *Imperial Gothic: Religious Architecture and High Anglican Culture in the British Empire, c. 1840–1870* (New Haven, CT, 2013); Hardwick, *Anglican British World*.

An Evangelical Empire?

Of Sir James Stephen it was said that 'he, more than any other man, virtually governed the Colonial Empire'.[173] Even allowing for exaggeration, the foregoing has shown that there was truth in this. Stephen's career coincided with a period when Evangelicals wielded disproportionate weight in colonial affairs. They also imbued the rhetoric of imperial governance with providential certainty. 'Can we suppose otherwise than it is our office to carry civilization and humanity, peace and good government, and, above all, the knowledge of the true God, to the uttermost ends of the earth?' asked the report of Buxton's Select Committee on Aborigines (1837).[174] Evangelical influence in the Colonial Office would never again reach the heights of the 1810s or the 1830s. Stephen himself unwittingly played a part in this: his 1837 Rules and Regulations encouraged the centralization of power via the systematic collection and use of statistics, thereby diminishing the role that extra-governmental organizations played and eroding the importance of personal acquaintances and connections.[175] The voluntarization of Anglicanism overseas, too, eroded another pillar of Evangelical strength. What remained was the pervasive if vague assumption that British rule was divinely ordained: a providential reward for a nation whose global strength rested not on technology or wealth but on the moral example she set. It was a comforting myth, and a self-serving one. But its long afterlife serves to highlight the deep roots it had put down in national institutions and ideas. The following chapters pursue this theme further.

---

[173] Henry Taylor, *Autobiography*, 2 vols (London, 1885), II: 301.
[174] *Report of the Parliamentary Select Committee on Aboriginal Tribes* (London, 1837), 105.
[175] Laidlaw, *Colonial Connections*, 169–99.

Plate 4: S.W. Fores, *Sternhold and Hopkins at Sea or a Stave out of Time*. Etching, hand-coloured, 1809.

Chapter Five
Patriotism, Piety and Patronage: Evangelicals and the Royal Navy

The naval action at the Basque Roads in April 1809 was not Admiral James Gambier's finest hour. With the French Atlantic fleet at his mercy he havered, refusing to commit his main force even when fire-ships commanded by the dashing young firebrand Thomas Cochrane (1775–1860) caused panic. Or so caricaturists had it. *STERNHOLD and HOPKINS at SEA or a Stave out of Time*, published by S.W. Fores of Picca-dilly in August, has Gambier droning through an uninspiring psalm while Cochrane begs him in vain to capitalize on French confusion. On the wall is a chart not of the French coast but of the Holy Land. A lank-haired chaplain holds up his hands in horror at the interruption, lamenting that Cochrane 'is quite insensible of the beauties of Divine Poetry'! Rumours abounded that 'Dismal Jimmy' Gambier had busied himself marshalling his sailors for church parade. Naturally, he requested a court-martial to clear his name. It was followed anxiously by Evangelicals, who saw it as a trial not just of Gambier's actions but his beliefs, too, and hailed his acquittal as a double vindication. Minutes taken by the shorthand writer and BFBS activist W.B. Gurney (1777–1855) were rushed into print, while Wilberforce praised his friend as 'a true specimen of Christian hero-ism'.[1] While the episode has often been taken to show that Gambier and those like him were 'more fitted for the organ-loft than the quarter-deck', this should be treated with scepticism.[2] There were plenty of celebrated officers who were known to combine piety with professional skill, men like Sir James Saumarez (1757–1836), Jahleel Brenton (1770–1844) and James Hillyar (1769–1843).[3] Indeed, Evangelicals were sensitive about Gambier

---

[1] W.B. Gurney, *Minutes of a Court Martial Holden on Board His Majesty's ship Glad-iator* (Portsmouth, 1809); Georgiana, Lady Chatterton (ed.), *Memorials, Personal and Historical of Admiral Lord Gambier*, 2 vols (London, 1861), II: 328–9.

[2] 'Pamphlets on Methodism', *Gentleman's Magazine*, 100 (1830), 242.

[3] Richard Blake, *Evangelicals in the Royal Navy, 1775–1815: Blue Lights and Psalm-Sing-ers* (Woodbridge, 2008), 174–224.

precisely because they set so much store by the equation of piety with professionalism, a connection that the movement's publicists had painstakingly forged in the preceding decade.[4] Perceptions of the affair have, moreover, been warped by Cochrane's self-justifying autobiography and his many modern acolytes. Among his fellow professionals he was not popular: they found him insufferably arrogant and, whatever they thought about Gambier, deplored Cochrane's misuse of a parliamentary seat as a bully-pulpit against a brother officer.[5]

More revealing for our purposes was another episode from the Basque Roads action. Ever since Trafalgar, when he had commanded the 'fighting *Temeraire*', the hotheaded Rear-Admiral Eliab Harvey (1758–1830) had bragged about his prowess, which he felt had not been recognized.[6] Yet even he surpassed himself when he was passed over for command of the attacking force in favour of Cochrane. This was not Gambier's choice: he seems to have been instructed by the Admiralty to place the relatively junior Cochrane in charge, probably as a sop to the latter's oppositionist allies in parliament. Nevertheless, in a shocking breach of discipline Harvey stormed into Gambier's cabin to protest, exploding as he departed to all in earshot that:

> This is not the first time I have been lightly treated and that my services have not been attended to in the way they deserved, because I am no canting Methodist, no hypocrite, no psalm-singer, and do not cheat old women out of their estates by hypocrisy and canting.[7]

Inevitably, Harvey was court-martialled and dismissed from the service. But he was far from being alone in feeling that religiosity, or at least a nauseating show of it, had lately become a necessary condition for advancement. In the *Naval Chronicle*, a barometer for opinion among naval officers, 'E.G.F.' hinted that 'puritans' and 'fanatics' had not sufficiently rewarded Harvey for his earlier services.[8] The perception that that Navy was becoming tinged with 'enthusiasm' also had a broader currency. 'The Methodists', warned

---

4   Gareth Atkins, 'Christian Heroes, Providence and Patriotism in Wartime Britain, 1793–1815', *Historical Journal*, 58 (2015), 393–414.

5   Cochrane's *Autobiography of a Seaman* (1860) in turn provoked Gambier's niece, Lady Georgiana Chatterton, to respond with *Memorials of Lord Gambier* (1861).

6   James Greig (ed.), *The Farington Diary*, 8 vols (London, 1922–8), V: 173.

7   'Court martial of Admiral Harvey, 22 May 1809', National Archives, Admiralty, Courts Martial Papers, 1809 May, PRO ADM 1/5396, The mysterious final accusation probably derived from Elizabeth Bouverie's bequest of the Teston estate to Middleton in 1798. He, as executor, was left open to allegations of underhand dealings.

8   'Correspondence', *Naval Chronicle*, 21 (1809), 475–6.

Sydney Smith in 1808, '... are attacking the Army and Navy. The principality of Wales and the East-India Company, they have already acquired.'[9]

We saw in the previous chapter how Evangelicals exploited connections, parliamentary influence and pious opinion to gain leverage over colonial appointments and policy. In investigating how and why they gained influence in naval affairs, this chapter provides a further piece of the same jigsaw. This story is largely untold. For although Richard Blake has ably demonstrated how the new piety reshaped professional norms and institutional morality, to assume that Evangelicals cared only about enforcing religious observance and winning souls is not just anachronistic but misleading. Here, as elsewhere, they were consummate 'insiders', developing a powerful patronage network in naval administration in the 1780s and 90s and at the Admiralty in the 1800s that took advantage of their access to Pitt and his circle, spanning parliament, naval administration and the sea-going officer corps.[10] The navy was thus an important sphere of Evangelical activity. It was also one of several contexts where they were drawn into party politics, notwithstanding the efforts of Wilberforce and the 'Saints' in parliament to cultivate an impression of independency. The survival of the Evangelical nexus was closely linked to that of Pittite administrations.

Initially, then, this chapter explores the career of Sir Charles Middleton, ennobled in 1805 as Lord Barham, his nephew James Gambier and the circle surrounding them.[11] Next, it charts how their influence was propagated through appointments in the 1780s and 90s, before examining the consequences of the Middleton–Gambier nexus for the Saints' political position at Westminster and for Evangelical prospects of advancement in the navy. 'Sir Charles is the best man of business I know,' remarked William Pitt to his friend Wilberforce, 'but he would do anything for a *Methodist*.'[12] In the final section the perspective broadens to consider the place of the navy in the wider Evangelical project. It argues that they sought to harness and redirect what Timothy Jenks has called 'victory culture': the slogans, images and associations that British naval successes conjured up. That culture was so vibrant precisely because it was contested, as rival groups tried to claim it as their own, glossing their sectional aspirations as patriotic endeavours

[9]   [Sydney Smith],'Ingram on Methodism', *Edinburgh Review*, 11, 22 (Jan. 1808), 361.
[10] Richard Blake, *Evangelicals*.
[11] Previous work on Middleton's religion is derived chiefly from published sources and therefore misses much that lies beyond Wilberforce and his coterie. See e.g. Michael E. Moody, 'Religion in the Life of Charles Middleton, First Baron Barham', in C. Robert Cole and Michael E. Moody (eds), *The Dissenting Tradition: Essays for Leland H. Carlson* (Athens, OH, 1975), 140–63.
[12] Wilberforce, *Life*, II: 212.

that ought to command universal support. The navy, in short, was a potent embodiment of Britishness on which Evangelicals were eager to put their stamp. Hence the avidity with which they pursued influence in it, and the anxieties of hostile observers regarding their growing weight.

Sir Charles Middleton and his Milieu

Charles Middleton was born in 1726, the twelfth child of Robert, a collector of customs, and his wife Helen, at Bo'ness in Linlithgowshire. He entered the navy in 1741 as captain's servant, passed his lieutenant's examination in 1745 and attained post-rank in 1759 when he was appointed to command the frigate *Arundel*. It was not a meteoric rise: Middleton married Margaret Gambier, the niece of his first Captain, Samuel Mead(e) (d. 1774), in December 1761 and, in 1763, with the end of the Seven Years' War in sight, was content to decline another sea-going appointment to become a gentleman farmer. The outbreak of war in North America saw a return to service, but merely as commander of a succession of guardships, and it was only his appointment as Comptroller in August 1778 by the First Lord, the Earl of Sandwich (1718–1792), that placed him in a position of prominence. Middleton's relatively sudden rise from obscurity has been a topic of debate. Like Sandwich, Middleton owned East India stock, and the two men also moved in similar circles: N.A.M. Rodger suggests that they may have met at the Concerts of Ancient Music, to which both were subscribers.[13] With a staff of only about a hundred, the new head of the Navy Board faced daunting responsibilities, ranging from financial procedures, manning and the royal dockyards, 'the largest industrial organization in Britain, probably in Europe, possibly in the world', to liaison between the Admiralty, Treasury, Victualling and Ordnance Boards.[14] Moreover, war against the Bourbon powers made expansion of the fleet imperative. Untested he undoubtedly was, but Middleton's workaholic appetite for tackling mountains of correspondence, perfecting technological innovations and pushing for administrative change made him an astute appointee.[15] One subordinate remarked

[13]   Roger Morriss, 'Charles Middleton, Lord Barham, 1726–1813', in Peter Le Fevre and Richard Harding (eds), *Precursors of Nelson: British Admirals of the Eighteenth Century* (London, 2000), 304; N.A.M. Rodger, *The Insatiable Earl: a Life of John Montagu, Fourth Earl of Sandwich, 1718–1792* (London, 1993), 160.

[14]   Roger Morriss, *Naval Power and British Culture 1760–1850* (Aldershot, 2004), 4.

[15]   R.J.B. Knight, 'The Introduction of Copper Sheathing into the Royal Navy, 1779–1786', *Mariner's Mirror*, 59 (1973), 175–92; M.E. Condon, 'The Establishment of the Transport Board – a Subdivision of the Admiralty – 4 July 1794', *Mariner's Mirror*, 57

admiringly in 1782 that 'the Controller is the most indefatigable and able of any in my time', adding that 'the load of business he Goes through at the Board, at the Treasury, the Admiralty, and his own house, is astonishing, and what I am confident no other man will be able to execute'.[16] Middleton's reach was extended still further by the connections that his post entailed with mercantile networks, through the contracting of government victualling and shipping contracts and through his position as one of the Elder Brethren of Trinity House, which controlled the movement of shipping on the Thames.

Relations between Sandwich and Middleton were seldom straightforward. Middleton repeatedly fired off blistering letters taking his superior to task for the state of the dockyards, naval discipline and the disposition of the fleet, and hinting that Sandwich was a slacker, as well as intriguing behind his back with the Secretary of State for the American Colonies, George Germain (1716–1785). Yet Sandwich came to appreciate Middleton's professional merits nonetheless, the latter being created a baronet in October 1781. While the two men's correspondence was, until recently, used to sustain nineteenth-century myths about Sandwich's incompetence, in reality it reveals more about the junior man's prickliness, arrogance and ambition. After his patron's resignation in 1782 Middleton crossed swords with a succession of First Lords – Keppel, Howe and Chatham – often making extravagant claims about his own merits and demanding greater influence over policy and appointments, usually unsuccessfully.[17] That this behaviour was tolerated says much about his competence, but it also hints at political connections. Pitt's rise to power in late 1783 was significant. Through his mother, Middleton was related to Henry Dundas, Scottish Lord Advocate and increasingly important as an electoral power-broker north of the border. Secret service money lubricated Middleton's election as MP for Rochester in 1784, while the marriage of his niece, another Margaret Gambier (d. 1818) and a noted beauty, to the Prime Minister's second cousin William Morton Pitt in 1785 further cemented his position in the Pittite political elite.[18] Throughout the late 1780s Middleton was in close contact with the Premier, who encouraged and perhaps judiciously humoured his

---

(1972), 69–84; I. Lloyd Phillips, 'The Evangelical Administrator: Sir Charles Middleton at the Navy Board, 1778–90' (unpublished D.Phil. Thesis, University of Oxford, 1974); John E. Talbott, *The Pen and Ink Sailor: Charles Middleton and the King's Navy, 1778–1813* (London, 1998).

[16] William Gregson to Lord Shelburne, 20 Dec. 1782, cited in Lloyd Phillips, 'Evangelical Administrator', 301–2.

[17] Rodger, *Insatiable Earl*, xiii–xviii, 159–71.

[18] Chatterton (ed.), *Gambier*, I: 6.

reforming schemes. Prime-ministerial latitude paid off: the smooth mobilization of the navy during the Nootka Sound crisis of 1789–90 owed much
to Middleton's painstaking programme of rebuilding and repair.[19]

It was a programme that seemingly suffered little from Middleton's sab-
batarian reluctance to allow dockyard work on Sundays except in direst
emergencies.[20] His reservations may have stemmed from his Presbyterian
upbringing, but they were almost certainly bolstered by his conversion to
heart religion at around the time of his marriage. He was introduced to
'that source of every comfort' through his wife, and he wrote movingly of
his debt to her in a black-edged mourning letter to his friend, the Moravian
minister Christian Ignatius La Trobe, shortly after her death.[21] Information
concerning the Middletons' early married life is patchy, but it is possible
to trace the contours of their religious and social world. For a time they
seem to have come under the influence of George Whitefield and attended
a chapel of the Countess of Huntingdon's Connexion.[22] But from 1763
onwards, they made their country home with Margaret's childhood friend
Elizabeth Bouverie (d. 1798) at Teston in Kent. It was through her that they
were introduced to the bluestocking philanthropist Hannah More during
the late 1770s.[23] 'I dined yesterday with Captain and Mrs Middleton,' More
wrote in 1776. 'There are so few people I meet with in this good town to
whom one can venture to recommend sermons, that the opportunity is
not to be missed.'[24] Although Roger Morriss reckons Middleton's religion
to have been 'censorious and Calvinistic' this may overamplify the available
evidence.[25] True, he was a difficult man and was a friend of the eccentric
predestinarian MP Richard Hill, but by the early 1780s he was also dining
with the much sunnier and more urbane young parliamentarian William
Wilberforce.[26] The Middletons had a town house in Mayfair, where Margaret – a talented painter with interests in literature – entertained cultured

[19]   Knight, 'Copper Sheathing', 175–92.
[20]   Phillips, 'Evangelical Administrator', 30.
[21]   Middleton to Charles Ignatius La Trobe, 17 Dec. 1792, National Maritime Museum,
       Greenwich, Papers of Middleton, Charles, Admiral, 1st Baron Barham, 1726–1813,
       MID/2/28/2. For more on La Trobe see J.C.S. Mason, *The Moravian Church and the
       Missionary Awakening in England, 1760–1800* (Woodbridge, 2001), 114–42.
[22]   William Jay, *Memoirs of the Life and Character of the Late Rev. Cornelius Winter*
       (2nd edn: London, 1812), 151; Blake, *Evangelicals*, 38–9.
[23]   See Anne Stott, *Hannah More: the First Victorian* (Oxford, 2003), 68.
[24]   William Roberts, *Memoirs of the Life and Correspondence of Mrs. Hannah More*, 4
       vols (London, 1834), I: 77.
[25]   Roger Morriss, 'Middleton, Charles, First Baron Barham (1726–1813)', *ODNB*.
[26]   Hannah More to Elizabeth Bouverie, 28 Dec. 1797, cited in Chatterton, *Gambier*, I:
       335; Wilberforce, *Life*, I: 75; III: 223, 370, 340; IV: 122.

visitors that included Johnson, Boswell, Garrick and Reynolds.[27] By the time Charles became Comptroller, he moved in circles that had a decidedly unsectarian feel. In 1781 his erstwhile shipboard surgeon, James Ramsay, now ordained, was appointed to the living at Teston, which lay in the gift of the Bouverie family, and it can be assumed that by this time the Middletons were observant Anglicans.[28] One of their closest friends was the Bishop of London, Beilby Porteus, who was sympathetic to Evangelical moral zeal but hardly an Evangelical himself, and certainly no Calvinist. His affectionate account of Teston's picturesque delights and pious company, *A Brief Account of Three Favourite Country Residences* (1808), was worlds away from the dour fanaticism sometimes associated with 'Calvinism'.[29]

Teston became significant in the explosion of philanthropy that took place in the 1780s. Older activists like the merchant and Marine Society founder Jonas Hanway and the prison reformer John Howard were both friends of Middleton, but Teston was also a crucible for anti-slavery. Ramsay in particular was a key figure, having served as Middleton's surgeon on HMS *Arundel* in the 1750s, where a stomach-churning encounter with a British slave ship ravaged by dysentery made a lasting impression upon him. He sought ordination and, serving parishes in St Kitts during the 1760s and 70s, ministered to slaves there, while penning searing attacks on their mistreatment by planters and government officials. On returning permanently to Britain with his family in late 1781, Ramsay became Middleton's confidential secretary, continuing to write against slavery but also assisting in the reform of the Navy Board.[30] Quakers had spoken out against slavery long since, but Ramsay and the Teston group were a catalyst for the growth of pressure-group politics within the Anglican establishment. 'Teston cabinets' eventually included More, Porteus, Thomas Clarkson, the black emancipist Olaudah Equiano and the La Trobes, Benjamin (1728–1786) and Charles.[31] It was there that parliamentary action was first mooted and it was probably Margaret Middleton who suggested Wilberforce as frontman

---

[27] For their circle, see Roberts, *Hannah More*, I: 77, 93, 146, 185, 207, 238, 253, 277, 317, 398; II: 13, 24, 81, 106, 110, 156, 226, 253; III: 9, 15, 53, 96, 226.

[28] Folarin Shyllon, *James Ramsay the Unknown Abolitionist* (Edinburgh, 1977), 13, 120–1; James Watt, 'James Ramsay, 1733–1789: Naval Surgeon, Naval Chaplain and Morning Star of the Anti-Slavery Movement', *Mariner's Mirror*, 81 (1995), 160.

[29] Beilby Porteus, *A Brief Account of Three Favourite Country Residences* ([n.p.], 1806?), 13–18.

[30] Blake, *Evangelicals*, 58. In London he stayed with Wilberforce or at Middleton's town house. Wilberforce, *Life*, I: 205, 209, 211, 214, 217, 222.

[31] Watt, 'James Ramsay', 156–70; Christopher Leslie Brown, *Moral Capital: Foundations of British Abolitionism* (Chapel Hill, NC, 2006), 333–77.

for the abolition campaign.[32] Ramsay died in 1789, apparently from stress brought about by overwork and by attacks from the West Indian lobby. Yet although the epicentre of the campaign moved elsewhere, this would always remain, for More, 'the Runnymede of the negroes'.[33] Margaret died in 1792 and Elizabeth Bouverie in 1798, but the house and estate were left in the care of Sir Charles and remained a place of retreat for friends like More, Wilberforce and Porteus.[34]

Teston was also an important place for Middleton's extended family. It provided a home for many of his grandchildren, since the marriage of his only child Diana (1762–1823) to the Rutland landowner and MP Gerard Noel Edwards (1759–1838) had not been a success. In part this was down to differences in temperament – Edwards was a compulsive speculator who sank most of his inherited income in the affairs of an unsuccessful bank – but it also owed something to Diana Middleton's overt brand of evangelical religiosity, an eccentricity which her husband did not share. 'You have a certain sacred Mischief in your Piety as to temporal matters', he wrote in 1814, 'which much impugns in my Mind the soundness of your religious opinions.'[35] For much of their lives the couple lived apart, meaning that their fourteen surviving children (whose surname changed when their father became Gerard Noel Noel in 1798) were taken under the wing of the Middletons at Teston. Sir Charles had little respect for his feckless son-in-law, and so took upon himself the task of rebuilding the shattered family fortunes. His letters to Noel senior smack of a lack of respect bordering on contempt. 'My feelings are daily worked at seeing your young men without a home and dependent upon their Acquaintance for a meal', he grumbled in 1805.[36] If their father could not provide for them, Middleton decided, he would call upon connections elsewhere. The results bespeak his influence: two of the Noel grandsons became naval officers; four became Anglican clergymen; the eldest, Charles, was elected MP for Rutland in 1808 and became a firm ally of the Saints.[37] Further pious links were created in the marriage of another grandchild, the saintly Louisa (c. 1785–1816), to the Evangelical banker W.H. Hoare in

[32] Charles Ignatius La Trobe, *Letters to My Children* (London, 1851), 22–3; Wilberforce, *Life*, I: 142–6.

[33] Roberts, *Hannah More*, II: 156.

[34] Sir John Knox Laughton, *Letters and Papers of Charles, Lord Barham: Admiral of the Red Squadron, 1758–1813*, 3 vols (London, 1907–11), II: xxiv–xxv.

[35] Gerard Noel Noel to Diana, Lady Barham, 14 March 1814, Record Office for Leicestershire, Leicester and Rutland, Records of the Noel Family, DE3214/395/34.

[36] Barham to Gerard Noel, 17 July 1805, DE3214/292/29.

[37] Egerton Brydges (ed.), *Collins's Peerage of England*, 9 vols (London, 1812), IX: 247.

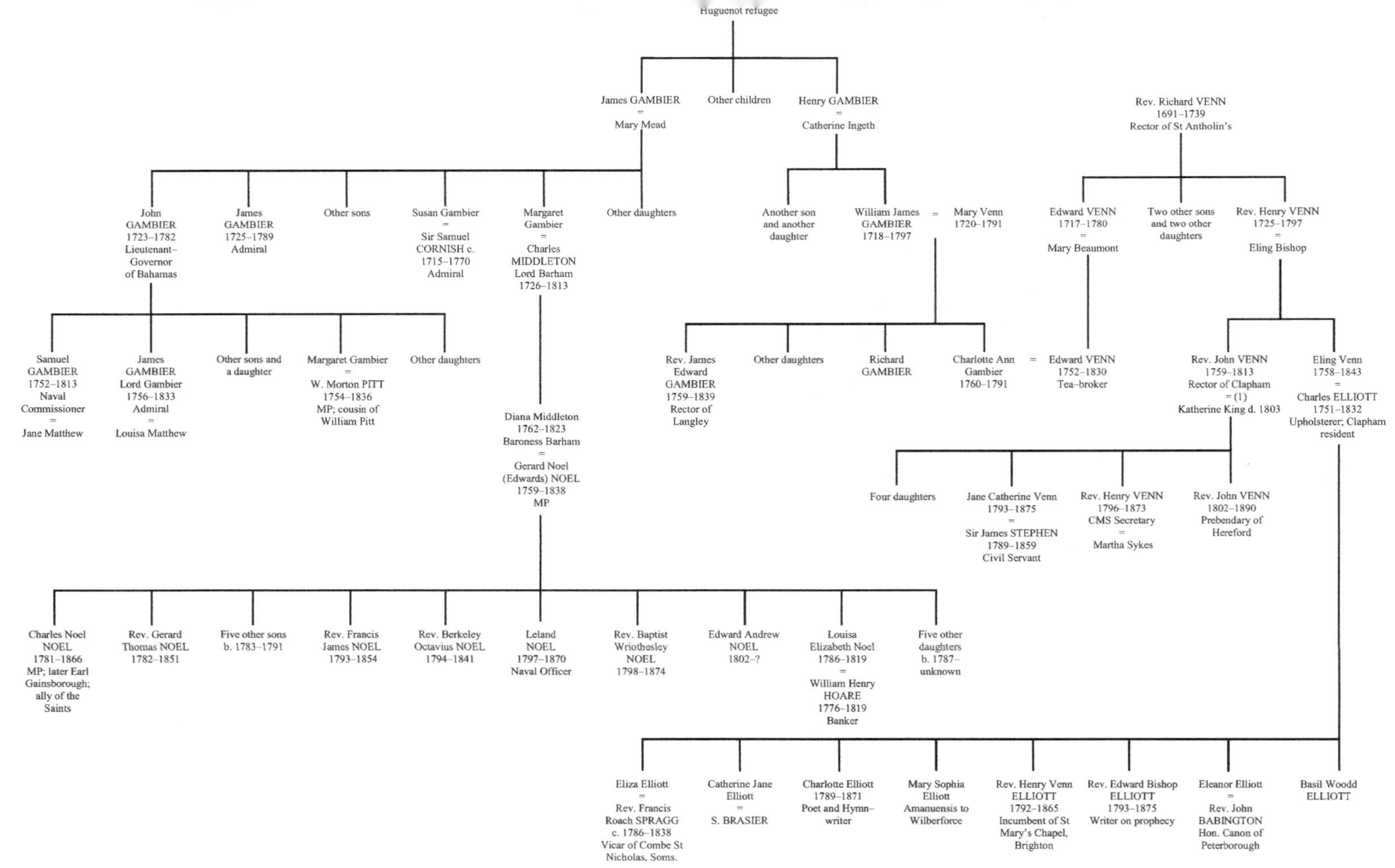

Figure 3: Gambier, Middleton, Noel, Stephen, Venn and Elliott Families

1807. Later on Lady Barham, as Diana Noel became on the death of her father, used her fortune to found her own connexion of chapels in the Gower peninsula of South Wales, which she ruled autocratically in a style that her cantankerous father might well have recognized.[38]

Promoting Piety

Even before the political advent of Wilberforce and the Saints in the 1780s and 90s, then, Middleton was embedded in the world of metropolitan Evangelicalism. But what of Pitt's comment that he 'would do anything for a Methodist'? Behaviour manuals on how those in positions of authority were to comport themselves were a feature of the 1790s.[39] One of the most widely read was Thomas Gisborne's *An Enquiry into the Duties of Men in the Higher and Middle Classes of Society* (1794). Strongly flavoured with cultured Evangelical piety, it set out the ideal roles and responsibilities of a range of professionals and public men. Given the wartime context, it is not surprising that Gisborne provided copious advice on military duties and on the behaviour of naval officers in particular. Lest professionals scoff at advice proffered by a clerical landlubber based in landlocked Staffordshire, Gisborne took pains to acknowledge his sources: 'an Officer of very high rank in his Majesty's Naval Service' and a naval captain recently rewarded 'in the most public and distinguished manner.'[40] From this and other clues, it is clear that the former was Middleton, whom Gisborne probably met through his Cambridge friend and contemporary Wilberforce. The former Comptroller sounds forth on the role of chaplains, the necessity of holding divine service and on the importance of captains as role models and moral enforcers. Whether or not Middleton also supplied advice on patronage, as is likely, it is safe to say that he would have agreed with what Gisborne had to say about it. 'There are various stations in the Navy and Army which confer on those who occupy them a right of patronage and promotion,' he began.

---

[38]   Grayson Carter, *Anglican Evangelicals: Protestant Secessions from the Via Media, c. 1800–1850* (Oxford, 2001), 17–18.

[39]   Leonore Davidoff and Catherine Hall, *Family Fortunes: Men and Women of the English Middle Class, 1780–1850* (London, 1987), 107–48; William Van Reyk, 'Christian Ideals of Manliness in the Eighteenth and Early Nineteenth Centuries', *Historical Journal*, 52 (2009), 1053–73.

[40]   Thomas Gisborne, *An Enquiry into the Duties of Men in the Higher and Middle Classes of Society* (London, 1794), 194n., 202n.

Every such right ought to be considered as a public trust, and exercised with a strict regard to desert. He who from interested views or private attachment promotes a favourite, a friend, or a relation, to a post of which he is unworthy, betrays sordid principles or an unskilful judgement; discourages meritorious exertion throughout the service; and perhaps prepares for his country some severe stroke to be experienced in distant years.[41]

Illegitimate influence, then, might be attended with dire consequences. Nevertheless, Gisborne continued, the idea that public interest was to take precedence over private connections ought not to prevent the conscientious commander from taking religion into account. Far from it: 'let him distinguish by his notice those who live christian lives; and allow to virtuous conduct every degree of reasonable weight in the granting of favours, and the distribution of preferment'.[42] Believers, Gisborne argued, were not only more zealous opponents of vice but were braver too.

One who fitted this description was Middleton's nephew, James Gambier. Gambier had been brought up effectively as a son at Teston before being sent to sea at an early age. After spending much of the 1780s on half pay, he returned to active service in 1793 as captain of HMS *Defence*. During his time ashore Gambier was a regular attender at the Lock Chapel in London, where Thomas Scott preached to a congregation drawn from the Evangelical *beau monde*.[43] Now those same connections helped him to man his ship. John Venn was instrumental in canvassing for possible chaplains for him. Gambier, he told a colleague, was a 'serious man' who wanted 'a serious Chaplain for his ship'. 'Could you recommend him one?'[44] Gambier chose other officers, too, for their piety. The *Defence* quickly became known in the fleet as a 'praying ship', earning its captain the mocking soubriquet 'Dismal Jimmy'.[45] Even so, recalled one midshipman later on, 'our Captain had an uncle who was one of the Lords of the Admiralty, and through whose influence the ship was well manned'.[46] Mockery gave way to plaudits after the Battle of the Glorious First of June in 1794, when

---

[41]   *Ibid.*, 200–1.

[42]   *Ibid., Enquiry*, 206.

[43]   John Scott, *The Life of the Rev. Thomas Scott* (4th edn: London, 1822), 315n. See this volume, 67–8.

[44]   John Venn to Edward Edwards, Aug. 1793, CRL, Church Missionary Society Unofficial Papers, Venn Papers, XCMSACC/ACC/81/C20.

[45]   Chatterton, *Gambier*, I: 248.

[46]   Michael Lewis (ed.), *Sir William Henry Dillon, K.C.H., Vice-Admiral of the Red: A Narrative of my Professional Adventures*, 2 vols (London, 1953–6), I: 96.

Gambier's courageous handling of the *Defence* earned him the gratitude of Earl Howe (1726–1799) and brought him a knighthood, a gold medal and, in 1795, promotion to flag-rank. Gambier was, then, Gisborne's recently rewarded naval captain and his comments on the benefits of instructing a ship's young men in religion as well as arithmetic were relayed in detail.[47] 'Gambier well spoken of,' recorded a delighted Wilberforce during a visit to Portsmouth.[48] More significant in terms of weight within the service was Gambier's appointment to the Board of Admiralty, where he served from 1795–1801 and again in 1804–6 and 1807–8.

While Gambier's rise was not wholly owing to his uncle, then, it served to reinforce an increasingly solid Evangelical bloc in the naval upper echelons. Ambrose Serle (1742–1812), appointed Secretary to the Navy Board in the dying months of Middleton's Comptrollership, was another key figure. Serle was a seasoned public servant, having held positions in the Colonial Department from 1768–76 before accompanying Howe to America, then taking up a place at the Board of Trade on his return in 1778.[49] A friend of preachers such as William Romaine, John Newton, Augustus Montague Toplady and Legh Richmond (1772–1827), Serle was a devotional writer and librettist of note, whose *Horae Solitariae* (1776) and *Christian Remembrancer* (1787) were republished well into the nineteenth century.[50] His introduction to Middleton in June 1789 came through his erstwhile employer Lord Dartmouth, Secretary of State for the Colonies between 1772 and 1775 and another prominent Evangelical.[51] The new colleagues immediately hit it off. Their correspondence frequently turned to religious matters ('I can be well content with my present retirement, enjoying mercies which the world can neither give nor take away,' wrote Serle in his second letter), but the new Secretary also became a professional confidant of the Comptroller, sharing his concerns about the Board's inefficiency and lethargy.[52] These frustrations eventually boiled over when Middleton resigned in early 1790. As a parting gesture he proposed to promote his friend to the Clerkship of the Acts, but Serle's polite refusal was revealing:

[47] Gisborne, *Enquiry*, 193–4.
[48] Wilberforce, *Life*, II: 57–8. In 1795 Wilberforce recorded dinner with 'two Gambiers', John Newton and Ambrose Serle. Wilberforce, *Life*, II: 84.
[49] J.M. Collinge, *Office-Holders in Modern Britain, VII: Navy Board Officials 1660–1832* (London, 1978), 137; Edward H. Tatum junior (ed.), *The American Journals of Ambrose Serle, Secretary to Lord Howe, 1776–1778* (San Marino, CA, 1940), xii.
[50] Serle supplied the libretto for La Trobe's *Dawn of Glory*. La Trobe, *Letters*, 55.
[51] Serle to Middleton, 19 June 1789, Middleton Papers, MID/1/168/1.
[52] Serle to Middleton, 8 Sept. 1789, Middleton Papers, MID/1/168/2.

Religion itself may suffer from the undistinguishing Calumny of my pursuing a sordid secular Interest, while I profess to live for a better. Men, and particularly those about us, who cannot enter into your patriotic and disinterested views in this case, will most assuredly judge from their own Motives concerning our's [*sic*], and give us no Credit for Professions, in the Establishment of which we establish too temporal and visible Interest.[53]

Appearances mattered, in other words; but one wonders what Middleton, who was undoubtedly highly ambitious, made of his colleague's comment. Serle resigned too, but like Ramsay became a valued member of the Middleton family circle.[54]

Middleton returned eagerly to office in May 1794 when he was called to the Admiralty as a naval lord. The Pitt government, eager to demonstrate its reforming credentials to the Portland Whigs, was creating a new Transport Board to prevent wasteful inter-board competition: it was constituted in July. Middleton had pestered a succession of superiors on the matter ever since the American War, and was consequently given full rein to put his ideas into practice.[55] Being in part under the supervision of the Secretary of State for War, Dundas, the new Board also provided Middleton with a prime chance to bring together some congenial Scottish cronies, to the chagrin of many within the navy. His countrymen Hugh Christian (1747–1798) and Philip Patton (1739–1815) – a distant relation – were put in place as chairman and sea commissioner, while Ambrose Serle became third member of the board, continuing there until his death in 1812. Other positions were filled by former Navy Board officials.[56] Middleton's appointment brought opportunities to pull further strings. Thus in 1794 he canvassed Dundas to support the candidacy of James Gambier's brother, Samuel (1752–1813), for an EIC Directorship, unsuccessfully as it turned out.[57] It comes as no surprise, however, to learn that Samuel was made Secretary to the Navy Board in August 1795 – despite having no experience of naval affairs – and

[53] Serle to Middleton, 25 Feb. 1790, 7 Apr. 1790, Middleton Papers, MID/1/168/7, 168/9.

[54] See, for example, Ambrose Serle's letters to Charles Noel on the death of the latter's wife, 13, 21, 29 Nov., 3 Dec. 1811, Record Office for Leicestershire, Leicester and Rutland, Records of the Noel Family, DE3214/493/95-8.

[55] Middleton to Chatham, 27 Jan. 1794, National Archives, William Pitt, First Earl of Chatham: Papers, PRO 30/8/365, fos. 62–4.

[56] Condon, 'Transport Board', 79; Middleton to John Deas Thompson, 10 Dec. 1803, Middleton Papers, MID/13/1/45.

[57] Middleton to Dundas, 28 May 1794, Melville Papers, BL Add. MS. 41079, fos. 7–8.

promoted to Naval Commissioner the following year.[58] Robert Gambier Middleton (1774–1837), another nephew, was raised to post-rank in 1794. Another James Gambier – a cousin – enjoyed a succession of diplomatic appointments in the 1790s and early 1800s.[59] Eventually Middleton over-played his hand, making himself so obnoxious in power struggles between Dundas and Earl Spencer, the new First Lord, that the latter forced him to resign, after barely a year in post. Nevertheless, he would have been cheered by the appointment of Sir James Gambier as junior naval lord, in March 1795, which he had lobbied for and was still there to witness.[60]

Notwithstanding Middleton's second and seemingly final departure in November 1795, there was a growing awareness among Evangelicals out-side the navy that they could call upon well-placed friends inside it. As we saw in the previous chapter, Middleton was instrumental in planning and co-ordinating the Sierra Leone expedition and the First Fleet to Botany Bay, and helped to place pious figures in key positions. But his influence, and that of Gambier, was not limited to the early years of these ventures. Through them the SLC constantly badgered the Admiralty for better naval protection and stronger escorts.[61] Private philanthropic bodies, too, were emboldened to come forward. The LMS, for instance, called upon the Serle–Middleton–Gambier axis in attempting to place missionaries on one of Bligh's voyages, as well as for advice regarding its first ship, the *Duff*, in 1795–6.[62] (William Shrubsole [1759–1829] was a shipwright at Sheerness, a clerk at the Bank of England, a member of Whitefield's Tabernacle and one of the founders of the LMS, and it is likely that he, too, was known to Middleton.)[63] Similarly, in surmounting an 1800 Privy Council travel ban, the Moravian Missionary Society applied to Serle via La Trobe, who armed himself with a letter of recommendation from their mutual friend Porteus as reserve ammunition. Here was Evangelical networking *par excellence*, for ultimately it was a word from Gambier, at the Admiralty, which did the trick. William Huskisson, Under-Secretary of State for War, issued the nec-essary exemption, assuring La Trobe that 'your Missionaries shall go. They do good, wherever they are, and there is no reason for detaining *them* on

[58] Collinge, *Navy Board Officials*, 102.
[59] William Battersby, *James Fitzjames: The Mystery Man of the Franklin Expedition* (Stroud, 2010), 25–30.
[60] Edward J. Eliot to George Pretyman-Tomline, 15 Feb. 1795, Kent History and Library Centre, Stanhope of Chevening Manuscripts, U1590 S5 C35/1.
[61] See e.g. Evan Nepean to William Wilberforce, 10 Jan. 1800, Bodl., MSS Wilberforce, d.17, fo. 99.
[62] A. Skevington Wood, *Thomas Haweis, 1734–1820* (London, 1957), 203–19.
[63] Rodger, *Insatiable Earl*, 169.

suspicion.'[64] Gambier was again solicited by the LMS in late 1808 to arrange conveyance for their India missionaries, a request he supported, but which was refused by the EIC. The sympathetic letter sent by the Senior Clerk to the Admiralty, John Dyer (c. 1777–1847), another LMS supporter, illustrates the extent of Evangelical penetration of the navy. 'I fear that political considerations when governed by worldly policy will always interpose insuperable objections to any formal sanction,' he explained apologetically.[65] Elsewhere, though, there was more success. Joseph Hughes of the Bible Society could announce in June 1809 that a co-conspirator in the Transport Office – Serle, probably – had 'offered his services in sending the Scriptures to Foreign parts by trusty gentlemen to whom he has frequent access'.[66] These links prefigured later philanthropic-naval collaboration, such as the West Africa Squadron and the disastrous Niger Expedition of 1841–2.

The Saints and Pittite Politics

Pitt's resignation in 1801 had significant implications for the Middleton–Gambier nexus. At the Admiralty, Spencer was replaced by the Earl of St Vincent (1735–1823), a sea-going disciplinarian who had little patience with politicians and even less with administrators.[67] The resulting purge saw the removal of the existing board and their replacement with a more compliant crew: Gambier, by this time Vice-Admiral, was banished first to the Channel Fleet and then appointed Lieutenant-Governor and naval Commander-in-Chief of distant Newfoundland. St Vincent's knife was sharper still in his dealings with the civilian boards, which he condemned as *'rotten to the very core',* implementing a series of ever deeper cuts.[68] Middleton initially warmed to the arrival of a fellow reformer, but became alarmed at St Vincent's destructive dockyard policy. Sea officers, he opined drily

---

[64]   La Trobe, *Letters*, 54–8.

[65]   John Dyer to London Missionary Society, 10 Jan. 1809, cited in Penelope Carson, *The East India Company and Religion, 1698–1858* (Woodbridge, 2012), 99. J.C. Sainty, *Office-Holders in Modern Britain, VIII: Admiralty Officials 1660–1870* (London, 1975), 122.

[66]   Leslie Howsam, *Cheap Bibles: Nineteenth-Century Publishing and the British and Foreign Bible Society* (Cambridge, 1991), 155. See also Thomas Shuttleworth Grimshawe, *A Memoir of the Rev. Legh Richmond* (London, 1829), 300.

[67]   See John R. Breihan, 'The Addington Party and the Navy in British Politics, 1801–1806', in Craig L. Symond (ed.), *New Aspects of Naval History* (Annapolis, MD, 1981), 163–89.

[68]   St Vincent to Spencer, 24 Aug. 1797, cited in J.S. Tucker, *Memoirs of Admiral the Right Hon. The Earl of St Vincent*, 2 vols (London, 1844), I: 423.

to Wilberforce, 'have very little knowledge of the Civil branches of the Navy and are in general inimical to those who conduct it.'[69] The former Comptroller was well aware that the current system was confused and ramshackle, but he also knew that it could be made to work, complaining all the while that if his advice had been followed decades before, the current upheaval might have been avoided.[70] St Vincent, for his part, was intent upon eliminating personal enemies. He loathed Middleton, calling him 'a compound of paper and packthread' and a corrupt 'scotch packhorse', and blasting him as a supporter of Pitt and a desk-sailing bureaucrat.[71] Open pamphleteering against 'the harpies and hydras that sting, and pollute, and prey upon the public' was paralleled by partisan investigations that sought to slur those who had crossed him. The Pittite Sir Home Popham (1762–1820) was indicted on fabricated evidence, while Sir Andrew Snape Hamond (1738–1828), Middleton's friend and successor at the Navy Board, was pilloried in the press and forced to defend himself in the Commons.[72]

Historians remain divided as to whether St Vincent was a well-meaning maverick or a vicious megalomaniac.[73] Either way, he was desperate to place amenable figures in key positions. At the Admiralty this was straightforward: commissioners were political appointments and therefore subject to ministerial fiat. At the Navy Board it was harder: its members were civil servants set in place by Letters Patent, liable for dismissal only on grounds of gross misconduct. The result was a power struggle between a pro-Pitt faction at the Board and a pro-St Vincent faction at the Admiralty, made all the more bitter by St Vincent's employment of informers and 'the most abusive letters that ever were written from one Board to another'.[74] In the event, his brinkmanship was matched by the stubbornness of Hamond and the Navy Board. Others, however, cracked more easily: Sir Evan Nepean

[69]   Middleton to Wilberforce, 23 Dec. 1802, Bodl., MSS Wilberforce, c.47 fos. 91–2.

[70]   Laughton, *Barham Letters*, II: 218; Middleton to Wilberforce, n.d. [1804-5],Bodl., MSS Wilberforce, c.47 fo. 93.

[71]   St Vincent to Markham, 16 May 1806, cited in Clements Markham (ed.), *Selections from the Correspondence of Admiral John Markham during the Years 1801–4 and 1806–7* (London, 1904), 49–50; Jervis to Nepean, May 1797, cited in O.A. Sherrard, *Life of Lord St Vincent* (London, 1933), 113.

[72]   N.A.M. Rodger, *The Command of the Ocean: a Naval History of Britain, 1649–1815* (London, 2004), 479.

[73]   David Bonner Smith (ed.), *Letters of Admiral of the Fleet the Earl of St. Vincent whilst First Lord of the Admiralty, 1801–1804*, 2 vols (London, 1922-7), II: 1–18; Roger Morriss, 'St Vincent and Reform, 1801–04', *Mariner's Mirror*, 69 (1983), 269–90; Rodger, *Command of the Ocean*, 477.

[74]   William Marsden, *A Brief Memoir of the Life and Writings of the late William Marsden* (London, 1838), 103n.

(1752–1822), another Middleton ally, resigned as Admiralty Secretary.[75] Middleton deplored the mounting dysfunction. 'To carry on reforms,' he remarked pithily, 'Zeal, Knowledge – Application and Principle are all necessary – But where are these to be found? Not I fear in men, who are hungry and thirsty after places.'[76] Anxiety about his own interest probably helped to shape his views – several protégés retained places in the endangered Navy Office – but like many others he worried about the parlous state of the service as it struggled to rearm after the Peace of Amiens.[77] During Pitt's political exile at Walmer Castle, he and Middleton had discovered a shared interest in farming.[78] More significant, though, was the advice he provided on naval matters, and when Pitt commenced his parliamentary attack on the Addington government in early 1804 on this issue, he did so armed with professional expertise, much of it from Middleton.[79] He was backed by Wilberforce, who asserted that 'he had not found a single professional man in the navy, who had not professed himself privately and confidently to him in the highest degree dissatisfied with the conduct of the Admiralty', predictably so given his intimacy with Middleton.[80] Addington fell a month later.

Loyal followers now claimed their rewards. Gambier was brought back to the Admiralty, then in December 1804 Middleton returned to office as head of a new Commission for Revising and Digesting the Civil Affairs of the Navy, designed both to draw the sting from the Commission of Naval Enquiry set up by St Vincent and to implement Middleton's 1780s reform programme.[81] This process was, however, derailed when the tenth report of the Commission of Naval Enquiry came out in spring 1805, accusing Dundas (now Viscount Melville) of tolerating the misuse of public funds. After a heated all-night debate on a motion of censure brought by the

[75] John Barrow, *An Auto-Biographical Memoir of Sir John Barrow, Bart., Late of the Admiralty* (London, 1847), 258.

[76] Middleton to Wilberforce, 23 Dec. 1802, Bodl., MSS Wilberforce, c.47 fos. 91–2.

[77] Correspondents who had thanked him in 1790 and were still in office included Charles Derrick and Edward Falkingham. Derrick's *Memoirs of The Rise and Progress of the Royal Navy* (1806) were dedicated to Barham. Derrick to Middleton, 15 March 1790, Middleton Papers, MID/1/43/2; Falkingham to Middleton, n.d., MID/1/63.

[78] Middleton to Thompson, 24 Dec. 1802, Middleton Papers, MID/13/1/37.

[79] Wilberforce, *Life*, III: 90, 96, 119, 149; Memorandum 'On the state of the Navy', Middleton to John Deas Thompson, 18 July 1803, cited in Laughton, *Barham Letters*, III: 15–21, 31–5; Middleton to John Fordyce, 3 March 1804, Melville Papers, BL Add. MS. 41079, fos. 51–2.

[80] *Parliamentary Debates from the Year 1803 to the Present Time*, 1 (22 Nov. 1803–29 March 1804), col. 896.

[81] Thompson to Middleton, 6 Dec. 1804, Middleton Papers, MID/1/186/10.

Foxite Samuel Whitbread and a knife-edge division decided by the Speaker's casting vote, Melville had no choice but to resign. 'We can get over Austerlitz,' lamented Pitt, 'but we can never get over the tenth report.'[82] Opposition newspapers crowed. To widespread surprise, however, Pitt passed over the obvious frontrunners, the Earl of Buckinghamshire (1760–1816) and Charles Yorke (1764–1834), and opted instead to replace Melville with Middleton, whom he ennobled as Baron Barham. The choice of a pen-pushing 'superannuated Methodist' was to some a baffling choice.[83] Yet the appointment made sense professionally: Barham and Gambier already commanded a web of protégés in naval administration, and were well-placed to administer a navy unsettled by St Vincent's austerities.[84] It was also politically expedient for a weakened Premier anxious to bolster his tottering ministry. Whereas Wilberforce's speech expressing his 'utter detestation' at Melville's conduct had been one of the nails in his coffin during the censure debate, Barham's elevation was calculated to 'catch the votes of Wilberforce and Co. now and then'.[85] This raises the point that while the Saints as parliamentarians could and did sanctimoniously disavow partisan considerations, often to the surprise and frustration of ministers, they acted in conjunction with others who did not. Barham refused to abandon his relative and patron, consoling him that a return to action might be imminent and later extending a warm invitation to Teston as a rest-cure after 'the persecution and anguish of mind' to which he had been subjected.[86] This was not wholly selfless: Charles Noel had been brought to town in 1804 to meet his grandfather's patrons, and was now ordered to make a point of attendance at Melville's impeachment proceedings, 'however distant he may be from Town'.[87] Melville might yet be in a position to reward those who stood by him.

If critics were astonished by Barham's rise, Evangelicals were delighted. They rejoiced in the appointment of one 'who, we know, *prays* for the success of his measures', seeing in its unexpectedness evidence of

[82] Thorne, *HoP*, III: 642.

[83] Thomas Creevey to J. Currie, 11 May 1805, cited in John Gore (ed.), *Creevey* (London, 1948), 22.

[84] C.I. Hamilton, *The Making of the Modern Admiralty: British Naval Policy-Making, 1805–1927* (Cambridge, 2011), pp. 6–41.

[85] *Parliamentary Debates*, 4 (13 Mar.–14 May 1805), *col 318*; Creevey to Currie, 11 May 1805, cited in Gore, *Creevey*, 22.

[86] Middleton to Melville, 27 Apr. 1805, Melville Papers, BL Add. MS. 41079, fo. 133; Barham to Melville, 13 June 1806, BL Add. MS. 41079, fo. 134.

[87] Middleton to Noel, n.d., [1804], Records of the Noel Family, DE3214/548/41; Middleton to Thompson, 24 March 1805, Middleton Papers, MID/13/1/80.

divine interposition.[88] 'When I wrote to you last', More told Wilberforce breathlessly,

> I did not think that a few hours wou'd have shower'd on the head of our Host the accumulated honour of a Peerage and then of 1st Lord of the Admiralty... There is something Providential in the whole History which he gave us last night. Strange! that the plans which he has been framing for near twenty years, and had thrown aside in utter despair, he shou'd now be called himself to put into Execution in the Plenitude of Power. May God give him grace and health.[89]

News of the crushing victory at Trafalgar in November elicited still more extravagant commentary. Amid patriotic outpourings about Nelson and his 'band of brothers', Evangelicals reflected smugly that the 'true Christian' installed at Admiralty House had been the real operative cause. 'To his activity and prudence, no small share of praise, on account of this victory, is generally ascribed', gushed the *Christian Observer*.[90] While Wilberforce had long been a public figure, this was the first time that a self-avowed 'serious Christian' had been placed at the centre of strategic and political affairs, and pious publicists rushed to capitalize on it.

Leaving aside its symbolic resonances, Barham's elevation also had material value. Admiralty patronage was vast and the favour of the First Lord highly sought after. 'I declare to you that since my coming to this board, I have made but one master and commander', he wearily told one correspondent. 'When I read over the claims before me, from admirals and captains for their children, from the king's ministers, members of parliament, peers, and eminent divines ... I do not see when I am to make another.'[91] Such remarks, however, should be taken with a pinch of salt. Noels, Gambiers and Middletons all appeared on promotion lists: Robert Gambier Middleton, for example, became Dockyard Commissioner at

---

[88] Roberts, *Hannah More*, III: 232; [James Stephen], 'Preface to the Fourth Edition', in *War in Disguise; or, the Frauds of the Neutral Flags* (4th edn: London, 1806), ix–xix, excerpted in 'View of Lord Barham's Naval Administration', *Christian Observer*, 5 (1806), 747–50.

[89] More to Wilberforce, n.d., [May 1805], Rubinstein Library, Duke University, Wilberforce Papers, Wilberforce Papers, Box 1, Folder 5.

[90] 'Great Britain. Thanksgiving Day', *Christian Observer*, 4 (1805), 711.

[91] Barham to Cornwallis, late 1805, cited in G. Cornwallis-West, *The Life and Letters of Admiral Cornwallis* (London, 1927), 494.

Gibraltar on £1,000 a year.[92] Sought-after frigate commands and lucrative dockyard posts went to other connections, many of them pious. It is also significant that Barham's papers contain numerous requests from co-religionists eager to advance clients, including Wilberforce, Serle, Noel, Hill, Morton Pitt and Porteus, the preacher C.E. de Coetlogon and the East India Director Charles Grant, not to mention Peter La Touche, Henry Thornton and his brother Robert, all financiers.[93] Barham resigned when the ministry dissolved after the death of Pitt in early 1806. But even then, Gambier retained a tight grip on patronage matters. Portland's ministry brought him back to the Board from 1807–8, where his already formidable authority was heightened by the inexperience of the new First Lord, Mulgrave (1755–1831), a soldier by profession who leant heavily on his veteran colleague.[94] An excess of junior officers, a lack of vacancies and the centralization of appointments compounded a sense in the profession that political influence mattered more than sea-going experience.[95] 'What I ask of the Admiralty they never comply with,' wrote Vice-Admiral Collingwood (1748–1810) to his sister in 1808. '[Your correspondent] should go to Admiral Gambier, who had the direction and all the patronage of the navy since Lord Mulgrave was at the Board.'[96]

William Henry Dillon's *Narrative of my Professional Adventures* allows us to examine Gambier's influence more closely.[97] A one-time midshipman under Gambier on the *Defence*, Dillon (1779–1857) benefited enormously from his patron's success thereafter, being shuffled rapidly from ship to ship in order to gain promotion and prize money. 'It was therefore desirable to be on good terms with him.'[98] Dillon does not seem to have been especially religious himself: he was on the *Defence* because he had other connections. But his impression that pious men were favoured is borne out by other evidence about Gambier's officers. The First Lieutenant, 'Mr Lobb', for instance, was 'of a religious turn', and his stop-start career prior to joining the *Defence* was transformed thereafter: by 1806 William Grenville

---

[92] *Steel's Original and Correct List of the Royal Navy* (February–May 1805); Collinge, *Navy Board Officials*, 122.

[93] For Barham's patronage requests see Middleton Papers, MID/4 and MID/14.

[94] It may also be significant that Mulgrave's father, like Middleton, had been a protégé of Sandwich in the 1770s and 80s. Rodger, *Insatiable Earl*, 156–8.

[95] Samantha Cavell, *Midshipmen and Quarterdeck Boys in the British Navy, 1771–1831* (Woodbridge, 2012), 113–58.

[96] Collingwood to his sister, 25 June 1808, cited in Edward Hughes (ed.), *The Private Correspondence of Admiral Lord Collingwood* (London, 1957), 247–8.

[97] Lewis, *Dillon*, I: 97, 100–2, 110.

[98] *Ibid.*, 164.

(or Granville) Lobb (d. 1814) was Dockyard Commissioner at Malta.[99] Twysden, the Third Lieutenant, 'swore frequently', but was connected with More and Middleton, and did well.[100] Several of Gambier's protégés followed him into later commands: the chaplain, William Hawtayne (c. 1754–1822), accompanied him in 1807 on the expedition to Copenhagen, as well as on board the *Caledonia* in the Channel in 1808–9.[101] Another Evangelical, Francis Austen (1774–1865), became his flag captain on *Neptune* in 1801. Recent suggestions that Austen's career was impeded by his association with Gambier seriously underestimate the latter's clout: Austen was kept in almost constant employment on *Canopus* (1805), *St Albans* (1807) and *Caledonia* (1811), all marks of favour at a time when commands were increasingly scarce.[102] Others, like Edward Ratsey (c. 1775–1867), Thomas Whinyates (1755–1806), Thomas Twysden (1765–1801) and Charles Hawtayne (1752–1857), William's son, also did well. In fact, of those who served under Gambier in the 1790s, ten reached post-rank, nine of them in or around his time at the Admiralty between 1795 and 1808.[103] Five made the next step to flag.[104] While it is difficult to draw such detailed conclusions about those from beyond his entourage, it is significant that his flag captain in 1809 at the Basque Roads was another pious man, William Bedford (c. 1764–1827); Admiral Sir Robert Stopford (1768–1847), too, was known to be a praying commander.

Even after stepping down from the Admiralty again in May 1808, Gambier remained a figure of substance. He was rewarded for his leadership of the controversial Copenhagen expedition in 1807 with parliamentary thanks and a peerage, and in 1808 he hoisted his flag as commander-in-chief of

[99]   Collinge, *Navy Board Officials*, 122.

[100]   Chatterton, *Gambier*, I: 292.

[101]   Lewis, *Dillon*, I: 96; John Marshall, *Royal Naval Biography*, 8 vols (London, 1823–35), 1st supplement, 263; National Archives, ADM 37/1238, Admiralty: Ships' Musters (Series II), Ship: *Caledonia*, 1 Aug. 1808–28 Feb. 1809.

[102]   Brian Southam, *Jane Austen and the Navy* (2000), 106–10. Francis, was brother of Jane Austen and eventually became Admiral of the Fleet, while another brother and naval officer, James (1765–1819), was related by marriage to Gambier's wife, Louisa Matthew. Park Honan, *Jane Austen: Her Life* (1987), 90, 162.

[103]   Thomas Twysden (1794), William Grenville Lobb (1795), Hon. Philip Wodehouse (1796), Andrew Smith, (1797), Charles Worsley Boys, John Riboleau, Alexander Becher (1802), Edward Ratsey (1806), Charles Sibthorpe Hawtayne (1807), William Henry Dillon (1808). National Archives, ADM 35/504, Navy Board: Navy Pay Office: Ships' Pay Books (Series III), Ship: *Defence*, 1793 May 21-1794 Jul. For further information, see David Syrett and R.L. DiNardo (eds), *The Commissioned Officers of the Royal Navy, 1660–1994* (Aldershot, 1994).

[104]   Dillon, Hawtayne, Ratsey, Riboleau and Smith.

the Channel Fleet, which position he retained until 1811. The controversies surrounding his behaviour at the Basque Roads have already been noted. But it is clear that what really counted against Gambier in the eyes of his fellow officers was not any perceived shortage of bravery or surfeit of piety, but his relative lack of active experience. It was this that weighed against him in 1810, when he was passed over as First Lord when Mulgrave left the Admiralty. For although Gambier knew the Prime Minister, Spencer Perceval, another deeply religious man, the two were not especially close; and while the King thought much of Gambier's character and courage, he observed astutely that 'his professional abilities are not held in the highest estimation'.[105] When he left the Channel Fleet in 1811 he had scarcely been to sea in two years.[106] Yet this was not quite the end of his public career. After hauling down his flag, Gambier led the British diplomatic team that negotiated peace with the United States in late 1814, and was awarded a G.C.B. in 1815. He was already, like Lord Teignmouth, a much respected ·Evangelical elder statesman, being made the first President of the Church Missionary Society in 1812 as the CMS armed itself for the 'Pious Clause' campaign. In retirement he added weight to the African Institution and naval charities, appearing frequently on philanthropic platforms and chairing London meetings.

Evangelicals and 'Victory Culture'

As the navy wound down at the end of the war, opportunities for the deployment of patronage became fewer and further between. Only those with Admiralty influence could realistically hope for active employment, meaning that the same centralizing forces that had placed preferment at the disposal of Barham and Gambier now counted against their protégés. There remained several 'blue lights' who were prepared to fly the flag for 'serious' piety, some of them prominent, such as Rear-Admiral Sir Charles Vinicombe Penrose (1759–1830), commander of the Mediterranean fleet. But they do not seem to have been part of a connected religious-professional nexus. This lack of a distinctive Evangelical 'party' was, paradoxically, an indirect consequence of the networks that this article has traced. As Richard Blake has argued, an important but overlooked aspect of Barham's time at the Admiralty was the revised *Regulations and Instructions* of 1806,

---

[105] Spencer Walpole, *The Life of the Rt. Hon. Spencer Perceval*, 2 vols (London, 1874), II: 83.

[106] *Parliamentary Debates*, 19 (22 Feb.–10 May 1811), 382.

which beefed up the framework for shipboard chaplains and reinforced the idea that there ought to be a service with a sermon on a Sunday.[107] Evangelicals did not, then, stand out as much as they once had. But, in any case, the idea that they were alone in their concern for shipboard morality and religious observance has long seemed suspect. The so-called 'Chaplains' Charter' of 1812 that improved pay, pensions and conditions of service, and gave John Owen (1754–1823), Chaplain-General to the Army, responsibility for the forces as a whole, was a government initiative.[108] It should be seen as part of the 'church reform' measures set in train by Spencer Perceval, the Ryder brothers, Nicholas Vansittart and Lord Liverpool, which were intended to defend and reassert the importance of the Church of England by enforcing residence, raising curates' pay and providing funding for new churches.[109] The provision of New Testaments and Prayer Books at government expense, another plank of the 1812 measure, was probably prompted as much by the spread of nonconformity as by sailors' perceived irreligion. To be sure, these initiatives were supported by Gambier and his ilk. But in the navy, as elsewhere, there were plenty of figures who supported a range of moralizing endeavours without identifying with partisan labels: men such as Edward Hawke Locker (1777–1849), Secretary (1819) and then Commissioner (1824) at Greenwich Naval Hospital, a regular correspondent of Wilberforce and John Bird Sumner and author of *Popular Lectures, on the Bible and Liturgy* (1821). Directors of the Hospital at around this period also included J.J. Angerstein and Samuel Thornton, while Locker replaced another evangelical, John Dyer, as Secretary.[110]

Nevertheless, as with Bible and missionary societies ashore, Evangelical-led voluntarism was a cause for potential friction. Some officers welcomed the activities of bodies such as the Naval and Military Bible Society (1779; refounded 1804) and British and Foreign Seamen and Soldiers' Friend Society (1813), and hortative journals such as the *New Sailors' Magazine and Naval Chronicle* (1827), all of which sought to remedy a perceived shortage in the availability of religious literature. Hitherto supplies of books and Bibles had depended on requests from individual captains for parcels of books

[107] Blake, *Evangelicals*, 140–73; see also *New Establishment of Pay and Half-Pay for Navy Chaplains* (London, 1812).

[108] Michael Snape, *The Royal Army Chaplains' Department, 1796–1953* (Woodbridge, 2007), 34–56. For broader context, see N.A.M. Rodger, 'The Naval Chaplain in the Eighteenth Century', *Journal for Eighteenth-Century Studies*, 18 (1995), 33–45.

[109] Stewart J. Brown, *The National Churches of England, Ireland, and Scotland, 1801–46* (Oxford, 2001), 62–74

[110] Philip Newell, *Greenwich Hospital: a Royal Foundation, 1692–1983* ([Holbrook], 1984), 125.

from the SPCK.[111] Others, however, were satisfied with that system and saw interference in it as a threat to the chain of command. They also regarded the non-denominational and often strongly dissenting composition of such bodies with suspicion. In 1816, for instance, the evangelistic activities of Sir George Grey (1676–1828), Commissioner at Portsmouth Dockyard, and his wife Lady Mary (1770–1858) became the subject of an Admiralty enquiry when the chaplain, Tufton Scott (1760–1832), accused the Greys of allowing apprentices to dodge chapel services via their garden in order to attend dissenting services in the town.[112] Later on Samuel Cole (c. 1767–1839), Senior Chaplain at Greenwich Hospital from 1827, domestic chaplain to the Duke of Clarence and, thanks to his royal patron, effectively the leading clergyman in the navy, took pains to ensure that 'no Books or Tracts [would be] circulated in His Majesty's Navy but such as were to be found on the printed List of the SPCK'.[113] There were, then, differences over how best to implement religious provision that mirrored similar debates on land.

Where Evangelicals undoubtedly were very successful indeed was in using their connections in the navy and their philanthropic investment in it to market the advantages of their creed. Among the earliest examples of this was the Naval and Military Bible Society, founded in 1779. By the turn of the nineteenth century it was in seemingly terminal decline brought about by lack of public interest and the deaths of its original proponents.[114] Like the younger CMS, its annual sermon was held at St Ann Blackfriars, in London, but the meagre returns from this and from other scattered collections meant that its financial situation was parlous.[115] This all changed in 1804–5 when a media-savvy consortium of bankers and metropolitan clergy resurrected it.[116] Their interest was not, as might be assumed, piqued by Trafalgar, although that almost certainly secured its prosperity thereafter; this was an endeavour that emerged from the period of invasion panic that preceded it. In its first incarnation it had been run by nonconformists and open to all. Now, rank and affluence were given more weight: whereas the NMBS had originally been administered by a committee of twenty-one subscribers, a guinea now bought a year's governorship; ten

---

[111] Snape, *Redcoat*, 67–89; Blake, *Evangelicals*, 82–4.

[112] Roald Kverndal, 'Grey [née Whitbread], Mary, Lady Grey (1770–1858)', *ODNB*; Blake, *Religion in the British Navy, 1815–1879*, 52. Mary Grey was a daughter of Samuel Whitbread.

[113] *Ibid.*, 54n.

[114] *The First Bible Society* (London, 1874).

[115] *An Account of the Naval and Military Bible Society* [*NMBS*] (London, 1804), 4.

[116] Led by the lawyer William Cardale, the bankers Ambrose Martin and W.H. Hoare, and three Eclectic clergymen, Josiah Pratt, William Goode and Basil Woodd.

guineas secured it for life.[117] Meetings were moved to Hatchard's bookshop on Piccadilly, a rendezvous of the Evangelical upper crust. The results were striking. Over the next decade a host of MPs and peers enlisted, being joined by a glittering array of naval and military names: admirals Saumarez and Gambier; Earl Spencer and the Earl of Radnor (1750–1828), Lord Willoughby de Broke (1738–1816), Lieutenant-General Robert Manners (1758–1823). Its figureheads were still more exalted: the Patron was the Commander-in-Chief, Frederick, Duke of York (1763–1827); the Vice-Patron the Duke of Gloucester, the President the Archbishop of Canterbury, Charles Manners-Sutton (1755–1828). The addition in 1815 of Wellington and Lord Liverpool brought further cachet.[118] While annual reports faithfully enumerated the books sent to regiments and ships, unusual effort went into parading prestigious supporters.

The equation of philanthropy with patriotism was not a new one. It had been central to the success of the Marine Society in the 1750s and 60s, for instance.[119] But it was undoubtedly deployed to great effect by Evangelical spokespeople, and all the more so amid the mounting optimism that attended British successes in Europe in the 1810s. 'We are sitting here like officers on the home staff,' crowed Henry Thornton in 1812,

> receiving and giving dinners among Christians, Lords and Baronets, and MPs talking around our dessert table of the progress of Bible Societies and foreign Missions and enjoying the eminence of the religiousness of the day somewhat in the same manner in which the officers of the Duke of York's table delight in hearing of the capture of Cuidad [*sic*] Rodrigo or the battle of Barossa.[120]

Evangelical publicists did everything they could to capitalize on the mood. 'Where then is the Briton who loves his king and his country,' one NMBS report asked, 'who will not cordially lend his aid to put the Bible into the hands of their intrepid defenders?'[121] There was no shortage of officers prepared to extol the qualities of soldiers and sailors who habitually read their Bibles.[122] Naturally, the NMBS was not the only society to play this card. Applications from seamen desperate for 'an anchor of the soul' made

---

[117] *Report of the Proceedings of the NMBS* (1806), 13–14.

[118] *NMBS Reports* (1806–15), passim.

[119] James Stephen Taylor, *Jonas Hanway, Founder of the Marine Society: Charity and Policy in Eighteenth-Century Britain* (London, 1985).

[120] Henry Thornton to John Bowdler, 16 Feb. 1812, 'Family Letterbook and Recollections', CUL, Thornton Family Letters and Papers, MS Add.7674/1/N, fos. 328–9.

[121] *Account*, 6.

[122] *Report* (1815), 18–19.

excellent publicity material for the BFBS. Some accounts were more believable than others: the *Christian Observer* reported implausibly that sailors in a recent shipwreck had dashed to rescue their Bibles before taking to the boats.[123] Years later, the clergyman Robert Wolfe (fl. 1803–1840s) would claim that religious observance transformed captured British seamen in France. 'I have been through a depot of 1500 sailors, and not seen one drunken man!' exclaimed one astonished observer.[124] Similar evidence was adduced repeatedly in the post-war period to argue that courage and audacity need not be sacrificed to sailors' reformation. Much was made of the provision of Bibles for Germans serving in the army and navy, for the Sea Fencibles and militia and even for French and Spanish prisoners of war in their own languages. Britain's duty was to all.[125]

Table 2: Admirals as Philanthropic Patrons[126]

Name	Societies	Patron	President	V-President	Committee	Governor
Lord Barham	22	1	1	4	1	3
Lord Gambier	39	3	3	11	2	3
Lord Radstock	18	-	1	4	2	3
Lord Saumarez	20	-	3	1	1	6
Earl Spencer	19	1	-	8	1	2

At the other end of the social scale, charities scrambled to secure celebrity endorsements from naval officers. While the NMBS could claim Admirals Exmouth (1757–1833), Northesk (1758–1831), Saumarez and Torrington (1768–1831), the BFBS announced proudly in 1813 that Gambier, Harvey and Murray (1759–1819) had come forward on its behalf.[127] Naval luminaries were especially sought after to head BFBS auxiliaries in port towns:

---

[123] 'Naval and Military Bible Society', *Christian Observer*, 9 (1810), 186.

[124] R.B. Wolfe, *English Prisoners in France* (London, 1830), 89.

[125] E.g. *Reports of the British and Foreign Bible Society ... Volume the First, for the Years 1805, to 1810, inclusive* (London, 1810), 139.

[126] Information from Brown, *Fathers of the Victorians*, 351–60. Barham and Gambier were undoubtedly evangelicals, as, according to the *ODNB*, was Spencer, who was a national vice-president of the BFBS. Saumarez participated in a broad range of groups, including the BFBS, LSPCJ, NMBS, CMS, SPCK and NSS: see John Ross, *Memoirs and Correspondence of Admiral Lord de Saumarez*, 2 vols (London, 1838), II: 298–9. Radstock was an active recruiter for the Vice Society – see M.J.D. Roberts, *Making English Morals: Voluntary Association and Moral Reform in England, 1787–1886* (Cambridge, 2004), 79 – but he departed the BFBS when it was attacked in 1805. Mrs Thornton to Hannah More, n.d., 1805, 'Family Letterbook and Recollections', CUL, Thornton Papers, Add. MS. 7674/1/N, fo. 203.

[127] 'Chester Auxiliary Bible Society', *Christian Observer*, 12 (1813), 60.

Admirals Bertie and Bligh at Southampton in 1815 and Governor Richard Creyke (c. 1746–1826) of the Plymouth Royal Naval Hospital, for the Plymouth, Plymouth Dock and Stonehouse Auxiliary.[128] By 1821 Lord Exmouth was a national Vice-President, serving also as President of the Merchant Seamen's Auxiliary in London.[129] Radstock (1753–1825), Saumarez, Spencer and Barham all represented multiple societies, while Gambier excelled them all as member of thirty-nine, patron of three, governor of three, committee member of two, vice-president of eleven and president of another three.[130] Piety mattered, but prestige was just as important: had he been alive Horatio Nelson (1758–1805) would certainly have been enlisted, personal scandals notwithstanding.[131] Among the more surprising recruits was Vice-Admiral Harvey. Now President of the South-West Essex Auxiliary Bible Society, he observed seemingly without irony that 'the distribution of the Bible must be attended with the happiest effects' and that 'there was the highest state of discipline on board those ships in which the Bible was most read'.[132] Whether or not Harvey really had undergone a change of heart, religious-style moralizing was now fashionable and, as the war began to turn against Napoleon in the early 1810s, philanthropic receipts boomed. The NMBS was among the chief recipients: annual collections climbed from just under £200 in 1804 to almost £4,500 in 1813–14. The real new departure, however, was in convincing a broad swathe of the upper and middle classes that morality and military success were intertwined. By exhorting people to dip into their pockets and showing where those funds were going, the NMBS and other societies were effectively creating a religious 'home front', where private philanthropy might visibly bolster state provision, sanctifying both the giver and the nation in the process.[133]

Pious valour sold well in the new climate. Even the unremarkable memoirs of Major-General Andrew Burn of the Marines attracted numerous

---

[128] 'Southampton Branch Bible Society', *Christian Observer*, 14 (1815), 123; *Reports of the British and Foreign Bible Society ... Volume the Second, for 1811, 1812, and 1813* (London, 1813), 331.

[129] *Reports of the British and Foreign Bible Society ... Volume the Sixth, for 1820 and 1821* (London, 1821), [1821], iv, 94.

[130] Ford K. Brown, *Fathers of the Victorians: the Age of Wilberforce* (Cambridge, 1961), 351–60; Ross, *Correspondence of de Saumarez*, II: 298–9.

[131] Notwithstanding the Mary Anne Clarke affair, the Duke of York appears to have been retained as a philanthropic patron.

[132] 'South-West Essex Auxiliary Bible Society', *Christian Observer*, 11 (1812), 539.

[133] For similar developments across Europe, see Joanna Innes, 'State, Church and Voluntarism in European welfare, 1690–1850', in Innes and Hugh Cunningham (eds), *Charity, Philanthropy, and Reform from the 1690s to 1850* (Basingstoke, 1998), 15–65.

subscribers from among the great and good.[134] Many ordered multiple copies, indicating that even accounts of pedestrian careers might usefully be distributed. For poorer consumers there were cheap pamphlets and tracts. One of the bestsellers was *The Retrospect*, published anonymously in 1816. By the 1840s it had gone through at least twenty editions. Its writer, Richard Marks (1778–1847), was living proof of the well-worn contention that the best Christian was also the best officer. After he left the sea he sought ordination, but the career recounted in the *Retrospect* rivalled that of any far-fetched fictional sea-dog: two shipwrecks in the same year; heroism at Trafalgar; near-fatal illness; fights with fellow officers; and a brush with death when a clowning colleague shot a stone through his hat. His tracts were produced in enormous numbers, eventually achieving a circulation of over a million copies in Britain, the United States and beyond. Combining pithy description with an expert grasp of nautical idiom, Marks made ordinary characters his mouthpieces in much the same way that Hannah More's Cheap Repository Tracts had done in the 1790s.[135] The message was all the more powerful because it was made to come not from chaplains but from fellow sailors. In *Conversation in a Boat*, for instance, 'Harry Williams' relates his testimony to 'Tom Brown': 'I was once as mad-brained and thoughtless a fellow as ever sailed out of Shields harbour.' He goes on to answer his friend's objections, concluding that now it is faith only that enables him to face death fearlessly: 'never let it be said that religion and the Bible unfitted Harry Williams from doing his duty.'[136] Just as important as direct proselytism was Marks's Bunyanesque use of maritime existence as a source of metaphors for the religious life. Taken together, the *Nautical Essays* map the perils that attend the sailor's earthly 'voyage', exhorting readers to avoid shipwreck – grog, women and swearing – and pointing them towards the heavenly port.[137] As with many tracts they may well have been read more by donors than by their intended readers; but they were part of the extraordinary post-war growth of missions to seamen.[138]

---

[134] John Allen (ed.), *Memoirs of the Life of the Late Major-General Andrew Burn*, 2 vols (London, 1815), I: 'List of Subscribers'.

[135] Susan Pedersen, 'Hannah More Meets Simple Simon: Tracts, Chapbooks and Popular Culture in Late Eighteenth-Century England', *Journal of British Studies*, 25 (1986), 84–113.

[136] Richard Marks, *The Seaman's Friend* (London, 1850), 50, 83.

[137] [Richard Marks], *Nautical Essays; or, a Spiritual View of the Ocean and Maritime Affairs* (London, 1818).

[138] Roald Kverndal, *Seamen's Missions: their Origins and Early Growth* (Pasadena, CA, 1986).

The Navy and Providence in Post-War Britain

By 1816 the mood had broadened into full-blown euphoria. No-one could have predicted the elevation of 'the obscure inhabitants of a little cheerless island, far to the north of the favoured region of philosophy, and literature, and liberty, and politeness, and wit', proclaimed the *Christian Observer*. 'But behold these obscure islanders, with all the world in array against them, at once raised into the benefactors and deliverers of that world – humbling the proud with one hand, and saving the miserable with the other.'[139] The idea that having won the war Britain now had a global destiny to fulfil was a powerful one. In the months after Waterloo, pulpits rang with proclamations of an era in which missionary zeal and steam-powered print would transmit the gospel around the globe.[140] Integral to that vision was British seapower. Since at least the 1790s exegetes had elided British fleets with the 'Ships of Tarshish' of Isaiah 60: 9, a prophecy that talked about the restoration of Israel to its homeland.[141] Such interpretations were congenial to the nascent Christian Zionist movement, but they also melded into a more diffuse sense of maritime destiny. Penrose, writing as 'A.F.Y', thought that the navy might be directly harnessed to missionary purposes: 'Nelson and his followers would have harassed our enemies beyond their resources by carrying a British army from place to place with ease and rapidity ... and by proper attention we might spread the power of the gospel to all nations and languages by the same means', he observed.[142] At the time this was pure fantasy; but within a few years collaboration between missionaries and naval officers was a fact of life in the Pacific and elsewhere.[143] The fascination of the pious press with the exploits of the West Africa Squadron, and of Arctic exploration voyages and the faith of those who served on them, reflected the purchase of these ideas. So too did the growing attention given to missions, morals and education among soldiers and seamen. For it suited the Victorians to imagine that their well-scrubbed bluejackets and redcoats were men of simple but certain faith. This fitted them to act as agents for a nation that saw its global role less in terms of geopolitics than civilizing mission. It was a very different world from that of Barham and Gambier. But it was one whose foundations they had laid.

---

[139] 'Review of Owen's History of the Bible Society', *Christian Observer*, 15 (1816), 729.

[140] See e.g. Thomas Chalmers, *Thoughts on Universal Peace* (Glasgow, 1816).

[141] Gareth Atkins, '"Isaiah's Call to England": Doubts about Prophecy in Nineteenth-Century Britain', *Studies in Church History*, 52 (2016), 381–97.

[142] 'Correspondence', *Naval Chronicle*, 29 (1813), 476.

[143] Samson, *Imperial Benevolence*; Blake, *Religion in the British Navy, 1815–1879*, 173–272.

Plate 5: John Bacon and Samuel Manning, Memorial to Charles Grant. Marble, St George's Church, Bloomsbury, c. 1825.

Chapter Six
'Small Detachments of Maniacs'? Evangelicals and the East India Company

In St George's Church in Bloomsbury is a marble memorial. A life-size male figure lounges in a reverie, his pen resting in one hand and a scroll in the other. He reclines on the bosom of a severe classical female: Faith, cradling a large cross. She points – summoning him, perhaps – towards heaven. The seated figure has turned away from his desk and his eyes follow her gesture. The symbolism is apt: the subject was a man of business and he expired in the midst of his work, returning from a day in the City of London and dying of a heart attack at home, soon after family prayers.[1] He was, the inscription proclaims, Charles Grant: Chairman of the EIC, one of its Directors for many years and MP for Inverness, and a member of William Wilberforce's inner circle. The focus of his memorial was, however, very specific. It writes Grant up as a Christian empire-builder: one whose business life was shaped by his faith and dedicated to the promulgation of that faith abroad. Beneath him, a turbaned cherub lifts the veil on an impressive list of achievements:

PROMOTION OF CHRISTIAN MISSIONS IN THE EAST – ECCLESIASTICAL ESTABLISHMENT IN INDIA – PURCHASE OF PROTESTANT CHURCH AT CALCUTTA – ESTABLISHMENT OF EAST INDIA-COLLEGE AT HERTFORD – RENEWAL OF THE COMPANY'S CHARTER IN MDCCCXIII

The text inscribed at the base of the memorial is still more laudatory.

THIS MONUMENT IS CONSECRATED BY THE EAST INDIA COMPANY, AS A TRIBUTE OF RESPECT AND AFFECTION TO THE PERSON WHOSE NAME IT BEARS, AS A RECORD OF THEIR HUMBLE GRATITUDE TO THE SUPREME BEING,

[1] 'Charles Grant, Esq', *Annual Biography and Obituary*, 9 (1825), I: 31; Henry Morris, *The Life of Charles Grant* (London, 1904), 387–9.

FOR THE LONG CONTINUED BENEFITS WHICH THEY DERIVED FROM THE
COUNSELS AND LABOURS OF THEIR LAMENTED DIRECTOR,
AND AS AN ENDURING MEMORIAL OF THE PRINCIPLES WHICH THEY DESIRE
TO RENDER PREVALENT
IN THE ADMINISTRATION OF THE IMMENSE DOMINIONS WHICH IT HAS
PLEASED PROVIDENCE TO CONFIDE TO THEIR CHARGE.

Behind this declaration of consensus, however, lay controversy. The scheme was put forward at a Special Court of the EIC on 17 December 1823.[2] Notwithstanding the encomiums heaped on the dead man by the London banker and MP John Smith, cousin of Wilberforce, several speakers were sceptical. William Fullerton Elphinstone (1740–1834) opposed singling Grant out: were not all Company men honest?[3] The radical MP Joseph Hume (1777–1855) thought Grant's commercial reputation overrated and attacked him at length for restricting Company patronage to a select few families.[4] Little was said about the dead man's religion. But no-one present could have been unaware that he had championed the spread of Protestant Christianity in the Company's possessions. Elphinstone's suggestion that the memorial should be paid for by Grant's friends was thus barbed. Those petitioning the Company to pay, Evangelicals and Quakers for the most part, were doing so because they wanted to seize control of public narratives surrounding the nation's largest company. Debates about India were also debates about the character of British dominion overseas and few issues ignited hotter contention than religion, especially during renewals of the Company's charter in 1793, 1813 and 1833.[5] The Grant memorial was not intrinsically valuable – it probably cost around 1,000 guineas – but it was nonetheless a high-stakes affair. The success of the proposal, fifty-four votes to twenty-nine, speaks volumes for the ability of Evangelicals to put their convictions into practice. Even the production of the memorial hints at their influence: it was carved by Samuel Manning senior (1786–1842), partner of the Evangelical sculptor John Bacon junior, apparently from a slab of marble originally intended for a statue of John Wesley.[6]

---

[2]   'Debate at the East-India House', *Asiatic Journal and Monthly Register for British India and its Dependencies*, 17 (1824), 57.

[3]   *Ibid.*, 62–4.

[4]   *Ibid.*, 64–71.

[5]   Penelope Carson, *The East India Company and Religion, 1698–1858* (Woodbridge, 2012).

[6]   *Illustrated London News*, June 30, 1849, 436.

As should be clear from Chapter 2, this was closely linked to the advance of the new piety among the shareholding classes. But it also points to networks of Company officials, military and naval officers, merchants and clergymen that enabled Evangelicals to influence appointments and policy: networks that have never been fully explored. The reasons for this neglect are not difficult to discern. The earliest English histories of Christianity in India were hagiographical: they portrayed the struggles of individual protagonists with climate, cultural difference and unsympathetic officialdom.[7] They concentrated overwhelmingly on missions, drawing sharp divisions between Evangelicals and their supposedly timeserving contemporaries. Twentieth-century Anglican historians reacted against this, producing accounts that emphasized ecclesiastical structures.[8] Mid and late twentieth-century research into Christian missions, some of it from nationalist or subaltern perspectives, tended to downplay the importance of western agents, to stress their cultural myopia and, more recently, to show how they helped, sometimes unwittingly, to refashion and reinforce the authority of the belief systems they encountered.[9] An aversion to top-down Eurocentricism continues to shape research agenda.[10] Moreover, while it was once fashionable to emphasize the role of philosophic systems – Evangelicalism and Utilitarianism above all – in shaping British India in the early nineteenth century, historians of governance emphasize how preserving peace and maximizing profit usually trumped programmatic thinking.[11] Most significantly, revisionists have questioned the notion that missionaries were always and everywhere agents of empire, reminding us that that they did not restrict themselves to areas of imperial control and

[7]   E.g. James Hough, *The History of Christianity in India: from the Commencement of the Christian Era*, 5 vols (London, 1839–60); John William Kaye, *Christianity in India: An Historical Narrative* (London, 1859); W.H. Carey, *Oriental Christian Biography*, 3 vols (Calcutta, 1850–2).

[8]   E.g. Eyre Chatterton, *A History of the Church of England in India* (London, 1924); M.E. Gibbs, *The Anglican Church in India, 1600–1970* (Delhi, 1972).

[9]   See discussions in John C.B. Webster, *Historiography of Christianity in India* (Oxford, 2012), 15–33; Robert Eric Frykenberg, *Christians and Missionaries in India* (Grand Rapids, MI, 2003), 1–32. See also Brian K. Pennington, *Was Hinduism Invented? Britons, Indians, and the Colonial Construction of Religion* (New York, 2005); Parna Sengupta, *Pedagogy for Religion: Missionary Education and the Fashioning of Hindus and Muslims in Bengal* (Berkeley, CA, 2011).

[10]   E.g. Dana L. Robert (ed.), *Converting Colonialism: Visions and Realities in Mission History, 1706–1914* (Grand Rapids, MI, 2008); Richard Fox Young (ed.), *India and the Indianness of Christianity* (Grand Rapids, MI, 2009).

[11]   E.g. Robert Travers, *Ideology and Empire in Eighteenth-Century India: the British in Bengal* (Cambridge, 2007); Jon Wilson, *The Domination of Strangers: Modern Governance in Eastern India, 1780–1835* (Basingstoke, 2008).

showing that they could be sharp critics of imperialism and even champions of indigenous nationalism.[12]

This chapter does not pretend to be a comprehensive history of Evangelicalism in India; nor does it engage closely with what Indians thought of Evangelicals or of the engagements between them.[13] It proceeds instead from the observation that military rule and the Company's trading monopoly made working against the grain difficult.[14] By necessity, then, but also by conviction, Evangelicals came to focus on reshaping the Company from within. It is therefore significant that although the Whig churchman Sydney Smith could glibly despise the attempts of 'small detachments of maniacs' to take on the misguided but majestic ancient faiths of India, he was equally concerned by the potency of Evangelical interests at Leadenhall Street and in Calcutta.[15] It is also significant that although many of the protagonists of what follow were Scots, they usually championed Anglican causes, being relatively unconcerned about ecclesiastical distinctions and seeing the development of an Indian Church establishment as essential. This chapter largely eschews well-known symbolic successes such as the 'Pious Clause' campaign of 1813: it is concerned instead with longer continuums: social influence and institutional penetration. This has important implications for how we redraw Evangelical India. First, it suggests that they thrived not despite existing systems, as they frequently claimed, but because of them. They excelled at exploiting civil, military and ecclesiastical patronage. Second, and perhaps more controversially, it suggests that Evangelicals were not solely or even necessarily mostly concerned with direct proselytization. Among their main bugbears was religious indifference among the Company elite, which they saw as fatal to the reputation of Christianity among subject peoples. This was compounded by the Company's religious neutrality, which seemed to deny the very truth of Christianity. In India, as in Britain, then, the support of the powerful was a precondition for

[12]　Brian Stanley, *The Bible and the Flag: Protestant Mission and British Imperialism in the Nineteenth and Twentieth Centuries* (Leicester, 1990); Andrew Porter, *Religion versus Empire? British Protestant Missionaries and Overseas Expansion, 1700–1914* (Manchester, 2004); Geoffrey A. Oddie, *Missionaries, Rebellion and Proto-Nationalism: James Long of Bengal, 1814–87* (Abingdon, 2013).

[13]　For a stimulating exploration of the latter question, see Homi Bhabha, 'Signs Taken for Wonders: Questions of Ambivalence and Authority under a Tree outside Delhi, May 1817', *Critical Inquiry*, 12 (1985), 144–65.

[14]　This argument draws on Jeffrey Cox, *Imperial Fault Lines: Christianity and Colonial Power in India, 1818–1940* (Stanford, CA, 2002), and Ian Copland, 'Christianity as an Arm of Empire: the Ambiguous Case of India under the Company, c. 1813–1858', *Historical Journal*, 49 (2006), 1025–54.

[15]　[Sydney Smith], 'Indian Missions', *Edinburgh Review*, 12, 23 (1808), 179.

structural change. It follows, third, that this created unexpected alliances with figures who shared some if not all of their priorities, not to mention generating tensions, too: with reformers bent on reducing the Company and its patronage, pragmatists keen to avert unrest and nonconformists who demanded liberty to proselytize.

What follows is organized into three sections that overlap chronologically. The first explores the world of serious piety in white Calcutta and further afield in the decades either side of 1800. The second considers how Evangelical scholarship and investment in print bought them privileged access to power in India and related institutions in the opening decades of the new century. The third outlines the longer-term development of patronage networks across the first half of the century. As will become clear, Evangelicals did not attain all of their objectives: the Christian Company they tried to create remained elusive. But they did succeed in creating a powerful subculture that allowed them to influence policy and, just as importantly, the tone of British rule.

Evangelical Calcutta, c. 1770–c. 1820

In 1797, amid the heat and humidity of Calcutta, David Brown (1762–1812) met an old friend 'in a most unexpected manner'. Presented with some old books 'by a native', he found a copy of *Parochialia; or Observations on the Discharge of Parochial Duties*, by his friend and spiritual father William Jesse (c. 1739–1815).[16] The remembrance transported him back a quarter of a century and halfway across the world to the Yorkshire wolds, where, as Vicar of Hutton Cranswick near Driffield, Jesse had first preached to him the doctrine of atonement. Brown was a product of the Yorkshire networks charted in Chapter 1: he was schooled at Scarborough before attending Hull Grammar School and Magdalene College, Cambridge. In 1785 he interrupted his studies to become Superintendent of the Bengal Military Orphan Asylum, being ordained deacon and married to a Miss Robinson (d. 1794) of Hull on the eve of his departure.[17] 'The foundation, under God, which you laid in me, and upon which the beloved man of God, Joseph Milner, of blessed memory, built, has never been shaken; "Jesus Christ and him crucified" has been almost my only theme,' he assured his mentor.[18] The importance of modern 'print capitalism' in creating and sustaining notions

---

[16] [Charles Simeon], *Memorial Sketches of the Rev. David Brown* (London, 1816), 294.
[17] *Ibid.*, 142–9.
[18] *Ibid.*, 294.

of national identity has long been recognized.[19] But Brown's serendipitous encounter is an eloquent reminder that print also provided the joining sinews for more particular imagined communities. Religious journals were eagerly awaited by fellow believers abroad, and by the early nineteenth century 'missionary intelligence' remitted home was coming to provide a significant proportion of those journals' content. Other print genres were conceived to bind together far-flung communities. Among the most poignant – and under-examined – are the volumes reproducing monuments, epitaphs and excerpts from funeral sermons from British India: testimony to the terrifying mortality rates among European inhabitants and to the desire of bereaved relatives and acquaintances to 'view' graves they could not visit.[20] Brown is a case in point. His posthumous biography, *Memorial Sketches* (1816), was written by his widow, Frances (d. 1822), edited by Charles Simeon, published by the Strand booksellers Cadell and Davies and funded by a subscription among the leading lights of Evangelical Calcutta. The sum of 19,300 rupees – around £2,500 – was raised from only a hundred names, including military officers, some of the highest-ranking civilian officials of Bengal and their families.[21]

This interchange matters because Evangelical networks did not just radiate from centre to periphery, but often developed piecemeal, being only later plumbed into broader systems. From at least the 1770s there existed an Evangelical community in Calcutta.[22] Evidence of how that community operated in its early decades is sparse. One key figure was Grant, but it is clear from his biography that he was not the first or the most prominent citizen of Calcutta to become 'serious'. First arriving in 1768, he became Secretary of the Board of Trade in 1775, but was devastated by the deaths of his two daughters from smallpox in 1776, within nine days of one another. Bleakly convinced that this was a sign of the 'just displeasure of God' at his gambling and financial imprudence, he was thrown into spiritual crisis. It may be significant that Grant never used the word 'conversion'. Like many of his contemporaries, the shift towards vital religion seems to have represented more a deepening of existing beliefs than the adoption of fresh principles. It drew on a variety of sources: his and his wife Jane's Presbyterian

---

[19]   Benedict Anderson, *Imagined Communities: Reflections on the Origin and Spread of Nationalism* (rev. edn: London, 2006), 1–8.

[20]   See Trev Lynn Broughton, 'The *Bengal Obituary*: Reading and Writing Calcutta Graves in the Mid Nineteenth Century', *Journal of Victorian Culture*, 15 (2010), 39–59.

[21]   [Simeon], *Memorial Sketches*, [pp. vi–viii].

[22]   For early nineteenth-century Calcutta, see P.J. Marshall, 'The white town of Calcutta under the rule of the East India Company', *Modern Asian Studies*, 34 (2000), 307–31.

upbringings; the counsel of J.C. Diemer (c. 1750–1792), a German SPCK missionary; 'certain books' of religious instruction lent by John Shore, a member of the Revenue Council; the influence of William Chambers (1748–1793), 'a man', Grant reported, 'whom religion animates and directs', Interpreter in the Supreme Court and, from his days in the Madras Civil Service, a friend of the famous Lutheran missionary C.F. Schwartz (1726–1798).[23] Although Grant's later biographer pronounced these to be 'clear lights shining amidst the surrounding darkness', their piety did not prevent them from mixing in Calcutta society.[24] Both Grant and Shore admired the Judge and Orientalist Sir William Jones (1746–1794): perhaps surprisingly given his deism, his Indophilia and his openly syncretistic attitude to non-Christian religions. Indeed, Shore was Jones's first biographer.[25] The three illegitimate children Shore left in India – one baptized in 1777 and the other two in 1785 – further underlines that distinctions between the 'godly' and the 'worldly' cannot always be neatly drawn.[26] In the opinion of the first Baptist missionary to Bengal, the quarrelsome John Thomas (1757–1801), who arrived there in 1786, Grant mingled too closely with 'the world': 'reputation is a snare', he opined in his journal, 'to those who are called to follow Him who made Himself of no reputation.'[27] Evangelical churchmen, for their part, were sympathetic to Baptist and LMS missions but averse to anything that might endanger their privileged position.[28]

Grant's new-found seriousness did not prevent his advancement.[29] In 1780 he became Commercial Resident at Malda, where he also started a mission with the help of his assistant, George Udny (c. 1760–1830), another Scots Company man, whose brother, Robert (d. 1794), was also part of the Evangelical scene. George Udny took over Malda when Grant became a member of the Calcutta Board of Trade in 1787, himself becoming a member of the Board in 1799 and serving on the Supreme Council from 1801–7. Grant's position owed much to the offices of Shore, but it also underlines how Evangelical uprightness and imperial reformism overlapped in the

---

[23] Charles John Shore, *Memoirs of the Life and Correspondence of John, Lord Teignmouth*, 2 vols (London, 1843), I: 111; Morris, *Charles Grant*, 64–5. See also Thomas M. Curley, *Sir Robert Chambers: Law, Literature, and Empire in the Age of Samuel Johnson* (Madison, WN, 1998), 182–4.

[24] Morris, *Charles Grant*, 64.

[25] John Shore, *Memoirs of the Life, Writings and Correspondence, of Sir William Jones* (2nd edn: London, 1806).

[26] Ainsley T. Embree, 'Shore, John, First Baron Teignmouth (1751–1834)', *ODNB*.

[27] Morris, *Charles Grant*, 103–4; C.B. Lewis, *The Life of John Thomas* (London, 1873), 66.

[28] See e.g. David Brown to Charles Simeon, n.d., Dec. 1809, Ridley Hall, Cambridge, Charles Simeon Papers.

[29] Morris, *Charles Grant*, 64.

post-Hastings era. Earl Cornwallis (1738–1805) came to India in 1786 with a brief to retrench spending and eliminate corruption, and Shore became his 'right hand'.[30] He was soon joined by Grant. While Cornwallis appreciated his new subordinate's energy and integrity, he was – like many among the authorities – not prepared to lend official support to Grant's schemes for native proselytization, which he thought might provoke unrest.[31] Even Shore worried that the dissemination of Christianity 'with the declared support and authority of the Government' would excite alarm. When he was Governor General in the 1790s he instead recommended the building of chapels in military stations, suggesting that the natural (i.e. illegitimate) children of soldiers could act as bridges to native communities.[32] Hence Grant's attempts to interest Christians at home in his ideas. With Brown and Chambers he spent many months drawing up a 'Proposal for Establishing a Protestant Mission in Bengal and Behar'. It was despatched in mid 1787 to the Archbishop of Canterbury, the Secretary of the SPCK, the Countess of Huntingdon, William Wilberforce and several leading gospel clergymen. Nothing came of it, but it brought Grant and his coadjutors to the notice of a range of metropolitan Christians.[33]

When Grant left India for good in 1790 he established himself in London. The pious businessman Thomas Raikes, a friend and correspondent during the 1780s, secured him a house, while Edward Parry, 'a brother Civilian, with whom Grant had been intimate in Bengal', now living at Little Dunham in Norfolk, introduced him to John Venn, whom he recommended as tutor for Grant's sons.[34] At some point in late 1790 or early 1791 Grant met Wilberforce and the Thornton brothers and in October 1794 he moved into Glenelg, his new house at Battersea Rise, Clapham, next door to Henry Thornton and Wilberforce. Immediately striking from the correspondence of the 'Saints' is how close their growing interest in India brought them to the Pitt administration. Grant returned to England with a minute knowledge of Company affairs and the effusive recommendation of Cornwallis and in February 1791 he and his cousin Sir James Grant (1750–1808), also a Company man, dined with Pitt, Lord Grenville (1759–1834) and Dundas at Wilberforce's house in Palace Yard.[35] Dundas was President of the India

---

[30] *Ibid.*, 147.
[31] *Ibid.*, 122.
[32] Shore, *Lord Teignmouth*, I: 291.
[33] Carson, *East India Company*, 27–31.
[34] Morris, *Charles Grant*, 160. For this milieu, see Michael M. Hennell, *John Venn and the Clapham Sect* (London, 1958), 81–3; Anne Stott, *Wilberforce: Family and Friends* (Oxford, 2012), 51–4.
[35] Morris, *Charles Grant*, 168.

Board of Control, and after their meeting Grant was consulted frequently by his countryman on revenue and settlement matters.[36] He was also instrumental in persuading Shore to accept the Governor-Generalship in 1792, although Grant declined Dundas's suggestion that he accompany his friend as a member of the Supreme Council.[37] Another Clapham intimate, Pitt's pious brother-in-law E.J. Eliot, was expected to become Governor General in 1797 until illness ruled him out. For a time there were hints that Grant was to be Governor of Bombay, while he again turned down the offer of a place on the Supreme Council in 1800.[38] His eminence did not enable him to alter the legal status of missions, as he hoped: he was unsuccessful in attempting to open India to missionaries during charter renewal in 1793. More important was his election as a Director in 1794, unopposed, after an unprecedentedly short poll: a tell-tale sign of Dundas's influence. Grant's power reached its apogee between 1804 and 1815, when he was continuously Chairman, Deputy Chairman or power behind the throne. This allowed him to stuff the Bengal and Madras presidency chaplaincies with 'serious' men, most of them carefully selected by Charles Simeon from among Cambridge's brightest and best.[39]

Before he left India, Grant had helped to acquire the 'Old Mission Church' in Calcutta from an SPCK missionary, the Swede Johann Zachariah Kiernander (1711–1799), in 1787. The purchase was opportunistic and its legal status uncertain: the Old Church remained formally owned by the SPCK. Arrangements had a ramshackle feel: newly arrived from England, Brown agreed to minister there in addition to his official role at the Orphan Asylum and as chaplain to the 6th Battalion at Fort William.[40] The building was not prepossessing. 'In 1787, it was a clumsy, unplastered brick edifice, of small dimensions, and choked up with old houses,' wrote an observer.

> Within, it was exceedingly uncouth; with a brick pulpit built against a wall; and its aisle, rough uncovered tiling. A few rude benches and pews of unpainted plank, formed the general seats, with a small number of chairs, without pews, for the gentry: and it was calculated to accommodate only about two hundred persons. It was indeed most

---

[36] Henry Dundas to Marquess Cornwallis, 17 Sep. 1792, cited in Charles Ross (ed.), *Correspondence of Charles, First Marquess Cornwallis*, 3 vols (2nd edn: London, 1859), I: 215.

[37] Shore, *Lord Teignmouth*, I: 221.

[38] Morris, *Charles Grant*, 199–200.

[39] See Ridley Hall, Charles Simeon Papers.

[40] Morris, *Charles Grant*, 101–2.

comfortless; and was pronounced by the then society of Calcutta, utterly unsuitable for the reception of an European congregation.[41]

It was, however, well situated, just off fashionable Tank (later Dalhousie) Square in the heart of the city, just around the corner from Customs House and the EIC Writers' Buildings. Gradually it was improved, with the addition of an organ, 'a handsome pulpit and desks', elegant pillars, better lighting and ventilation and, as the congregation increased, galleries and extensions. 'At length it formed altogether a most pleasing coup d'oeil, surprisingly contrasted with its somewhat revolting appearance before.'[42] The High Church clergyman-architects of the mid-nineteenth century vividly described by Alex Bremner would anathematize such gimcrack classicism as emblematic of a 'debased' Low Church, lay-led religiosity that they countered with Gothic purism and heightened episcopal authority.[43] Late-Hanoverian Evangelicals would doubtless have retorted that they needed to improvise in a situation where religious provision was patchy at best. The SPCK was unable to fill the pulpit: it appointed ministers to it twice, in 1789–90 and 1797, but neither lasted more than a year. The congregation therefore took matters into their own hands, establishing an Evangelical Fund in 1802 in order to support a long-term ministry there. By 1808, when an official chaplain was appointed at the behest of Grant, the transfer of power was complete.[44]

The new man, Thomas Truebody Thomason (1774–1829), was another high-calibre product of Magdalene College, Cambridge: a wrangler, twice Norrisian prizewinner, Fellow of Queens' College and curate to Simeon at Holy Trinity.[45] His arrival cemented the strategic importance of the Old Church. Already in 1790 Grant discerned increasing attendance and by 1808 the weekly congregation numbered around 800.[46] To some extent this reflected the growth of the European community, which St John's Church – the 'official' presidency church and later the cathedral – was inadequate to accommodate. It also coincided with changes in the complexion of Calcutta society. To the Baptist missionary William Carey (1761–1834) the shift was

---

[41] [Simeon], *Memorial Sketches*, 117–20.

[42] *Ibid.*, 119.

[43] G.A. Bremner, *Imperial Gothic: Religious Architecture and High Anglican Culture in the British Empire, c. 1840–70* (New Haven, CT, 2013), 1–20.

[44] E.T. Sandys, 'One Hundred and Forty-Five Years at the Old or Mission Church, Calcutta – III', *Bengal Past and Present*, 11 (1915), 244–57. The patronage was given to the CMS in the 1860s.

[45] John Sargent, *The Life of the Rev. T.T. Thomason* (London, 1833).

[46] Morris, *Charles Grant*, 127; [Simeon], *Memorial Sketches*, 119.

pronounced: while only a handful of people 'cared about the Gospel' when he arrived in 1793, by around 1810 there was 'scarcely a place where you can pay a visit without having an opportunity of saying something about true religion': judges and civil servants invited him to family prayers.[47] This was facilitated by connections between the two Anglican churches, which lay across Tank Square from one another. As Junior Chaplain from 1794 and then Senior Presidency Chaplain from 1797, Brown ministered at both. Grant paid large sums for extension and refurbishment at the 'New Church' and, whenever it was closed for building work, 'the Governor General and suite, with the whole congregation, have gladly availed themselves of the one kept open solely by Mr. Brown's fostering affections'.[48] The government, for its part, undertook to liquidate the debts and defray the running expenses of the Old Church, in especial recognition, Brown's biographer claimed, of the benefit it rendered to the community.[49] While this claim seems fanciful – the Company held itself responsible for all churches that ministered to Europeans – it is certainly true that there were close links with the Company establishment. On 23 September 1804, the anniversary of the seminal Battle of Assaye, Brown preached there before the Governor General and his brother, Major-General Sir Arthur Wellesley, the victorious commander. 'Here,' observes Brown's biographer, 'Britain's Wellington has suffered the graceful tear stealing from the heart, to adorn his manly cheek; on being reminded from this pulpit, that it was "God who covered his head in the day of battle".'[50] Through endeavours such as the Female Orphan Institution (1815), which was Thomason's initiative, and local Bible Society and CMS branches, it was also bound closely into the fabric of Calcutta's nascent civil society.[51] In 1824 Thomason was advanced to the cathedral by Bishop Heber, a mark of the broad esteem in which he was held.[52]

Establishment piety in Calcutta thus had a noticeably Evangelical flavour. Several of the leading families who attended the Old Church were 'serious'.[53] Among the most eminent was John Walter Sherer (d. 1846), who by 1816 was Accountant-General to the Company and a Director of

[47] Eustace Carey, *Memoir of William Carey* (London, 1836), 513.
[48] [Simeon], *Memorial Sketches*, 117–20.
[49] *Ibid.*, 121–2.
[50] *Ibid.*, 120.
[51] Sargent, *T.T. Thomason*, 251. See also Abhijit Gupta, 'The Calcutta School-Book Society and the Production of Knowledge', *English Studies in Africa*, 57 (2014), 55–65.
[52] Sargent, *T.T. Thomason*, 296–300.
[53] Sandys, 'One Hundred and Forty-Five Years', 245–8.

the Bank of Calcutta.[54] He was married to Mary (1783–1859), sister of the chaplain Daniel Corrie (1777–1837), who was in turn married to Elizabeth (1789–1836), daughter of one of the Evangelical Trustees, William Myers (1758–1817). The Sherers lived in 'Chouringee', a row of magnificent white mansions overlooking the Maidan parade ground, grandly porticoed, surrounded by luxuriant gardens and guarded by tall gates and porters' lodges: 'the residences of the great Sahibs of Calcutta'.[55] Another Evangelical Chowringhee resident was John Herbert Harington (1765–1828), civil servant, judge, member of the Supreme Council and eventually President of the Board of Trade.[56] The Old Church and its congregation also acted as a node for connections in the Calcutta hinterland. David Brown's idyllic country residence at Aldeen, a few miles north along the Hooghly River, was close to Serampore, the Danish enclave where the Baptists Carey and his fellow Baptists, William Ward (1769–1823) and Joshua Marshman (1768–1837), established their famous mission and press in 1800, free from Company interference.[57] Carey had first found employment as superintendent at the indigo factory in Malda, which under first Grant and then Udny was the centre of a system of manufacture, evangelism and Bengali schools for plantation workers in the surrounding villages. Its personnel included Grant's cousin William Grant (d. 1807); the archaeologist and engraver Henry Creighton (1764–1807); and the linguist John Ellerton (1768–1820).[58] Further off but co-ordinated to some extent from Calcutta were the activities of Evangelical officers in Benares and of the Muslim convert, Abdul Masih (1776–1827), in Agra.[59] Also noticeable was the presence of Evangelical piety among the Company military and the regular regiments stationed in Bengal. Efforts to school the children of soldiers and local inhabitants sometimes flourished only briefly. Equally, though, there were plenty of stations where chaplains were given a hearing. While

---

[54] Edward Dodwell and James Samuel Miles, *Alphabetical List of the Honourable East India Company's Bengal Civil Servants, from the year 1780, to the year 1838* (London, 1839), 458–61.

[55] Sophia Kelly (ed.), *The Life of Mrs Sherwood, Chiefly Autobiographical* (London, 1857), 469.

[56] Dodwell and Miles, *Bengal Civil Servants*, 228–9.

[57] John Clark Marshman, *The Life and Times of Carey, Marshman and Ward. Embracing the History of the Serampore Mission*, 2 vols (London, 1859). For Aldeen, see Kelly, *Life of Mrs Sherwood*, 471–4.

[58] George Elwes Corrie and Henry Corrie, *Memoirs of the Right Rev. Daniel Corrie* (London, 1847), 59; Michael Andrew Laird, *Missionaries and Education in Bengal, 1793–1837* (Oxford, 1972).

[59] See also Avril A. Powell, 'Creating Christian Community in Nineteenth-Century Agra', in Young, *Indianness of Christianity*, 82–107.

it is impossible to give precise figures, memoirs and philanthropic sub-scription lists suggest that 'serious religion' was a growing characteristic of the officer corps.[60] Among the most famous converts was the Evangelical novelist Mary Martha Sherwood (1775–1851), wife of a Captain in the 53rd Foot, whose biography provides an affectionate and colourful account of Christianity in military cantonments.

Integral to these developments were the 'serious' chaplains, a string of whom were appointed through Simeon and Grant. Claudius Buchanan in 1796, Daniel Corrie and Joseph Parson (1780–1835) in 1805, Henry Martyn and Thomas Thomason in 1808 and Thomas Robertson (1788–1846) in 1812 all went to Bengal; Marmaduke Thompson (1776–1851) in 1806, Henry Harper (1791–1865) in 1814, James Traill (1785–1849) and James Hough (1789–1847) in 1815, Edward Martin Jackson (d. 1821), William Malkin (1791–1874) and Charles Church (1785–1822) in 1816 all went to Madras, where they joined Richard Hall Kerr, who had ministered there since 1793.[61] Thomas Robinson junior (1790–1873) went to the smaller establishment at Bombay in 1816 and Thomas Carr (1788–1859) joined him in 1817. The presence of several others who favoured the CMS or attended Queens' College, Cambridge or St Edmund Hall, Oxford, points to others who probably shared their views.[62] The notion that such men were somehow inferior in quality or education to their metropolitan brethren seems fanciful. By English standards such posts were exceptionally well-paid – the salary was around £900 by 1834 – and they frequently attracted high-calibre fig-ures.[63] Being drawn from long-established networks, those hand-picked by Simeon and Grant arrived in India with webs of acquaintance ready-made. Once there they continued to meet: Aldeen became an unofficial

---

[60] E.g. An Officer [Moyle Sherer], *Sketches of India* (2nd edn: London, 1824), 133–4; 214, 217–18; 321–2, 333–4; *Familiar Letters from the Rev. Daniel Corrie, a Military Chaplain in the E.I. Company, to a Subaltern Officer in the same Service* (Cocker-mouth, 1856); Henry Martyn, *Christian India; or, an Appeal on Behalf of 900,000 Christians in India, who want the Bible* (Calcutta, 1811).

[61] Kerr's cousin Thomas also served between 1807 and his death in 1811.

[62] Details from Frank Penny, *The Church in Madras*, 3 vols (London, 1904–22), II: 356–86, and John C. Bennett, 'Charles Simeon and the Anglican Evangelical Missionary Movement: a Study of Voluntaryism and Church-Mission Tensions' (unpublished Ph.D. Thesis, University of Edinburgh, 1992), 401–6. Bennett identifies several oth-ers whom Simeon may have influenced and who may or may not have served in India: Henry Cotterill (d. 1876), Joseph Crosthwaite (d. en route to India, 1816), An-thony Hammond (1797–1855), Frederick Spring (d. 1843) and Christopher Winter (d. 1822).

[63] Daniel O'Connor, *The Chaplains of the East India Company, 1601–1858* (London, 2012)

transit-camp where they stayed between postings, convalesced and shared ideas. In November 1806, for instance, Brown hosted the recently arrived Corrie, Parson and Thompson, who collectively agreed to promote the BFBS, to forward translations of the Bible, and to report to one another on their progress. 'After prayer we separated.'[64] Such gatherings multiplied in later years.[65] They also corresponded regularly with friends in Britain through both official and unofficial channels. 'You cannot confer a greater favour,' wrote Corrie to Simeon from the garrison at Cawnpore in 1811, 'than by forwarding to this country, supplies of Christian Guardians, Eclectic Reviews, Christian Observers, &c. We can lend them about, and they are read with much avidity, and excite much conversation about religious books.'[66] Such networks were self-perpetuating, remitting information on vacancies to contacts to have them filled by congenial candidates.

Small wonder, then, that when the firmly unevangelical Bishop Middleton arrived in Calcutta in 1814 he was dismayed to find that 'almost every body [*sic*]' in white Calcutta was a member of the Bible Society.[67] The lack of provision made for his accommodation doubtless heightened Middleton's awareness that he was a late arrival: George Udny reported incredulously how he had to offer the Bishop a room in order to prevent him being put up at a tavern.[68] Once he had been found a 'palace' at Chowringhee, Middleton would have discovered that his next-door-neighbour Sherer and his near neighbour Harington were leading lights in numerous charitable institutions, among them auxiliaries of the BFBS (1811) and CMS (1817).[69] It was a measure of the Bible Society's reach beyond Calcutta that the auxiliary printed no fewer than 1,000 copies of the early reports of the parent society for circulation.[70] As in Britain, not everyone who participated did so through Evangelical conviction. One of the most prominent was the high-ranking civil servant Charles Lushington (1785–1866), a reforming Whig who championed the School-Book Society (1817) as a tool for liberating Hindu society from backwardness.[71] The success of societies whose

---

[64] Corrie and Corrie, *Memoirs*, 54.

[65] *Ibid.*, 436, 440–1.

[66] *Ibid.*, 200.

[67] Middleton to Norris, 3 Jun. 1815, cited in E.A. Varley, *The Last of the Prince Bishops: William Van Mildert and the High Church Movement of the Early Nineteenth Century* (Cambridge, 1992), 78

[68] George Udny, n.d., [November?] 1814, in Morris, *Charles Grant*, 333–4.

[69] C. Lushington, *The History, Design and Present State of the Religious, Benevolent and Charitable Institutions Founded by the British in Calcutta and its Vicinity* (Calcutta, 1824).

[70] Corrie and Corrie, *Memoirs*, 190n.

[71] John Statham, *Indian Recollections* (London, 1832), 371–2, 387–9.

elected committees, dominated by laymen and including avowed nonconformists, owed nothing at all to episcopal authority can only have compounded Middleton's discomfort. The relationship between the Company
and the newly formed ecclesiastical establishment, moreover, remained
uncodified. Evangelicals could bypass the bishop entirely: the BFBS committee, for instance, met at Fort William College, while government provided generous grants for the Orphan Asylum and other philanthropic
endeavours.[72] The bishop, for his part, could threaten the independence of
the Old Church. 'The Bishop is jealous of my Church, and unless effectual
measures are taken to prevent it, he will deprive Calcutta of this blessing,'
Thomason told Josiah Pratt, imploring him to mobilize influential CMS
supporters at home in his defence.[73] There was even friction in Middleton's
new cathedral, whose select (i.e. self-perpetuating) vestry was championed
by Evangelical chaplains against not just reform-minded inhabitants of
Calcutta but their own bishop, too.[74] Middleton's foundation of SPCK District Committees in the three presidency capitals and of Bishop's College,
Calcutta, marked an attempt to build an alternative power-base, although
even these could not be quarantined from Evangelical involvement: chaplains tended also to be members of the SPCK.[75]

These developments were mirrored in other presidencies, albeit on a
smaller scale. In Bombay the Governor, Sir Evan Nepean, was instrumental
both in persuading the Directors to increase the official complement of
chaplains and in the foundation of a Bible Society Auxiliary (1813), which
was supported by 'some of the most respectable Gentlemen of the presidency'.[76] In Madras the key figure was R.H. Kerr (1769–1808), appointed
chaplain by the governor in 1793 in a manner that later generations would
regard as irregular: he was only priested in 1802.[77] This did not, however,
prevent him from becoming Senior Chaplain (1801–4, 1804–8) which position he used to lobby for an increase in chaplains' numbers and to campaign

---

[72] *Reports of the British and Foreign Bible Society ... Volume the Second, for 1811, 1812,
and 1813* (London, 1813), 241–5.

[73] Thomason to Pratt, 14 Aug. 1816, CRL, Church Missionary Society Archive, North
India Mission, XCMS/B/OMS/C I1 E1/32.

[74] Joseph Hardwick, 'Vestry Politics and the Emergence of a Reform 'Public' in Calcutta, 1813–36', *Historical Research*, 84 (2011), 90–1.

[75] M.E. Gibbs, 'The First Hundred and Fifty Years', in R.W. Bowie and I.D.L. Clark (eds),
Bishop's College, Calcutta (Calcutta, 1970). Reproduced at http://anglicanhistory.
org/india/bishops1970/, last accessed 5 July 2018.

[76] John Owen, *The History of the Origin and First Ten Years of the British and Foreign
Bible Society*, 2 vols (London, 1816), II: 461–5.

[77] 'Some Account of the Life of the Late Reverend Dr Kerr', *Christian Observer*, 11
(1812), 80–6, 150–7.

for moral improvement. 'At last it was found impossible to get up a play, or even a monthly assembly,' recalled an admiring contemporary. 'In consequence, the Pantheon ... was actually shut up, and ordered to be sold.'[78] At the Military Male Orphan Asylum where Kerr ministered, 'orphans' (i.e. the illegitimate children of European soldiers) worked a printing press that published religious tracts and sermons for circulation around India and Ceylon, as well as being official printer to the government. Kerr found strong support among the leading inhabitants of the city: the building of a new church in 'Black Town' between 1796 and 1801 was funded by a subscription. He had cordial relations with a succession of governors, being strongly encouraged by Lord William Bentinck and his wife, Lady Mary (d. 1843), as well as the Chief Judge, Sir Thomas Strange (1756–1841). While it is difficult to avoid the impression that Kerr's activities attracted support simply because he was active and conscientious, he was hailed by later Evangelical commentators, who assumed that the Danish Halle missions of the SPCK were moribund and that he and his ilk superseded them. Buchanan revealingly told him in 1807 that he was 'the representative and sole public supporter of the Christian religion in the peninsula.'[79] Still, attitudes to Evangelicals undoubtedly hardened in some quarters after the Vellore Mutiny of 1806, when Bentinck was recalled. Plans for a Madras Bible Society Auxiliary were summarily slapped down by his successor.

The Company Establishment and the Vernacular Bible Project, c. 1800–1850

Major John Scott-Waring (1747–1819) was annoyed. A former Bengal army officer and agent of Warren Hastings (1732–1818), now in London, he was convinced that the indiscretions of missionaries were to blame for the unrest at Vellore. He was thus scandalized to find one of them on the Company payroll. In a series of polemics fired off during 1807 and 1808 he reported incredulously that 'Mr William Carey ... enjoys a salary ... of eight hundred pounds a year, as teacher of the Bengalee and Sanscrit languages,' as well as rooms in Fort William College: this despite being a Baptist and flouting regulations preventing unauthorized proselytization.[80] 'I cannot ... subscribe to the justice of your panygerick [sic] on Mr. William Carey as he

---

[78] Hough, *History of Christianity*, IV: 233–4.

[79] *Ibid.*, IV: 160

[80] Major Scott Waring, *Observations on the Present State of the East India Company* (4th edn: London, 1808), liii. See also Jörg Fisch, 'A Pamphlet War on Christian Missions in India 1807–1809', *Journal of Asian History*, 19 (1985), 22–70.

is called in the list of persons employed by the EIC. The *Reverend* Mr. Carey as the Bible Society denominates him, or *Brother Carey*, the name he goes by at Serampore,' Scott-Waring waspishly told an Evangelical opponent.[81] 'To suppose that a people, tremblingly alive as the natives of India are on every subject that may by possibility touch their religion, can view such proceedings without the utmost apprehension and alarm for their future security, would be an absurdity of which no unprejudiced man is capable.'[82] Perhaps he was right to be alarmed. Carey's multiple identities bespoke not just the strength of the new piety but its exploitation of grey areas: non-governmental institutions and personal commitments that Company policy was powerless to prevent. He also embodied the growing entanglement of Evangelicalism and officialdom. Among the chief reasons for that was what may be termed the vernacular Bible project: the Evangelical conviction that all that was needed for the conversion of the world was enough copies of the Scriptures in people's mother tongues. Crucial to that project was infrastructure – presses; type; translators; distribution networks; the elementary education that allowed Bibles to be read – and Evangelicals poured enormous resources into this. As this section will show, that made them important partners even in places where the authorities tried to remain disinterested, not least in and around the Company.

The symbiosis between Evangelicalism and the establishment in Bengal emerged at around the turn of the nineteenth century. The catalyst was the arrival as Governor General of the Earl of Mornington (1760–1842), soon to become Marquess Wellesley, in 1798. An associate of Pitt and a supporter of Wilberforce's anti-slavery campaign, Wellesley was no paragon of virtue: he married his mistress and on his return to England scandalized even aristocratic London with his voracious womanizing. But he was nevertheless part of a generation for whom the defeat of the French and the extension of British rule abroad required the enforcement of public morality and close Church–state links. He arrived in Calcutta determined to raise standards of behaviour, seeing gambling and sexual immorality among Company officials as inimical to the image of godlike probity that he sought to instil in the minds of the ruled. The translation of the outspoken Claudius Buchanan from a military post to a presidency chaplaincy in late 1799 placed Evangelicals close to the centre of the new regime.[83] It also allowed them to put their own spin on it. In February 1800

[81] Major Scott Waring, *A Letter to the Rev. John Owen* (London, 1808), 32.
[82] *Ibid.*, xv
[83] For Buchanan, see Allan K. Davidson, *Evangelicals and Attitudes to India, 1786–1813* (Sutton Courtenay, 1990).

Buchanan preached before the government on the day of thanksgiving for the defeat of Tipu Sultan (1750–1799), damning French-inspired atheism and holding out Christianity as the rock on which British and Indian social stability ought to be based. This impressed Wellesley: he ordered copies of Buchanan's sermon to be distributed across British India and sent home to the EIC Directors.[84] From around this time, Brown recalled, there was 'an open and general acknowledgement of the Divine Providence'.[85] '[Wellesley] has been the saviour of India to Britain,' gushed Corrie.[86]

The effects were material as well as moral. 'Merit is patronized' crowed Buchanan, '... and young men of good inclinations have the best opportunities of improvement.'[87] This was particularly evident at Fort William College, Wellesley's 'Oxford of the East', founded in 1800. If Government House, conceived at around the same time, was meant to dazzle observers architecturally, the College was designed to impress them intellectually and culturally. By acquainting all civil servants with 'the history, languages, customs and manners of the people of India, with the Mahommedan and Hindu codes of law and religion', it would turn 'a temporary and precarious acquisition' into 'a sacred trust and a permanent possession', or so Wellesley hoped.[88] It was lavishly staffed, with generous prizes to reward industry.[89] And it also strengthened connections between the institutional church and the colonial state: instruction in the principles of Christianity was to be one of the College's purposes and those at its head were to be clergymen on the Company establishment. It is not clear how much of this can be ascribed to Buchanan, who had become one of Wellesley's closest collaborators, but he was certainly one of the College's chief apologists. 'The whole direction of the College lies with me,' he boasted. 'Every paper is drawn up by me and everything that is printed is revised by me.'[90] He became Vice-Provost and Professor of Greek, Latin and English Classics, while Brown was made Provost, with responsibility for morals and discipline. These were natural appointments given their status in the presidency, but

[84] Hugh Pearson, *Memoirs of the Life and Writings of the Rev. Claudius Buchanan*, 2 vols (Oxford, 1817), I: 185–91.
[85] [Simeon], *Memorial Sketches*, 303.
[86] Corrie and Corrie, *Memoirs*, 56–7.
[87] Pearson, *Claudius Buchanan*, I: 190.
[88] 'Extract from the Governor General's NOTES ... with respect to the Foundation of a College at Fort William, August 1800', *Papers Relating to East Indian Affairs, Part IV: 24 Nov. 1812–22 July, 1813, Volume 10* (London, 1813), 5, 9
[89] See Thomas Roebuck, *The Annals of the College of Fort William* (Calcutta, 1819).
[90] Buchanan to Charles Grant, n.d. 1801, cited in Pearson, *Claudius Buchanan*, I: 219–20.

it is likely that Wellesley also used them to draw the sting out of potential criticism at home: such an expensive enterprise was always likely to prove controversial. In peddling the merits of his provosts he commended 'Mr Brown's character' as 'well known in England, and particularly so to some members of the Court of Directors', reminding readers that Buchanan was an intimate of Bishop Porteus and 'Dr Milner, Master of Queen's [sic] College'.[91] J.H. Harington became Professor of the Laws and Regulations of the British Government in India; Carey was Professor of Sanskrit, Bengali and Marathi; Thomason was later made examiner in Arabic.[92] Among the early cohorts were several notably pious men – W. Butterworth Bayley (1782– 1860), Robert Merttins Bird (1788–1853) and William Wilberforce Bird junior (1784–1857) – who would later rise to high offices in the Company.[93]

It would be misleading to suggest that Fort William College as an institution inculcated Evangelical principles. Employing as it did a mixture of white teachers and Indian *pundits*, it also acted as a seedbed for the 'Bengal Renaissance', a cultural, intellectual and social reform movement that promoted classical Indian literature and vernacular education, and for the associated Brahmo Samaj movement. Yet it is impossible to understand the world of Ram Mohan Roy (1772–1833) and his contemporaries without appreciating how multiply embedded evangelicals were in it. While in Britain their co-religionists were increasingly hostile towards 'Hindu' culture, in India there was a strong strand of positive evangelical Orientalism: Harington and Carey were, for instance, leading members of the Asiatic(k) Society of Bengal, as well as initially supporting the Hindu College, established in 1816 to educate the sons of rich Indian families, which became the cradle of 'Young India'.[94] English ideas of educational 'improvement', missionary-sponsored scholarship and indigenous reformism and proto-nationalism were inter-braided streams.[95] Biblical translators, whose desire to spread the gospel among the influential led them to focus on elite languages such as Persian and Sanskrit, also shaped literary trends. Carey worked closely alongside Bengali intellectuals to produce not just Bible translations but vernacular dictionaries and an edition of the early Hindu epic *Ramayana*.[96] Indeed, so valuable were his linguistic expertise and connections that Wellesley and Buchanan regarded his participation as indispensable to the

[91] 'Extract from the Governor General's NOTES', 17.
[92] Roebuck, *College of Fort William*, Appendix IV, 53–4; Sargent, *T.T. Thomason*, 204.
[93] Roebuck, *College of Fort William*, Appendix V, 58–80.
[94] David Kopf, *British Orientalism and the Bengal Renaissance: the Dynamics of Indian Modernization, 1773–1835* (Berkeley, CA, 1969), 179–85.
[95] Pennington, *Was Hinduism Invented?*, 139–66.
[96] *Ibid.*, 77–80.

success of the College. In exchange for his involvement as a teacher, government agreed to reconcile itself to the (illegal) presence of the Serampore Baptists.[97] It was also relevant that Serampore had a Sanskrit press: it was contracted to do the college's printing, an arrangement that dispelled at a stroke the financial problems that had dogged the mission. By 1805 Ward was running at least three presses in 'more commodious premises' and, thanks to the efforts of native type-cutters such as Panchanan Karmakar (d. c. 1804) and his son-in-law Monohar Karmakar (fl. 1800s and possibly after), could print in Bengali, Urdu, Oriya, Tamil, Telegu, Kanarese and Marathi.[98] Products of the College via Serampore thus ranged from classical Persian or Sanskrit poetry to legal textbooks to Arabic or Hindustani Bibles, alongside Grammars and Dictionaries, many of them written by missionaries and their collaborators and all of them appearing under the patronage of government, either explicit or implied.[99] If religious neutrality remained the Company's declared policy, there were numerous individuals who blurred the boundaries, such as the LMS missionary Robert Morrison (1782–1834), whose Chinese Grammar was published at the College, and whose work as 'Chinese Secretary to the Honorable [*sic*] Company's Supercargoes at Canton' (i.e. translator) was as useful to the Company as it was to the Bible project.[100]

Paradoxically, the most serious threat to the Evangelical position at Fort William was Grant, now dominant at Leadenhall Street. Like his fellow directors, Grant deplored the expense of Wellesley's project, but he also feared that it might promote an 'assimilation to Eastern opinions'.[101] There were also tactical considerations to bear in mind: like his colleagues Parry and Teignmouth, Grant was wary of being tarred as an 'enthusiast', and worried that Buchanan's tactless (and self-promoting) pro-missionary lobbying might damage his own hard-won credibility in the Company.[102] Hence the leading part he played in the establishment of Haileybury College in Hertfordshire in 1805. Hence also on 1 January 1807 the 'reduction' of Fort William College. With it expired the positions of Provost and Vice-Provost. The irrepressible Buchanan was, however, already considering alternative ways of mobilizing. In the dying months of his Provostship he drew up what was effectively a propaganda leaflet for Serampore, detailing its activities and

---

[97] *Ibid.*, 56. See also Carson, *East India Company*, 57–60.

[98] Kopf, *British Orientalism*, 76–80

[99] See e.g. Roebuck, *College of Fort William*, 419–25.

[100] *Ibid.*, 421. For Morrison, see Christopher A. Daily, *Robert Morrison and the Protestant Plan for China* (Hong Kong, 2013).

[101] Ainslie T. Embree, *Charles Grant and British Rule in India* (London, 1962), 191.

[102] Simeon to Grant, 26 April 1809, Ridley Hall, Charles Simeon Papers.

calling for funds to translate the Bible into fifteen oriental languages. This was printed and despatched at government expense to civil and military officers across India, 'many of whom had never heard of the Serampore Mission before', with a letter from Buchanan in his soon-to-be-discontinued official capacity. 'The design received encouragement from every quarter: and a sum of about 1600l. was soon raised.'[103] The BFBS declined to sponsor it formally, but was prepared to donate £1,000 a year for three years.[104] Thus although 1807 was undoubtedly a setback, there remained close links between Fort William and Serampore. The Evangelical faction retained significant clout at the diminished College through Harington, who became President of its Council, and Carey, who was also a personal friend of the Earl of Minto (1751–1813), Governor General from 1806–13.

Buchanan's appeal, however, pointed to the possibilities inherent in more fleet-footed forms of organization. Crucial in Calcutta was the arrival of the Bible Society, whose honed publicity and ostensibly uncontroversial programme acted, as in Britain, not only as a motor for fundraising, but also as a way of gaining political leverage. Brown's appeal on its behalf from the pulpit of the Old Church on 1 January 1810 elicited 9,000 rupees to distribute 'Tamul' Bibles in Tanjore, which sum included contributions from the chaplains and the leading inhabitants of the city, as well as 2,000 rupees from the Commander-in-Chief of the army, Lieutenant-General George Hewett (1750–1840).[105] Prominent supporters enabled pressure to be brought to bear on government, such as in 1813, when a public address signed by thirteen of 'the most respectable people' elicited 10,000 rupees (about £1,250) to help print an edition of the Malay Bible.[106] Calcutta's religious public and its chaplains also proved influential in publicizing developments at faraway Travancore, on the Malabar coast, where Colonel Colin Macaulay and then Colonel John Munro (1778–1858), both 'serious Christians', effectively ruled as Company Resident and *Diwan* (Prime Minister), the former from 1800–10 and the latter until 1819.[107] Both men sponsored conversion to Christianity, taking an especial interest in the Syrian Christians of the region and encouraging the CMS 'Mission of Help' and its foundation of Kottayam College in 1818. Interest was piqued by Henry Martyn's

---

[103] Owen, *Bible Society*, II: 3, 6.

[104] Davidson, *Evangelical Attitudes to India*, 222–6.

[105] Owen, *Bible Society*, II: 23–31. Henry Martyn, *Christian India; or, an Appeal on Behalf of 900,000 Christians in India, who want the Bible* (Calcutta, 1811), i.

[106] Hough, *History of Christianity*, IV: 378.

[107] Cheriyan, *The Malabar Christians and the Church Missionary Society, 1816–1840* (Kottayam, 1935); R.N. Yesudas, *Colonel John Munro in Travancore* (Trivandrum, 1977).

sermon *Christian India; or, an Appeal on Behalf of 900,000 Christians in India, who want the Bible* (1811), which also launched the Calcutta Auxiliary Bible Society, and by Claudius Buchanan's bestselling *Christian Researches in Asia* (1811), both of which presented the venerable but degraded Syrian Church as dry kindling which Bibles would ignite.[108] The 'Bibliotheca Biblica', a repository for the distribution of Bibles in oriental languages, coupled with a translation library, was a reflex of the same urge.[109] 'The port of Calcutta is the annual resort of multitudes from all quarters ... of Armenian Greeks from the Archipelago; Arabians, Jews, Turks, and Malays; "some of almost every nation under heaven",' proclaimed the publicity. 'Opportunities occur of sending from this port the Scriptures in every direction throughout the whole East.'[110] From the first decade of the century onwards, elementary education in both English and vernacular languages expanded rapidly, almost all of it supplied by missionary organizations.[111]

Calcutta was thus now part of a rapidly coalescing system of Anglo-American missions spanning India and the Middle East. If many of the ideas, books and people that comprised that system emanated from London, there was also a lively exchange between points in it. There were close parallels between the Calcutta institution and the press and Bible depot founded at Malta in 1815. Established, likewise, in a British jurisdiction that was notionally neutral on religious questions, its projectors envisaged using mass-produced Bibles to reach places and people that missionaries could not, chiefly in the Ottoman Empire.[112] Its founder, William Jowett (1787–1855) of the CMS, deliberately emulated Buchanan in producing his own *Christian Researches in the Mediterranean* (1822) and *Christian Researches in Syria and the Holy Land* (1825), which conjured up grandiose visions of a new apostolic age in which vernacular Bibles and tracts might be transmitted across the Levant, travelling in African trade caravans or along Christian and Muslim pilgrimage routes, reviving ancient churches as they went.[113] By the early 1820s Malta and Calcutta were points in a ramifying network of individuals and stations throughout the Middle East,

---

[108] Sargent, *T.T. Thomason*, 208.
[109] Corrie and Corrie, *Memoirs*, 149. Claudius Buchanan, *Christian Researches in Asia* (Cambridge, 1811), 224–8.
[110] *Reports of the BFBS, Volume the Second*, 20–5.
[111] See Sutapa Dutta, *British Women Missionaries in Bengal, 1793–1861* (London, 2017), 19–34, for an excellent summary.
[112] See Gareth Atkins, 'William Jowett's Christian Researches: British Protestants and Religious Plurality in the Mediterranean, Syria and the Holy Land, 1815–30', *Studies in Church History*, 51 (2015), 216–31.
[113] *Proceedings of the Church Missionary Society* (1817), Appendix V, 149.

Asia and India, including the Reverend Henry Leeves (1790–1845), BFBS representative at Constantinople; Robert Pinkerton (1780–1859), the Bible Society's roving agent; John Paterson (1776–1865) and the St Petersburg Bible Society; the Scottish 'Astrachan' Mission; Samuel Gobat (1799–1879) and Christian Kugler (c. 1800–1830) in Egypt and Abyssinia; and Karl Gottlieb Pfander (1803–1865), at Shusha in Persia.[114] There were also close contacts with other parts of the evangelical 'Eastern Empire': LMS posts in South Africa and the Pacific, and CMS and BFBS personnel in Australia and New Zealand.

For the burgeoning philanthropic bureaucracy in London, India was a strategic lynchpin. Their activities and their links with the American Board for Congregational Foreign Missions (1810) and the Basel *Evangelische Missionsgesellschaft* (1815) were geared towards exploiting it. By later standards aspects of that infrastructure look embarrassingly ad hoc. The earliest CMS missionaries, for instance, lodged with the former Sierra Leone governor William Dawes at Bledlow in Buckinghamshire, where Nathaniel Gilbert, a former SLC chaplain, was incumbent. The curriculum was ostensibly sound: it comprised Arabic and Susoo for those destined for West Africa; Arabic, Persian and Hindustani for India; and for both groups tropical medicine, astronomy, mathematics, 'Mechanical Arts' and instruction in how to build 'good plain comfortable houses'.[115] But when Dawes was forced to vacate his residence, Thomas Scott at nearby Aston Sandford – enlisted to give occasional tuition in divinity – found himself solely responsible for their studies, including Susoo and Arabic, 'of neither of which languages he has any knowledge', and which he tried to decipher with the help of his rusty Hebrew, a situation exacerbated by the fact that most of his students were German.[116] Yet if this sounds amateurish, it is worth remembering that clerical education did not on the whole take place in the universities, where mastery of the Greek and Latin classics remained the blue riband of intellectual achievement. Vocational skills and specific knowledge were acquired through study and often residence with clerical tutors.[117] Even once the CMS became a larger concern it continued to employ this model: between 1816 and 1825 trainees lodged

[114] Thomas O'Flynn, *The Western Christian Presence in the Russias and Qājār Persia, c.1760–c.1870* (Leiden, 2017)

[115] Stuart Piggin, *Making English Missionaries, 1789–1858: the Social Background and Training of British Protestant Missionaries to India* (Sutton Courtenay, 1984), 190–1.

[116] John Scott, *The Life of the Rev. Thomas Scott* (4th edn: London, 1822), 381.

[117] Sara Slinn, *The Education of the Anglican Clergy, 1780–1839* (Woodbridge, 2017), 109–98.

with the Secretary, Edward Bickersteth, who doubled as tutor, a situation that changed only with the opening of the Church Missionary Institution at Islington.

Moreover, as Nile Green has rightly pointed out, university dons, clerics and missionaries did not occupy separate worlds.[118] Clerical networks used to identify candidates for service abroad were also employed to find scholars who would labour in the same cause: the Evangelical orientalist Thomas Pell Platt (1798–1852), for instance, studied with Henry Jowett at Little Dunham prior to his admission to Trinity College, Cambridge, in 1816, where he was elected Fellow in 1820 and Tyrwhitt Hebrew Scholar in 1821, becoming the Bible Society's librarian at around the same time. More famous was Samuel Lee, a Shropshire joiner and autodidact 'discovered' and sponsored through Queens' College by the CMS from 1813 onwards. His almost miraculous rise thereafter owed much to the influence of his co-religionists: he received his B.A. in 1818; an M.A. by royal mandate in 1819, the same year that he was elected to the Sir Thomas's Professorship of Arabic; and the Regius Professorship of Hebrew in 1831. Lee's career also serves to underline the lack of hard-and-fast boundaries between the universities and the committee rooms of Bible and missionary societies: for although his elevation to a chair 'naturally closed his official connection with the Church Missionary Society', it did not prevent him from being Oriental Tutor at Islington between 1825 and 1831.[119]

It also illustrates how the demands of the vernacular Bible project could shape scholarly priorities: Lee edited Bibles, Testaments or significant sections of them in Syriac, Malay, Arabic, Coptic, Persian and Hindustani, as well as writing histories of the Abyssinian and Syrian churches, in both of which CMS agents took a close interest.[120] With the missionary Thomas Kendall (1778–1832) and the New Zealanders Hongi Hika (c. 1772–1828) and Waikato (c. 1790–1877), who visited Britain at the behest of the CMS in 1820–1, Lee produced the first Maori dictionary.[121] One of Lee's collaborators was another high-ranking Evangelical, J.D. MacBride (1778–1868), who held the Lord Almoner's Readership (later Professorship) in Arabic at Oxford from 1813–68, while Thomas Robinson junior returned from

[118] Nile Green, 'Parnassus of the Evangelical Empire: Orientalism and the English Universities, 1800–50', *Journal of Imperial and Commonwealth History*, 40 (2012), 337–55.

[119] Piggin, *Making Evangelical Missionaries*, 195-6.

[120] [Anna Mary Lee], *A Scholar of a Past Generation: A Brief Memoir of Samuel Lee* (London, 1896).

[121] Judith Binney, *The Legacy of Guilt: a Life of Thomas Kendall* (2nd edn: Wellington, 2005), 68-79.

Madras to be Lord Almoner's Professor of Arabic at Cambridge from 1837–54. The inaugural Boden Professor of Sanskrit at Oxford, Horace Hayman Wilson (1786–1860), by contrast, was too much a champion of Hindu culture for Evangelicals to approve of him: he also left in India several illegitimate children. Yet his chair was an Evangelical initiative. It was established in 1832 with monies left by Lieutenant-Colonel Joseph Boden (d. 1811) of the Bombay Native Infantry to enable his countrymen 'to proceed in the conversion of the natives of India to the Christian religion by disseminating a knowledge of the sacred scriptures'. The language of the bequest and the fact that his daughter attended an Evangelical church in Cheltenham imply that he, too, held 'serious' beliefs.[122]

Green's notion that Evangelicals dominated oriental scholarship in the first half of the nineteenth century is overblown. But they undoubtedly influenced scholarly priorities, cultural agenda and indeed policy. By the mid 1810s, Gambier on behalf of the CMS and Teignmouth on behalf of the BFBS could plausibly act as though they *were* the establishment, presenting Maori chiefs at court, hosting Persian diplomats and corresponding with Syrian and Greek patriarchs. When Mirza Salih (1790?–1845) and five other Muslim students came to Britain between 1815 and 1819 to investigate the 'European sciences', it was natural that they should encounter serious piety at every turn.[123] Study with the pious mathematician Olinthus Gregory at the Royal Military Academy in Woolwich introduced them into a world of Evangelical acquaintanceship: they met Hannah More at Cowslip Green (to their mutual incomprehension); toured the 'madrasas' of Oxford with MacBride and John Hill (1786–1855) of St Edmund's College, and of Cambridge with Lee and Milner; and took a close interest in the printing side of the Bible Society. The students' friend and patron was Sir Gore Ouseley (1770–1844), a Persian scholar and former Ambassador in Tehran. Ouseley was a deeply devout man who had befriended Henry Martyn during the latter's final journey and illness, assisted in correcting Martyn's Persian translation of the New Testament and worked to bring it to fruition, both in Persia and during his visit to the Tsar's court in St Petersburg.[124] On his

---

[122] Green mistakenly suggests that no appointment was made, and his vague comment that Wilson had 'evangelical connections' is unhelpful. His characterization of Stephen Reay (Laudian Professor, 1840–61) as 'crypto-evangelical' is also wrong: what he imagines to be a pamphlet offering a 'spirited defence' of the CMS was in fact a vitriolic attack on it: Green, 'Parnassus', 345–6.

[123] Nile Green, *The Love of Strangers: What Six Muslim Students Learned in Jane Austen's London* (Princeton, NJ, 2016).

[124] Robert Pinkerton to BFBS Committee, 20 Sep., 1 Oct. 1814, cited in *Reports of the BFBS ... Volume the Third, for the Years 1814 and 1815* (London, 1815), 318–20.

return he became a vice-president of the BFBS. Whether or not he was Evangelical is unclear, but he shows how readily Evangelical causes became also national causes in global contexts.[125]

A 'Christian Raj'? Patronage Networks and Piety, c. 1800–58

William Taylor Money (1769–1834) was strapped for cash. A former officer in the Company navy, Superintendent of the Bombay Marine Board and President of the Asiatic Society of Bombay, his finances were eroded by his election as MP for Wootton Bassett in 1816 and destroyed by his agents' corrupt mismanagement of his Java estate. It was therefore natural that he should seek election as a Director, which lucrative position he secured in 1818. In Bombay he had acted alongside Nepean in pushing Evangelical causes, and in parliament he assisted Wilberforce and T.F. Buxton's anti-slavery campaign and spoke against 'godless' radicalism. He was intimate with the pious great and good. Hannah More wrote him gossipy letters; Charles Simeon was a family friend; Daniel Wilson was a confidant.[126] But if piety pervades his surviving correspondence, the whiff of patronage is just as pungent. The army officer and 'canting' courtier-turned-Wesleyan Benjamin Bloomfield (1768–1846) wrote repeatedly during the 1820s for places in the Company military;[127] the devout Irish peer Lord Roden (1788–1870) enquired after military and naval positions;[128] the CMS sought to place a potential chaplain: 'we have applied without success to Mr Grant and Mr Parry'.[129] Money in turn was a frequent supplicant on behalf of his connections, foremost among them his sons, three of whom followed him into Company service.[130] An enquiry about a cadetship in 1824 elicited a

[125] James Reynolds, 'Memoir', in Sir Gore Ouseley, *Biographical Notices of Persian Poets* (London, 1846), lxiii–lxv, cxiv–cxv, cciii–ccvi. See e.g. Sir Gore Ouseley to Lord Teignmouth, 20 Sep. 1814, CUL, BSA/F3/Shore, British and Foreign Bible Society Archive, BSA/F3/Shore/29.

[126] See LPL, William Taylor Money Letters, DS/UK/3153.

[127] Benjamin Bloomfield to Money, 24 Jun., 28[?] Jun., 15 Jul 1820; 24 Jun. 1823; 27 Mar. 1827; 1 Jul. 1829; 21 Jan. 1832, LPL, Money Letters, DS/UK/3153, fos 1–16.

[128] Roden to Money, n.d. [1822]; 1 Mar., 9 Apr. 1822, LPL, Money Letters, DS/UK/3153, fos 55–62.

[129] Daniel Wilson to Money, 21 Mar. [1819], LPL, Money Letters, DS/UK/3153, fos 153–4.

[130] Robert Cotton Money (1803–1835), EIC Civil Service; George William Money (1806–1830), 3rd Bengal Light Cavalry; David Inglis Money (1807–1880), EIC Civil Service: Judge of Calcutta High Court. John Burke and John Bernard Burke, *A Geneaological and Heraldic Dictionary of the Landed Gentry of Great Britain and*

pained reply from Robert Grant regarding the impossibility of satisfying every request that his late father received. 'To little purpose did we spend, not *hours* but *days*,' he lamented, 'in adjusting the relative priorities of the names in my father's pocket-book' after his death.[131]

For there was nothing unusual about Money's pursuit of patronage. 'I have long been solicited by my friend Mr. Grant the E.I. Director (who was out by Rotation last year and is a Candidate at the ensuing Election), to canvass him for all my acquaintance, who had votes,' Wilberforce breathlessly told a correspondent in 1807. '... He is in danger, and He in particular desires me to apply to your Lordship.'[132] A year later Wilberforce was writing again, this time on behalf of John Hudleston (1746–1835), a Director, onetime MP and ally of the Saints whose re-election to the Company was threatened because of his strong support for anti-slavery.[133] Grant's long membership of the Court of Directors and repeated election to the Chairmanship (1804–5; 1807–9; 1815) made him a pivotal figure, especially in his careful selection of chaplains, a privilege reserved for the Chairs.[134] Yet his dominance has been exaggerated, both by hagiographers and by contemporary critics bent on damning him as a canting member of Dundas's 'Scotch' cousinhood. There were others, too, whom Evangelicals might count upon: chairs or deputy chairs such as George Smith (1805), Edward Parry (1806–8), Robert Thornton (1812–13) and William Thornton Astell (1809–10; 1823–4; 1828–9). Beyond the ranks of the Company proper, devout churchmen were also well represented among the 'Commissioners for the Affairs of India', i.e. the Indian Board of Control, which was comprised of Privy Counsellors and members of the government.[135] The Earl of Harrowby (1804, 1809), his brother Richard Ryder (1809–12), Spencer Perceval (1807–12) and Nicholas Vansittart (1812–23) all served, although given their ministerial loyalties and political ambivalence towards the Saints, too much should not be read into this. One very decided Evangelical was Lord Ashley, the future Earl of Shaftesbury (1801–85), who served from 1828–30, being determined to

Ireland, 2 vols (London, 1846–7), II: 875–6; Frederick Charles Danvers, et al., *Memorials of Old Haileybury College* (Westminster, 1894).

[131] Robert Grant to Money, 17 Mar. 1824, LPL, Money Letters, DS/UK/3153, fos 31–2.

[132] Wilberforce to Bishop of Lincoln, 20 April 1807, Kent History and Library Centre, Stanhope of Chevening Manuscripts, U1590 S5 04/12.

[133] As Resident of Tanjore, Hudleston knew the missionary C.F. Schwartz, and wrote the text for Bacon's memorial to him in St Mary's Church, Fort St George. Penny, *Church in Madras*, I: 502.

[134] Morris, *Charles Grant*, 220.

[135] Thomas Pennell, 'Board of Control – List of the Commissioners Appointed for the Management of the Affairs of India', in *Thirty-First Annual Report of the Deputy Keeper of the Public Records* (London, 1870), 367–71.

promote 'good government and Christianity', and who retained a strong interest in Indian affairs.[136] Also significant were the long tenure of Teignmouth (1807–28) and the presidency of Charles Grant junior from 1830–4, during which time his brother Robert was also a member of the Board.

It is important not to assume that these always acted as a coherent group: like members of any interest, Evangelicals owned multiple obligations. Nor should we conclude, anachronistically, that they limited themselves to moral causes. Their unpublished correspondence is dotted with countless requests on behalf of friends and family, some but by no means all of them justified in terms of the advance of religion. 'The desire to promote the election of their friends, and participate in the patronage' was, after all, among the foremost motivations for investing in Company stock.[137] Nevertheless, Evangelicals were aware of the importance of friends in high places, and with good reason. East India patronage consisted not only of appointments to the civil, military, medical and marine branches of the Company: it also included places on the home establishment – clerkships at Leadenhall Street, positions at Haileybury, the military college at Addiscombe and at the recruiting depots for European soldiers – as well as hundreds of lower-ranking posts in Company premises across London, such as labourers, door-keepers, porters and firelighters.[138] After 1784, the new Board of Control effectively made the Governor General, governors and commanders-in-chief into government appointments, but this still left high-ranking places at the directors' disposal, from staff officers in the Company's armies to presidency law officers. Subject to the consent of the Archbishop of Canterbury and the Bishop of London, they could also appoint chaplains. Vacancies were divided into twenty-eight parts: the Chairman, the Deputy Chairman and the President of the Board of Control received two each, and the other twenty-two directors were given one apiece. Naturally, the value of this was the subject of frequent speculation. Robert Grant estimated in 1813 that a director's patronage was worth £7,000 to £8,000 a year, while Joseph Hume thought £12,025 more realistic, equating to £24,050 apiece for the Chairs.[139] Not surprisingly, Grant senior was a jealous defender of Company privileges, taking umbrage at Wellesley's suggestion that positions in India should depend on their performance at Fort William College.

---

[136] Diary, 6 August 1828, cited in Edwin Hodder, *The Life and Work of the Seventh Earl of Shaftesbury*, 3 vols (London, 1886), I: 104.

[137] Cited in H.V. Bowen, *The Business of Empire: the East India Company and Imperial Britain* (Cambridge, 2008), 85.

[138] J.M. Bourne, 'The Civil and Military Patronage of the East India Company, 1784–1858' (unpublished Ph.D. thesis, University of Leicester, 1997), esp. 83–90.

[139] *Ibid.*, 86.

This usurpation of the directors' rights was one of the chief reasons for his hostility to Wellesley.[140]

It also provided impetus for the foundation of Haileybury College: an attempt, critics alleged, to expand Grant's fiefdom. It is important, however, to see through Joseph Hume's jibes and Sydney Smith's scaremongering about directors bent on 'introduc[ing] ... their own particular tenets' to the inmates.[141] For one thing it exaggerates Grant's reach. 'Though we may not see so much as you and I would desire of deep religious impressions produced on the minds of your young men, while they are all in your seminary,' Wilberforce consoled him, 'yet the mere circumstance of grounding them in the principles of Christianity and of morals may be of immense importance.'[142] Only a handful of appointments went to Evangelicals: William Dealtry was Professor of Mathematics and Natural Philosophy from 1805–13; Robert Anderson (1792–1843) was Assistant Professor in the Oriental Department from 1820–5; the popular preacher Henry Melvill (1798–1871) was Principal from 1844 until the College's closure in 1857; Sir James Stephen was Professor of History and Political Economy from 1855–7.[143] More important, as Callie Wilkinson has argued, was how Haileybury created an Anglo-Indian ruling caste in which 'fifty or sixty families formed a kind of society within a society, connected through friendship, kinship, and patronage.'[144] That world was shot through with pious connections. The frequency with which names such as Bayley, Bird, Grant, Gambier, Grote, Harington, Money, Raikes, Shore, Thomason and Udny appear on the college roll bears eloquent testimony to how Evangelical patrons advanced recruits from like-minded families.[145] Robert Merttins Bird, for instance, owed his opening to his distant cousin George Smith.[146] Below the Company 'aristocracy' lay a multitude of lesser figures: the brothers of Benjamin Jowett (1817–1893), for instance, brought up in a prominent pious family, obtained cadetships through Lord Ashley,

---

[140] Embree, *Charles Grant*, 186–95.
[141] [Sydney Smith], 'Ingram on Methodism', *Edinburgh Review*, 11, 22 (Jan. 1808), 355.
[142] Wilberforce to Grant, 24 Sep. 1804, cited in Morris, *Charles Grant*, 247.
[143] Danvers, et al., *Memorials of Old Haileybury*, 20–3. Anderson was later ordained and married Ellen-Mary Shore, daughter of Teignmouth: Shore, *Lord Teignmouth*, II: 529, 571; Ellen-Mary Anderson, *Practical Religion Exemplified* (2nd edn: London, 1845).
[144] Callie Wilkinson, 'The East India College Debate and the Fashioning of Imperial Officials, 1806–1858', *Historical Journal*, 60 (2017), 964.
[145] Danvers, et al., *Memorials of Old Haileybury*.
[146] Peter Penner, *The Patronage Bureaucracy in North India: the Robert M. Bird and James Thomason School, 1820–1870* (Delhi, 1986), 10–11.

William (d. 1850) as an ensign to Madras in 1842 and Alfred (d. 1858) as a surgeon in 1846.[147]

During the 1810s and 20s Evangelical complaints about the weakness of their position and the irreligiosity of the Company bore less and less relation to reality. In 1819, for instance, Grant was still bemoaning 'the want of Churches, and yet more of Chaplains', which he saw as 'a scandal and a reproach' to the Company. 'What little has been done in the course of the last fifteen years ... has been effected against constant ill will in one part of the Court.'[148] While there was truth in this, it overlooked the fact that the Company had always been committed to supporting Christian ministry among the European inhabitants, a principle it continued to uphold. After the accession of extensive territories in the Madras Presidency in the 1800s, the Court of Directors increased the number of chaplains there from fifteen to eighteen, as well as taking the initiative in church and chapel provision for new military stations: of twenty-three constructed between 1808 and 1832, fifteen were built and furnished by the government and two were assisted with grants, the others being built through private initiative (one of them by the CMS).[149] Even for the latter, funding was available to pay for maintenance and running costs.[150] By 1835 the Bengal chaplaincy establishment stood at thirty-seven, Madras at twenty-three and Bombay at fifteen.[151] Government also supported a number of Church of Scotland chaplains and Catholic priests, the latter chiefly with an eye to Irish and continental Europeans in its service. From 1812 – in parallel with developments in the British armed forces – Prayer Books and Bibles (the latter in both England and Gaelic) were distributed to garrisons and chaplains at Company expense. Likewise, the Company marched in step with the British army when it opted in 1825 to supply Bibles and Prayer Books *gratis* to any British soldier who could read, a policy extended to European servicemen in 1827.[152] Libraries were set up at various stations under chaplains' supervision, the prescribed books including standard religious works. Evangelicals

---

[147] Evelyn Abbott and Lewis Campbell, *The Life and Letters of Benjamin Jowett*, 2 vols (London, 1897), I: 18–19.

[148] Charles Grant to William Taylor Money, 18 Oct. 1819, LPL, Money Letters, DS/UK/3153, fos 21–3.

[149] Penny, *Church in Madras*, II: 52–7.

[150] *Ibid.*, I: 648–51.

[151] The number on station and in good health at any one time was smaller. Martin Montgomery, *History of the British Colonies*, 5 vols (2nd edn: London, 1835), I: 464–76. By around 1850 total numbers of chaplains had roughly doubled: O'Connor, *Chaplains*, 119.

[152] Penny, *Church in Madras*, II: 308.

certainly approved of these developments and claimed credit for them: the Naval and Military Bible Society made much of its supplying Bibles at a loss, to the tune of 50,000 in the decade after 1825.[153] As in Britain, however, care was taken by the authorities to control the distribution of such literature. Evangelicals were only part of a broader shift towards formalizing religious provision.[154]

More significant was their growing hold over the ecclesiastical hierarchy. When Calcutta fell vacant in 1831, Charles Grant junior, now President of the Board of Control, used Daniel Wilson to approach a string of Evangelical luminaries: William Dealtry (now Rector of Clapham), Henry Raikes (Canon Chancellor of Chester) and Charles Hoare (Archdeacon of Winchester). All turned it down. It was at this point that Wilson realized that he himself might be called to accept. Although his combativeness and 'Calvinism' proved hard for Earl Grey's government to swallow, Wilson was consecrated in April 1832.[155] Grant was also able to pressurize a recalcitrant and parsimonious Court of Directors to expand the Church establishment in India when the Company charter was renewed in 1833. The premature deaths of the first four bishops of Calcutta – Middleton, Reginald Heber, Thomas James (1786–1828) and John Matthias Turner (1786–1831) – were, he opined, caused by overexertion in a vast diocese that stretched from Cape Colony to New South Wales. The SPCK, SPG and CMS, 'a large portion of the public' and the Archbishop of Canterbury, he pointed out, agreed.[156] The result was two new bishoprics at Madras and Bombay.[157] Wilson, meanwhile, set sail for an ecclesiastical establishment where Evangelicals were in a position of near-dominance. Their strength and seniority among the chaplains helped to ensure that they already held the three archdeaconries: Daniel Corrie (Calcutta, 1823); Thomas Robinson junior (Madras, since 1825); and Thomas Carr (Bombay, 1833). All owed their initial advancement to Evangelical patrons, but all had proved themselves since: Corrie and Robinson were advanced by the non-Evangelical but sympathetic Bishop Heber. Even so, they were opposed in some quarters. Corrie's position as *de facto* diocesan during the long intervals in between bishops dismayed the SPG-appointed professors of Bishop's College. They

[153] *An Appeal in Behalf of the Naval and Military Bible Society* (London, 1835), 3.

[154] Sharon Murphy, *The British Soldier and his Libraries, c. 1822–1901* (London, 2016), 29–92.

[155] Josiah Bateman, *The Life of the Right Rev. Daniel Wilson*, 2 vols (London, 1860), I: 278–87.

[156] Grant to Chairman and Deputy Chairman, 12 Jun. 1832, cited in *Further Papers Respecting the Company's Charter (5.)* ([London], 1833), 67–9.

[157] Penny, *Church in Madras*, II: 350–1.

resented what they saw as interference and held Corrie's churchmanship to be suspect, also quarrelling with Robinson.[158]

Evangelicals could, though, afford to play a long game. 'The College is calculated to become a great instrument of good,' Corrie assured the CMS in 1827, 'and will not always be in the hands of its present professors. I hold it therefore of importance to maintain the connection.'[159] He now became first Bishop of Madras, while Carr became Bishop of Bombay. Further positions were thus opened up. Henry Harper became Archdeacon of Madras. Thomas Dealtry (1795–1861), another member of the Old Church axis, became Archdeacon of Calcutta, being succeeded in 1850 by John Henry Pratt (1809–1871), Wilson's domestic chaplain, when Dealtry was consecrated Bishop of Madras.[160] Dealtry's episcopal successor was Frederick Gell (1820–1902), probably himself a Broad Churchman, but also the son of Philip Gell (1783–1870), the Evangelical Rector of Derby. The second Bishop of Bombay was John Harding (1805–1874), a strong anti-ritualist, who was selected by the Archbishop of Canterbury, John Bird Sumner. It has been argued that India deprived Evangelicals of much-needed clerical talent in the 1830s.[161] Yet that notion exaggerates the gap between Britain and India. If Evangelicals felt under-represented on the episcopal bench in England, they knew well that they monopolized it in India. Daniel Wilson used his position as a platform to intervene at home, such as when he attacked the Oxford Movement from the late 1830s onward.[162]

Nevertheless, there was no sea-change in Company policy. Leading presidency figures of the 1810s and 20s such as Charles Metcalfe (1785–1846) and John Adam (1779–1825) in Bengal, Mountstuart Elphinstone (1779–1859) and John Malcolm (1769–1833) in Bombay and Thomas Munro (1761–1827) in Madras were only too aware that British rule rested on the loyalty of the sepoy army, and regarded attempts to interfere in Indian laws and institutions as foolhardy.[163] Granted, there were avenues for Evangelicals to exercise influence. The case of two American missionaries who

---

[158] Gibbs, 'First Hundred and Fifty Years'; [Elizabeth Fenton], *The Journal of Mrs Fenton* (London, 1901), 174–5. A. Westcott, *Our Oldest Indian Mission* (Madras, 1897), 50.

[159] Gibbs, 'First Hundred and Fifty Years'.

[160] Pratt might have succeeded Wilson had the decision not been made after the Mutiny to avoid anyone linked to missions. I. Cave Brown, 'The Venerable Archdeacon Pratt, Archdeacon of Calcutta: a Sketch', *Mission Life*, 3, n.s. (1872), 163–9.

[161] Ian S. Rennie, 'Evangelicalism and English Public Life, 1823–1850' (unpublished Ph.D. thesis, University of Toronto, 1962), 76.

[162] Andrew Atherstone (ed.), *The Journal of Bishop Daniel Wilson of Calcutta, 1845–1857* (Woodbridge, 2015), xxxi–xli.

[163] Carson, *East India Company*, 152.

arrived illegally at Bombay in 1813 was pleaded by Nepean, Money and George Udny, as well as several chaplains: instead of being sent home they went to Ceylon.[164] Thomason was close to Lord Moira (1754–1826), from 1816 the Marquess of Hastings, Governor General from 1813–23. Moira frequently attended the Old Church; he took Thomason as his chaplain on progresses through the provinces; and he commissioned him in early 1814 to draw up a plan for the education of the Indian population.[165] Moira also contributed to Baptist schools from his private funds, while Lady Hastings (1780–1840) was also instrumental in the establishment of the Calcutta School Book and Schools Societies, both of which received government grants.[166] Yet Moira and his successors refused to countenance anything that smacked of official coercion regarding religion. They ignored calls to have Sabbath observance enforced, while increasingly vociferous Evangelical opposition to the Company's collection of 'pilgrim tax' from those attending Hindu festivals and the participation of its officers in such rites fell on deaf ears. Their social priorities, Corrie thought, indicated their lack of zeal. 'Our Friday evening [services] have been but irregularly attended,' Corrie lamented to Sherer in 1826. 'The Government dinners have, no doubt, interfered; and next Friday Lady A[mherst, the Governor General's wife,] has an "at home." Shall we ever have "the powers that be" on our side?'[167] 'The most painful thing in the present administration is, that our duty as Christians is not recognised ... [N]ot a rupee, or a smile of approbation must come from Government.'[168]

The mood shifted only slightly during the tenure of Lord William Bentinck, between 1828 and 1835, whose campaign against *sati* – widows' self-immolation – and efforts to prevent discrimination against Christian converts Evangelicals cheered.[169] Yet Bentinck's liberal-minded pietism set him at odds with their commitment to a Christian establishment: he clashed with Daniel Wilson regarding the latter's attempts to assert episcopal authority over chaplains, ostentatiously attending dissenting chapels as well as the established church and declaring that it was the 'whole

[164] Thomas Smith and John O. Choules, *The Origin and History of Missions*, 2 vols (Boston, MA, 1834), II: 242–7. Thomason letter, n.d., cited in John Sargent, *T.T. Thomason*, 209.

[165] *Ibid.*, 214.

[166] Carson, *East India Company*, 159–60.

[167] Corrie and Corrie, *Memoir*, 386.

[168] *Ibid.*, 448.

[169] The Evangelical aristocrat Lady Olivia Sparrow was his sister-in-law. John Rosselli, *Lord William Bentinck: the Making of a Liberal Imperialist, 1774–1839* (Berkeley, CA, 1974), 61–6.

Christian church, whose cause in this heathen country we are to cherish'.[170]
On the subject of education, too, Bentinck was more ambivalent than
Evangelical agitators could have wished. In some respects his views paral-
lelled those of Thomas Babington Macaulay: although he was wary of the
'anti-Oriental' thrust of Macaulay's famous 'Minute on Education', the two
men agreed that schooling was integral to the 'improvement' of India: an
unobtrusive way of achieving what impatient missionaries sought by more
risky means.[171] He approved of the work of the Church of Scotland minister Alexander Duff (1806–1878), whose elite English-medium General
Assembly Institution, founded in 1830, became Calcutta's most prestigious
college, and was emulated by John Wilson (1804–1875) in Bombay and John
Anderson (1805–1855) in Madras. Yet Bentinck was also at pains to disso-
ciate government from missionary activity, refusing to countenance direct
grants to missionary schools and supporting Ram Mohan Roy's 'Hindu
College', which eschewed religious teaching entirely.[172] 'In many ways',
asserts Robert Frykenberg, 'the Indian Empire actually was a Hindu Raj', a
statement informed by Frykenberg's focus on Madras but which holds true
for the 1830s, by which time government was spending more than 10 *lakhs*
(a million rupees) a year on Hindu charities and institutions.[173]

The biggest bone of contention for Evangelicals was the 'Pilgrim Tax'.
Under the influence of Charles Grant at the Board of Control, in early
1833 the Directors signed and sent a Revenue Despatch calling for its discontinuation. Bentinck declined to implement it; so too did his successor,
Lord Auckland (1784–1849). The result was an uproar against government
support for 'idolatry'. Evangelicals were provided with ammunition in 1836
when a sepoy was killed at a Hindu religious festival. Bishop Corrie produced a 'Memorial praying for equal religious toleration to all subjects of
the state', calling for the full implementation of the Court's 1833 order: the
withdrawal of Company sanction for all ceremonies. It was signed by 201
prominent people, including thirteen chaplains, thirty-seven missionaries,
thirty-one civilians and no fewer than 111 military men.[174] The Evangelical
Commander-in-Chief of the Madras army, Sir Peregrine Maitland, forbade
his soldiers to participate in such occasions and was reprimanded. He
resigned in 1838, returning to Britain where he was hailed as a martyr and

[170] Carson, *East India Company*, 187.
[171] *Ibid.*, 194–8.
[172] *Ibid.*, 195.
[173] Robert Eric Frykenberg, 'Religion and Company Raj in South India', *Fides et Historia*,
17 (1985), 13; Copland, 'Arm of Empire', 1033.
[174] 'Memorial Praying for Equal Religious Toleration to All Subjects of the State', *Friend
of India*, 3 Nov. 1836.

founded the Anti-Idolatry Connexion League.[175] The Governor of Bombay, Robert Grant, and his equally Evangelical adviser, James Farish (1791–1873), sought more quietly to discontinue gestures of official respect, arguing that no government servant 'be they Hindu, Mussulman or Christian' ought to be compelled to participate in rites they did not profess.[176] 'As I prefer to follow the Lord Jesus Christ,' wrote Robert Nelson (fl. 1816–1842), an Evangelical sub-collector, 'I must renounce the service of the East India Company.'[177] In Britain this was dynamite. The lawyer and pamphleteer John Poynder (1779/80–1849) called for the abandonment of 'an unhallowed source of profit', lambasting the Company in the Court of Proprietors.[178] The Archbishop of Canterbury, William Howley (1766–1848) and the Bishop of London, Charles James Blomfield (1786–1857), took up the cudgels in the House of Lords.[179] Upholders of the status quo were forced to back down. 'I own I am afraid of the violence of your Saints and our Saints', wrote John Cam Hobhouse (1786–1869), President of the Board of Control, to Auckland, 'and I prefer attempting some compromise with that fierce and foolish party.'[180]

Evangelicals never managed to elicit the unambiguous statement that they desired. Yet, as Ian Copland has argued, the distinction between Christianity and the Company became increasingly blurred during the 1830s and 40s. Under the Council of Education, established in 1839, annual state grants-in-aid rose from £30,000 to £190,000 in 1852–3, the vast majority of which subsidized missionary schools. Christians became adept at using the idea of 'toleration' to ensure that the Company gave no countenance to other religions, while regulations against Christian instruction and the presence of Bibles in government-run schools were relaxed, to the disquiet of Hindu and Muslim observers.[181] Missionary presses had always attracted government custom, but the profits thus generated now

---

[175] Nancy Gardner Cassels, *Religion and Pilgrim Tax under the Company Raj* (New Delhi, 1987), 111–15, 128–31. See e.g. *Letters of Lieutenant-General Sir P. Maitland ... on the Compulsory Attendance of the British and Native Troops at Idolatrous and Mohammedan Festivals and Processions ...* (London, 1841). See also 'A Lady' [Julia Charlotte Maitland], *Letters from Madras During the Years 1836–1839* (new edn: London, 1861).

[176] Cassels, *Pilgrim Tax*, 116.

[177] *Ibid.*, 131.

[178] John Poynder, *Speech of John Poynder, Esq. at a General Court of Proprietors of the East India Company, on the 21st December, 1836...* (London, 1837), 1.

[179] Cassels, *Pilgrim Tax*, 121.

[180] Hobhouse to Auckland, 30 Aug. 1837, cited in Carson, *East India Company*, 215.

[181] Robert Eric Frykenberg, 'Modern Education in South India, 1784–1854: its Roots and its Role as a Vehicle of Integration under Company Raj', *American Historical*

took on a sinister aspect. It was not that Indians resisted modernity: it was missionaries' relentless association of technological advances with the advent of Christianity that bred resentment.[182] Indeed, civil servants and military officers often took the lead in missionary initiatives: the 'Himalaya Mission' was founded at Simla in 1840, while the victorious British army concluded the Second Anglo-Sikh War in 1849 by raising a thanksgiving subscription for the CMS.[183] The number of converts was small: around 90,000 at mid century.[184] But the growing piety of the Company's servants made its protestations of neutrality look increasingly hollow. The critic of British rule Francis Horsley Robinson (1801–1856) observed gloomily that this was because large swathes of India had fallen into Evangelical hands. 'There is, at least under the Bengal and Agra governments, hardly any man at the Presidency or in the interior ... who does not adhere to this party.'[185] It was an *'imperium in imperio'* that sidelined its critics and suppressed alternative opinions. The discontinuation of patronage, Robinson hoped, might shake its hegemony, but anyone truly interested in the welfare of India would need to tackle it head-on.[186]

Having come through Haileybury, Addiscombe or Fort William College together, and sharing the same convictions, this milieu was further knit together by a web of intermarriage. To dip into it at any point is to find a bewildering array of connections.[187] James Thomason (1804–1853), Lieu-tenant-Governor of the North-West Provinces, was a son of the chaplain Thomas Thomason and married Maynard Eliza Grant (c. 1811–1839), daugh-ter of James William Grant (1788–1865), a cousin and appointee of Charles. James's sister Frances Mary (1816–1842) married Sir Robert Montgomery (1809–1887), Governor of the Punjab from 1859–65. Or to look elsewhere: Samuel Thornton's grandson Edward Parry Thornton (1811–1893) went to India in 1830–1 as assistant to Robert Merttins Bird, his distant cousin, Collector at Gorakhpur. Bird in his turn was married to Jane (1792–1821), daughter of the chaplain David Brown; while another daughter, Hannah

---

Review, 91 (1986), 54–61; C.A. Bayly, *Empire and Information: Intelligence Gathering and Social Communication in India, 1780–1870* (Cambridge, 1996), 212–46.

[182] *Ibid.*, 243–5.

[183] James Long, *Hand-Book of Bengal Missions, in Connexion with the Church of Eng-land* (London, 1848), 160–9; Eugene Stock, *The History of the Church Missionary Society*, 4 vols (London, 1899–1916), II: 205–6.

[184] Copland, 'Arm of Empire', 1048.

[185] Francis Horsley Robinson, *What Good May Come out of the India Bill* (London, 1853), 34.

[186] *Ibid.*, 35.

[187] Unless otherwise indicated, all details in this paragraph are drawn from *ODNB*

Elizabeth, married William Wilberforce Bird the younger, Deputy Governor of Bengal and acting Governor General.[188] Bird's sister Mary (1789–1834) was a pioneer of 'zenanah mission', i.e. work with women segregated under the purdah system.[189] And so on. There were undoubtedly regions of particular strength. Thomason and his colleague John Russell Colvin (1807–1857) in the North-West Provinces between 1843 and 1857, and the brothers Henry (1806–1857) and John Lawrence (1811–1879), who served as successive Governors of the Punjab between 1846 and 1859, created the so-called 'Punjab system', which combined reform of taxes and land-tenure with strong support for missions. Close to these socially and in religious terms were the Scottish Presbyterian Muir brothers, especially William (1819–1905), whose position as Lieutenant-Governor of the North-West Provinces owed much to his connection with Thomason.[190] They gathered around them officials who shared their values: what has been dubbed the 'Bird–Thomason school'.[191] Though religion never induced Thomason to favour incompetence, his obituarist less-than-delicately reflected, 'it sometimes diminished his dislike of palpable mediocrity'![192] Indian resentment at overt and covert Christianization undoubtedly played a large part in the events of 1857–8. The 'Mutiny' sparked deep debates in Britain about the wisdom or otherwise of such policy and, under Crown control, religious neutrality was reaffirmed by royal proclamation. Publicly most Evangelicals toed the line; some, indeed, acknowledged that aspects of missionary activity were imprudent.[193] Nevertheless, attitudes in many quarters undoubtedly continued to resemble those of Thomason, who at an official examination of a government school publicly vindicated official neutrality while recommending Christianity to the boys' attention. '*You know* my heart is with you,' was his parting comment to the future bishop Thomas Valpy French (1825–1891).[194]

[188]   The latter's father, also William Wilberforce Bird, was prominent in evangelical circles at Cape Town. Joseph Hardwick, *An Anglican British World: the Church of England and the Expansion of the Settler Empire, c. 1790–1860* (Manchester, 2014), 172.

[189]   Rosemary Seton, *Western Daughters in Eastern Lands: British Missionary Women in Asia* (Santa Barbara, CA, 2013), 31–2.

[190]   Avril A. Powell, *Scottish Orientalists and India: the Muir Brothers, Religion, Education and Empire* (Woodbridge, 2010), esp. 75–99.

[191]   Penner, *Patronage Bureaucracy*, 350–5.

[192]   *Ibid.*, 103.

[193]   Tim Allender, 'Anglican Evangelism [*sic*] in North India and the Punjabi Missionary Classroom: the Failure to Educate "the Masses", 1860–77', *History of Education*, 32 (2003), 273–88.

[194]   Herbert Birks, *The Life and Correspondence of Thomas Valpy French*, 2 vols (London, 1895), I: French, 40.

'Asia Minor'

At the founding of the Pershore Bible Society Auxiliary in the late 1820s Thomas Thomason, on furlough from India and the guest of honour, challenged the solemnity of the occasion by placing his small goddaughter on his lap on the meeting platform: 'we old East Indians scorn to do anything like other people', her mother exclaimed proudly.[195] Old East Indians also flocked together: by the 1880s the London suburb of Bayswater was mockingly referred to as 'Asia Minor'.[196] In the first half of the century, though, they retired to Cheltenham. The spa waters were marketed for their benefits to those whose health had been impaired through residence in the tropics. Not the least attraction was Francis Close (1797–1882), incumbent of the parish church between 1826 and 1856. Close's attacks on horse-racing, Sabbath-breaking and the stage earned him the unflattering nickname of 'parish pope': he helped to ensure that Cheltenham was genteel without being quite as dangerously fashionable as it had once been.[197] He attracted enormous and admiring congregations and was enthusiastically supported by the 'Lieutenant-General Close Brigade', a tight-knit group of military officers, many of whom had served in India.[198] With their assistance he built four district churches, whose pulpits he filled with Evangelical curates; he also constructed infant and national schools; revived the grammar school; founded and for many years controlled Cheltenham College; and established in 1847 a Church of England Training College for teachers.[199] To Charles Simeon, who appointed him, Cheltenham under Close was 'a heaven upon earth'. To the ex-Company families in Close's congregations, it was a microcosm of the milieu in which they had spent much of their lives. As yet India had not yielded the harvest of conversions they hoped for; indeed, it never would. But in many respects they had achieved what they set out to do.

---

[195] Kelly, *Life of Mrs Sherwood*, 512–13.

[196] Elizabeth Buettner, *Empire Families: Britons and Late-Imperial India* (Oxford, 2004), 219–27.

[197] William Edwin Adams, *Memoirs of a Social Atom*, 2 vols (London, 1903), I: 11–23.

[198] Stuart Fraser, 'Exiled from Glory: Anglo-Indian Settlement in Nineteenth-Century Britain, with Especial Reference to Cheltenham' (unpublished Ph.D. thesis, University of Gloucester), 112–30.

[199] Alan F. Munden, *A Cheltenham Gamaliel: Dean Francis Close of Cheltenham* (Cheltenham, 1997); Khim Harris, *Evangelicals and Education: Evangelical Anglicans and Middle-Class Education in Nineteenth-Century England* (Carlisle, 2004), 127–56.

Conclusion:
Britannia Converted?

The 1825 Report of the British and Foreign Bible Society records an unusual donation to the Society's library. Listed below Bible editions and tracts in various languages was a painting by 'Thomas Stothard, Esq. R.A.'[1] *Britannia Recommending the Sacred Records to the Attention of the Different Nations of the World* – the probable title – was presented by the Baptist miniature painter and publisher Robert Bowyer (1758–1834) and was almost certainly given to mark the twentieth anniversary of the BFBS, which fell in 1824. The original does not seem to be extant. But from a rare contemporary print its main lineaments are clear. The 'sacred records' occupy the central position. They are held by two angels who present them to the peoples of the world as a revelation from the Triune deity, symbolized by the dove and triangle. In a metaphor so frequently invoked that it became a cliché, the Bible dispels dark clouds of ignorance: clouds that perhaps also evoke the bleak backdrop of global warfare against which the Bible Society was founded in 1804. Because Britannia's helmet and trident are now conspicuously laid aside. She points the nations towards the Scriptures: their representatives include a kneeling black slave at the bottom left, recognizable from abolitionist publicity ('Am I not a Man and a Brother?'), and a robed, shaven-headed Buddhist monk at the bottom right. It is not subtle. But it is revealing nonetheless. By giving their guineas, supporters of the BFBS were not only spreading the gospel but investing in a benevolent empire whose global grip rested on moral rather than military pre-eminence. And in the twenty years since the Society's foundation, it had witnessed success beyond its founders' wildest dreams. If support for it had once been viewed as outré, a place on a subscription list now placed its holder in the company of bankers, merchant princes, bishops, MPs, aristocrats and royal dukes. Measures were afoot, the *Christian Observer* reflected, 'for the conversion and happiness of an ignorant and perishing world'. Among them it cited

[1]   *Reports of the British and Foreign Bible Society ... Volume the Eighth, for the Years 1825, 1826, and 1827* (London, [1827?], 113.

Plate 6: Thomas Stothard, *Britannia Recommending the Sacred Records to the Attention of the Different Nations of the World*. Etching by Henry William Worthington, c. 1824.

'Bible and missionary institutions, books, tracts, education, reading-clubs, peace societies, the progress of civil liberty and ecclesiastical equality ... infant schools, mechanics' institutes, joint stock companies for public improvements, &c.'[2] The millennial reign of Christ and the triumph of busy do-goodery were practically synonymous.

If the image of Britannia converted encapsulates what Evangelicals were trying to do, this book has thrown new light how they went about it. It has charted the development of Evangelical networks in the Church of England, the City of London, the East India Company, the Royal Navy and in broader officialdom, both in Britain and abroad. It has shown, too, how this gave Evangelicals disproportionate influence over the discourses surrounding those institutions, and thus over the tone of public life. For if their embrace of voluntarism and the forms of organization that facilitated it have rightly been seen as marking a shift towards the consumeristic,

[2]   'Review of Works on Prophecy and the Millennium', *Christian Observer*, 24 (1825), 496.

market-driven religion of the nineteenth century, establishment Evangelicals were also masterly manipulators of an older set of tools. They therefore prospered in a dynamic establishment which did not just suppress radicalism but pre-empted damaging demands for change by advancing a reform agenda of its own.[3] Evangelicals were well placed to speak to that institutional culture, imbuing its buzzwords – professionalism, economy, reform – with moral and providential significance. It follows from this that Evangelicals were not the unthinking reactionaries that 1960s social historians loved to hate. We have seen repeatedly how they pursued their own agenda, weathering attacks from 'rational Christians' on the freethinking religious 'left' and from High Churchmen on the ecclesiastical 'right', flirting with Pittites and Foxites as necessary, and withstanding vicious abuse from radicals who denounced them as pro-regime patsies and po-faced 'Enemies of Laughter'.[4] Just as importantly, though, we have seen that Evangelicals were seldom as embattled as they or their hagiographers felt. They operated within a broadly Protestant culture that often welcomed their initiatives. And even if not all of their contemporaries agreed that Britannia needed to be converted, or approved of their methods, Evangelicals forged fruitful coalitions with other groups in order to achieve their goals.

All this has important implications for our understanding of what Evangelicalism was, how it operated and how it should be situated within late-Hanoverian politics and public life. It also suggests that existing chronologies need to be revisited. Two narratives have predominated. One emphasizes long-term continuity, seeing 'the imponderable pressure of the Evangelical discipline' as moulding Regency raffishness into Victorian seriousness,[5] and, in more recent accounts, shaping class and gender norms.[6] Boyd Hilton's reading of the period from c. 1785–1865 as an 'Age of Atonement' in which providentialism dominated social and economic

---

[3] See esp. Philip Harling, *The Waning of 'Old Corruption': Economical Reform, 1779–1846* (Oxford, 1996); Boyd Hilton, *A Mad, Bad, and Dangerous People: England, 1783–1846* (Oxford, 2006). For a summary of the historiography, see Arthur Burns and Joanna Innes, *Rethinking the Age of Reform: Britain, 1780–1850* (Oxford, 2003), 1–70.

[4] Vic Gatrell, *City of Laughter: Sex and Satire in Eighteenth-Century London* (London, 2006), 417–573.

[5] G.M. Young, *Victorian England: Portrait of an Age* (London, 1936), 1. The older literature is vast: see e.g. Maurice J. Quinlan, *Victorian Prelude: a History of English Manners, 1700–1830* (repr. London, 1965); Muriel Jaeger, *Before Victoria: Changing Standards and Behaviour, 1787–1837* (2nd edn: London, 1967).

[6] See esp. Leonore Davidoff and Catherine Hall, *Family Fortunes: Men and Women of the English Middle Class, 1780–1850* (London, 1987).

thought is now established orthodoxy.[7] Against this, however, scholars who have studied Evangelicalism as a movement have tended to emphasize discontinuity. From the mid-1820s, it is maintained, infighting fragmented Evangelicals and turned them in on themselves, just as an ageing generation of leaders was beginning to bow out.[8] The 'Age of Elegance', as Ford K. Brown put it, was succeeded by the 'Bleak Age', as the movement forged by Wilberforce, More and Simeon was 'slowly reconstituted' by 'a different kind of Evangelical'. Such, Brown reckoned, is the fate of all religious movements: 'as means come more and more to be taken for ends, leaders become less important, followers more; genuine beliefs harden into doctrinaire convictions and once heartfelt truths become shibboleths.' 'Great moral societies', he went on, 'grow into huge moral bureaux, good parish priests become platform preachers, organizers and religious executives'.[9] By the 1830s, he concluded, Evangelicalism had decisively lost its grip on the great and good. David Bebbington's focus is on culture rather than politics, but his work, too, posits a seminal shift in the 1820s, when romanticism began to unsettle a movement forged in the context of enlightened rationalism.[10] These narratives are not mutually exclusive: they reflect different angles on the same picture and there is some overlap between them, not least in Hilton's reading of tussles between post- and premillennial readings of providence. Nevertheless, given the tensions between these interpretations, it is worth re-examining them in the light of the findings of this book.

---

[7] Boyd Hilton, *The Age of Atonement: the Influence of Evangelicalism on Social and Economic Thought, 1785–1865* (Oxford, 1988).

[8] Ernest Marshall Howse, *Saints in Politics: the Clapham Sect and the Growth of Freedom* (Toronto, 1952), 138–65; Ford K. Brown, *Fathers of the Victorians: the Age of Wilberforce* (Cambridge, 1961), 518–20; David Newsome, *The Parting of Friends: the Wilberforces and Henry Manning* (London, 1966); Ernest R. Sandeen, *The Roots of Fundamentalism: British and American Millenarianism, 1800–1930* (Chicago, IL, 1970), 3–41; Ian Bradley, 'The Politics of Godliness: Evangelicals in Parliament, 1784–1832' (unpublished D.Phil. thesis, University of Oxford, 1974), 251–69; W.H. Oliver, *Prophets and Millennialists: the Uses of Biblical Prophecy in England from the 1790s to the 1840s* (Auckland, 1978), 99–149; Roger H. Martin, *Evangelicals United: Ecumenical Stirrings in Pre-Victorian Britain, 1795–1830* (Metuchen, NJ, and London, 1983), 194–203; John Wolffe, *The Protestant Crusade in Great Britain, 1829–1860* (Oxford, 1991), 29–64; Timothy C.F. Stunt, *From Awakening to Secession: Radical Evangelicals in Switzerland and Britain, 1815–35* (Edinburgh, 2000).

[9] Brown, *Fathers of the Victorians*, 518–19.

[10] D.W. Bebbington, *Evangelicalism in Modern Britain: a History from the 1730s to the 1980s* (London, 1989), 75–104. See also 'Ian S. Rennie, 'Evangelicalism and English Public Life, 1823–1850' (unpublished Ph.D. thesis, University of Toronto, 1962).

The End of the 'Age of Wilberforce'?

Undoubtedly there was what Bebbington calls a 'troubling of the water' between the mid 1820s and early 1830s, as economic crashes, missionary failures, political upheavals and cholera outbreaks incubated more apocalyptic and doctrinaire strains of piety.[11] Bible Society meetings degenerated into shouting matches over whether the scriptures should be distributed with the Apocrypha, or whether meetings ought to begin with Trinitarian prayers.[12] Behind the vehemence of self-appointed prophets such as Robert and Alexander Haldane (1800–1882), Henry Drummond (1786–1860) and Edward Irving lay a Romantic yearning for spiritual intensity and emotional assurance that was opposed to the slightest hint of accommodation with 'the world'.[13] Not for them the careful compromises of moderate Calvinism: 'would you say of your friend that he was moderately honest, or wish your wife to be moderately virtuous?'[14] Their predestinarianism was granitic and certain, the product of a hard-edged scriptural literalism that made them impatient with the fuzzy answers of their forebears. Indeed, some of their most blistering invective was directed at the ageing Evangelical establishment, whose quasi-Arminian 'works-righteousness' and expediency they lashed mercilessly. Irving blasted the prevailing obsession with 'money, money, money', denouncing the pursuit of 'the highest names upon a subscription list' as marks of a Church that had been 'perverted by usefulness'.[15] 'By looking upon the world itself as to be converted in the mass, instead of looking at it as the mass out of which the children of God are to be chosen and drawn forth ... after it has yielded the appointed number of God's elect,' he raged, the Evangelical establishment had confused eternal salvation with social improvement.[16] The *Christian Observer* and its allies, railed the *Morning Watch*, were 'willing to keep the peculiarities and essentials of Christianity out of sight ... to secure prebendaries, archdeaconries

---

[11] Bebbington, *Evangelicalism*, 75.
[12] Martin, *Evangelicals United*, 123–46; Stunt, *Awakening to Secession*, 239–82; Grayson Carter, *Anglican Evangelicals: Protestant Secessions from the Via Media, c. 1800–1850* (Oxford, 2001), 152–94.
[13] Ralph Brown, 'Victorian Anglican Evangelicalism: the Radical Legacy of Edward Irving', *Journal of Ecclesiastical History*, 58 (2007), 675–704.
[14] Cited in 'Review of Cottle's Strictures on Antinomianism', *Christian Observer*, 22 (1823), 725.
[15] Edward Irving, *For Missionaries after the Apostolical School* (London, 1825), xvi, 129; Edward Irving (ed. and trans.), *The Coming of Messiah in Glory and Majesty*, 2 vols (London, 1827), I: xlviii.
[16] Edward Irving, *The Last Days: a Discourse on the Evil Character of These, our Times* (London, 1828), 490.

and chancellorships' from the Whig grandees with whom they consorted.[17] The preparedness of Wilberforce to accept Catholic emancipation, of the Grant brothers to take office under the Whigs, or of Zachary Macaulay to promote the new secular London University (the 'godless institution on Gower Street') was hardly reassuring.

Yet the idea that all this betokened a changing of the guard, as 'Record-ite' extremism eclipsed the moderation of the 'Christian Observer School', has been exaggerated, as Joseph Stubenrauch has also recently suggested.[18] Evangelical difficulties had more to do with the challenges inherent in holding together a broad-based movement and the penumbra of philanthropic concerns around it. After all, the metropolitan urbanity of the *Christian Observer* had never been to all tastes, and while the ultra-Tory *Record* was probably right to boast that it was now the 'parsons' paper', many among the gospel clergy had hitherto preferred to take the Toryish *Christian Guardian* in any case.[19] The 'Saints' had always been to the 'left' of their clerical brethren on questions of Church and state, their longstanding support for Catholic emancipation being a case in point. Nor did the pious world necessarily split along generational lines. Hannah More was among several elderly figures who deplored the reforms of 1828–32, disinheriting her beloved 'Tom' Macaulay for his part in the passing of the Reform Act.[20] Divisions within the BFBS were certainly traumatic. 'We all thought that the B[ible] Soc[iet]y was so simple in its form and its object that none of the frailties of mortality could touch it,' Marianne Thornton lamented, 'and that, whereas in all other societies there might be some chance of jarring discords, this alone was secure from all the conflicts which belong to human undertakings.'[21] But despite greater volatility in its income from the mid 1820s as most of the Scottish auxiliaries cut loose, by the early 1840s it was regularly receiving over £100,000 a year, a figure approached only by the SPCK.[22] There remained a broad optimism about the spread of the gospel through the application of organized philanthropy. 'Ours,' Sir James Stephen declared, 'is the age of societies ... For the cure of every sorrow

[17] 'The Record Newspaper and Christian Observer', *The Morning Watch*, 4 (1832), 236.

[18] Joseph Stubenrauch, *The Evangelical Age of Ingenuity in Industrial Britain* (Oxford, 2016), 250–4.

[19] Josef L. Altholz, 'Alexander Haldane, the *Record*, and Religious Journalism', *Victorian Periodicals Review*, 20 (1987), 23–31.

[20] Anne Stott, *Hannah More: the First Victorian* (Oxford, 2003), 328–30.

[21] Marianne Thornton to Hannah More, n.d., CUL, Thornton Family Letters and Papers, MS Add.MS.7674/1/F10.

[22] Martin, *Evangelicals United*, 128–31; W. Canton, *The History of the British and Foreign Bible Society*, 5 vols (London, 1904–10), II: 151, 453.

by which our land or our race can be visited, there are patrons, vice-presidents, and secretaries.'[23] Stephen was being playful, and he also thought that 'Exeter Hall' could be narrow-minded; but he was also expressing genuine sentiments. By the mid 1830s, moreover, the movement was regrouping, helped by the secession of disruptive figures such as the hyper-Calvinist Henry Bulteel.[24] The postmillennial euphoria of the 1810s was never quite recaptured. But the temperate premillenarian Adventism that displaced it marked a decisive rejection of the apocalyptic exultancy and charismatic experimentation of Irving, Drummond and the rest.[25] By the 1850s the acute 'Church in danger' crisis had subsided. Church- and school-building on a massive scale had largely restored Anglican confidence. The collapse of Chartism, the rise of Liberal consensus politics and the mid-Victorian economic boom all helped to dispel the eschatological anxieties of earlier years. It also helped that the Whigs were not the anti-clerical iconoclasts of fevered Tory imaginations. Indeed, it was a Whig Premier, Lord John Russell (1792–1878), who elevated the gentle but firmly evangelical John Bird Sumner to be Archbishop of Canterbury in 1848.

Those few gospel ministers who seceded in this period were thus swimming against strong currents that had long been flowing in the other direction, and which continued to do so. There were well-worn arguments for staying put. If asked, many clergymen would have probably cited the apostle Paul: 'a little leaven leaveneth the whole lump' (Galatians 5: 9). They held themselves largely aloof, for instance, from the Evangelical Alliance, founded in 1846 to express pan-denominational, transnational solidarity against rationalism and romanism.[26] In large part this was because they could build on robust inherited foundations. Clerical education societies, colleges at Oxford and Cambridge and a strong associational culture helped to ensure that Evangelicals continued to grow as a proportion of the clergy, reaching perhaps a third of the total – around 6,000 out of 18,000, by one estimate – by the 1850s.[27] They also continued to ascend the ecclesiastical ranks. Thanks to the Earl of Shaftesbury's influence on Lord Palmerston (1784–1865) and to the Prime Minister's own predilection for active

---

23 [Sir James Stephen], 'The Clapham Sect', *Edinburgh Review*, 80, 161 (1844), 306.

24 Carter, *Anglican Evangelicals*, 187–94.

25 Gareth Atkins, 'Anglican Evangelical Theology, c. 1820–1850: the Case of Edward Bickersteth', *Journal of Religious History*, 38 (2014), 1–19; Martin Spence, *Heaven on Earth: Reimagining Time and Eternity in Nineteenth-Century British Evangelicalism* (Eugene, OR, 2015), 55–64.

26 John Wolffe, 'The Evangelical Alliance in the 1840s: an Attempt to Institutionalise Christian Unity', *Studies in Church History*, 23 (1986), 333–46.

27 [W. J. Conybeare], 'Church Parties', *Edinburgh Review*, 98, 200 (1853), 338.

clergymen who would avoid riling dissenters, Evangelical representation among the bishops rose markedly in the mid 1850s, with the elevation of men such as Henry Montagu Villiers (1813–1861) to Carlisle, Charles Baring (1807–1879) to Gloucester and then Bristol, Robert Bickersteth (1816–1884) to Ripon and John Thomas Pelham (1811–1894) to Norwich. They retained around a third of the episcopal bench thereafter, as well as providing prominent colonial bishops, such as Charles Perry (1807–1891) of Melbourne.[28] Patronage trusts guaranteed their hold over strategic livings in London and in provincial towns and cities.[29] They were especially strong in places where the middle classes congregated for business or pleasure: Bath, Birmingham, Bradford, Bristol, Cheltenham, Clifton, Derby, Hull, Leeds, Liverpool, Manchester, Nottingham, Norwich, Plymouth, Sheffield and Sunderland.[30] But given the too-easily invoked stereotype of the kid-gloved watering-place minister, beloved of his female flock, it is important not to ignore the many hundreds who happily ministered in rural parishes and market towns.[31]

If it makes little sense to divide clerical Evangelicalism at 1825 or 1833, the foregoing chapters suggest that other facets of the movement cannot be shoehorned into that chronology either. The networks surrounding Barham and Gambier in the navy, for instance, rose and fell between the 1780s and the mid 1810s, more or less within the period of the Revolutionary and Napoleonic Wars. Evangelical influence in the City of London, by contrast, had a much longer, more diffuse existence. Pious influence in colonial affairs was in many ways episodic, revolving around Sierra Leone in the 1790s and 1800s, the Colonial Office in the 1810s and 20s and the prominent role of Charles Grant junior, from 1835 Lord Glenelg, in the governments of Earl Grey and Lord Melbourne (1779–1848). The Evangelical networks that riddled the EIC continued to shape policy and the tone of British rule up to and beyond the Crown takeover in 1858. All this

---

[28]　John Wolffe, 'Lord Palmerston and Religion: a Reappraisal', *English Historical Review*, 120 (2005), 907–36.

[29]　Wesley D. Balda, '"Spheres of Influence": Simeon's Trust and its Implications for Evangelical Patronage' (unpublished Ph.D. thesis, University of Cambridge, 1981).

[30]　Andrew Atherstone, 'Anglican Evangelicalism', in Rowan Strong (ed.), *The Oxford History of Anglicanism, Volume III: Partisan Anglicanism and its Global Expansion, 1829–c. 1914* (Oxford, 2017), 171.

[31]　The definitive history of the Evangelical parish in our period has yet to be written, although see Owen Chadwick, *Victorian Miniature* (Cambridge, 1960), for a brilliantly evocative cameo case-study. See also Rod W. Ambler, 'Evangelicals and the Establishment: Evangelical Identity in a Nineteenth-Century Market Town', in Mark Smith (ed.), *British Evangelical Identities Past and Present* (Milton Keynes, 2008), 74–84.

raises the point that 'generationality' is always a highly subjective notion. It lends itself to retrospective construction and depends on selectivity to make sense. Although several aged luminaries went to their reward in the 1830s – Wilberforce and More in 1833; Teignmouth in 1834; Simeon in 1836; Macaulay in 1838 – they had long taken a back seat in Evangelical affairs. Indeed, Wilberforce himself was already limiting his public commitments in the early 1820s. Equally, though, there were plenty of leading figures whose careers confound the chronology of the 'Age of Wilberforce': Daniel Wilson and Edward Bickersteth, for example, rose to prominence in the 1810s and died in the 1850s, while mid-Victorian clerical giants such as Hugh Stowell (1799–1865) and Hugh McNeile (1795–1879) were already making their names by the 1820s.[32] Of course, historians have to cut their cloth somewhere. It is true that the euphoria of the 'anni mirabiles' between around 1810 and 1825, when pious philanthropy seemed to carry all before it, was never recaptured. And it is certain that the troubled decade that followed repelled some who might once have thrown in their lot with such projects. Nevertheless, that period marked the slowing of a never-to-be-repeated boom rather than the beginning of a bust. Neither J.C.D. Clark's focus on 1828–32 nor the choice of 1829 as a sharper dividing line between volumes in the recent *Oxford History of Anglicanism* works well for the movement we have been discussing.

No 'Clapham Sect'?

One of my aims when I began this project was to show that the notion of a small, tightly defined Clapham Sect has misled historians as to the nature and extent of Evangelicalism as a movement. It was natural, of course, for loyal filial biographers like Sir James Stephen to mourn the passing of the genteel world of their parents. 'Oh where are the people who are at once really religious, and really cultivated in heart and in understanding, the people with whom we could associate as our fathers used to associate with each other?' he lamented in 1845. 'No "Clapham Sect" nowadays.'[33] Yet in ranging beyond the leafy gardens and genteel villas of suburban Surrey, as this book has consistently sought to do, the notion of wholesale generational shift that has long shaped perceptions of the end of the 'Age of Wilberforce'

---

[32] See also Michael Murray Hennell, *Sons of the Prophets: Evangelical Leaders of the Victorian Church* (London, 1979).

[33] Sir James Stephen, *Letters: With Biographical Notes by his Daughter, Caroline Emelia Stephen* ([London?], 1907), 87.

becòmes harder to sustain. So too does the explanatory weight given to the change of tone that is usually associated with it. While the journey of the younger Wilberforces away from the piety of their youth was undoubtedly prompted in part by the 'negativity', 'narrowness' and 'anti-intellectualism' of segments of the Evangelical movement in the years either side of 1830, there was more to it than that. Such accusations were hardly new; and there remained plenty of prominent figures who had come to maturity in, and shared the attitudes of, the sunnier 1810s and early 1820s. It was not as though Tractarianism was optimistic and broad-minded: morbid introspection was, indeed, central to its attraction. Its reaction against Evangelicalism consisted at least as much in a rejection of its comfortable complicity with the Liberal spirit of the age as in revulsion at the antics of 'prophetical' extremists.[34]

Nevertheless, hostile novelistic caricatures, such as John Henry Newman's jargonizing Mr Freeborn in *Loss and Gain* (1848) or Anthony Trollope's oily Mr Slope in *Barchester Towers* (1857) have too often been accepted as being drawn from life, while accounts of George Eliot's blistering attack on the real-life John Cumming (1807–1881), Minister of the National Scottish Church in Covent Garden, usually ignore the fact that he drew huge and approving congregations.[35] Such treatments lend themselves to a slightly snobbish sense of teleology, as though numbers can be ignored because the right sort of people were coming to disavow an obviously backward creed. In reality, the journeys of John Henry Newman, Francis William Newman (1805–97) or George Eliot (1819–1880) away from the piety of their youth were anything but inevitable or straightforward or, indeed, complete: Evangelicalism left lasting marks.[36] In making these points it should be emphasized that I am not interested in exonerating Evangelical 'faults': throughout this book I have sought simply to explain why they acted as they did and how they fitted into contemporary public life. It cannot be denied that the 1840s and 50s witnessed a mounting cultural and intellectual backlash against middle-class moral and economic 'puritanism'.[37] But nor can it be denied that this was because the networks established in earlier decades remained hugely influential and were in many places still growing.

---

[34]   See Gareth Atkins, 'Evangelicals', in Frederick D. Aquino and Benjamin J. King (eds), *The Oxford Handbook of John Henry Newman* (Oxford, 2018), 189–90.

[35]   [George Eliot], 'Evangelical Teaching: Dr Cumming', *Westminster Review*, 64 (1855).

[36]   David Hempton, *Evangelical Disenchantment: Nine Portraits of Faith and Doubt* (New Haven, CT, 2008). See also Atkins, 'Evangelicals'.

[37]   Hilton, *Age of Atonement*, 255–339.

Why, then, did the tale of generational change become so ingrained? One obvious but seldom explored reason is that it fitted neatly into the narratives that nineteenth-century Church parties wanted to tell about themselves. Anglo-Catholics reared on accounts of the 'high-and-dry' Hanoverians were on the whole sympathetic to evangelical revivalism, which they saw as breathing new life into dead forms, but they also insisted that Evangelical churchmanship was defective. Hence it had stagnated, they argued, being overtaken by richer, more ecclesiastically 'authentic' expressions of Christianity.[38] 'One Cecil or Simeon is as much more than a thousand Closes, Barings or McNeiles as one rifled cannon is to all the pea-shooters of schoolboys,' sneered the *Church Times*.[39] Liberal Churchmen, likewise, drew stark intergenerational contrasts. The gossipy essayist W.J. Conybeare (1815–1857) posited a disjunction between the compassionate common sense of 'the party of Milner, Martyn, and Wilberforce' and the shibboleths of 'the extreme party which calls itself by the same name': prophecy, proto-Zionism and razor-edged sabbatarianism. 'The disgust but too justly excited by the eccentric offspring has alienated some reasonable men from the sober-minded parent.'[40] Perhaps the worst culprits, however, were Evangelicals themselves. Despite and indeed because they enjoyed influence beyond their forefathers' wildest dreams, they could be painfully nostalgic about an earlier, more heroic age.[41] The jubilee and centenary commemorations of the great philanthropic societies showered pious readers with souvenir volumes rejoicing in the growth of late-Hanoverian seedlings into mighty oaks, but they also elicited the gloomy reflection that the giants who planted them no longer bestrode the land. In the final third of the century, as the Evangelical tide perceptibly began to ebb, affectionate retrospectives about the golden age intensified. Yet narratives of decline arguably reveal more about the Evangelical psyche than they do about what actually happened. Christ's warning against false prophets, 'Woe unto you, when all men shall speak well of you' (Luke 6: 26), had always echoed uncomfortably in Evangelical ears. Even during their palmiest periods, they were nagged by doubts as to whether or not their success indicated divine favour. Writing in 1807, against a backdrop of burgeoning pious influence and anti-slavery triumphs, Thomas Scott could still yearn for an infusion of the rough-and-ready pioneering spirit. 'I ... prefer the Newtons, Venns,

---

[38] See e.g. Sabine Baring-Gould, *The Church Revival. Thoughts Thereon and Reminiscences* (London, 1914).

[39] 'The Church Association', *Church Times*, 4 Nov. 1870, 467.

[40] [Conybeare], 'Church Parties', 277, 284.

[41] Atherstone, 'Anglican Evangelicalism', 165–73.

nay Berridges, the old warm-hearted men, with all their imperfections,' he sighed, 'to these *sang-froid* young men.'[42]

If too much weight has been given to the movement's real or imagined shortcomings in accounting for its decline, too little attention has been given to the cumulative effect of mid-century political and cultural changes on the world in which Evangelicals had operated so successfully. Joseph Stubenrauch has helpfully suggested that the period between the French Revolution and the Great Exhibition was a 'distinct period in British religious history' marked by the confident evangelical exploitation of technological modernity.[43] The periodization and themes of this book owe something to that story. Yet I have also insisted that politics and public institutions mattered, and that Evangelicalism derived much of its impact from its combination of 'Hanoverian' and 'Victorian' methods and tools. While Stubenrauch is probably right to suggest that Evangelicalism turned in on itself in the 1860s and 70s, this was partly because that successful formula had already lost its potency. This process, however, was multifaceted and it took place only gradually, in the twenty years or so after the 1832 Reform Act. There is not room here to explore it in detail. But it is possible to delineate some broad contours. One dimension was political. Evangelicalism had thrived in and helped to create an age of pressure groups – the peace movement and the Anti-Corn Law League, for instance – which fell between the old and mainly local system of politics that characterized the high eighteenth century and the central and local party political structures of the later nineteenth century. But the levers that had served them well were now no longer so effective in a world of Liberal public opinion. Patronage was, for instance, neither as prevalent nor as acceptable as it had once been. Although personal connections remained central to ecclesiastical appointments, elsewhere during the 1830s and 40s patronage was coming to be regarded with suspicion. It can also be observed that Evangelicals were no longer so far ahead of the curve organizationally. The voluntarism that had once marked them out as trend-setters was fast becoming the standard way of funding religious projects.[44]

Partly as a consequence of this, dwindling state support for religious establishments was unsettling rather than devastating. More threatening were the hares it set running. There were undoubted affinities between Evangelicals and the Oxford Movement, especially in the early 1830s, when

---

[42] John Scott, *The Life of the Rev. Thomas Scott* (4th edn: London, 1822), 396.

[43] Stubenrauch, *Evangelical Age of Ingenuity*, 250.

[44] Sarah Flew, *Philanthropy and the Funding of the Church of England, 1856–1914* (London, 2015).

many gospel ministers echoed the Tracts for the Times, denouncing national apostasy in terms every bit as apocalyptic as John Keble (1792–1866).[45] Over time, however, their differences became clear. The Tractarians revelled in their extremism, declaring their spiritual independence from a compromised state and grounding their authority instead on apostolic succession. Their anti-Erastian elevation of the Church and clergy as the main or even the sole agents of social and spiritual renewal was at odds with the commitment of Evangelicals to lay leadership and to pursuing improvement through a wide range of state and quasi-state bodies.[46] Nonconformists, meanwhile, many of them now enfranchised, were increasingly opposed to anything that connected religious affiliation with political privileges: they, too, thought Christianity worked best when it was forced to stand on its own two feet.[47] Evangelical attachment to the 'dismal science' of political economy and proximity to the business world, meanwhile, was coming under attack by commentators concerned about the 'Condition of England' question.[48] With increasingly tight lines being drawn on all sides between politics and religion, the Church and the world, commerce and Christianity, the idea of bringing about widespread change through capturing the institutional high ground looked not just grubby but fanciful.

All of these shifts were compounded by an increasingly febrile partisan atmosphere within the Church of England. Evangelicals had, it is true, often defined themselves against the Orthodox mainstream, but they had also operated within similar paradigms on questions of theology, ecclesiology and Church–state relations.[49] Now, the emergence of Tractarianism and the maturation of Liberal Churchmanship produced visions of the national Church that clashed sharply with one another.[50] This did not

[45] Parallels have long been drawn between the Oxford Movement and different species of Evangelicalism. See Yngve Brilioth, *Evangelicalism and the Oxford Movement* (London, 1934), 1–53; Newsome, *Parting of friends*, 12–16; Peter B. Nockles, 'The Oxford Movement and Evangelicalism: Parallels and Contrasts in Two Nineteenth-Century Movements of Religious Revival', in Robert Webster (ed.), *Perfecting Perfection: Essays in Honour of Henry D. Rack* (Cambridge, 2016), 233–59.

[46] S.A. Skinner, *Tractarians and the 'Condition of England': the Social and Political Thought of the Oxford Movement* (Oxford, 2004).

[47] Timothy Larsen, *Friends of Religious Equality: Nonconformist Politics in Mid-Victorian England* (Woodbridge, 1999), 79–136.

[48] For an original take on this, see Dominic Janes, *Victorian Reformation: the Fight over Idolatry in the Church of England, 1840–1860* (Oxford, 2009), 4–25, 51–92.

[49] Peter B. Nockles, *The Oxford Movement in Context: Anglican High Churchmanship, 1860–1857* (Cambridge, 1994), esp. 48–9, 106–11, 150–2, 190–8, 228–48.

[50] Stewart J. Brown, *The National Churches of England, Ireland, and Scotland, 1801–46* (Oxford, 2001), 168–323.

happen overnight: the Tractarians made plenty of noise, but their impact should not be exaggerated before, say, the mid 1850s. Orthodox church-men still dominated the ecclesiastical hierarchy.[51] Evangelicals, though, were numerous, and well integrated into the establishment. They had a marked sense of identity, built up over many years, and a strong sense of what they stood for. But by necessity and choice they had also become a Church party, geared less towards expansion than to defending what they had gained. In some senses, as we have seen, they had succeeded in 'Converting Britannia'. Viewed another way, however, their universal vision had become a pipedream.

---

[51]   See e.g. Arthur Burns, *The Diocesan Revival in the Church of England, c. 1800–1870* (Oxford, 1999); Jeremy Morris, *The High Church Revival in the Church of England: Arguments and Identities* (Brill, 2016), 1–40; Nicholas Dixon, 'The Activity and In-fluence of the Established Church in England, c. 1800–1837' (unpublished Ph.D. the-sis, University of Cambridge, 2019).

Bibliography

Manuscript Sources and Archival Collections

Bodleian Library, Oxford

MSS Wilberforce, Wilberforce Family Papers, 1726–[c. 1900].

MS Wilberforce, Additional Wilberforce Papers, 1771–1872.

MS Eng. Lett. c. 789, Papers of Henry Handley Norris, letters, c. 1812.

Ms Eng. c. 6397-8, Correspondence and Papers of Edward Bickersteth, Rector of Watton (1786–1850), letters, 1815–59.

St. Edmund Hall MS. 66-7, Diaries of the Revd John Hill, 1803–6, 1820–55.

Bristol Record Office

28048, Deeds and Documents relating to the Harford Family, including the Blaise Castle Estate, 1575–1918, correspondence, diaries and papers of J.S. Harford junior, and Louisa his wife, 1789–1875.

British Library, London

Add. MS 12131, Collection of Papers Relative to Sierra Leone, 1792–8.

Add. MS 35126-35133, Original Letters addressed to Arthur Young, 1743–1820.

Add. MS 35129, fo. 411, Wilberforce Election Meeting, of Friends, New London Tavern, Cheapside, 13 May 1807.

Add. MS 35424, 35649, Hardwicke Papers, letters from William Wilberforce, 1801–11.

Add. MS 38323, 38191, 38258, 38288, 38289, 38416, Correspondence and Papers of the 2nd Earl of Liverpool, correspondence between William Wilberforce, Liverpool, Nicholas Vansittart and others, 1800–22.

Add. MS 40096, Correspondence and Papers of Vice-Admiral Cuthbert Collingwood, letters, 1805.

Add. MS 40343, Correspondence and Papers, official and private, of the Right Hon. Sir Robert Peel, letters, 1820s.

Add. MS 40862, Ripon Papers, letters from William Wilberforce to Nicholas Vansittart, 1821–2.

Add. MS 40862, Rose Papers, letters from William Wilberforce to George Rose, 1806.

Add. MS 41079, Melville Papers, letters from Sir Charles Middleton, Lord Barham, to Henry Dundas, Viscount Melville, c. 1788–1806.

Add. MS 41267A, 41267B, Clarkson Papers, 1787–1853.

Add. MS 42377, Miscellaneous Letters and Papers, letters from William Wilberforce to Henry Gauntlett, 1820–32.

Add. MS 43845, fo. 25, Sturge Papers, Sir James Stephen to Joseph Sturge, 4 Oct. 1844.

Add. MS 46844A, 46844A, Letters to the Rev. Thomas Hartwell Horne, 1822–71.

Add MS 59846, Miscellaneous Letters and Papers, letters from William Wilberforce to Gerald Noel Noel (Edwards), 1780–2, and Charles Noel Noel, 1828.

Add. MS 63084, Blakeney Collection, Correspondence of Zachary Macaulay, chiefly letters from Hannah More and William Wilberforce, 1796–1825.

IOR/B/263-4, General Court Minutes (Proprietors), 12 Apr. 1797–23 Sep. 1807.

IOR/H/729-30, Letterbooks of David Scott, letters to William Wilberforce and Charles Grant, 1797–9.

IOR/ L/AG/14/5/25-35, East India Company Stock Records, Main Stock Ledgers, 5 Jul. 1791–5 Apr. 1818.

OIR 253.0954, S.J. McNally, *The Chaplains of the East India Company* (unpublished, India Office Library and Records, 1976).

Cadbury Research Library, University of Birmingham

XCMS/B/OMS/I/C I1 E1-2, Church Missionary Society Archive, North India Mission, Early Correspondence, 1815-20.

XCMS/G/AC/3, Church Missionary Society Archive, Home Correspondence Letter Books, 1824–90.

XCMS/G/AC/3, Church Missionary Society Archive, Incoming Home Correspondence, 1799–1867.

XCMSACC/ACC/81/C19-22, Church Missionary Society Unofficial Papers, Letters and Papers of Henry Martyn and his friends, 1802–7.

XCMSACC/ACC/81/C19-22, Church Missionary Society Unofficial Papers, Venn Papers, Letters of John Venn, 1777–1813.

XCMSACC/ACC/81/C35, Church Missionary Society Unofficial Papers, Venn Papers, Letters of Henry Venn of CMS, 1755–1877.

XCMSACC/ACC/81/C47-52, Church Missionary Society Unofficial Papers, Venn Papers, Letters of the King Family, 1755–1808.

XCMSACC/ACC/81/C68-73, Church Missionary Society Unofficial Papers, Venn Papers, Letters and Papers of the Thornton Family, 1760–1809.

XCMSACC/ACC/81/C95, Church Missionary Society Unofficial Papers, Papers of the Havergal Family, 1816–86.

Cambridge University Library

BSA/F3/Shore, British and Foreign Bible Society Archive, Letters to John Shore, Lord Teignmouth, 1795–1833.

BSA/F4/1/1/1, British and Foreign Bible Society Archive, London Secretaries' Association Minutebook, 1819–48.

MS Add.7674, Thornton Family, Letters and Papers, c. 1742–1881.

SPCK.MS A1/37, SPCK Archive, Committee Minute Book, 1815–16.

SPCK.MS B1, SPCK Archive, Annual Reports, 1793–1835.

Canterbury Cathedral Library

CCA-U210/3/1-2 Inglis/Harrison Papers, correspondence of R.H. Inglis, 1815–33.

Devon Heritage Centre, Exeter

1148M/7/ Acland of Killerton Papers, correspondence of Sir Thomas Dyke Acland, 10th Baronet, 1812–42.
1148M/7/7, Acland of Killerton Papers, correspondence of Revd Thomas Fisher, 1815–40.

Dorset History Centre, Dorchester

D-WIB/C/87, Williams of Bridehead, Littlebredy, Archive, letters from Revd Charles James Hoare to J.W. Cunningham, 1801–17.

Durham University Library

Add MS 1025/105, Letters of Thomas Gisborne, 1797–1822.
GB-0033-GRE-B, Political and Public Papers of Charles, 2nd Earl Grey, letters from various, including William Wilberforce, Sydney Smith, Thomas Clarkson, Zachary Macaulay and others, 1769–1846.

Hampshire Record Office, Winchester

92M95, F2/19/1-40, Baring (Northbrook) Family Papers, General Correspondence and Memoranda of Sir Thomas Baring, 1810s–1830s.
26M62/F/C1-1420, Calthorpe of Elvetham Papers, correspondence with Wilberforce Family, Elliott Family, Olivia Sparrow, Joseph John Gurney and others, 1800s–1830s.

Harrowby Manuscripts Trust, Sandon Hall, Stafford

Harrowby MSS, 1st ser., vol 4, Family Correspondence, 1803–9.
Harrowby MSS, 1st ser., vols 8–17, General Correspondence, 1784–1847.
Harrowby MSS, 2nd ser., vol. 40, Supplementary Volume.
Harrowby MSS, 3rd ser., vols 56–62, Letters, 1727–1830.
Harrowby MSS, 3rd ser., vols 102–5, Letters and Papers of the Right Reverend the Hon. Henry Ryder, D.D., 1777–1887.

Hull History Centre

C DFW, Papers of William Wilberforce, 1695–1831.

Hull University, Brynmor Jones Library

DTH/1, Papers of Thomas Perronet Thompson relating to Sierra Leone, 1804–38.

Huntington Library, San Marino, California

Papers of Zachary Macaulay, 1793–1888 [Microfilm: Adam Matthew Publications, *Abolition and Emancipation, Part 1: Papers of Thomas Clarkson, William Lloyd Garrison, Zachary Macaulay, Harriet Martineau, Harriet Beecher Stowe and William Wilberforce from the Huntington Library* (Marlborough, 1997)]
mssLR, Edward Hawke Locker Papers, letters from J.B. Sumner and C.R. Sumner, 1821–42.

John Rylands University Library, Manchester

GB 133 English MS 11221, Correspondence of Henry Raikes, c. 1832–49.

Kent History and Library Centre, Maidstone

U194, Family papers and correspondence of the Gambier and Howe Families, letters of Venn family, Revd J.E. Gambier, Charles Noel Noel and others, 1792–1808.

U1590/S5/C38, Stanhope of Chevening Manuscripts, Pitt Papers, correspondence and personal papers of William Pitt, Letters to the Bishop of Lincoln, 1801, 1807.

U1590/S5/O1-4, Stanhope of Chevening Manuscripts, Pitt Papers, autograph letters from colleagues, 1782–1827.

Lambeth Palace Library

DS/UK/3153, William Taylor Money letters, 1808–31.

Library and Museum of Freemasonry, London

Minutes of the Hall Committee, Volume 4, 10 Jan. 1788–14 Nov. 1810.

Messrs Hoares Bank, London

Customer Ledgers, 1790s–1810s.

HFM/26, William Henry Hoare Material, 1800s–1810s.

Private Ledgers, 1793–1856.

National Archives, Kew

ADM 1/5396, Courts Martial Papers, 1809 May [Court martial of Admiral Harvey, 22 May 1809].

ADM 35/504, Navy Board: Navy Pay Office: Ships' Pay Books (Series III), Ship: *Defence*, 1793 May 21–1794 Jul.

ADM 37/1238, Admiralty: Ships' Musters (Series II), Ship: *Caledonia*, 1 Aug. 1808–28 Feb. 1809.

CO 138, Colonial Office and Predecessors: Jamaica, Entry Books, 1661–1872.

CO 267, Colonial Office and Predecessors: Sierra Leone Original Correspondence, 1664–1951.

PRO 30/8/183, 189, William Pitt, First Earl of Chatham: Papers, letters to William Pitt jun., c. 1788–1805.

PRO 30/8/365, William Pitt, First Earl of Chatham: Papers, letters from Sir Charles Middleton and others to the 2nd Earl of Chatham, 1780s–1800s.

National Maritime Museum, Greenwich, London

AGC/M/11, Letters, Sir Charles Middleton to William Wilberforce, 16 Dec. 1801.

MID/1-2, Papers of Middleton, Charles, Admiral, 1st Baron Barham, 1726–1813, correspondence.

MID/4, Papers of Middleton, Charles, Admiral, 1st Baron Barham, 1726–1813, letters of application and thanks for commissions, 1805–6.

MID/13/1, In-Letters from Middleton, 1778–1813.

MID/14, Register of Applications to the Admiralty for Commissions, 1805.

YOR/6, Yorke, Charles Philip (First Lord Of The Admiralty), 1764–1834, letters from Sir James Gambier, 1810.

New College, Edinburgh

MS CHA 3-4, The Chalmers Collection, correspondence with Edward Bickersteth, William Wilberforce, Charles Grant, Zachary Macaulay, Thomas Babington and others, 1810s–1840s.

North Yorkshire County Record Office, Northallerton

ZFW/7/2 Rev. Christopher Wyvill (1738–1822) Political Papers, correspondence with William Wilberforce, 1784–1807.

Record Office for Leicestershire, Leicester and Rutland

DE3214 Records of the Noel Family, Earls of Gainsborough and Viscounts Campden, of Exton, Rutland and Chipping Campden, Glos., correspondence, 1785–1838.

Ridley Hall, Cambridge

Charles Simeon Papers, letters to Charles Grant, 1805–15.
John Newton Special Collection, letters to John Thornton, 1773–78.
Richard Cecil Special Collection, notebooks and reminiscences, c. 1810.

Royal Bank of Scotland Archives, Edinburgh

PT, Pole, Thornton, Down, Free and Scott Archives, Thornton and Wilberforce family correspondence and business papers, 1770–1875.

Rubenstein Library, Duke University, Durham, North Carolina

[Microfilm: Adam Matthew Publications, *Abolition and Emancipation, Part 6: Papers of William Wilberforce, William Smith, Iveson Brookes, Francis Corbin and related records from the Rare Books, Manuscript and Special Collections Library, Duke University* (Marlborough, 1997)]
RL.01224, William Smith Papers, 1785–1860, correspondence, c. 1787–1825.
RL.01381, Wilberforce Papers, correspondence, 1782–1837 and undated.

Senate House Library Archives, London

MS 797/I/5464-72, Booth Family Papers, letters from Colin to Kenneth Macaulay, 1810–34.
MS 797/I/5587-5670, Booth Family Papers, letters from Zachary Macaulay, 1799–1831.

Trinity College, Cambridge

GBR/0016/MAYOR/B2-16, Papers of the Mayor and related families, Mayor Family Papers, 1780–1916.
GBR/0016/MAYOR/D1-8, Papers of the Mayor and related families, Bickersteth Family Papers, 1799–1849.
Trinity/BABINGTON, Boxes 26–7, Papers of the Babington Family of Rothley Temple, letters of Zachary Macaulay to Thomas Babington, 1791–1835.

York Libraries and Archives

GRF/3, Gray Family of Gray's Court Papers, Account books, 1774–1844.

GRF/4, Gray Family of Gray's Court Papers, Correspondence, 1751–1932.

GRF/5, Gray Family of Gray's Court Papers, Diaries of Faith Gray and William Gray, 1764–1841.

Printed Primary Sources

Contemporary Books and Articles

Allen, John (ed.), *Memoirs of the Life of the Late Major-General Andrew Burn*, 2 vols (London, 1815)

Allen, W., *Life of William Allen, with Selections from his Correspondence*, 3 vols (London, 1846)

Anderson, Ellen-Mary, *Practical Religion Exemplified by Letters and Passages from the Life of the late Rev. Robert Anderson, Perpetual Curate of Trinity Chapel, Brighton* (2nd edn: London, 1845)

Anon., *The Annual Subscription Charities and Public Societies in London* (London, 1823)

Barrow, John, *An Auto-Biographical Memoir of Sir John Barrow, Bart., Late of the Admiralty* (London, 1847)

Bateman, Josiah, *The Life of the Rev. Henry Venn Elliott, M.A.* (London, 1868)

——, *The Life of the Right Rev. Daniel Wilson D.D., Late Lord Bishop of Calcutta and Metropolitan of India. With Extracts from his Journals and Correspondence*, 2 vols (London, 1860)

[Bean, James], *Zeal Without Innovation* (London, 1808)

'Bell, Currer' [Charlotte Brontë], *Shirley*, 3 vols (London, 1849)

Benson, Joseph (ed.), *The Works of the Rev. John Wesley*, 17 vols (London, 1809–13)

Biddulph, T.T., *Baptism, a Seal of the Christian Covenant* (London, 1816)

——, *Practical Essays on the Morning and Evening Services of the Church of England*, 3 vols (4th edn: London, 1809)

Birks, Thomas Rawson, (ed.), *Memoir of the Rev. Edward Bickersteth*, 2 vols (3rd edn: London, 1852)

Blomfield, Alfred, *A Life of Charles James Blomfield*, 2 vols (London, 1863)

Bonner, George, *Memoir of the Life of the Right Rev. Reginald Heber, D.D.* (Cheltenham, 1833)

Braithwaite, Joseph Bevan (ed.), *Memoirs of Joseph John Gurney: with Selections from his Journal and Correspondence*, 2 vols (Norwich, 1854)

Brenton, Edward Pelham, *Life and Correspondence of John, Earl of St Vincent*, 2 vols (London, 1838)

Brougham, Henry, *Historical Sketches of Statesmen who Flourished in the Time of George III*, 2 vols (London, 1839)

Brown, Abner William, *Recollections of the Conversation Parties of the Rev. Charles Simeon* (London, 1863)

Brydges, Egerton (ed.), *Collins's Peerage of England*, 9 vols (London, 1812)

Buchanan, Claudius, *Christian Researches in Asia* (Cambridge, 1811)

——, *Memoir of the Expediency of an Ecclesiastical Establishment for British India: both as the Means of Perpetuating the Christian Religion among our own Countrymen; and as a Foundation for the Ultimate Civilization of the Natives* (London, 1805)

——, *A Sermon, Preached at the New Church of Calcutta, before the Right Honorable [sic] the Earl of Mornington, Governor General, &c. &c. &c. on Thursday, February 6th, 1800; being the Day Appointed for a General Thanksgiving* (Calcutta, 1800)

——, *The Star in the East* (2nd edn: London, 1809)

Budd, Henry, *A Memoir of the Rev. Henry Budd, M.A.* (London, 1855)

Burgess, Thomas, *A Charge Delivered to the Clergy of the Diocese of St David's in September 1813* (2nd edn: Durham, 1813)

Burke, John, and John Bernard Burke, *A Geneaological and Heraldic Dictionary of the Landed Gentry of Great Britain and Ireland*, 2 vols (London, 1846–7)

[Burn, Andrew], *Who Fares Best, the Christian or the Man of the World?* (London, 1789)

[——], *The Christian Officer's Panoply: Containing Arguments in Favour of a Divine Revelation.* (London, 1789)

Burrow, E.J., *A Second Letter Addressed to the Rev. William Marsh* (2nd edn: London, 1819)

Burton, Charles James, *A Short Inquiry into the Character and Designs of the British and Foreign Bible Society* (Canterbury, 1817)

Buxton, Charles (ed.), *Memoirs of Sir Thomas Fowell Buxton, Baronet: with Selections from his Correspondence* (London, 1848)

Buxton, Thomas Fowell, *The Speech of Thomas Fowell Buxton Esq. at the Egyptian Hall, on the 26th November, 1816, on the Subject of the Distress in Spitalfields* (London, 1816)

'Buxton, Thomas Fowell' [William Hone], *The Distress of the People, the Blessed Effects of the Pitt System, Described, in a Speech at Length, at a Meeting for Sufferings, in the Egyptian Hall, Mansion House* (London, 1816)

Campbell, John (ed.), *Letters and Conversational Remarks, by the Late Rev. John Newton* (New York, 1811)

Carey, Eustace, *Memoir of William Carey* (London, 1836)

Carey, W.H., *Oriental Christian Biography*, 3 vols (Calcutta, 1850–2)

Carey, William, *An Enquiry into the Obligations of Christians, to use Means for the Conversion of the Heathen* (Leicester, 1792)

Carus, William, *Memoirs of the Life of the Rev. Charles Simeon* (London, 1847)

Cecil, Richard, *Discourses of the Honourable and Reverend William Bromley Cadogan* (London, 1798)

——, *Memoirs of John Bacon* (London, 1801)

[——] (ed.), *Memoirs of the Rev. John Newton* (2nd edn: London, 1808)

——, *Memoirs of the Rev. William Bromley Cadogan, M.A.* (London, 1798)

Chalmers, Thomas, *Thoughts on Universal Peace* (Glasgow, 1816)

Chatterton, Lady Georgiana (ed.), *Memorials, Personal and Historical of Admiral Lord Gambier, G.C.B.*, 2 vols (London, 1861)

Cheyne, Sarah Anne, *Reminiscences, Personal and Biographical, of Thomas Hartwell Horne* (London, 1862)

Churton, Edward, *Memoir of Joshua Watson* (2nd edn: London, 1863)

Clarkson, Thomas, *History of the Rise, Progress and Accomplishment of the Abolition of the African Slave-Trade by the British Parliament*, 2 vols (London, 1808)

'Clergyman of the Diocese, A' [Charles Thomas Longley], *The Lord Bishop of Ripon's Cobwebs to Catch Calvinists* (London, 1838)

The Clerical Guide, or Ecclesiastical Directory (London, 1817)

The Clerical Guide, or Ecclesiastical Directory (corr. edn: London, 1821)

The Clerical Guide, or Ecclesiastical Directory (new edn: London, 1836)

'Clericus', *A Letter to the Right Reverend the Bishop of Gloucester in Vindication of his Lordship's Refusal to Accept a Vice-Presidentship of an Auxiliary Bible Society at Gloucester* (Canterbury, 1813)

Cobbett, William, 'Dissenters' [1811], in John M. Cobbett and James Paul Cobbett (eds), *Selections from Cobbett's Political Works*, 6 vols (London, 1835), IV: 42–60.

Collingwood, G.L. Newnham, *A Selection from the Public and Private Correspondence of Vice-Admiral Lord Collingwood: Interspersed with Memoirs of his life*, 2 vols (London, 1828)

Colquhoun, John C., *William Wilberforce: his Friends and his Times* (2nd edn: London, 1867)

[Conybeare, W. J.], 'Church Parties', *Edinburgh Review*, 98, 200 (1853), 272–342.

Cooper, Edward, *Conduct of the Clergy in Supporting the Bible Society Vindicated* (London, 1818)

Corrie, George Elwes, and Henry Corrie, *Memoirs of the Right Rev. Daniel Corrie* (London, 1847)

'Country Clergyman, A' [Thomas Sikes], *An Address to Lord Teignmouth, President of the British and Foreign Bible Society, Occasioned by his Address to the Clergy of the Church of England* (London, 1805)

——, *A Second Letter to Lord Teignmouth, Occasioned by his Lordship's Letter to the Rev. Christopher Wordsworth, D.D.* (London, 1810)

Cowan, Thomas C., *A Brief Account of the Reasons which have Induced the Revd T.C. Cowan to Secede from the Established Church* (2nd edn: Bristol, 1817)

[Creevey, Thomas], *A Guide to the Electors of Great Britain upon the Accession of a New King* (London, 1820)

Cunningham, John William, *Church of England Missions* (London, 1814)

Dealtry, William, *A Sermon Preached in the Chapel of the East-India College, Hertfordshire, on Sunday, November 12, 1809* (London, 1809)

——, *A Letter Addressed to the Rev. Dr. Wordsworth, in Reply to his 'Reasons for Declining to become a Subscriber to the British and Foreign Bible Society'* (2nd edn: London, 1810)

Doddridge, Philip, *The Rise and Progress of Religion in the Soul* (London, 1745)

Dodwell, Edward, and James Samuel Miles, *Alphabetical List of the Honourable East India Company's Bengal Civil Servants, from the year 1780, to the year 1838* (London, 1839)

——, *Alphabetical List of the Honourable East India Company's Bengal Civil Servants, from the year 1798, to the year 1839* (London, 1839)

——, *Alphabetical List of the Officers of the Indian Army; with the Dates of their Respective Promotion, Retirement, Resignation, or Death, whether in India or in Europe, from the Year 1760, to the Year 1834 Inclusive* (London, 1838)

Dudley, Charles Stokes, *An Analysis of the Bible Society throughout its Various Parts* (London, 1821)

[Eliot, George], 'Evangelical Teaching: Dr Cumming', *Westminster Review*, 64 (1855), 436–62.

Faber, G.S., *The Many Mansions in the House of the Father, Scripturally Discussed, and Practically Considered, with Prefatory Memoir by Francis A. Faber* (London, 1854)

Familiar Letters from the Rev. Daniel Corrie, a Military Chaplain in the E.I. Company, to a Subaltern Officer in the same Service (Cockermouth, 1856)

Fawcett, John, *An Account of the Life, Ministry and Writings of the Late Rev. John Fawcett, D.D.* (London, 1818)

Freshfield, J.W., *Remarks on the 'Counter-Address' to the Inhabitants of Hackney, on the Proposed Formation of an Auxiliary Bible Society; and on a Paper Entitled 'Both Sides of the Question' &c. &c.* (London, 1812)

[Fry, Thomas], *Domestic Portraiture; or, the Successful Application of Religious Principle in the Education of a Family* (London, 1833)

Forster, Charles (ed.), *Thirty Years' Correspondence between John Jebb, D.D., F.R.S., and Alexander Knox*, 2 vols (London, 1834)

Gisborne, Thomas, *An Enquiry into the Duties of Men in the Higher and Middle Classes of Society in Great Britain, Resulting from their Respective Stations, Professions and Employments* (London, 1794)

——, *An Enquiry into the Duties of the Female Sex* (London, 1797)

——, *A Letter to the Right Reverend the Lord Bishop of Gloucester, on the Subject of the British and Foreign Bible Society* (London, 1815)

——, *The Substance of the Speech of the Rev. Thomas Gisborne, M.A., on April 8th 1812 in the County Hall at Stafford, at a Meeting Convened for the Purpose of Forming a Staffordshire Auxiliary Bible Society* (London, 1812)

Gladstone, W.E., 'The Evangelical Movement, its Parentage, Progress, and Issue', in Gladstone, *Gleanings of past years*, 7 vols (London, 1879), VII: 201–41.

Goode, William, *A Memoir of the Late Rev. William Goode* (2nd edn: London, 1828)

Grimshawe, Thomas Shuttleworth, *A Memoir of the Rev. Legh Richmond, A.M.* (London, 1829)

Gunning, Henry, *Reminiscences of the University, Town, and County of Cambridge from the Year 1780*, 2 vols *(London, 1854)*

Gurney, J.J., *Chalmeriana; or, Colloquies with Dr Chalmers* (London, 1853)

——, *Familiar Sketch of the Late William Wilberforce* (London, 1838)

——, *Substance of a Speech Delivered at a Public Meeting on the Subject of British Colonial Slavery* (London, 1824)

Gurney, W.B., *Minutes of a Court Martial Holden on Board His Majesty's Ship Gladiator, in Portsmouth Harbour, on Wednesday, the 26th Day of July, 1809* (Portsmouth, 1809)

Haldane, Alexander, *The Lives of Robert Haldane of Airthrey, and of his Brother, James Alexander Haldane* (3rd edn: London, 1853)

Haldane, Robert, *The Books of the Old and New Testaments proved to be Canonical, and their Verbal Inspiration Maintained and Established* (6th edn: Edinburgh, 1853)

Hare, Augustus J.C., *The Gurneys of Earlham*, 2 vols (London, 1895)

Harford, John S., *Recollections of William Wilberforce, Esq.* (London, 1864)

Hazlitt, William, *The Spirit of the Age* (London, 1825)

Heber, Amelia, *The Life of Reginald Heber*, 2 vols (London, 1830)

Hoare, Charles James, *Remains of the Late Rev. Charles John Paterson, B.A.* (London, 1838)

——, *The Blessed Death of the Righteous: a Funeral Sermon* (London, 1847)

Hoare, Prince, *Memoirs of Granville Sharp* (London, 1820)

Hough, James, *The History of Christianity in India: from the Commencement of the Christian Era*, 5 vols (London, 1839-60)

Housman, R.F., *The Life and Remains of the Rev. Robert Housman* (London, 1841)

Hume, Joseph, *The Substance of the Speech of Mr Joseph Hume at the East India House on the 6th October 1813, upon the Motion for an Increase in the Salaries to the Directors of the East-India Company* (London, 1814)

Irving, Edward (ed. and trans.), *The Coming of Messiah in Glory and Majesty*, 2 vols (London, 1827)

——, *The Last Days: a Discourse on the Character of These, our Times* (London, 1828)

——, *For Missionaries after the Apostolical School* (London, 1825)

Jay, William, *Memoirs of the Life and Character of the Late Rev. Cornelius Winter* (2nd edn: London, 1812)

Jerram, James (ed.), *The Memoirs and a Selection from the Letters of the Late Reverend Charles Jerram, M.A.* (London, 1855)

Jowett, William, *Memoir of the Rev. W.A.B. Johnson* (London, 1852)

Kaye, John William, *Christianity in India: An Historical Narrative* (London, 1859)

Kelly, Sophia (ed.), *The Life of Mrs Sherwood, Chiefly Autobiographical* (London, 1857)

King, John, *Memoir of the Rev. Thomas Dykes, LL.B.* (London, 1849)

Knight, James (ed.), *Sermons and Miscellaneous Works of the Rev. Samuel Knight, A.M., with a Memoir by William Knight*, 2 vols (Halifax, 1828)

La Trobe, Charles Ignatius, *Letters to my Children* (London, 1851)

'Lady, A' [Julia Charlotte Maitland], *Letters from Madras during the Years 1836–1839* (new edn: London, 1861)

Laurence, Richard, *An Attempt to Illustrate those Articles of the Church of England which the Calvinists improperly consider Calvinistical* (Oxford, 1805)

Lavington, George, *The Enthusiasm of Methodists and Papists Considered*, ed. Richard Polwhele (London, 1820)

Leifchild, John, *Memoir of the Late Rev. Joseph Hughes* (London, 1835)

Le Mesurier, Thomas, *The Nature and Guilt of Schism* (Oxford, 1807)

Letters of Lieutenant-General Sir P. Maitland ... Late Commander-in-Chief in Madras on the Compulsory Attendance of the British and Native Troops at Idolatrous and Mohammedan Festivals (London, 1841)

Lewis, C.B., *The Life of John Thomas* (London, 1873)

Lloyd, Richard, *A Reply to Letters Illustrative of Recent Transactions in the Town of Midhurst, including Two Letters from the Rev. Thomas Lloyd, to the Rev. John Sargent and an Interesting Account of the Recent Conduct and Present State of the Rev. Robert Taylor, Late Curate of Midhurst* (London, 1819)

——, *Two Letters Addressed to a Young Clergyman, Illustrative of his Clerical Duties in these Times of Innovation and Schism, with an Appendix, containing an Account of a Recent Attempt to Institute an Auxiliary to the British and Foreign Bible Society in the Parish of Midhurst* (London, 1818)

Long, James, *Hand-Book of Bengal Missions, in Connexion with the Church of England* (London, 1848)

Ludlam, William, and Thomas Ludlam, *Essays, Scriptural, Moral, and Logical* (1807)

Lushington, C., *The History, Design and Present State of the Religious, Benevolent and Charitable Institutions Founded by the British in Calcutta and its Vicinity* (Calcutta, 1824)

Macaulay, Kenneth, *The Colony of Sierra Leone Vindicated* (London, 1827)

Macaulay, Zachary, *A Letter to His Royal Highness the Duke of Gloucester* (2nd edn: London, 1815)

MacQueen, James, *The Colonial Controversy* (Glasgow, 1825)

Madden, Samuel, *Memoir of Reverend Peter Roe* (Dublin, 1862)

Mant, Richard, *An Appeal to the Gospel, or an Inquiry into the Justice of the Charge, Alleged by Methodists and other Objectors, that the Gospel is not Preached by the National Clergy* (Oxford, 1812)

——, *Two Tracts, Intended to Convey Correct Notions of Regeneration and Conversion, According to the Sense of Holy Scripture, and the Church of England* (London, 1815)

[March Phillipps, Lucy Frances], *Records of the Ministry of the Rev. E.T. March Phillipps* (London, 1862)

[Marks, Richard], *Nautical Essays: or, a Spiritual View of the Ocean and Maritime Affairs: with Reflections on the Battle of Trafalgar and other Events* (London, 1818)

——, *The Seaman's Friend* (London, 1850)

Marryatt, Joseph, *Thoughts on the Abolition of the Slave Trade, and Civilization of Africa; with Remarks on the African Institution, and an Examination of the Report of their Committee, Recommending a General Registry of Slaves in the British West India Islands* (London, 1816)

Marsh, Catherine, *The life of the Revd William Marsh* (London, 1867)

Marshman, John Clark, *The Life and Times of Carey, Marshman and Ward. Embracing the History of the Serampore Mission*, 2 vols (London, 1859)

Marsden, J.B., *Memoirs of the Life and Labours of the Rev. S. Marsden* (London, 1838)

——, *Two Sermons on the Life, Ministry and Death of the Late Rev. Richard Marks* (London, 1847)

Marsden, William, *A Brief Memoir of the Life and Writings of the Late William Marsden* (London, 1838)

Marsh, Herbert, *A Comparative View of the Churches of England and Rome* (2nd edn: London, 1816)

——, *An Inquiry into the Consequences of Neglecting to Give the Prayer Book with the Bible* (4th edn: Cambridge, 1812)

——, *The National Religion the Foundation of National Education* (5th edn: London, 1811)

Marshall, John, *Royal Naval Biography*, 8 vols (London, 1823–35)

Martyn, Henry, *Christian India; or, an Appeal on Behalf of 900,000 Christians in India, who want the Bible* (Calcutta, 1811).

Maurice, F.D., *Reasons for not Joining a Party in the Church* (London, 1841)

Middelton, J.W., *An Ecclesiastical Memoir of the First Four Decades of the Reign of George the Third* (London, 1822)

Middleton, Erasmus, *Evangelical Biography*, 4 vols (London, 1807)

Milner, Isaac, *An Account of the Life and Character of the Late Rev. Joseph Milner* (London, 1804)

——, (ed.), *The Works of the Late Rev. Joseph Milner, A.M.*, 8 vols (London, 1810)

Milner, Mary, *The Life of Isaac Milner, D.D.* (London, 1842)

Montgomery, Martin, *History of the British Colonies*, 5 vols (2nd edn: London, 1835)

More, Hannah, *An Estimate of the Religion of the Fashionable World, by One of the Laity* (London, 1808)

——, *Thoughts on the Importance of the Manners of the Great to General Society* (London, 1788)

Motherwell, M.C., *A Memoir of the Late Albert Blest* (Dublin, 1843)

Mozley, Thomas, *Reminiscences Chiefly of Oriel College and the Oxford Movement*, 2 vols (London, 1882)

Natt, John, *Posthumous Sermons* (2nd edn: London, 1855)

Newton, John, *Memoirs of the Life of William Grimshaw* (London, 1799)

Norris, Henry Handley, *The Origin, Progress, and Existing Circumstances, of the London Society for Promoting Christianity among the Jews. An Historical Inquiry* (London, 1825)

——, *A Practical Exposition of the Tendency and Proceedings of the British and Foreign Bible Society* (London, 1813)

——, *A Respectful Letter to the Earl of Liverpool, Occasioned by the Speech Imputed to his Lordship at the Isle of Thanet Bible Society Meeting* (2nd edn: London, 1823)

O' Byrne, R., *A Naval Biographical Dictionary*, 2 vols (London, 1849)

O'Callaghan, A., *The Bible Society against the Church and State: and the Primitive Christians, the Reformers, and the Bible, against the Bible Society* (London, 1817)

O'Donnoghue, Hallifield Cosgayne, *A Familiar and Practical Exposition of the Thirty-Nine Articles of Religion of the United Church of England and Ireland* (London, 1816)

'Officer, An' [Moyle Sherer], *Sketches of India* (2nd edn: London, 1824)

The Original Letters of the Rev. John Newton, A.M., to the Rev. W. Barlass (London, 1819)

Ostler, Edward, *The Life of Admiral Viscount Exmouth* (London, 1835)

'Orthodox Clergyman, An', *Consideration of the Probable Effects of the Opposition of the Orthodox clergy to their Evangelical Brethren* (London, 1818)

Otter, William, *The Life and Remains of the Rev. Edward Daniel Clarke, LL.D.* (London, 1824)

——, *A Vindication of Churchmen who Become Members of the British and Foreign Bible Society, in a Letter to a Friend at Cambridge; being an Answer to Dr Marsh's Pamphlet upon that Subject* (Cambridge, 1812)

Ouseley, Sir Gore, *Biographical Notices of Persian Poets* (London, 1846)

Overton, John, *The True Churchmen Ascertained: or, an Apology for those of the Regular Clergy of the Establishment, who are Sometimes called Evangelical Ministers: Occasioned by the Publications of Drs. Paley, Hey, Croft; Messrs. Daubeny, Ludlam, Polwhele, Fellowe; the Reviewers, &c. &c.* (2nd edn: York, 1802)

Owen, John [of the Bible Society], *The History of the Origin and First Ten Years of the British and Foreign Bible Society*, 3 vols (London, 1816–20)

——, *A Letter to a Country Clergyman* (London, 1805)

Owen, John, *Memoir of the Rev. Thomas Jones* (London, 1851)

Pearson, H.N., *Memoirs of the Life and Writings of the Rev. Claudius Buchanan*, 2 vols (Oxford, 1817)

Pearson, John, *The Life of William Hey, Esq., F.R.S.*, 2 vols (London, 1822)

Peckard, Peter, *Justice and Mercy Recommended* (London, 1788)

Pellew, George, *The Life and Correspondence of the Right Hon. Henry Addington, First Viscount Sidmouth*, 3 vols (London, 1847)

Pickering, Danby (ed.), *The Statutes at Large, from Magna Charta to the end of the Eleventh Parliament of Great Britain, Anno 1761, Continued*, 46 vols (Cambridge, 1763–1807)

Porteus, Beilby, *A Brief Account of Three Favourite Country Residences: to which is added – Death: a Poetical Essay first Printed at Cambridge in the Year 1759* ([London?], [c. 1808])

Poynder, John, *Speech of John Poynder, Esq. at a General Court of Proprietors of the East India Company, on the 21st December, 1836, upon a Motion for Carrying into Effect the Letter of the Court of Directors of 20th February 1833, which ordered the Withdrawal of British Patronage and Support from the Worship and Service of Idolatry, and the Extinction of all Taxation arising from the Superstitions of Heathenism* (London, 1837)

Pratt, John H. (ed.), *Eclectic Notes* (London, 1856)

——, and Josiah Pratt junior, *Memoir of the Rev. Josiah Pratt, B.D., Late Vicar of St. Stephen's Coleman Street, and for Twenty-One Years Secretary of the Church Missionary Society* (London, 1849)

[Pratt, Josiah], *Propaganda: Being an Abstract of the Designs and Proceedings of the Incorporated Society for Propagating the Gospel in Foreign Parts* (London, 1819)

—— (ed.), *The Works of the Rev. Richard Cecil, M.A., late Rector of Bisley, and Vicar of Chobham, Surrey: and Minister of St. John's-Chapel, Bedford-Row, London, with a Memoir of his Life*, 3 vols (London, 1816)

'Presbyter of the Church of England, A', *Papers Occasioned by Attempts to Form Auxiliary Bible Societies in Various Parts of the Kingdom* (London, 1812)

'Protestant Party, One of the', *Random Recollections of Exeter Hall, in 1834–1837* (London, 1838)

Pym, R. (ed.), *Memoirs of the Late Rev. William Nunn* (London, 1842)

Raffles, Sophia, *Memoir of the Life and Public Services of Sir Thomas Stamford Raffles* (London, 1830)

Raikes, H., *Memoirs of the Life of Vice-Admiral Sir Jahleel Brenton* (London, 1855)

Randolph, John, *A Charge Delivered to the Clergy of the Diocese of London, at his Primary Visitation* (Oxford, 1810)

Redford, George, and John Angell James, *The Autobiography of the Rev. William Jay: with Reminiscences of some Distinguished Contemporaries* (2nd edn: London, 1855)

Rees, R.O., *Mary Jones, y Gymraes fechan heb yr un Beibl: a sefydliad y Feibl-Gymdeithas* [Mary Jones, the Welsh Girl without a Bible: the Organisation of the Bible Society] (Wrexham, 1879)

Report from the Clergy of a District in the Diocese of Lincoln Convened for the Purpose of Considering the State of Religion (London, 1800)

Roberts, William, *Memoirs of the Life and Correspondence of Mrs. Hannah More*, 4 vols (2nd edn: London, 1834)

Robinson, Francis Horsley, *What Good May Come out of the India Bill* (London, 1853)

Roebuck, Thomas, *The Annals of the College of Fort William* (Calcutta, 1819)

Ross, J., *Memoirs and Correspondence of Admiral Lord de Saumarez*, 2 vols (London, 1838)

Ryder, Henry, *A Sermon Before the Incorporated Society for the Propagation of the Gospel in Foreign Parts; at their Anniversary Meeting in the Parish Church of St Mary Le Bow, on Friday, February 19, 1819* (London, 1819)

——, *A Sermon Preached for the Benefit of St Mary's School, in Leicester, in Pursuance of the Request of the Late Vicar* (Lutterworth, 1813)

——, *A Sermon Preached in the Cathedral of Wells before the Diocesan Association of the Members of the Society for Promoting Christian Knowledge* (London, 1818)

——, *Three Sermons on Particular Occasions* (London, 1818)

Sargent, John, *A Memoir of the Rev. Henry Martyn* (10th edn: London, 1830)

——, *The Life of the Rev. T.T. Thomason* (London, 1833)

Scott, John, *An Inquiry into the Effects of Baptism* (London, 1815)

—— (ed.), *Letters and Papers of the Late Reverend Thomas Scott* (London, 1824)

——, *The Life of the Rev. Thomas Scott* (4th edn: London, 1822)

Scott, Thomas, *The Force of Truth: an Authentic Narrative* (London, 1779)

Scott Waring, Major [John], *A Letter to the Rev. John Owen* (London, 1808)

——, *Observations on the Present State of the East India Company* (4th edn: London, 1808)

Sharp, Granville, *The Law of Retribution; or, a Serious Warning to Great Britain and her Colonies* (London, 1776)

——, *A Short Sketch of Temporary Regulations (Until Better shall be Proposed) for the Intended Settlement on the Grain Coast of Africa near Sierra Leone* (3rd edn: London, 1788)

Shore, Charles, Second Lord Teignmouth, *Memoir of the Life and Correspondence of John Shore, Lord Teignmouth*, 2 vols (London, 1843)

——, *Reminiscences of Many Years*, 2 vols (Edinburgh, 1878)

Shore, John, *Memoirs of the Life, Writings and Correspondence, of Sir William Jones* (2nd edn: London, 1806)

Sidney, Edwin, *The Life, Ministry, and Selections from the Remains, of the Rev. Samuel Walker* (London, 1835)

——, *The Life of Lord Hill, G.C.B., Late Commander of the Forces* (London, 1845)

——, *The Life of Sir Richard Hill, Bart., M.P. for the County of Shropshire* (London, 1839)

——, *The Life of the Rev. Rowland Hill* (London, 1834)

Sikes, Thomas, *An Humble Remonstrance to the Lord Bishop of London, Vice-President of a New Association called the British and Foreign Bible Society* (London, 1806)

[Simeon, Charles] (ed.), *Memorial Sketches of the Rev. David Brown: with a Selection of his Sermons, Preached at Calcutta* (London, 1816)

——, *Dr Marsh's Fact; or, a Congratulatory Address to the Church-Members of the British and Foreign Bible Society* (Cambridge, 1813)

——, *Horae Homileticae*, 21 vols (London, 1832–3)

Sirr, J. D'A., *Memoir of the Honourable and Most Reverend Power Le Poer Trench, Last Archbishop of Tuam* (Dublin, 1845)

[Smith, Sydney], 'Remarks on the System of Education in Public Schools', *Edinburgh Review*, 16, 32 (Jul. 1810), 326–34

[——], 'Ingram on Methodism', *Edinburgh Review*, 11, 22 (Jan. 1808), 340–62

[——], 'Indian Missions', *Edinburgh Review*, 12, 23 (Apr. 1808), 151–81

[——], 'Styles on *Methodists and Missions*', *Edinburgh Review*, 14, 27 (Apr. 1809), 40–50

Smith, Theophilus Ahijah, *The Moral Reformation of Sailors* (Richmond, 1874)

Smith, Thomas, and John O. Choules, *The Origin and History of Missions*, 2 vols (Boston, MA, 1834)

Southey, Robert, Caroline Southey and Charles Robert Southey (eds), *The Life of the Rev. Andrew Bell*, 3 vols (London, 1844)

—— (ed.), *The Works of William Cowper*, 8 vols (London, 1854)

Spry, John Hume, *Christian Union Doctrinally and Historically Considered* (Oxford, 1816)

——, *An Enquiry into the Claims of the British and Foreign Bible Society, to the Countenance and Support of Members of the Established Church* (London, 1810)

——, *Farther [sic] Observations on the British and Foreign Bible Society in Answer to a Letter Addressed by the Right Hon. N. Vansittart, M.P., &c. &c. &c. to the Rev. Dr. Marsh* (London, 1812)

Statham, John, *Indian Recollections* (London, 1832)

Stephen, Sir George, *Anti-Slavery Recollections* (London, 1854)

——, *A Memoir of the Late James Stephen, one of the Masters in the High Court of Chancery, in relation to Slave Emancipation* (Brighton, 1875)

[Stephen, James], *Dangers of the Country* (London, 1807)

[——], *An Inquiry into the Right and Duty of Compelling Spain to Relinquish her Slave Trade in Northern Africa* (London, 1816)

[——], *War in Disguise; or, the Frauds of the Neutral Flags* (4th edn: London, 1806)

Stephen, Sir James, *Essays in Ecclesiastical Biography*, 2 vols (London, 1849)

[——], 'The Clapham Sect', *Edinburgh Review*, 80, 161 (Jul. 1844), 251–307

Sumner, John Bird, *Apostolical Preaching Considered in an Examination of St Paul's Epistles* (London, 1815)

Sumner, G.H., *Life of Charles Richard Sumner* (London, 1876)

Sweet, James Bradley, *A Memoir of the Late Henry Hoare, Esq.* (London, 1869)

Tatham, Edward, *A New Address to the Free and Independent Ministers of Convocation* (London, 1810)

Taylor, Henry, *Autobiography*, 2 vols (London, 1885)

Thomas, Josiah, *An Address to a Meeting Holden at the Town-Hall, in the City of Bath, under the Presidency of the Hon. and Rt. Rev. the Lord Bishop of Gloucester, on Monday, the First Day of December, 1817; for the Purpose of Forming a Church Missionary Society in that City; Word for Word as Delivered from Writing; with a Protest against the Establishment of such a Society in Bath* (5th edn: London, 1817)

——, *A Charge Delivered to the Reverend the Clergy of the Archdeaconry of Bath in 1819* (Bristol, 1819)

——, *Real Charity and Popular Charity: a Discourse* (London, 1819)

Thorpe, Robert, *A Letter to William Wilberforce, Esq, M.P. Vice President of the African Institution, &c. &c. &c., Containing Remarks on the Reports of the Sierra Leone Company, and African Institution: with Hints Respecting the Means by which an Universal Abolition of the Slave Trade might be Carried into Effect* (London, 1815)

——, *A Reply 'Point by Point' to the Special Report of the Directors of the African Institution* (London, 1815)

Tucker, J.S., *Memoirs of Admiral the Right Hon. The Earl of St Vincent*, 2 vols (London, 1844)

Urwick, W., *Biographic Sketches of James Digges La Touche Esq.* (Dublin, 1868)

Vaughan, Edward T., *Some Account of the Life, Ministry, Character, and Writings of the Late Rev. T. Robinson* (London, 1815)

Venn, Henry, junior (ed.), *The Life and a Selection from the Letters of the Late Rev. Henry Venn* (London, 1834)

Wadström, C.B., *An Essay on Civilization*, 2 vols (London, 1794–5)

Wakefield, Gilbert, *Memoirs of the Life of Gilbert Wakefield*, 2 vols (London, 1804)

Warner, Richard, *A Letter to the Hon. and Rt. Rev. Henry Ryder D.D., Lord Bishop of Gloucester, on the Admission to Holy Orders of Young Men Holding (what are Commonly Called) Evangelical principles* (Bath, 1818)

Watkins, Henry George, *Distress in Germany: a Sermon Preached at St Swithin's Church, on Sunday, Feb. 20, 1814* (London, 1814)

Wesley, John, *The Consequence Proved* (London, 1771)

Whately, Richard, *The Use and Abuse of Party-Feeling in Matters of Religion* (Oxford, 1822)

Wilberforce, Robert Isaac, and Samuel Wilberforce, *Correspondence of William Wilberforce*, 2 vols (London, 1840)

——, *The Life of William Wilberforce*, 5 vols (London, 1838)

Wilberforce, William, *An Appeal to the Religion, Justice and Humanity of the Inhabitants of the British Empire, in Behalf of the Negro Slaves in the West Indies* (London, 1823)

——, *A Practical View of the Prevailing Religious System of Professed Christians, in the Higher and Middle Classes in this Country, Contrasted with Real Christianity* (London, 1797)

——, *A Practical View of the Prevailing Religious System of Professed Christians, in the Higher and Middle Classes in this Country, Contrasted with Real Christianity* (14th edn: London, 1829)

——, *A Practical View of the Prevailing Religious System of Professed Christians, in the Higher and Middle Classes in this Country, Contrasted with Real Christianity, with an Introductory Essay by Daniel Wilson* (Glasgow, 1826)

Willis, William Downes, *Simony. A Sermon* (London, 1842)

Wilson, Daniel, *The Character of the Good Man as a Christian minister* (London, 1831)

[Wilson, Daniel], *A Defence of the Church Missionary Society against the Objections of the Rev. Josiah Thomas, M.A., Archdeacon of Bath* (11th edn: London, 1818)

——, *The Doctrine of Regeneration Practically Considered. A Sermon, Preached before the University of Oxford, at St Mary's, on Monday, February 24th 1817* (London, 1817)

——, *Motives for the Religious Education of the Poor. A Sermon, Preached at the Parish Church of St Mary's Islington, on Sunday Evening, December 11th 1825* (London, 1826)

[——], *A Respectful Address to the Most Rev. the Archbishops, the Right Rev. the Bishops, the Rev. the Clergy, and the Other Members of the Society for Promoting Christian Knowledge, on Certain Inconsistencies and Contradictions which have Appeared of late in the Books and Tracts of that Society* (London, 1816)

——, *The Substance of a Conversation with John Bellingham, the Assassin of the Late Right Hon. Spencer Perceval, on Sunday, May 17, 1812, the Day Previous to his Execution* (London, 1812)

Wolfe, R.B., *English Prisoners in France* (London, 1830)

Woodd, Basil, *A Family Record or Memoirs of the Late Rev. Basil Woodd* (London, 1834)

Wordsworth, Christopher, *Reasons for Declining to Become a Subscriber to the British and Foreign Bible Society, Stated in a Letter to a Clergyman of the Diocese of London* (London, 1810)

Young, Arthur, *An Enquiry into the State of the Public Mind amongst the Lower Classes and on the Means of Turning it to the Welfare of the State. In a Letter to William Wilberforce, Esq., M.P.* (London, 1798)

[Young, Arthur], *National Danger, and the Means of Safety. By the Editor of the Annals of Agriculture* (London, 1797)

Later Editions of Primary Sources

Atherstone, Andrew (ed.), *The Journal of Bishop Daniel Wilson of Calcutta, 1845–1857*, Church of England Record Society, 21 (Woodbridge, 2015)

Aspinall, Arthur (ed.), *The Diary of Henry Hobhouse* (London, 1947)

——(ed.), *The Later Correspondence of George III*, 5 vols (Cambridge, 1962–70)

——, and Anthony Smith (eds), *English Historical Documents 1783–1832* (London and New York, 1959)

Anon., *A Short Account of Successful Exertions in Behalf of the Fatherless and Widows after the War in 1814* (privately printed, 1871)

Betham-Edwards, M. (ed.), *The Autobiography of Arthur Young* (London, 1898)

Bevington, Merle M., *The Memoirs of James Stephen: Written by Himself for the use of his Children* (London, 1954)

Bonner Smith, David (ed.), *Letters of Admiral of the Fleet the Earl of St. Vincent whilst First Lord of the Admiralty, 1801–1804*, 2 vols (London, 1922–7)

Bloom, Edward A., and Lilian D. (eds), *The Piozzi Letters, Volume VI: 1817–1821* (Newark, NJ, and London, 2010)

Conybeare, W.J., 'Church Parties', ed. Arthur Burns, in Stephen Taylor (ed.), *From Cranmer to Davidson: a Church of England Miscellany*, Church of England Record Society, 7 (Woodbridge, 1999), 213–385.

Elder, J.R., *The Letters and Journals of Samuel Marsden, 1765–1838* (Dunedin, 1932)

Equiano, Olaudah, *The Interesting Narrative of the Life of Olaudah Equiano, or Gustavus Vassa, the African, Written by Himself*, ed. Werner Sollors (New Yorkand London, 2001)

Falconbridge, Anna Maria, *Narrative of Two Voyages to the River Sierra Leone during the Years 1791–1792–1793*, ed. Christopher Fyfe (Liverpool, 2000)

[Fenton, Elizabeth], *The Journal of Mrs Fenton* (London, 1901)

Gray, A., *Papers and Diaries of a York family, 1764–1839* (London, 1927)

Greig, James (ed.), *The Farington Diary*, 8 vols (London, 1922–8)

Headlam, Cuthbert (ed.), *The Letters of Lady Harriot Eliot, 1766–1786* (Edinburgh, 1914)

Hole, Robert (ed.), *Selected Writings of Hannah More* (London, 1996)

Hughes, Edward (ed.), *The Private Correspondence of Admiral Lord Collingwood* (London, 1957)

Knutsford, Viscountess, *Life and Letters of Zachary Macaulay* (London, 1900)

Kup, Alexander Peter, *Adam Afzelius: Sierra Leone Journal, 1795–1796* (Uppsala, 1967)

Laughton, J.K., *Letters and Papers of Charles, Lord Barham, Admiral of the Red Squadron, 1758–1813*, 3 vols (*London*, 1907–13)

Lewis, Michael (ed.), *Sir William Henry Dillon, K.C.H., Vice-Admiral of the Red: A Narrative of my Professional Adventures*, 2 vols (London, 1953–6)

Mackarness, George (ed.), *Some Private Correspondence of the Rev. Samuel Marsden and Family, 1794–1824* (Sydney, 1942)

Markham, Clements (ed.), *Selections from the Correspondence of Admiral John Markham during the Years 1801–4 and 1806–7* (London, 1904)

Newman, John Henry, *Apologia Pro Vita Sua and Six Sermons*, ed. Frank M. Turner (New Haven, CT, 2008)

Ross, Charles (ed.), *Correspondence of Charles, First Marquess Cornwallis*, 3 vols (2nd edn: London, 1859)

Ryan, A.N., *The Saumarez Papers: Selections from the Baltic Correspondence of Vice-Admiral Sir James Saumarez 1808–1812* (London, 1968)

Ryder, Henry, 'A Charge Delivered to the Clergy of the Diocese of Gloucester in the Year 1816', ed. Mark A. Smith, in Smith and Taylor (eds), *Evangelicalism in the Church of England c.1790–c.1890*, 51–107.

Stephen, Sir James, *Letters: With Biographical Notes by his Daughter, Caroline Emelia Stephen* ([London?], 1907)

Tatum, Edward H., junior (ed.), *The American Journals of Ambrose Serle, Secretary to Lord Howe, 1776–1778* (San Marino, CA, 1940)

Thackeray, William Makepeace, *The Newcomes: Memoirs of a Most Respectable Family*, ed. Arthur Pendennis; rev. edn D.J. Taylor (London, 1994)

——, *Vanity Fair* (rev. edn: London, 1994)

Thornton, Henry, *An Enquiry into the Nature and Effects of the Paper Credit of Great Britain*, ed. F.A. van Hayek (London, 1939)

Thornton, Samuel, *The Book of Yearly Recollections of Samuel Thornton, Esq., of Clapham, and Albury Park, in the County of Surrey* (London, 1891)

Trollope, Anthony, *Barchester Towers*, ed. Michael Sadleir and Frederick Page (repr. Oxford, 1991)

Wilberforce, Anna Maria (ed.), *Private Papers of William Wilberforce* (London, 1897)

Wraxall, N.W., *The Historical and Posthumous Memoirs of Sir Nathaniel William Wraxall 1772–1784*, ed. Henry B. Wheatley, 5 vols (London, 1884)

Wright, Thomas (ed.), *The Correspondence of William Cowper*, 4 vols (London, 1904)

Official Documents and Publications

An Account of the Naval and Military Bible Society from its Institution in 1780 to Lady-Day 1804 (London, 1804)

An Account of the Proceedings at the Green Man Inn, Blackheath, on Saturday, February 22, 1812, when an Auxiliary Society was Established for that very Populous Neighbourhood (London, 1812)

African Institution Annual Reports, 1807–27

An Appeal in Behalf of the Naval and Military Bible Society (London, 1835)

British and Foreign Bible Society Annual Reports, 1804–

Church Missionary Society Proceedings, 1801–

Further Papers Respecting the Company's Charter (5.) ([London], 1833)

Naval and Military Bible Society Annual Reports, 1811–

Naval and Military Bible Society Biennial Accounts, 1804–10

New Establishment of Pay and Half-Pay for Navy Chaplains, Admiralty Office, 9th March 1812 (London, 1812)

Papers Relating to East Indian Affairs, Part IV: 24 Nov. 1812–22 July, 1813, Volume 10 (London, 1813)

Prayer Book and Homily Society Annual Sermons and Proceedings, 1813–

Proceedings of the Public Meeting at Freemasons' Hall, on Thursday, the 25th of February, 1813, for the Purpose of Establishing an Auxiliary Society for Bloomsbury and South Pancras, in aid of the British and Foreign Bible Society (London, 1813)

Proceedings of the Public Meeting for the Purpose of Establishing an Auxiliary Bible Society for Hackney, Newington, Homerton, Clapham, Stamford-Hill, Newington-Green, Kingsland, Shacklewell, and Dalston (London, 1812)

Report of the Parliamentary Select Committee on Aboriginal Tribes (London, 1837)

Report of Proceedings at a Meeting held at the London Tavern, Tuesday, March 16, 1813, His Highness the Duke of Kent in the Chair, for the Formation of the North-East London Auxiliary Bible Society (London, 1813)

Report of Proceedings at the Meeting in the Egyptian Hall, in the Mansion House, on Thursday, August 6, 1812, the Right Hon. the Lord Mayor in the Chair, for the Purpose of Establishing the City of London Auxiliary Bible Society (London, 1812)

Reports of the Committees Formed in London in the Year 1814, for the Relief of the Unparalleled Distresses in Germany (London, 1814)

Sierra Leone Company Reports and Abstracts, 1791–1808

Society for Promoting Christian Knowledge, Annual Reports, 1793–1835.

Newspapers and Periodicals

Annual Biography and Obituary
Anti-Jacobin Review
Asiatic Journal and Monthly Miscellany
Asiatic Journal and Monthly Register for British India and its Dependencies
British and Foreign Anti-Slavery Reporter
British Review
British Critic
Christian Guardian
Christian Observer
Christian Remembrancer
Church Times
Cobbett's Weekly Political Register
Eclectic Review
Edinburgh Review
Evangelical Magazine
Friend of India
Gentleman's Magazine
John Bull
Missionary Magazine
Missionary Register
Monthly Repository of Theological and General Literature
Morning Chronicle
Morning Post
The Morning Watch
Naval Chronicle
Navy List
Orthodox Churchman's Magazine; or, a Treasury of Divine and Useful Knowledge
The Parliamentary History of England, from the Earliest Time until 1803
The Parliamentary Debates from the Year 1803 to the Present Time
Public Advertiser
Quarterly Review
The Record
Steel's Original and Correct List of the Royal Navy
The Times

Secondary Sources

Abbey, Charles J., and John H. Overton, *The English Church in the Eighteenth Century*, 2 vols (London, 1878)

Abbott, Evelyn, and Lewis Campbell (eds), *The Life and Letters of Benjamin Jowett*, 2 vols (London, 1897)

Acheson, Alan R., *A History of the Church of Ireland 1691–1996* (Dublin, 1997)

——, 'Trinity College, Dublin, and the Making of Irish Evangelicalism, 1790–1850', in Power (ed.), *Flight of Parsons*, 13–40

Ackerson, Wayne, *The African Institution (1807–1827) and the Antislavery Movement in Great Britain* (New York, Queenston, ON, and Lampeter, 2005)

Ackrill, Margaret, and Leslie Hannah, *Barclays: the Business of Banking 1690–1996* (Cambridge, 2001)

Aglionby, Francis Keyes, *The life of Edward Henry Bickersteth, D.D., Bishop and Poet* (London, 1907)

Allender, Tim, 'Anglican Evangelism [*sic*] in North India and the Punjabi Missionary Classroom: the Failure to Educate "the Masses", 1860–77', *History of Education*, 32 (2003), 273–88

Allpress, Roshan, 'William Wilberforce and "the Saints"', in Atkins (ed.), *Making and Remaking Saints*, 209–25

Altholz, Josef L., 'Alexander Haldane, the *Record* and Religious Journalism', *Victorian Periodicals Review*, 20 (1987), 23–31

——, *The Religious Press in Britain, 1760–1900* (Westport, CO, 1989)

Ambler, Rod W., 'Evangelicals and the Establishment: Evangelical Identity in a Nineteenth-Century Market Town', in Smith (ed.), *British Evangelical*, 74–84

Anderson, Benedict, *Imagined Communities: Reflections on the Origin and Spread of Nationalism* (rev. edn: London, 2006)

Andrew, Donna T., *Philanthropy and Police: London Charity in the Eighteenth Century* (Princeton, NJ, 1989)

Andrews, Robert M., *Lay Activism and the High Church Movement of the Late Eighteenth Century* (Leiden, 2015)

Annan, Noel, 'The Intellectual Aristocracy', in J.H. Plumb (ed.), *Studies in Social history: a Tribute to G.M. Trevelyan* (London, 1955), 243–87; reprinted in Noel Annan, *The Dons: Mentors, Eccentrics and Geniuses* (Chicago, IL, 1999), 304–42

Anderson, Olive, 'The Growth of Christian Militarism in Mid-Victorian Britain', *English Historical Review*, 86 (1971), 46–72

Anon., 'Friends and the Slave Trade: a Yorkshire Election Declaration, 1806', *Journal of the Friends' Historical Society*, 46 (1954), 65–6

Anstey, Roger, *The Atlantic Slave Trade and British Abolition, 1760–1810* (London, 1975)

——, and P.E.H. Hair (eds), *Liverpool, the African Slave Trade and Abolition* (Liverpool, 1976)

——, 'Parliamentary Reform, Methodism, and Anti-Slavery Politics, 1829–1833', *Slavery and Abolition*, 2 (1981), 209–26

Aquino, Frederick D., and Benjamin J. King (eds), *The Oxford Handbook of John Henry Newman* (Oxford, 2018)

Armstrong, A., *The Church of England, the Methodists, and Society, 1700–1850* (London, 1973)

Aston, Nigel, *Christianity and Revolutionary Europe, c. 1750–1830* (Cambridge, 2002)

Atherstone, Andrew, 'Anglican Evangelicalism', in Strong (ed.), *Oxford History of Anglicanism, Volume III*, 165–86

——, *Evangelical Mission and Anglican Church Order: Charles Simeon Reconsidered* (London, 2009)

Atkins, Gareth, Anglican Evangelical Theology, c. 1820–1850: the Case of Edward Bickersteth', *Journal of Religious History*, 38 (2014), 1–19

——, 'Christian Heroes, Providence and Patriotism in Wartime Britain, 1793–1815', *Historical Journal*, 58 (2015), 393–414

——, 'Evangelicals', in Aquino and King (eds), *Oxford Handbook of John Henry Newman*, 173–95

——, '"Isaiah's Call to England": Doubts about Prophecy in Nineteenth-Century Britain', *Studies in Church History*, 52 (2016), 381–97

—— (ed.), *Making and Remaking Saints in Nineteenth-Century Britain* (Manchester, 2016)

——, 'Piety and Plutocracy: the Social and Business World of the Thorntons', in Brown and Musson (eds), *Moggerhanger Park*, 183–99

——, 'Reformation, Revival and Rebirth in Anglican Evangelical Thought, c. 1780–c. 1830', *Studies in Church History*, 44 (2008), 164–74

——, 'Religion, Politics and Patronage in the Late-Hanoverian Navy, c. 1780–c. 1820', *Historical Research*, 88 (2015), 272–90

——, '"True Churchmen?" Anglican Evangelicals and History, c. 1770–1850', *Theology*, 115 (2014), 339–49

——, 'William Jowett's Christian Researches: British Protestants and Religious Plurality in the Mediterranean, Syria and the Holy Land, 1815–30', *Studies in Church History*, 51 (2015), 216–31

Bagster, Samuel, *Samuel Bagster of London, 1772–1851* (London, 1972)

Balleine, George R., *A History of the Evangelical Party in the Church of England* (2nd edn: London, 1951)

Barclay, H.F., and A. Wilson-Fox, *A History of the Barclay Family with Pedigrees from 1067 to 1933*, 3 vols (London, 1934)

Baring-Gould, Sabine, *The Church Revival: Thoughts Thereon and Reminiscences* (London, 1914)

——, *The Evangelical Revival* (London, 1920)

Barker, Juliet, *The Brontës* (London, 1994)

Bartlett, C.J., *Great Britain and Sea Power, 1815–1853* (Oxford, 1963)

Batalden, Stephen, Kathleen Cann and John Dean (eds), *Sowing the Word: the Cultural Impact of the British and Foreign Bible Society, 1804–2004* (Sheffield, 2004)

Battersby, William, *James Fitzjames: The Mystery Man of the Franklin Expedition* (Stroud, 2010)

Bayly, C.A., *Empire and Information: Intelligence Gathering and Social Communication in India, 1780–1870* (Cambridge, 1996)

——, *Imperial Meridian: the British Empire and the World, 1780–1830* (London, 1989)

Bebbington, David W., *The Dominance of Evangelicalism: the Age of Spurgeon and Moody* (Nottingham, 2005)

——, *Evangelicalism in Modern Britain: a History from the 1730s to the 1980s* (London, 1989)

——, 'The Islington Conference', in Maiden and Atherstone (eds), *Evangelicalism and the Church of England*, 48–67

Beerbuhl, Margrit Schulze, 'The Commercial Culture of Spiritual Kinship amongst German Immigrant Merchants in London, c. 1750–1830', in Lee (ed.), *Commerce and Culture*, 225–54

Belmonte, Kevin, *Hero for Humanity* (Colorado Springs, CO, 2002)

——, and Brian H. Edwards, *Travel with William Wilberforce: the Friend of Humanity* (Leominster, 2006)

Benham, William, *Catharine and Craufurd Tait, Wife and Son of Archibald Campbell, Archbishop of Canterbury* (London, 1879)

Bennett, Arthur, 'Robert Porten Beachcroft: Preacher and Pastor (1781–1830)', *Churchman*, 103 (1989), n.p.

Bennett, G.V., and J.D. Walsh (eds), *Essays in Modern English Church History* (London, 1966)

Best, G.F.A., 'The Evangelicals and the Established Church in the Early Nineteenth Century', *Journal of Theological Studies*, n.s., 10 (1959), 63–78

——, *Temporal Pillars: Queen Anne's Bounty, the Ecclesiastical Commissioners, and the Church of England* (Cambridge, 1964)

Bhabha, Homi, 'Signs Taken for Wonders: Questions of Ambivalence and Authority under a Tree outside Delhi, May 1817', *Critical Inquiry*, 12 (1985), 144–65

Bidwell, W.H., *Annals of an East Anglian Bank* (Norwich, 1900)

Binney, Judith, *The Legacy of Guilt: a Life of Thomas Kendall* (2nd edn: Wellington, 2005)

Binns, H.B., *A Century of Education: Being the Centenary History of the British & Foreign School Society 1808–1908* (London, 1908)

Birks, Herbert, *The Life and Correspondence of Thomas Valpy French*, 2 vols (London, 1895)

Blake, R.C., *Evangelicals in the Royal Navy, 1775–1815: Blue Lights and Psalm Singers* (Woodbridge, 2008)

——, *Religion in the British Navy, 1815–1879: Piety and Professionalism* (Woodbridge, 2014)

Bolitho, Hector, and Derek Peel, *The Drummonds of Charing Cross* (London, 1967)

Bolt, Christine, and Seymour Drescher (eds), *Anti-Slavery, Religion and Reform: Essays in Memory of Roger Anstey* (Folkestone, 1980)

Bonwick, James, *Australia's First Preacher: the Rev. Richard Johnson, First Chaplain of New South Wales* (London, 1898)

Borgen, Peder, 'George Wolff (1736–1828): Norwegian-born Merchant, Consul, Benevolent Methodist Layman, Close Friend of John Wesley', *Methodist History*, 40 (2001), 17–28

Bowen, Desmond, 'A.R.C. Dallas: the Warrior Saint', in Phillips (ed.), *View from the Pulpit*, 17–44

Bowen, H.V., *The Business of Empire: the East India Company and Imperial Britain, 1756–1833* (Cambridge, 2000)

——, N. Rigby and M. Lincoln (eds), *The Worlds of the East India Company* (Woodbridge, 2002)

Bradley, A.G., *Our Centenarian Grandfather* (London, 1922)

Bradley, Ian, *The Call to Seriousness: the Evangelical Impact on the Victorians* (London, 1976)

Braidwood, Stephen J., *Black Poor and White Philanthropists. London's Blacks and the Foundation of the Sierra Leone Settlement 1786–1791* (Liverpool, 1994)

Breihan, John R., 'The Addington Party and the Navy in British Politics, 1801–1806', in Symond (ed.), *New Aspects of Naval History*, 163–89

——, 'William Pitt and the Commission on Fees, 1785–1801', *Historical Journal*, 27 (1984), 59–81

Bremner, G.A., *Imperial Gothic: Religious Architecture and High Anglican Culture in the British Empire, c. 1840–1870* (New Haven, CT, 2013)

Brent, Richard, *Liberal Anglican Politics: Whiggery, Religion, and Reform, 1830–1841* (Oxford, 1987)

Brilioth, Yngve, *Evangelicalism and the Oxford Movement* (London, 1934)

Brock, M.G., and M.C. Curthoys (eds), *The History of the University of Oxford, VI: Nineteenth-Century Oxford, Part I* (Oxford, 1997)

Broughton, Trev Lynn, 'The *Bengal Obituary*: Reading and Writing Calcutta Graves in the Mid Nineteenth Century', *Journal of Victorian Culture*, 15 (2010), 39–59

Brown, Christopher Leslie, 'Evangelicals and the origins of anti-slavery in England', in *Oxford Dictionary of National Biography* online, http://www.oxforddnb.com, last accessed 18 Jan. 2019

——, *Moral Capital: Foundations of British Abolitionism* (Chapel Hill, NC, 2006)

Brown, Ford K., *Fathers of the Victorians: the Age of Wilberforce* (Cambridge, 1961)

Brown, Jane, and Jeremy Musson (eds), *Moggerhanger Park: an Architectural and Social History* (Ipswich, 2012)

Brown, Ralph, 'Victorian Anglican Evangelicalism: the Radical Legacy of Edward Irving', *Journal of Ecclesiastical History*, 58 (2007), 675–704

Brown, Stewart J., and Timothy Tackett (eds), *The Cambridge History of Christianity, VII: Enlightenment, Reawakening and Revolution, 1660–1815* (Cambridge, 2006)

——, *The National Churches of England, Ireland and Scotland, 1801–46* (Oxford, 2001)

Brown-Lawson, A., *John Wesley and the Anglican Evangelicals of the Eighteenth Century: a Study in Co-operation and Separation with Special Reference to the Calvinist Controversies* (Edinburgh, 1993)

Buettner, Elizabeth, *Empire Families: Britons and Late-Imperial India* (Oxford, 2004)

Burgess, H.J., *Enterprise in Education: The Story of the Work of the Established Church in the Education of the People prior to 1870* (London, 1958)

Burns, Arthur, *The Diocesan Revival in the Church of England, c. 1800–1870* (Oxford, 1999)

——, and Joanna Innes (eds), *Rethinking the Age of Reform: Britain 1780–1850* (Cambridge, 2003)

Byrn, John D., *Crime and Punishment in the Royal Navy: Discipline in the Leeward Islands Station, 1784–1812* (Aldershot, 1989)

Cannadine, David, *Lords and Landlords: the Aristocracy and the Towns 1774–1967* (Leicester, 1980)

Canton, W., *The History of the British and Foreign Bible Society*, 5 vols (London, 1904–10)

Carey, Hilary M., *God's Empire: Religion and Colonialism in the British World, c. 1801–1908* (Cambridge, 2011)

Carson, Penelope, *The East India Company and Religion, 1698–1858* (Woodbridge, 2012)

——, 'The British Raj and the Awakening of the Evangelical Conscience: The Ambiguities of Religious Establishment and Toleration, 1698–1833', in Stanley (ed.), *Christian Missions*, 45–70

Carter, Grayson, *Anglican Evangelicals: Protestant Secessions from the Via Media, c. 1800–1850* (Oxford, 2001)

Cassels, Nancy Gardner, *Religion and Pilgrim Tax under the Company Raj* (New Delhi, 1987)

Cave Brown, I., 'The Venerable Archdeacon Pratt, Archdeacon of Calcutta: a Sketch', *Mission Life*, 3, n.s. (1872), 163–9

Cavell, Janice, *Tracing the Connected Narrative: Arctic Exploration in British Print Culture, 1818–1860* (Toronto, 2008)

Cavell, Samantha, *Midshipmen and Quarterdeck Boys in the British Navy, 1771–1831* (Woodbridge, 2012)

Chadwick, Owen, *The Victorian Church*, 2 vols (London, 1966, 1970)

——, *Victorian Miniature* (Cambridge, 1960)

Chatterton, Eyre, *A History of the Church of England in India* (London, 1924)

Chapman, Stanley, *The Rise of Merchant Banking* (London, 1984)

Cheriyan, P., *The Malabar Christians and the Church Missionary Society, 1816–1840* (Kottayam, 1935)

Christopher, Emma, Cassandra Pybus and Marcus Rediker (eds), *Many Middle Passages: Forced Migration and the Making of the Modern World* (Oakland, CA, 2007),

——, 'The Slave Trade is Merciful Compared to [This]', in Christopher, Pybus and Rediker (eds), *Many Middle Passages*, 109–28

Clapham, John, *The Bank of England: a History*, 2 vols (Cambridge, 1944)

Clapp, Elizabeth J., and Julie Roy Jeffrey (eds), *Women, Dissent, and Anti-Slavery in Britain and America, 1790–1865* (Oxford, 2011)

Clark, J.C.D., *English Society 1688–1832: Ideology, Social Structure and Political Practice during the Ancien Regime* (Cambridge, 1985)

——, *English Society 1660–1832: Religion, Ideology and Politics during the Ancien Regime* (Cambridge, 2000)

Clark, Peter, *British Clubs and Societies, 1580–1800: the Origins of an Associational World* (Oxford, 2000)

Clarke, W.K. Lowther, *A History of the SPCK* (London, 1959)

Claydon, Tony, and Ian McBride, *Protestantism and National Identity: Britain and Ireland, c. 1650–c. 1850* (Cambridge, 1998)

Clayton, Helen, *To School Without Shoes: a Brief History of the Sunday School Society for Ireland, 1809–1979* ([Dublin(?)], n.d.)

Clinch, Anne, *A History of Langley in Kent* (Maidstone, 2007)

Clive, John, 'Review: FATHERS OF THE VICTORIANS: THE AGE OF WILBERFORCE. By Ford K. Brown...'. *Journal of Modern History*, 34 (1962), 337–8

Cnattingius, Hans, *Bishops and Societies: a Study of Anglican Colonial and Missionary Expansion, 1698–1850* (London, 1952)

Cocksworth, Christopher J., *Evangelical Eucharistic Thought in the Church of England* (Cambridge, 1993)

Coffey, John (ed.), *Heart Religion: Evangelical Piety in England and Ireland, 1690–1850* (Oxford, 2016)

——, '"Tremble, Britannia!": Fear, Providence and the Abolition of the Slave Trade, 1758–1807', *English Historical Review*, 127 (2012), 844–81

Cohen, Deborah, *Household Gods: the British and their Possessions* (New Haven, CT, 2006)

Cole, C. Robert, and Michael E. Moody (eds), *The Dissenting Tradition: Essays for Leland H. Carlson* (Athens, OH, 1975)

Coleman, Deirdre, *Romantic Colonization and British Anti-Slavery* (Cambridge, 2005)

Colley, Linda, *Britons: Forging the Nation 1707–1837* (New Haven, CT, 1992)

——, 'Whose Nation? Class and National Consciousness in Britain 1750–1830', *Past and Present*, 113 (1986), 98–117

Collinge, J.M., *Office-Holders in Modern Britain, VII: Navy Board Officials 1660–1832* (London, 1978)

Collinson, Patrick, *The Elizabethan Puritan Movement* (2nd edn: Oxford, 1990)

Condon, M.E., 'The Establishment of the Transport Board – a Subdivision of the Admiralty – 4 July 1794', *Mariner's Mirror*, 58 (1972), 69–84

Cookson, J.E., *The British Armed Nation, 1793–1815* (Oxford, 1997)

Ian Copland, 'Christianity as an Arm of Empire: the Ambiguous Case of India under the Company, c. 1813–1858', *Historical Journal*, 49 (2006), 1025–54

Cornwallis-West, G., *The Life and Letters of Admiral Cornwallis* (London, 1927)

Coupland, Reginald, *The British Anti-Slavery Movement* (2nd edn: London, 1964)

——, *Wilberforce, a Narrative* (Oxford, 1923)

Jeffrey Cox, *Imperial Fault Lines: Christianity and Colonial Power in India, 1818–1940* (Stanford, CA, 2002)

Cowie, Leonard W., 'Exeter Hall', *History Today*, 18 (1968), 390–7

Crane, Jane Miriam [née Havergal], *Records of the Life of the Rev. William H. Havergal, M.A.* (London, [1883])

Creighton, Mandell, *Memoir of Sir George Grey* (new edn: London, 1901)

Crimmin, P.K., 'The Financial and Clerical Establishment of the Admiralty Office, 1783–1806', *Mariner's Mirror*, 55 (1969), 299–309

Cunich, Peter, and others, *A History of Magdalene College Cambridge 1428–1988* (Cambridge, 1994)

Cunningham, Hugh, 'The Language of Patriotism, 1750–1914', *History Workshop Journal*, 12 (1981), 8–33

Curley, Thomas M., *Sir Robert Chambers: Law, Literature, and Empire in the Age of Samuel Johnson* (Madison, WN, 1998)

Currer-Jones, A., *William Dawes, R.M., 1762–1836* (Torquay, 1930)

Curtin, Philip D., *The Image of Africa: British Ideas and Action, 1780–1850*, 2 vols (Madison, WI, 1964)

Daily, Christopher A., *Robert Morrison and the Protestant Plan for China* (Hong Kong, 2013)

Danker, Ryan, *Wesley and the Anglicans: Political Division in Early Evangelicalism* (Downers Grove, IL, 2016)

Danvers, Frederick Charles, et al., *Memorials of Old Haileybury College* (Westminster, 1894)

Davenport, Rowland, *Albury Apostles* (Birdlip, 1970)

Davidoff, Leonore, and Catherine Hall, *Family Fortunes: Men and Women of the English Middle Class, 1780–1850* (London, 1987)

Davidson, Allan K., *Evangelicals and Attitudes to India, 1786–1813* (Sutton Courtenay, 1990)

Davies, G.C.B., *The Early Cornish Evangelicals, 1735–1760* (London, 1951)

——, *First Evangelical Bishop: Some Aspects of the Life of Henry Ryder* (London, 1958)

Davies, John G., *From Bridge to Moor: the History of Leeds Grammar School from its Foundation to 1854* (Leeds, 2002)

Davies, Rupert, and Gordon Rupp (eds), *A History of the Methodist Church in Great Britain*, 4 vols (London, 1965–88)

Davis, David Brion, *The Problem of Slavery in the Age of Revolution 1770–1823* (Ithaca, NY, 1975)

Davis, R.W., *Dissent in Politics, 1780–1830: the Political Life of William Smith, MP* (London, 1971)

Dening, Greg, *Mr Bligh's Bad Language: Passion, Power and Theatre on the 'Bounty'* (Cambridge, 1992)

Deutsch, Phyllis, 'Moral Trespass in Georgian London: Gaming, Gender, and Electoral Politics in the Age of George III', *Historical Journal*, 39 (1996), 637–56

Devereaux, Simon, 'Inexperienced Humanitarians? William Wilberforce, William Pitt, and the Execution Crisis of the 1780s', *Law and History Review*, 33 (2015), 839–85

Dewey, Clive, *The Passing of Barchester* (London, 1991)

Dinwiddy, J., *Christopher Wyvill and Reform* (York, 1971)

Ditchfield, G.M., *The Evangelical Revival* (London, 1998)

Dowland, David A., *Nineteenth-Century Anglican Theological Training: the Redbrick Challenge* (Clarendon, 1997)

Drescher, Seymour, *Abolition: a History of Slavery and Antislavery* (Cambridge, 2009)

——, *Capitalism and Antislavery: British Mobilization in Comparative Perspective* (London, 1987)

——, *The Mighty Experiment: Free Labour versus Slavery in British Emancipation* (New York, 2002)

——, 'Public Opinion and Parliament in the Abolition of the British Slave Trade', *Parliamentary History*, supplement (2007), 42–65

——, 'Public Opinion and the Destruction of British and Colonial Slavery', in Walvin (ed.), *Slavery and British Society*, 22–48

——, 'Whose Abolition? Popular Pressure and the Ending of the British Slave Trade', *Past and Present*, 143 (1994), 136–66

Élodie Duché, 'Charitable Connections: Transnational Financial Networks and Relief for British Prisoners of War in Napoleonic France, 1803–1814', *Napoleonica. La Revue*, 3 (2014), 74–117

Duffy, Michael, 'The French Revolution and British Attitudes to the West Indian Colonies', in Gaspar and Geggus (eds), *Turbulent Time*, 78–101

——, *The Younger Pitt* (Harlow, 1994)

Dumas, Paula E., *Proslavery Britain: Fighting for Slavery in an Era of Abolition* (New York, 2016)

Dunn, R.S., and M.M. Dunn (eds), *The World of William Penn* (Philadelphia, PA, 1986)

Durey, Jill, 'The Evangelicalism of Bishop Anthony Wilson Thorold (1825–1895), *Churchman*, 118 (2004), 151–64

Dutta, Sutapa, *British Women Missionaries in Bengal, 1793–1861* (London, 2017)

Ehrman, John, *The younger Pitt*, 3 vols (London, 1969–96)

Elbourne, Elizabeth, *Blood Ground: Colonialism, Missions, and the Contest for Christianity in the Cape Colony and Britain, 1799–1853* (Montreal, 2002)

——, 'The Foundation of the Church Missionary Society: the Anglican Missionary Impulse', in Walsh, Haydon and Taylor (eds), *Church of England, c. 1689–c. 1833*, 247–64

Eliot, Simon (ed.), *The History of Oxford University Press, Volume II: 1780–1896* (Oxford, 2013)

Elliott-Binns, L.E., *The Early Evangelicals: a Religious and Social Study* (London, 1953)

Eltis, David, *Economic Growth and the Ending of the Transatlantic Slave Trade* (Oxford, 1987)

——, and Stanley L. Engerman, 'The Importance of Slavery and the Slave Trade to Industrializing Britain', *Journal of Economic History*, 60 (2000), 123–44

Ely, Richard, 'From Sect to Church: Sir James Stephen's Theology of Empire', *Journal of Religious History*, 19 (1995), 75–91

Embree, Ainslie T., *Charles Grant and British Rule in India* (London, 1962)

Etherington, Norman (ed.), *Missions and Empire* (Oxford, 2005)

Fancourt, Mary St J., 'George Berkeley Mitchell 1776–1828', *Transactions of the Leicestershire Archaeological and Historical Society*, 61 (1980–1), 71–87

Farooq, Jennifer, *Preaching in Eighteenth-Century London* (Woodbridge, 2013)

Farrell, Stephen, '"Contrary to the Principles of Justice, Humanity and Sound Policy": the Slave Trade, Parliamentary Politics and the Abolition Act, 1807', *Parliamentary History*, supplement (2007), 141–202

The First Bible Society (London, 1874)

Fisch, Jörg, 'A Pamphlet War on Christian Missions in India 1807–1809', *Journal of Asian History* (1985), 22–70

Fisher, David (ed.), *The History of Parliament: the House of Commons, 1820–1832*, 7 vols (Cambridge, 2009)

Fitton, R.S., *The Arkwrights: Spinners of Fortune* (Manchester, 1989)

Fletcher, B. H., *Ralph Darling: a Governor Maligned* (Melbourne, 1984)

Flew, Sarah, *Philanthropy and the Funding of the Church of England, 1856–1914* (London, 2015)

Flynn, Michael, *The Second Fleet: Britain's Grim Convict Armada of 1790* (Sydney, 1993)

Follett, Richard R., *Evangelicalism, Penal Theory and the Politics of Criminal Law Reform in England, 1808–30* (Basingstoke, 2001)

Forsaith, Peter, and Geordan Hammond (eds), *Religion, Gender, and Industry* (Cambridge, 2011)

Forster, E.M., *Marianne Thornton, 1797–1887: a Domestic Biography* (London, 1956)

Foster, J., *Alumni Oxonienses: the Members of the University of Oxford, 1715–1886*, 4 vols (Oxford, 1887–8)

Franklin, Alexandra, and Mark Philp, *Napoleon and the Invasion of Britain* (Oxford, 2003)

Frey, Sylvia R. *Water from the Rock: Black Resistance in a Revolutionary Age* (Princeton, NJ, 1992)

Friedman, Terry, *The Eighteenth-Century Church in Britain* (New Haven, CT, 2011)

Frost, Alan, *Convicts and Empire: a Naval Question, 1776–1811* (Melbourne, 1980)

——, *Dreams of a Pacific Empire: Sir George Young's Proposal for a Colonization of New South Wales, 1784–5* (Sydney, 1980)

Fry, Michael, *The Dundas Despotism* (Edinburgh, 1992)

Frykenberg, Robert Eric, *Christians and Missionaries in India* (Grand Rapids, MI, 2003)

——, 'Modern Education in South India, 1784–1854: Its Roots and Its Role as a Vehicle of Integration under Company Raj', *American Historical Review*, 91 (1986), 37–65

——, 'Religion and Company Raj in South India', *Fides et Historia*, 17 (1985), 6–37

Furneaux, Robin, *William Wilberforce* (London, 1974)

Fyfe, Aileen, *Science and Salvation: Evangelical Popular Science Publishing in Victorian Britain* (Chicago, IL, 2004)

Fyfe, Christopher, *History of Sierra Leone* (London, 1962)

Gallant, Thomas W., *Experiencing Dominion: Culture, Identity, and Power in the British Mediterranean* (Notre Dame, IN, 2002)

Gascoigne, John, *Cambridge in the Age of the Enlightenment: Science, Religion and Politics from the Restoration to the French Revolution* (Cambridge, 1988)

——, *The Enlightenment and the Origin of European Australia* (Cambridge, 2002)

——, *Joseph Banks and the English Enlightenment: Useful Knowledge and Polite Culture* (Cambridge, 1994)

Gash, Norman, *Lord Liverpool: the Life and Political Career of Robert Banks Jenkinson, Second Earl of Liverpool, 1770–1828* (London, 1984)

Gaspar, David, and David Geggus (eds), *A Turbulent Time: the French Revolution and the Greater Caribbean* (Bloomington, IN, 1997)

Gatrell, Vic, *City of Laughter: Sex and Satire in Eighteenth-Century London* (London, 2006)

Gibbs, M.E., *The Anglican Church in India, 1600–1970* (Delhi, 1972)

——, 'The First Hundred and Fifty Years', in R.W. Bowie and I.D.L. Clark (eds), *Bishop's College, Calcutta* (Kolkata, 1970)

Gibson, William, *The Church of England 1688–1832: Unity and Accord* (London, 2001)

——, and Robert G. Ingram (eds), *Religious Identities in Britain, 1660–1832* (Aldershot, 2005)

——, 'The Tories and Church Patronage: 1812–30', *Journal of Ecclesiastical History*, 41 (1990), 266–74

Gidney, William Thomas, *The History of the London Society for Promoting Christianity Amongst the Jews: from 1809–1908* (London, 1908)

Gilbert, A.D., *Religion and Society in Industrial England: Church, Chapel and Social Change, 1740–1914* (Harlow, 1976)

Gilley, Sheridan, and Brian Stanley (eds), *The Cambridge History of Christianity, VIII: World Christianities, c. 1815–c. 1914* (Cambridge, 2007)

Gladwin, Michael, *Anglican Clergy in Australia, 1788–1850: Building a British World* (Woodbridge, 2015)

Glasson, Travis, *Missionary Anglicanism and Slavery in the Atlantic World* (New York, 2012)

Gleadle, Kathryn, *Borderline Citizens: Women, Gender and Political Culture in Britain, 1815–1867* (Oxford, 2009)

Godfrey, Richard T., Andrew Edmunds and Mark Hallett, *James Gillray and the Art of Caricature* (London, 2001)

Goldie, Mark, 'Voluntary Anglicans', *Historical Journal*, 46 (2003), 977–90

Gore, John (ed.), *Creevey* (London, 1948)

Götz, Norbert, 'The Good Plumppuddings' Belief: British Voluntary Aid to Sweden during the Napoleonic Wars', *International History Review*, 37 (2015), 519–39

——, 'Rationales of Humanitarianism: the Case of British Relief to Germany, 1805–1815', *Journal of Modern European History*, 12 (2014), 186–99

Gray, Arthur, and Frederick Brittain, *A History of Jesus College, Cambridge* (Cambridge, 1960)

Gray, Dennis, *Spencer Perceval: the Evangelical Prime Minister 1762–1812* (Manchester, 1963)

Green, Nile, *The Love of Strangers: What Six Muslim Students Learned in Jane Austen's London* (Princeton, NJ, 2016)

——, 'Parnassus of the Evangelical Empire: Orientalism and the English Universities, 1800–50', *Journal of Imperial and Commonwealth History*, 40 (2012), 337–55

Green, Samuel G., *The History of the Religious Tract Society for One Hundred Years* (London, 1899)

Green, V.H.H., *The Commonwealth of Lincoln College, 1427–1977* (Oxford, 1979)

——, *Religion at Oxford and Cambridge* (London, 1964)

Gregory, Jeremy, '*Homo Religiosus*: Masculinity and Religion in the Long Eighteenth Century', in Hitchcock and Cohen (eds), *English Masculinities*, 85–110

——, and Jeffrey Chamberlain (eds), *The National Church in Local Perspective* (Woodbridge, 2003)

——(ed.), *The Oxford History of Anglicanism, Volume II: Establishment and Empire, 1662–1829* (Oxford, 2017)

Gribben, Crawford and Andrew R. Holmes (eds), *Protestant Millennialism, Evangelicalism and Irish Society, 1790–2005* (Basingstoke, 2006)

Griffiths, D.N., 'Prayer-Book Translations in the Nineteenth Century', *The Library*, 6 (1984), 1–24

Grimble, Ian, *The Sea Wolf: the Life of Admiral Cochrane* (London, 1978)

Groseclose, Barbara, *British Sculpture and the Company Raj: Church Monuments and Public Statuary in Madras, Calcutta, and Bombay to 1858* (Cranbury, NJ, 1995)

Grounds, Douglas, *Son and Servant of Shropshire: the Life of Archdeacon Joseph (Plymley) Corbett* (Logaston, 2009)

Guinness, Michele, *The Guinness Legend* (Sevenoaks, 1989)

Gupta, Abhijit, 'The Calcutta School-Book Society and the Production of Knowledge', *English Studies in Africa*, 57 (2014), 55–65

Haakonssen, Knud (ed.), *Enlightenment and Religion: Rational Dissent in Eighteenth-Century Britain* (Cambridge, 1996)

Hague, William, *William Wilberforce: the Life of the Great Anti Slave-Trade Campaigner* (London, 2007)

Hair, P.E.H., 'Freetown Abused, 1809', *Durham University Journal*, 59 (1967), 152–60

Halévy, Elie, *The Birth of Methodism in England*, trans. Bernard Semmel (Chicago, IL, 1971)

——, *A History of the English People in the Nineteenth Century, I: England in 1815*, trans. E.I. Watkin and D.A. Barker (2nd edn: London, 1949)

Hall, Catherine, *Civilising Subjects: Metropole and Colony in the English Imagination 1830–1867* (Chicago, IL, 2002)

——, *Macaulay and Son: Architects of Imperial Britain* (London, 2012)

——, Nicholas Draper, Keith McClelland, Katie Donington and Rachel Lang, *Legacies of British Slave-Ownership: Colonial Slavery and the Formation of Victorian Britain* (Cambridge, 2014)

The Hall in the Garden: the Story of Freemasons' Hall (London, 2006)

Hamilton, C.I., *The Making of the Modern Admiralty: British Naval Policy-Making, 1805–1927* (Cambridge, 2011)

Harding, Alan, *The Countess of Huntingdon's Connexion: a Sect in Action in Eighteenth-Century England* (Oxford, 2003)

Hardwick, Joseph, *An Anglican British World: the Church of England and the Expansion of the Settler Empire, c. 1790–1860* (Manchester, 2014)

——, 'Vestry Politics and the Emergence of a Reform "Public" in Calcutta, 1813–36', *Historical Research*, 84 (2011), 87–108

Harford, A.M., *Annals of the Harford Family* ([London], 1909)

Harling, Philip, 'Leigh Hunt's *Examiner* and the Language of Patriotism', *English Historical Review*, 111 (1996), 1159–81

——, *The Waning of 'Old Corruption': Economical Reform, 1779–1846* (Oxford, 1996)

Harris, Khim, *Evangelicals and Education: Evangelical Anglicans and Middle-Class Education in Nineteenth-Century England* (Carlisle, 2004)

Harrison, Brian H., *Drink and the Victorians: the Temperance Question in England, 1815–1872* (London, 1971)

Harrison, J.F.C., *The Second Coming: Popular Millenarianism 1780–1850* (London, 1979)

Harvey, A.D., *Collision of Empires: Britain in Three World Wars, 1793–1945* (London, 1992)

Heasman, Kathleen, *Evangelicals in Action: an Appraisal of their Social Work in the Victorian Era* (London, 1962)

Helfman, Tara, 'The Court of Vice Admiralty at Sierra Leone and the Abolition of the West African Slave Trade', Yale Law Journal, 115 (2006), 1122–56

Hellmuth, Eckhardt (ed.), *The Transformation of Political Culture: England and Germany in the Late Eighteenth Century* (Oxford, 1990)

Hempton, David, *The Church in the Long Eighteenth Century* (London, 2011)

——, *Evangelical Disenchantment: Nine Portraits of Faith and Doubt* (New Haven, CT, 2008)

——, 'Evangelicalism and Reform, c. 1780–1832', in Wolffe (ed.), *Evangelical Faith and Public Zeal*, 17–37

——, *Methodism and Politics in English Society, 1750–1850* (London, 1984)

——, *Methodism: Empire of the Spirit* (New Haven, CT, 2005)

——, *Religion and Political Culture in Britain and Ireland* (Cambridge, 1996)

Hendrickson, Kenneth E., *Religion and the Public Image of the British Army, 1809–1885* (Madison, NJ, 1998)

Hennell, Michael M., *John Venn and the Clapham Sect* (London, 1958)

——, *Sons of the Prophets: Evangelical Leaders of the Victorian Church* (London, 1979)

Hervey, Thomas, *Life of the Rev. Samuel Settle* (Colmer, 1881)

Hill, Draper, *The Satirical Etchings of James Gillray* (New York, 1976)

Hilton, Boyd, *The Age of Atonement: the Influence of Evangelicalism on Social and Economic Thought, 1785–1865* (Oxford, 1988)

——, *A Mad, Bad, and Dangerous People? England, 1783–1846* (Oxford, 2006)

——, 'The Nineteenth Century', in Linehan (ed.), *St John's College, Cambridge*, 220–396

——, '1807 and All That: Why Britain Outlawed Her Slave Trade', in Peterson (ed.), *Abolitionism and Imperialism*, 63–83

Hitchcock, Tim, and Michèle Cohen (eds), *English Masculinities, 1660–1800* (London, 1999)

Himmelfarb, Gertrude, 'A Genealogy of Morals: from Clapham to Bloomsbury', in Himmelfarb, *Marriage and Morals among the Victorians* (London, 1986), 22–49

Hindmarsh, D. Bruce, *The Evangelical Conversion Narrative: Spiritual Autobiography in Early Modern England* (Oxford, 2005)

——, *John Newton and the English Evangelical Tradition: Between the Conversions of Wesley and Wilberforce* (Oxford, 1996)

Hoare, H.P.R., *Hoare's Bank: a Record, 1672–1955* (London, 1932)

Hochschild, Adam, *Bury the Chains: the British Struggle to Abolish Slavery* (London, 2005)

Hodder, Edwin, *The Life and Work of the Seventh Earl of Shaftesbury*, 3 vols (London, 1886)

Hole, Charles, *The Early History of the Church Missionary Society for Africa and the East* (London, 1896)

Hole, Robert, *Pulpits, Politics and Public Order in England, 1760–1832* (Cambridge, 1989)

Honan, Park, *Jane Austen: her Life* (London, 1987)

Hoock, Holger, *Empires of the Imagination: Politics, War and the Arts in the British World, 1750–1850* (London, 2010)

——, *The King's Artists: the Royal Academy of Arts and the Politics of British Culture 1760–1840* (Oxford, 2003)

Howsam, Leslie, *Cheap Bibles: Nineteenth-Century Publishing and the British and Foreign Bible Society* (Cambridge, 1991)

Howse, E.M., *Saints in Politics: the 'Clapham Sect' and the Growth of Freedom* (London, 1953)

Humphreys, A.L., *Piccadilly Bookmen: Memorials of the House of Hatchard* (London, 1893)

Hurwitz, Edith F., *Politics and the Public Conscience: Slave Emancipation and the Abolitionist Movement in Britain* (London, 1973)

Hutchings, Victoria, *Messrs Hoare Bankers: a History of the Hoare Banking Dynasty* (London, 2005)

Hutchinson, Mark, and John Wolffe, *A Short History of Global Evangelicalism* (New York, 2012)

Huzzey, Richard, *Freedom Burning: Anti-Slavery and Empire in Victorian Britain* (Ithaca, NY, 2012)

Hyam, Ronald, *Britain's Imperial Century 1815–1914* (London, 1976)

Hylson-Smith, Kenneth, *Bath Abbey: a History* (Bath, 2003)

——, *Evangelicals in the Church of England, 1754–1984* (Edinburgh, 1988)

Innes, Joanna, and Hugh Cunningham (eds), *Charity, Philanthropy, and Reform from the 1690s to 1850* (Basingstoke, 1998)

——, *Inferior Politics: Social Problems and Social Policies in Eighteenth-Century Britain* (Oxford, 2009)

——, 'Politics and Morals: the Reformation of Manners Movement in Later Eighteenth-Century England', in Hellmuth (ed.), *Transformation of Political Culture*, 57–118

——, 'State, Church and Voluntarism in European Welfare, 1690–1850', in Innes and Cunningham (eds), *Charity, Philanthropy, and Reform*, 15-65.

Jackson, Gordon, *Hull in the Eighteenth Century: a Study in Economic and Social History* (London, 1972)

Jacob, W.M., *Lay People and Religion in the Early Eighteenth Century* (Cambridge, 1996)

——, *The Clerical Profession in the Long Eighteenth Century, 1680–1840* (Oxford, 2007)

Jaeger, Muriel, *Before Victoria: Changing Standards and Behaviour, 1787–1837* (2nd edn: London, 1967)

Jakobsson, S., *Am I not a Man and a Brother?* (Uppsala, 1972)

James, C.L.R., *The Black Jacobins: Toussaint L'Ouverture and the San Domingo Revolution* (London, 1938)

Janes, Dominic, *Victorian Reformation: the Fight over Idolatry in the Church of England, 1840–1860* (Oxford, 2009)

Jay, Elisabeth, *The Religion of the Heart: Anglican Evangelicalism and the Nineteenth-Century Novel* (Oxford, 1979)

Jenkins, Brian, *Henry Goulburn 1784–1856: a Political Biography* (Liverpool, 1996)

Jenks, Timothy, *Naval Engagements: Patriotism, Cultural Politics and the Royal Navy 1793–1815* (Oxford, 2006)

Jennings, Judith, *The Business of Abolishing the Slave Trade, 1783–1807* (London, 1997)

Johnson, Leonard George, *General T. Perronet Thompson, 1783–1869: his Military, Literary, and Political Campaigns* (London, 1957)

Jones, H. K., *Butterworths: History of a Publishing House* (London, 1980)

Jupp, Peter, *British Politics on the Eve of Reform* (Basingstoke, 1998)

Kielstra, Paul Michael, *The Politics of Slave Trade Suppression in Britain and France, 1814–48: Diplomacy, Morality and Economics* (Basingstoke, 2000)

Kloes, Andrew, 'The Committee for the Relief of Distress in Germany: a Case Study of Co-operation and Solidarity between British Evangelicals and German Pietists during the Napoleonic Era', *Pietismus und Neuzeit*, 40 (2014), 163–201

Knaplund, Paul, *James Stephen and the British Colonial System 1813–1847* (Madison, WI, 1953)

Knight, Frances, *The Nineteenth-Century Church and English Society* (Cambridge, 1995)

Knight, Roger, *Britain Against Napoleon: the Organization of Victory, 1793–1815* (London, 2014)

——, 'The Introduction of Copper Sheathing into the Royal Navy, 1779–1786', *Mariner's Mirror*, 59 (1973), 175–92

——, *The Pursuit of Victory: the Life and Achievement of Horatio Nelson* (London, 2005)

——, 'Sandwich and Middleton Dockyard Appointments', *Mariner's Mirror*, 57 (1971), 175–92

Knox-Shaw, Peter, *Jane Austen and the Enlightenment* (Cambridge, 2004)

Kopf, David, *British Orientalism and the Bengal Renaissance: the Dynamics of Indian Modernization, 1773–1835* (Berkeley, CA, 1969)

Kriegel, Abraham D., 'A Convergence of Ethics: Saints and Whigs in British Antislavery', *Journal of British Studies*, 26 (1987), 423–58

Kverndal, Roald, *Seamen's Missions: their Origin and Early Growth* (Pasadena, CA, 1986)

Kynaston, David, *The City of London, I: a World of its Own 1815–1890* (London, 1994)

Laidlaw, Zoe, *Colonial Connections, 1815–45: Patronage, the Information Revolution and Colonial Government* (Manchester, 2005)

——, 'Investigating Empire: Humanitarians, Reform and the Commission of Eastern Inquiry', *Journal of Imperial and Commonwealth History*, 40 (2012), 749–68

Laird, Michael Andrew, *Missionaries and Education in Bengal, 1793–1837* (Oxford, 1972)

Laqueur, T.W., *Religion and Respectability: Sunday Schools and Working-Class Culture, 1780–1850* (New Haven, CT, 1976)

Larsen, Timothy, and Michael Ledger-Lomas (eds), *The Oxford History of Dissenting Traditions, Volume III: the Nineteenth Century* (Oxford, 2017)

——, *Friends of Religious Equality: Nonconformist Politics in Mid-Victorian England* (Woodbridge, 1999)

——, David W. Bebbington and Mark Noll (eds), *Biographical Dictionary of Evangelicals* (Leicester, 2003)

Latour, Bruno, *Reassembling the Social: an Introduction to Actor-Network Theory* (Oxford, 2005)

Laver, J., *Hatchard's of Piccadilly, 1797–1947: One Hundred and Fifty Years of Bookselling* (London, 1947)

Lawson, John, *A Town Grammar School through Six Centuries: a History of Hull Grammar School against its Local Background* (Oxford, 1963)

Le Fevre, Peter, and Richard Harding (eds), *Precursors of Nelson: British Admirals of the Eighteenth Century* (London, 2000)

Lean, Garth, *God's Politician: William Wilberforce's Struggle* (London, 1980)

Lecky, W.E.H., *History of England in the Eighteenth Century*, 8 vols (London, 1878–90)

Ledger-Lomas, Michael, 'Conder and Sons: Dissent and the Oriental Bible in Nineteenth-Century Britain', in Mandelbrote and Ledger-Lomas (eds), *Dissent and the Bible*, 205–32

——, 'Theology, Divinity, and Sermons', in Eliot (ed.), *History of Oxford University Press, Volume II*, 403–34

[Lee, Anna Mary], *A Scholar of a Past Generation: A Brief Memoir of Samuel Lee* (London, 1896)

Leighton-Boyce, J.A.S.L., *Smiths the Bankers 1658–1958* (London, 1958)

Leiner, Frederick C., *The End of Barbary Terror: America's 1815 War against the Pirates of North Africa* (Oxford, 2006)

Lester, Alan, and Fae Dussart, *Colonization and the Origins of Humanitarian Government: Protecting Aborigines across the Nineteenth-Century British Empire* (Cambridge, 2014)

——, *Imperial Networks: Creating Identities in Nineteenth-Century South Africa and Britain* (London, 2001)

Lewis, Donald M. (ed.), *The Blackwell Dictionary of Evangelical Biography, 1730–1860*, 2 vols (Oxford, 1995)

Lewis, Judith S., *Sacred to Female Patriotism: Gender, Class, and Politics in Late Georgian Britain* (London, 2003)

Lewis, Michael, *A Social History of the Navy, 1793–1815* (repr. Chatham, 2004)

Lincoln, Margarette, *Representing the Royal Navy: British Sea Power, 1750–1815* (Aldershot, 2002)

Linehan, Peter (ed.), *St John's College, Cambridge: a History* (Woodbridge, 2011)

Lloyd, Christopher, *The Navy and the Slave Trade* (London, 1949)

Lloyd, Gareth, *Charles Wesley and the Struggle for Methodist Identity* (Oxford, 2007)

Lloyd, Sarah, *Charity and Poverty in England, c. 1680–1820: Wild and Visionary Schemes* (Manchester, 2009)

——, 'Pleasing Spectacles and Elegant Dinners: Conviviality, Benevolence, and Charity Anniversaries in Eighteenth-Century London', *Journal of British Studies*, 41 (2002), 23–57

Lockley, Philip, *Visionary Religion and Radicalism in Early Industrial England: from Southcott to Socialism* (Oxford, 2013)

Lovegrove, Deryck W., *Established Church, Sectarian People: Itinerancy and the Transformation of English Dissent, 1780–1830* (Cambridge, 1988)

Lovejoy, Paul E., and Suzanne Schwarz (eds), *Slavery, Abolition, and the Transition to Colonialism in Sierra Leone* (Trenton, NJ, 2015)

Lovett, Richard, *The History of the London Missionary Society, 1795–1895*, 2 vols (London, 1899)

Machin, G.I.T., *The Catholic Question in English Politics, 1820–30* (Oxford, 1964)

——, *Politics and the Churches in Great Britain 1832 to 1868* (Oxford, 1977)

Macintosh, Neil K., *Richard Johnson, Chaplain to the Colony of New South Wales, his Life and Times, 1755–1827* (Sydney, 1978)

Madden, Deborah, *The Paddington Prophet: Richard Brothers's Journey to Jerusalem* (Manchester, 2010)

Maiden, John, and Andrew Atherstone (eds), *Evangelicalism and the Church of England in the Twentieth Century* (Woodbridge, 2014)

Major, Emma, *Madam Britannia: Women, Church, and Nation, 1712–1812* (Oxford, 2012)

Mallet, Bernard, *Thomas George, Earl of Northbrook G.C.S.I.: a Memoir* (London, 1908)

Mandelbrote, Scott, and Michael Ledger-Lomas (eds), *Dissent and the Bible in Britain, c. 1650–1950* (Oxford, 2013)

Marshall, P.J., *Problems of Empire: Britain and India, 1757–1813* (London, 1968)

——, 'The White Town of Calcutta under the Rule of the East India Company', *Modern Asian Studies*, 34 (2000), 307–31

Martin, Ged, 'Two Cheers for Lord Glenelg', *Journal of Imperial and Commonwealth History*, 7 (1979), 213–27

Martin, Roger H., *Evangelicals United: Ecumenical Stirrings in Pre-Victorian Britain, 1795–1830* (Metuchen, NJ, and London, 1983)

Mason, J.C.S., *The Moravian Church and the Missionary Awakening in England, 1760–1800* (Woodbridge, 2001)

Matthews, P.W., *History of Barclays Bank limited*, ed. A.W. Tuke, 2 vols (London, 1926)

Meacham, Standish, 'The Evangelical inheritance', *Journal of British Studies*, 3 (1963), 88–104

——, *Henry Thornton of Clapham, 1760–1815* (Cambridge, 1964)

Mellor, G.R., *British Imperial Trusteeship, 1783–1850* (London, 1951)

Midgley, Clare, *Women Against Slavery: the British Campaigns, 1780–1870* (New York NJ & London, 1992)

Mineka, Francis E., *The Dissidence of Dissent: the Monthly Repository, 1806–1838* (Chapel Hill, NC, 1944)

Moir, Martin, *A General Guide to the India Office Records* (London, 1985)

Moody, Michael E., 'Religion in the Life of Charles Middleton, first Baron Barham', in Cole and Moody (eds), *Dissenting Tradition*, 140–163

Morgan, Sue, and Jacqueline DeVries (eds), *Women, Gender and Religious Cultures in Britain, 1800–1940* (Abingdon, 2010)

Morris, Henry, *The Life of Charles Grant* (London, 1904)

——, *A Memorable Room: the Story of the Inception and Foundation of the British and Foreign Bible Society* (London, 1898)

Morris, Jeremy, *The High Church Revival in the Church of England: Arguments and Identities* (Brill, 2016)

Morris, R.J., *Class, Sect and Party. The Making of the British Middle Class: Leeds, 1820–50* (Manchester, 1990)

——, *Men, Women and Property in England, 1780–1870* (Cambridge, 2005)

Morriss, Roger, 'Charles Middleton, Lord Barham, 1726–1813', in Le Fevre and Harding (eds), *Precursors of Nelson*, 301–23

——, *Naval Power and British Culture 1760–1850: Public Trust and Government Ideology* (Aldershot, 2004)

——, 'St Vincent and Reform, 1801–04', *Mariner's Mirror*, 69 (1983), 269–90

Moule, H.C.G., *Charles Simeon* (new edn: Fearn, 1997)

——, *The Evangelical School in the Church of England* (London, 1901)

——, *Memories of a Vicarage* (London, 1913)

Mouser, Bruce L., 'African Academy – Clapham 1799–1806', *History of Education*, 33 (2004), 87–103

Munch-Petersen, Thomas, *Defying Napoleon: how Britain Bombarded Copenhagen and Seized the Danish Fleet in 1807* (Stroud, 2007)

Munden, Alan F., *A Cheltenham Gamaliel: Dean Francis Close of Cheltenham* (Cheltenham, 1997)

——, 'The Origin of Evangelical Anglicanism in Newcastle upon Tyne', *Archaeologia Aeliana*, 5 ser., 11 (1983), 301–7

Murphy, Sharon, *The British Soldier and his Libraries, c. 1822–1901* (London, 2016)

Namier, Lewis, and John Brooke (eds), *The History of Parliament: The House of Commons, 1754–1790*, 3 vols (London, 1964)

Newell, Philip, *Greenwich Hospital: a Royal Foundation, 1692–1983* ([Holbrook], 1984)

Newman, Gerald M., *The Rise of English Nationalism: a Cultural History, 1740–1830* (Basingstoke, 1997)

Newsome, David, 'Father and Sons', *Historical Journal*, 6 (1963), 295–310

——, *The Parting of Friends: a Study of the Wilberforces and Henry Manning* (London, 1966)

——, *The Victorian World Picture: Perceptions and Introspections in an Age of Change* (London, 1997)

Nockles, Peter, 'Church Parties in the Pre-Tractarian Church of England 1750–1833: the 'Orthodox' – Some Problems of Definition and Identity', in Walsh, Haydon and Taylor (eds), *Church of England, c. 1689–c. 1833*, 334–59

——, 'The Oxford Movement and Evangelicalism: Parallels and Contrasts in Two Nineteenth-Century Movements of Religious Revival', in Webster (ed.), *Perfecting Perfection*, 233–59

——, *The Oxford Movement in Context: Anglican High Churchmanship, 1760–1857* (Cambridge, 1994)

——, 'Recreating the History of the Church of England: Bishop Burgess, the Oxford Movement and Nineteenth-Century Reconstructions of Protestant and Anglican Identity', in Yates (ed.), *Bishop Burgess and his World*, 233–89

——, 'The Waning of Protestant Unity and Waxing of Anti-Catholicism? Archdeacon Daubeny and the Reconstruction of "Anglican" Identity in the Later Georgian Church, c. 1780–c. 1830', in Gibson and Ingram (eds), *Religious Identities in Britain*, 179–230

Noel, Emilia F., *Some Letters and Records of the Noel Family* (London, 1910)

Noel, Gerard, *Sir Gerard Noel MP and the Noels of Chipping Campden and Exton* (Chipping Campden, 2004)

Noll, Mark A., David W. Bebbington and George W. Rawlyk (eds), *Evangelicalism: Comparative Studies of Popular Protestantism in North America, the British Isles and Beyond, 1700–1900* (Oxford, 1994)

——, 'Revolution and the Rise of Evangelical Social Influence in North Atlantic Societies', in Noll, Bebbington and Rawlyk (eds), *Evangelicalism*, 113–36

——, *The Rise of Evangelicalism: the Age of Edwards, Whitefield and the Wesleys* (Leicester, 2004)

Norman, Edward, *Church and Society in England, 1770–1870* (Oxford, 1976)

O'Connor, Daniel, *The Chaplains of the East India Company, 1601–1858* (London, 2012)

O'Donnell, Jean, *John Venn and the Friends of the Hereford Poor* (Almeley, 2006)

O'Flynn, Thomas, *The Western Christian Presence in the Russias and Qājār Persia, c. 1760–c. 1870* (Leiden, 2017)

O'Gorman, Frank, 'Party Politics in the Early Nineteenth Century, 1812–1832', *English Historical Review*, 102 (1987), 63–88

O'Shaughnessy, Andrew J., *An Empire Divided: the American Revolution and the British Caribbean* (Philadelphia, PA, 2000)

Oddie, Geoffrey A., *Missionaries, Rebellion and Proto-Nationalism: James Long of Bengal, 1814–87* (Abingdon, 2013)

Oldfield, J.R., *Popular Politics and British Anti-Slavery* (Manchester, 1995)

——, 'Chords of Freedom': Commemoration, Ritual and British Transatlantic Slavery* (Manchester, 2007)

Oliver, W.H., *Prophets and Millennialists: the Uses of Biblical Prophecy in England from the 1790s to the 1840s* (Oxford, 1978)

Oman, Charles, *Wellington's Army, 1809–1814* (London, 1912)

Ovenden, Toby, 'The Cobbs of Margate: Evangelicalism and Anti-Slavery in the Isle of Thanet, 1787–1834', *Archaeologia Cantiana*, 133 (2013), 1–32

Overton, John H., *The English Church in the Nineteenth Century, 1800–1833* (London, 1894)

Paracka, Daniel J., *The Athens of West Africa: A History of International Education at Fourah Bay College, Freetown, Sierra Leone* (New York, 2003)

Parkinson, C. Northcote, *Edward Pellew, Viscount Exmouth, Admiral of the Red* (London, 1934)

Parsons, Gerald and others (eds), *Religion in Victorian Britain*, 5 vols (Manchester, 1988)

Pascoe, C.F., *Classified Digest of the Records of the Society for the Propagation of the Gospel in Foreign Parts, 1701–1892* (London, 1898)

Patten, John A., *These Remarkable Men: the Beginnings of a World Enterprise* (London, 1945)

Payne, Reider, *Ecclesiastical Patronage in England, 1770–1801: a Study of Four Family and Political Networks* (Lewiston, ME, Queenston, ON, and Lampeter, 2010)

Peake, Charles F., 'Henry Thornton in the History of Economics: Confusions and Contributions', *Manchester School*, 63 (1995), 283–96

Pedersen, Susan, 'Hannah More Meets Simple Simon: Tracts, Chapbooks and Popular Culture in Late Eighteenth-Century England', *Journal of British Studies*, 25 (1986), 84–113

Pennell, Thomas, 'Board of Control – List of the Commissioners Appointed for the Management of the Affairs of India', in *Thirty-First Annual Report of the Deputy Keeper of the Public Records* (London, 1870), 367–71

Penner, Peter, *The Patronage Bureaucracy in North India: the Robert M. Bird and James Thomason School, 1820–1870* (Delhi, 1986)

Pennington, Brian K., *Was Hinduism Invented? Britons, Indians, and the Colonial Construction of Religion* (New York, 2005)

Penny, Frank, *The Church in Madras*, 3 vols (London, 1904–22)

Pereiro, James, 'Ethos' and the Oxford Movement: at the Heart of Tractarianism* (Oxford, 2008)

Perkin, Harold, *The Origins of Modern English Society, 1780–1880* (London, 1969)

Perriton, Linda, 'The Parochial Realm, Social Enterprise and Gender: the Work of Catharine Cappe and Faith Gray and others in York, 1780–1820', *Business History*, 59 (2017), 202–30

Peterson, Derek R. (ed.), *Abolitionism and Imperialism in Britain, Africa, and the Atlantic* (Athens, OH, 2010)

Philips, C.H., and D. Philips, 'Alphabetical List of Directors of the East India Company from 1758 to 1858', *Journal of the Royal Asiatic Society* (1941), 325–47

——, *The East India Company, 1784–1834* (repr. Manchester, 1961)

Phillips, I. Lloyd, 'Lord Barham at the Admiralty, 1805–6', *Mariner's Mirror*, 64 (1978), 217–33

Phillips, P.T. (ed.), *The View from the Pulpit* (Toronto, 1978)

Phillips, Sibyl, *Glorious Hope: Women and Evangelical Religion in Kent and Northamptonshire, 1800–1850* (Northampton, 2004)

Piggin, Stuart, 'The American and British Contributions to Evangelicalism in Australia', in Noll, Bebbington and Rawlyk (eds), *Evangelicalism*, 290–309

——, *Evangelical Christianity in Australia: Spirit, Word and world* (Melbourne and Oxford, 1996)

——, *Making Evangelical Missionaries, 1789–1858: the Social Background and Training of British Protestant Missionaries to India* (Sutton Courtenay, 1984)

Pollard, Arthur, and Michael Hennell, *Charles Simeon (1759–1836)* (London, 1959)

——, 'Evangelical Parish Clergy, 1820–40', *Church Quarterly Review*, 159 (1958), 387–95

Pollock, John, *Wilberforce: God's Statesman* (London, 1977)

Port, M.H., *Six Hundred New Churches* (London, 1961)

Porter, Andrew, '"Commerce and Christianity": the Rise and Fall of a Nineteenth-Century Missionary Slogan', *Historical Journal*, 28 (1985), 597–621

——, *Religion versus Empire? British Protestant Missionaries and Overseas Expansion, 1700–1914* (Manchester, 2004)

Postle, Martin, *Angels and Urchins: the Fancy Picture in Eighteenth-Century British Art* (Nottingham, 1998)

Powell, Avril A., 'Creating Christian Community in Nineteenth-Century Agra', in Young (ed.), *Indianness of Christianity*, 82–107

——, *Scottish Orientalists and India: the Muir Brothers, Religion, Education and Empire* (Woodbridge, 2010)

Power, Thomas P. (ed.), *A Flight of Parsons: the Divinity Diaspora of Trinity College Dublin* (Eugene, OR, 2018)

Pratt, David H., *English Quakers and the First Industrial Revolution* (New York and London, 1985)

Prest, J. M., 'Review: FORD K. BROWN. *Fathers of the Victorians, the Age of* Wilberforce' *Economic History Review*, n.s., 15 (1963), 555–6

Prinsep, Charles C., *Records of the Services of the Honourable East India Company's Civil Servants in the Madras Presidency. From 1741 to 1858* (London, 1885)

Price, A.C., *A History of the Leeds Grammar School* (Leeds, 1919)

Price, Jacob M., 'The Great Quaker Business Families of Eighteenth-Century London: the Rise and Fall of a Sectarian Patriciate', in Dunn and Dunn (eds), *World of William Penn*, 363–99

Pybus, Cassandra, *Epic Journeys of Freedom: Runaway Slaves of the American Revolution and their Global Quest for Liberty* (Boston, MA, 2006)

——, '"A Less Favourable Specimen": the Abolitionist Response to Self-Emancipated Slaves in Sierra Leone, 1793–1808', *Parliamentary History*, supplement (2007), 97–112

Quinlan, Maurice J., *Victorian Prelude: a History of English Manners, 1700–1830* (repr. London 1965)

Railton, Nicholas M., *No North Sea: the Anglo-German Evangelical Network in the Middle of the Nineteenth Century* (Leiden, 2000)

Railton, Peter, *Hull Schools in Victorian Times* (Hull, 1995)

Raven, James, *The Business of Books: Booksellers and the English Book Trade, 1450–1850* (New Haven, CT, 2007)

Reardon, Bernard M.G., *From Coleridge to Gore: a Century of Religious Thought in Britain* (London, 1971)

Reckord, Mary, 'The Colonial Office and the Abolition of Slavery', *Historical Journal*, 14 (1971), 723–34

Reynolds, J.S., *The Evangelicals at Oxford, 1735–1871* (2nd edn: Abingdon, 1975)

Richardson, David, Suzanne Schwarz and Anthony Tibbles (eds), *Liverpool and Transatlantic Slavery* (Liverpool, 2007)

Richardson, Sarah, *The Political Worlds of Women: Gender and Politics in Nineteenth-Century Britain* (Abingdon, 2012)

Rimmington, Gerald T., 'Thomas Robinson: Evangelical Clergyman in Leicester, 1774–1813', *Transactions of the Leicestershire Archaeological and Historical Society*, 75 (2001), 105–17

Rivers, Isabel, 'The First Evangelical Tract Society', *Historical Journal*, 50 (2007), 1–22

Robert, Dana L. (ed.), *Converting Colonialism: Visions and Realities in Mission History, 1706–1914* (Grand Rapids, MI, 2008)

Roberts, M.J.D., *Making English Morals: Voluntary Association and Moral Reform in England, 1787–1886* (Cambridge, 2004)

——, 'The Society for the Suppression of Vice and its Early Critics, 1802–1812', *Historical Journal*, 26 (1983), 159–76

Roberts, Richard and David Kynaston (eds), *The Bank of England: Money, Power and Influence 1694–1994* (Oxford, 1995)

Robinson, Arthur R.B., *The Counting House: Thomas Thompson of Hull 1754–1828 and his Family* (York, 1992)

Rodger, N.A.M., *The Command of the Ocean: a Naval History of Britain, 1649–1815* (London, 2004)

——, *The Insatiable Earl: a Life of John Montagu, Fourth Earl of Sandwich, 1718–1792* (London, 1993)

——, 'The Naval Chaplain in the Eighteenth Century', *British Society for Eighteenth-Century Studies*, 18 (1995), 33–45

——, *The Wooden World: an Anatomy of the Georgian Navy* (London, 1986)

Rosman, Doreen M., *Evangelicals and Culture* (London, 1984)

Rosselli, John, *Lord William Bentinck: the Making of a Liberal Imperialist, 1774–1839* (Berkeley, CA, 1974)

Rowell, Geoffrey, *Hell and the Victorians* (Oxford, 1974)

Russell, Anthony, *The Clerical Profession* (London, 1980)

Russell, George W.E., *The Household of Faith: Portraits and Essays* (London, 1902)

Rutz, Michael A., *The British Zion: Congregationalism, Politics, and Empire, 1790–1850* (Baylor, TX, 2011)

——, 'The Politicizing of Evangelical Dissent, 1811–1813', *Parliamentary History*, 20 (2001), 187–207

Ryan, Maeve, '"A Moral Millstone"?: British Humanitarian Governance and the Policy of Liberated African Apprenticeship, 1808–1848,' *Slavery and Abolition*, 37 (2016), 399–422

Ryder, Thomas Dudley, *A Memoir of the Hon. and Rt. Rev. Henry Ryder, D.D.*, ed. A.P. Ryder (London, 1886)

Sadleir, Michael, *Archdeacon Francis Wrangham, 1769–1842* (Oxford, 1937)

Sainty, J.C., *Office-Holders in Modern Britain, VIII: Admiralty Officials 1660–1870* (London, 1975)

Sambrook, James (ed.), *William Cowper: The Task and Selected Other Poems* (London, 1994)

Samson, Jane, *Imperial Benevolence: Making British Authority in the Pacific Islands* (Honolulu, HI, 1998)

Sandeen, Ernest R., *The Roots of Fundamentalism: British and American Millenarianism, 1800–1930* (Chicago, IL, 1970)

Sanderson, F.E., 'The Liverpool Abolitionists', in Anstey and Hair (eds), *Liverpool, the African Slave Trade and Abolition*, 196–238

Sandys, E.T., 'One Hundred and Forty-Five Years at the Old or Mission Church, Calcutta – III', *Bengal Past and Present*, 11 (1915), 244–57

Scanlan, Padraic, *Freedom's Debtors: British Antislavery in Sierra Leone in the Age of Revolution* (New Haven, CT, 2017)

——, 'The Rewards of their Exertions: Prize Money and British Abolitionism in Sierra Leone, 1807–1823', *Past and Present*, 25 (2014), 113–42

Schama, Simon, *Rough Crossings: Britain, the Slaves and the American Revolution* (London, 2005)

Schofield, T.P., 'Conservative Political Thought in Britain in Response to the French Revolution', *Historical Journal*, 29 (1986), 601–22

Schwarz, Suzanne, 'Commerce, Civilization and Christianity: the Development of the Sierra Leone Company', in Richardson, Schwarz and Tibbles (eds), *Liverpool and Transatlantic Slavery*, 252–76

Scotland, Nigel, *Evangelical Anglicans in a Revolutionary Age 1789–1901* (Carlisle, 2004)

——, *John Bird Sumner, Evangelical Archbishop* (Leominster, 1995)

Searby, Peter (ed.) *A History of the University of Cambridge, III: 1750–1870* (Cambridge, 1997)

Seeley, M., *The Later Evangelical Fathers* (2nd edn: London, 1914)

Semmel, Bernard, *The Methodist Revolution* (London, 1974)

Semmel, Stuart, *Napoleon and the British* (New Haven, CT, 2004)

Sengupta, Parna, *Pedagogy for Religion: Missionary Education and the Fashioning of Hindus and Muslims in Bengal* (Berkeley, CA, 2011)

Seton, Rosemary, *Western Daughters in Eastern Lands: British Missionary Women in Asia* (Santa Barbara, CA, 2013)

Severn, Derek, 'The Bombardment of Algiers, 1816', *History Today*, 28 (1978), 31–9

Shaen, Margaret J., *Memorials of Two Sisters: Susanna and Catherine Winkworth* (London, 1908)

Sharp, Andrew, *The World, the Flesh and the Devil: the Life and Opinions of Samuel Marsden in England and the Antipodes, 1765–1838* (Auckland, 2016)

Shaw, A.G.L., *Sir George Arthur, Bart., 1784–1854* (Melbourne, 1980)

Shaw, Ian J., *High Calvinists in Action: Calvinism and the City* (Oxford, 2002)

Sherrard, O.A., *Life of Lord St Vincent* (London, 1933)

Shyllon, Folarin, *James Ramsay the Unknown Abolitionist* (Edinburgh, 1977)

Simon, M. (ed.), *Aspects de l'Anglicanisme* (Paris, 1974)

Sirota, Brent, *The Christian Monitors: the Church of England and the Age of Benevolence, 1680–1730* (New Haven, CT, 2014)

——, 'Robert Nelson's *Festivals and Fasts* and the Problem of the Sacred in Early Eighteenth-Century England', *Church History*, 84 (2015), 556–84

Skinner, S.A., *Tractarians and the 'Condition of England': the Social and Political Thought of the Oxford Movement* (Oxford, 2004)

Slinn, Sara, *The Education of the Anglican Clergy, 1780–1839* (Woodbridge, 2017)

Smith, E.A., 'The Yorkshire Elections of 1806 and 1807: a Study in Electoral Management', *Northern History*, 2 (1967), 66–72

Smith, Mark A., (ed.), *British Evangelical Identities Past and Present: Aspects of the History and Sociology of Evangelicalism in Britain and Ireland* (Milton Keynes, 2008)

——, and Stephen Taylor (eds), *Evangelicalism in the Church of England c.1790–c.1890*, Church of England Record Society, 12 (Woodbridge, 2004)

——, 'Henry Ryder and the Bath CMS: Evangelical and High Church Controversy in the Later Hanoverian Church', *Journal of Ecclesiastical History*, 62 (2011), 726–43

——, *Religion in Industrial Society: Oldham and Saddleworth 1740–1865* (Oxford, 1994)

——, 'Thomas Burgess, Churchman and Reformer', in Yates (ed.), *Bishop Burgess and his World*, 5–40

Smyth, Charles, 'The Evangelical Movement in Perspective', *Cambridge Historical Journal*, 7 (1941–3), 160–74

——, *Simeon and Church Order: a Study of the Origins of the Evangelical Revival in Cambridge in the Eighteenth Century* (Cambridge, 1940)

Smyth, John, *In this Sign Conquer: the Story of the Army Chaplain* (London, 1968)

Snape, Michael, *The Redcoat and Religion: the Forgotten History of the British Soldier from the Age of Marlborough to the Eve of the First World War* (London, 2005)

——, *The Royal Army Chaplains' Department, 1796–1953: Clergy under Fire* (Woodbridge, 2007)

Soloway, R.A., *Prelates and People: Ecclesiastical Social Thought in England, 1783–1852* (London, 1969)

Southam, Brian, *Jane Austen and the Navy* (London, 2000)

Spence, Martin, *Heaven on Earth: Reimagining Time and Eternity in Nineteenth-Century British Evangelicalism* (Eugene, OR, 2015)

Spring, David, 'Aristocracy, Social Structure, and Religion in the Early Victorian Period', *Victorian Studies*, 6 (1962–3), 263–80

——, 'The Clapham Sect: some Social and Political Aspects', *Victorian Studies*, 5 (1961), 35–48

Srinivastava, B.B., *Sir John Shore's Policy towards the Indian States* (Allahabad, 1981)

St Clair, William, *The Reading Nation in the Romantic Period* (Cambridge, 2004)

——, *The Grand Slave Emporium: Cape Coast Castle and the British Slave Trade* (rev. edn: London, 2007)

Stanley, Brian, '"An Ardour of Devotion": the Spiritual Legacy of Henry Martyn', in Young (ed.), *Indianness of Christianity*, 108–26

——, 'Anglican Missionary Societies and Agencies in the Nineteenth Century', in Strong (ed.), *The Oxford History of Anglicanism, Volume III*, 116–40

——, *The Bible and the Flag* (Leicester, 1990)

——, 'Christian Missions, Antislavery and the Claims of Humanity, c. 1813–1873', in Gilley and Stanley (eds), *Cambridge History of Christianity, VIII*, 443–57

——(ed.), *Christian Missions and the Enlightenment* (Grand Rapids, MI, & Cambridge, 2001)

——, 'The Evangelical Revival, the Missionary Movement, and Africa', in Noll, Bebbington and Rawlyk (eds), *Evangelicalism*, 310–26

——, *The History of the Baptist Missionary Society* (Edinburgh, 1992)

Stirling, A.M.W., *The Ways of Yesterday* (London, 1930)

Stock, Eugene, *The History of the Church Missionary Society*, 4 vols (London, 1899–1916)

Stoneman, David, 'Richard Bourke: for the Honour of God and the Good of Man', *Journal of Religious History*, 38 (2014), 341–55

Stott, Anne, *Hannah More: the First Victorian* (Oxford, 2003)

——, 'Hannah More and the Blagdon Controversy, 1799–1802', in Smith and Taylor (eds), *Evangelicalism in the Church of England c.1790–c.1890*, 1–50

——, *Wilberforce: Family and Friends* (Oxford, 2012)

Strong, Rowan, *Anglicanism and Empire, 1700–1850* (Oxford, 2007)

——(ed.), *The Oxford History of Anglicanism, Volume III: Partisan Anglicanism and its Global Expansion, 1829–c. 1914* (Oxford, 2017)

Stubenrauch, Joseph, *The Evangelical Age of Ingenuity in Industrial Britain* (Oxford, 2016)

Stunt, Timothy C.F., *From Awakening to Secession: Radical Evangelicals in Switzerland and Britain 1815–35* (Edinburgh, 2000)

——, 'Geneva and British Evangelicals in the Early Nineteenth Century', *Journal of Ecclesiastical History*, 32, 1 (1981), 35–46

Sugden, David, *Nelson: a Dream of Glory* (London, 2004)

Sussman, Charlotte, *Consuming Anxieties, Consumer Protest, Gender and British Antislavery, 1713–1833* (Stanford, CA, 2000)

Sutherland, L.S., and L.G. Mitchell (eds), *The History of the University of Oxford, V: the Eighteenth Century* (Oxford, 1986)

Swift, David E., *Joseph John Gurney: Banker, Reformer, and Quaker* (Middletown, CT, 1962)

Symond, Craig L. (ed.), *New Aspects of Naval History* (Annapolis, MD, 1981)

Syrett, David, and R.L. DiNardo (eds), *The Commissioned Officers of the Royal Navy, 1660–1994* (Aldershot, 1994)

Talbott, John E., *The Pen and Ink Sailor: Charles Middleton and the King's Navy, 1778–1813* (London, 1998)

Taylor, Gordon, *The Sea Chaplains: a History of the Chaplains of the Royal Navy* (Oxford, 1978)

Taylor, James Stephen, *Jonas Hanway, Founder of the Marine Society: Charity and Policy in Eighteenth-Century Britain* (London and Berkeley, CA, 1985)

Taylor, Michael, 'British Proslavery Arguments and the Bible, 1823–1833', *Slavery and Abolition*, 37 (2016), 139–58

Telford, John, *A Sect that Moved the World: Three Generations of Clapham Saints and Philanthropists* (London, 1907)

Temperley, Nicholas, 'The Lock Hospital Chapel and its Music', *Journal of the Royal Musical Association*, 118 (1993), 44–72

Tennant, Bob, *Corporate Holiness: Pulpit Preaching and the Church of England Mission-ary Societies, 1760–1870* (Oxford, 2013)

Thomas, Donald, *Cochrane: Britannia's Sea Wolf* (repr. London, 1999)

Thompson, Andrew C. (ed.), *The Oxford History of Dissenting Traditions, Volume II: the Long Eighteenth Century, c. 1689–c. 1828* (Oxford, 2018)

Thompson, David M., *Cambridge Theology in the Nineteenth Century: Enquiry, Contro-versy and Truth* (Aldershot, 2008)

——, *Baptism, Church and Society in Modern Britain from the Evangelical Revival to Baptism, Eucharist and Ministry* (Bletchley, 2005)

Thompson, E.P., *The Making of the English Working Class* (rev. edn: London, 1980)

Thompson, H.P., *Into All Lands: the History of the Society for the Propagation of the Gospel in Foreign Parts, 1701–1950* (London, 1951)

Thompson, Neville, *Earl Bathurst and the British Empire* (Barnsley, 1999)

Thorne, Susan, *Congregational Missions and the Making of an Imperial Culture in Nine-teenth-Century England* (Stanford, CA, 1999)

Thorne, R.G. (ed.), *The History of Parliament: The House of Commons, 1790–1820*, 5 vols (London, 1986)

Tolley, Christopher, *Domestic Biography: the Legacy of Evangelicalism in Four Nine-teenth-Century Families* (Oxford, 1997)

Tomkins, Stephen, *The Clapham Sect: how Wilberforce's Circle Transformed Britain* (Oxford, 2010)

——, *William Wilberforce* (Oxford, 2007)

Toon, Peter, *Evangelical Theology 1833–1856: a Response to Tractarianism* (London, 1979)

Torrance, John, 'Social Class and Bureaucratic Innovation: the Commissioners for Examining the Public Accounts 1780–1787', *Past and Present*, 78 (1978), 56–81

Tosh, John, *A Man's Place: Masculinity and the Middle-Class Home in Victorian Eng-land* (New Haven. CT, 1999)

Travers, Robert, *Ideology and Empire in Eighteenth-Century India: the British in Bengal* (Cambridge, 2007)

Turley, David, *The Culture of English Antislavery, 1780–1860* (London and New York, 1991)

Turner, F.M., *John Henry Newman: the Challenge to Evangelical Religion* (New Haven, CT, and London, 2002)

Turner, John Munsey, *Conflict and Reconciliation: Studies in Methodism and Ecumen-ism in England, 1740–1982* (London, 1985)

Turner, Michael J., 'The Limits of Abolition: Government, Saints and the "African Ques-tion", c.1780–1820', *English Historical Review*, 112 (1997), 319–57

Tute, Warren, *Cochrane: a Life of Admiral the Earl Dundonald* (London, 1965)

Twells, Alison, *The Civilising Mission and the English Middle Class, 1792–1850: the 'Hea-then' at Home and Overseas* (Basingstoke, 2009)

Twigg, John, *A History of Queens' College, Cambridge 1448–1986* (Woodbridge, 1987)

Twist, Anthony, *A Life of John Julius Angerstein, 1735–1823: Widening Circles in Finance, Philanthropy and the Arts in Eighteenth-Century London* (Lewiston, NJ, Queenston, ON, and Lampeter, 2006)

Tyson, John R., and Boyd Stanley Schlenther (eds), *In the Midst of Early Methodism: Lady Huntingdon and her Correspondence* (Lanham, MD, 2006)

Van Reyk, William, 'Christian Ideals of Manliness in the Eighteenth and Early Nineteenth Centuries', *Historical Journal*, 52 (2009), 1053–73

Vander Weyer, Martin, *Falling Eagle: the Decline of Barclays Bank* (London, 2000)

Varley, E.A., *The Last of the Prince Bishops: William Van Mildert and the High Church Movement of the Early Nineteenth Century* (Cambridge, 1992)

Vaudry, Richard W., *Anglicans and the Atlantic World: High Churchmen, Evangelicals, and the Quebec Connection* (Ithaca, NY, 2003)

Venn, J., and Venn, J.A., *Alumni Cantabrigienses: a Biographical List of all Known Students, Graduates and Holders of Office at the University of Cambridge, from the Earliest Times to 1900. Part 1. From the Earliest Time to 1751*, 4 vols (Cambridge, 1922–7)

——, *Alumni Cantabrigienses: a Biographical List of all Known Students, Graduates and Holders of Office at the University of Cambridge, from the Earliest Times to 1900. Part 2. From 1752 to 1900*, 6 vols (Cambridge, 1940–54)

Venn, John, *Annals of a Clerical Family* (London, 1904)

Virgin, Peter, *The Church in an Age of Negligence: Ecclesiastical Structure and Problems of Church Reform, 1700–1840* (Cambridge, 1989)

Wahrman, Dror, *Imagining the Middle Class: the Political Representation of Class in Britain, c. 1780–1840* (Cambridge, 1995)

——, '"Middle-Class" Domesticity goes Public: Gender, Class and Politics from Queen Caroline to Queen Victoria', *Journal of British Studies*, 32 (1993), 396–432

——, 'Percy's Prologue: from Gender Play to Gender Panic in Eighteenth-Century England', *Past and Present*, 159 (1998), 113–60

Walls, Andrew F., 'A Christian Experiment: the Early Sierra Leone Colony', *Studies in Church History*, 7 (1970), 107–29

Walpole, Spencer, *The Life of the Rt. Hon. Spencer Perceval*, 2 vols (London, 1874)

Walsh, John D., 'The Anglican Evangelicals in the Eighteenth Century', in Simon (ed.), *Aspects de l'Anglicanisme*, 87–102

——, Colin Haydon and Stephen Taylor (eds), *The Church of England, c. 1689–c. 1833: from Toleration to Tractarianism* (Cambridge, 1993)

——, 'Evangelicals and Predestination, 1730–1830' (private paper lent by the author, n.d.)

——, 'Joseph Milner's Evangelical Church History', *Journal of Ecclesiastical History*, 10 (1959), 174–87

——, 'Methodism at the End of the Eighteenth Century', in Davies and Rupp (eds), *History of the Methodist Church*, IV: 277–313

——, 'Origins of the Evangelical Revival', in Bennett and Walsh (eds), *Essays in Modern English Church History*, 132–62

——, and Stephen Taylor (eds), *The Papers of the Elland Society, 1769–1828* (forthcoming).

——, and Ronald Hyam, 'Peter Peckard: Liberal Churchman and Anti-Slave Trade Campaigner', *Magdalene College Occasional Papers*, 16 (1998)

——, 'Religious Societies: Methodist and Evangelical, 1738–1800', *Studies in Church History*, 23 (1986), 279–302

——, 'The Magdalene Evangelicals', *Church Quarterly Review*, 159 (1958), 499–511

Walvin, James, *The Abolition of the Atlantic Slave Trade: Origins and Effects in Europe, Africa and the Americas* (Madison, WI, 1981)

——, *England, Slaves and Freedom, 1776–1838* (London, 1986)

——(ed.), *Slavery and British Society, 1776–1846* (London, 1982)

Ward, Kevin, and Brian Stanley (eds), *The Church Mission Society and World Christianity, 1799–1999* (Grand Rapids, MI, 2000)

Ward, W.R., *Religion and Society in England, 1790–1850* (London, 1972)

——, *The Protestant Evangelical Awakening* (Cambridge, 1994)

Warner, Oliver, *William Wilberforce and his Times* (London, 1962)

Watt, James, 'James Ramsay, 1733–1789: Naval Surgeon, Naval Chaplain and Morning Star of the Anti-Slavery Movement', *Mariner's Mirror*, 81 (1995), 156–70

Watts, Michael R., *The Dissenters, Volume I: from the Reformation to the French Revolution* (Oxford, 1985)

——, *The Dissenters, Volume II: the Expansion of Evangelical Nonconformity* (Oxford, 1995)

——, *The Dissenters, Volume III: the Crisis and Conscience of Nonconformity* (Oxford, 2015)

Webster, A.B., *Joshua Watson: the Story of a Layman, 1771–1855* (London, 1954)

Webster, John C.B., *Historiography of Christianity in India* (Oxford, 2012)

Webster, Robert (ed.), *Perfecting Perfection: Essays in Honour of Henry D. Rack* (Cambridge, 2016)

Westcott, A., *Our Oldest Indian Mission* (Madras, 1897)

Whelan, Irene, 'The Bible Gentry: Evangelical Religion, Aristocracy, and the New Moral Order in the Early Nineteenth Century', in Gribben and Holmes (eds), *Protestant Millennialism*, 52–82

Iain Whyte, *Zachary Macaulay 1768–1838: The Steadfast Scot in the British Anti-Slavery Movement* (Liverpool, 2011)

Wilkinson, Callie, 'The East India College Debate and the Fashioning of Imperial Officials, 1806–1858', *Historical Journal*, 60 (2017), 943–69

Wilson, Bryan R., *Patterns of Sectarianism: Organisation and Ideology in Social and Religious Movements* (London, 1967)

Wilson, David R., 'Church and Chapel: Methodism as Church Extension', in Forsaith and Hammond (eds), *Religion, Gender, and Industry*, 53–76

Wilson, Ellen Gibson, *The Great Yorkshire Election of 1807*, ed. Edward Royle and James Walvin (Lancaster, 2015)

——, *John Clarkson and the African Adventure* (London, 1980)

——, *Thomas Clarkson: a Biography* (London, 1989)

Wilson, Jon, *The Domination of Strangers: Modern Governance in Eastern India, 1780–1835* (Basingstoke, 2008)

Wilson, Kathleen, 'The Island Race: Captain Cook, Protestant Evangelicalism and the Construction of English National Identity, 1760–1800', in Claydon and McBride, *Protestantism and National Identity*, 265–90

——, *The Sense of the People: Politics, Culture and Imperialism in England, 1715–1785* (Cambridge, 1985)

Wilson, Quentin Harcourt, 'Richard Conyers of Helmsley – the Adventures of an Eighteenth-Century Memoir' (private paper lent by the author, n.d.)

Wilson, Robert William Keith, *George Augustus Selwyn* (Farnham, 2014)

Wolffe, John, 'Clapham Sect' in *Oxford Dictionary of National Biography* online, http://www.oxforddnb.com, last accessed 18 Jan. 2019

——, 'The Evangelical Alliance in the 1840s: an Attempt to Institutionalise Christian Unity', *Studies in Church History*, 23 (1986), 333–46

——(ed.), *Evangelical Faith and Public Zeal* (London, 1995)

——, *The Expansion of Evangelicalism: the Age of Wilberforce, More, Chalmers and Finney* (Nottingham, 2006)

——, 'Lord Palmerston and Religion: a Reappraisal', *English Historical Review*, 120 (2005), 907–36

——, *The Protestant Crusade in Great Britain, 1829–1860* (Oxford, 1991)

——, 'William Wilberforce's *Practical View* (1797) and its Reception', *Studies in Church History*, 44 (2008), 175–84

Wood, A. Skevington, *Thomas Haweis, 1734–1820* (London, 1957)

Yates, Nigel (ed.), *Bishop Burgess and his World: Culture, Religion and Society in Britain, Europe and North America in the Eighteenth and Nineteenth Centuries* (Cardiff, 2007)

——, *The Religious Condition of Ireland, 1780–1850* (Oxford, 2006)

Yates, T.E., *Venn and Victorian Bishops Abroad: the Missionary Policies of Henry Venn and their Repercussions upon the Anglican Episcopate of the Colonial Period 1841–1872* (Uppsala, 1978)

——, *The Conversion of the Maori: Years of Religious and Social Change, 1814–1842* (Grand Rapids, MI, 2013)

Yeldham, Charlotte, *Maria Spilsbury (1776–1820): Artist and Evangelical* (Farnham, 2010)

Yesudas, R.N., *Colonel John Munro in Travancore* (Trivandrum, 1977)

Young, B.W., 'Religious History and the Eighteenth-Century Historian', *Historical Journal*, 43 (2000), 849–68

Young, G.M, *Victorian England: Portrait of an Age* (Oxford, 1936)

Young, Richard Fox (ed.), *India and the Indianness of Christianity: Essays on Understanding – Historical, Theological, and Bibliographical – in Honor of Robert Eric Frykenberg* (Grand Rapids, MI, 2009)

Ziegler, Philip, *The Sixth Great Power: Barings 1762–1929* (London, 1988)

Unpublished Theses

Allpress, Roshan, 'Making Philanthropists: Entrepreneurs, Evangelicals, and the Growth of Philanthropy in the British World, 1756–1840' (Unpublished D.Phil. Thesis, University of Oxford, 2015)

Atkins, Gareth, 'Wilberforce and his *Milieux*: the Worlds of Anglican Evangelicalism, c. 1780–1830' (Unpublished Ph.D. Thesis, University of Cambridge, 2009)

Balda, Wesley D., '"Spheres of Influence": Simeon's Trust and its Implications for Evangelical Patronage' (Unpublished Ph.D. Thesis, University of Cambridge, 1981)

Bennett, John C., 'Charles Simeon and the Anglican Evangelical Missionary Movement: a Study of Voluntaryism and Church-Mission Tensions' (Unpublished Ph.D. Thesis, University of Edinburgh, 1992)

Blake, R.C., 'Aspects of Religion in the Royal Navy, c. 1770–c. 1870' (Unpublished M.Phil. Thesis, University of Southampton, 1980)

Bourne, J.M., 'The Civil and Military Patronage of the East India Company, 1784–1858' (Unpublished Ph.D. Thesis, University of Leicester, 1997)

Bradley, Ian, 'The Politics of Godliness: Evangelicals in Parliament, 1784–1832' (Unpublished D.Phil. Thesis, University of Oxford, 1974)

Burnage, Sarah, 'The Works of John Bacon R.A. (1766–1799)', (Unpublished Ph.D. Thesis, University of York, 2007)

Carson, Penelope S.E., '"Soldiers of Christ": Evangelicals and India, 1780–1833' (Unpublished Ph.D. Thesis, University of London, 1988)

Dixon, Nicholas, 'The Activity and Influence of the Established Church in England, c. 1800–1837' (Unpublished Ph.D. Thesis, University of Cambridge, 2019)

Ervine, W.J.C., 'Doctrine and Diplomacy: some Aspects of the Thought of the Anglican Evangelical Clergy, 1797 to 1837' (Unpublished Ph.D. Thesis, University of Cambridge, 1979)

Evershed, William Anthony, 'Party and Patronage in the Church of England, 1800–1945: a Study of Patronage Trusts and Patronage Reform' (Unpublished D.Phil. Thesis, University of Oxford, 1985)

Fox, L.P., 'The Work of the Reverend Thomas Tregenna Biddulph' (Unpublished Ph.D. Thesis, University of Cambridge, 1953)

Fraser, Stuart, 'Exiled from Glory: Anglo-Indian Settlement in Nineteenth-Century Britain, with Especial Reference to Cheltenham' (Unpublished Ph.D. Thesis, University of Gloucester)

Hicks, Edward, '"Christianity Personified": Perceval and Pittism' (Unpublished D.Phil. Thesis, University of Oxford, 2018)

Kochav, Sarah, 'Britain and the Holy Land: Prophecy, the Evangelical Movement, and the Conversion and Restoration of the Jews, 1790–1845' (Unpublished D.Phil. Thesis, University of Oxford, 1989)

Melaas-Swanson, Barbara Jane, 'The Life and Thought of the Very Reverend Dr Isaac Milner and his Contribution to the Evangelical Revival in England' (Unpublished Ph.D. Thesis, University of Durham, 1993)

Mole, D.E.H., 'The Church of England and Society in Birmingham 1830–66' (Unpublished Ph.D. Thesis, University of Cambridge, 1961)

Munden, Alan F., 'The Anglican Evangelical Party and the Diocese of Carlisle in the Nineteenth Century, with Particular Reference to the Ministries of Bishop Samuel Waldegrave and Dean Francis Close' (Unpublished Ph.D. Thesis, University of Durham, 1987)

Phillips, I. Lloyd, 'The Evangelical Administrator, Sir Charles Middleton, at the Navy Board, 1778–1790' (Unpublished D.Phil. Thesis, University of Oxford, 1974)

Rennie, Ian S., 'Evangelicalism and English Public Life, 1823–1850' (Unpublished Ph.D. Thesis, University of Toronto, 1962)

Robin, A. de Quetteville, 'The Life of Charles Perry, Bishop of Melbourne (1847–1876), with Special Reference to the Significance of his Episcopate' (Unpublished Hulsean Prize Essay, University of Cambridge, 1964)

Steggles, Mary Ann, 'The Empire Aggrandized: a Study in Commemorative Portrait Statuary exported from Britain to her Colonies in South Asia, 1800–1939' (Unpublished Ph.D. Thesis, University of Leicester, 1993)

Steinhöfel, Antje, 'John Russell and the Impact of Evangelicalism and Natural Theology on Artistic Practice' (Unpublished Ph.D. Thesis, University of Leicester, 2005)

Stubley, P.D., 'Serious Religion and the Improvement of Public Manners: the Scope and Limitations of Evangelicalism in Hull 1770–1914' (Unpublished Ph.D. Thesis, University of Durham, 1991)

Walsh, John D., 'The Yorkshire Evangelicals in the Eighteenth Century, with Especial Reference to Methodism' (Unpublished Ph.D. Thesis, University of Cambridge, 1956)

Willmer, Haddon, 'Evangelicalism 1785 to 1835' (Unpublished Hulsean Prize Essay, University of Cambridge, 1962)

Web-based Sources

Australian Dictionary of Biography online, http://adb.anu.edu.au, last accessed 26 Sep. 2017

Biographical Dictionary of Sculptors in Britain, 1660–1851, http://liberty.henry-moore.org/henrymoore/index.php, last accessed 25 Jan. 2019

Clergy of the Church of England Database 1540–1835 (CCEd), last accessed 19 Jan. 2019

Dictionary of Canadian Biography online, http://www.biographi.ca/en, last accessed 27 Sep. 2017

Legacies of British Slave Ownership, http://www.ucl.ac.uk/lbs/, last accessed 16 Aug. 2018

Neil Jeffares, *Pastels and Pastellists*, http://www.pastellists.com, last accessed 7 Sept. 2017

Oxford Dictionary of National Biography online, http://www.oxforddnb.com, last accessed 19 Jan. 2019

Purchasing Power of British Pounds from 1270 to Present, https://www.measuringworth.com/calculators/ppoweruk/, last accessed 7 Sep. 2017

UK Public Spending, https://www.ukpublicspending.co.uk, last accessed 22 Feb. 2019

Index

Page numbers in italics refer to illustrations.

Printed and bound by CPI Group (UK) Ltd, Croydon, CR0 4YY

23/04/2024

14487822-0001